LEARNING IN GROUPS

Learning in groups in both face-to-face and online contexts allows students to have greater scope to negotiate meaning and express themselves and their own ideas. It also helps them to establish far more effective relationships and can play a central role in developing key professional skills, such as listening, presenting ideas, persuasion, self-direction, self-monitoring and team working.

This fully revised fourth edition of *Learning in Groups*, updated throughout with guidance on group learning and collaborating online, not only promotes understanding of group methods, but also develops group learning skills in students and tutors by showing a range of practical exercises and group experiences to be used.

The areas covered include:

- Characteristics of groups
- The place of leadership
- The processes of collaboration and communication
- How students learn
- Setting and structuring tasks
- Reflection and emotional intelligence
- The effects of the learning context
- Action research
- Assessment and evaluation of group work
- How to make learning more real

Practical and accessible, *Learning in Groups* includes case studies, exercises and training activities for both face-to-face and online contexts that add to its focus and depth. It is invaluable reading for all those involved in tutoring and training, and facilitating and moderating online, and will help to develop powerful groups skills for both tutors and students.

David Jaques is an independent educational and organisational consultant, and an experienced groupwork and teamwork trainer. He was previously Head of the Educational Methods Unit at Oxford Brookes University.

Gilly Salmon is a Professor of E-Learning at the University of Leicester, UK, and is author of a number of best-selling titles, including *E-Moderating* and *E-Tivities*. She was awarded a National Teaching Fellowship in 2006.

Visit www.learningingroups.com for more information.

LEARNING IN GROUPS

A HANDBOOK FOR FACE-TO-FACE AND ONLINE ENVIRONMENTS

Fourth edition

DAVID JAQUES AND GILLY SALMON

Routledge
Taylor & Francis Group

LONDON AND NEW YORK

First published by Croom Helm 1984
Second edition published by Kogan Page 1991
Third edition published by Kogan Page 2000

This edition published 2007 by Routledge
2 Park Square, Milton Park, Abingdon, Oxon OX14 4RN

Simultaneously published in the USA and Canada
by Routledge
270 Madison Ave, New York NY 10016

Routledge is an imprint of the Taylor & Francis Group, an informa business

© 1984, 1991, 2000, 2007 David Jaques and Gilly Salmon

Reprinted 2008

Typeset in Zapf Humanist
by Keystroke, 28 High Street, Tettenhall, Wolverhampton
Printed and bound in Great Britain by Bell & Bain Ltd, Glasgow

British Library Cataloguing in Publication Data
A catalogue record for this book is available from the British Library

Library of Congress Cataloging in Publication Data
A catalog record for this book has been requested

ISBN10: 0–415–36527–9 (hbk)
ISBN10: 0–415–36526–0 (pbk)
ISBN10: 0–203–01645–9 (ebk)

ISBN13: 978–0–415–36527–7 (hbk)
ISBN13: 978–0–415–36526–0 (pbk)
ISBN13: 978–0–203–01645–9 (ebk)

CONTENTS

11 DEVELOPING GROUP LEARNING   **273**

PREFACE TO THE 4TH EDITION

Since the first edition of this book appeared some 20 years ago a vast number of changes have taken place both in the principles of learning groups, in the techniques and technologies which support them, and in the many ways to lead them. So for this edition Gilly Salmon, whose books *E-Tivities* and *E-Moderating* have a strong focus on online group learning, has joined me as co-author. We have chosen not to write separate chapters about on and offline group work but rather to demonstrate how transferable so many of the principles and practice are by interweaving the two modalities and where appropriate, drawing comparisons.

This edition also includes several structural changes as well as updating, though it retains a similar basic structure and content to previous editions. Examples of more recent theory and practice in groups, both face-to-face and online, have been incorporated; exercises based on the text appear in the Appendix. New material on the fast-growing phenomenon of online learning groups, both synchronous and asynchronous and whether in its own right or as part of a blended course, has been incorporated where appropriate. However, since there is constant overlap between underlying theories and processes in such groups and in traditional face-to-face ones, it will serve little purpose constantly to remind readers that such and such applies equally to the online world, where, *mutatis mutandis*, it should be obvious with a little thought. The important difference, however, between the two modes is that the written word replaces speech and visual cues particularly in asynchronous online group interaction and leaves an audit trail or record of proceedings. And the time delay in asynchronous online group work which can sometimes run over a period of days or even weeks and across time zones is not usually conducive to instant feedback; but it does have the advantage of offering more time for reflection both in action and on action, particularly given the record of proceedings. (For a fuller treatment of working with groups online, see Salmon 2002 and 2004.)

We think of our intended readership as academics, teachers, instructors, tutors, trainers, moderators, student teachers, course designers, in fact anyone who is interested in the understanding and development of group learning and their own part in it.

David Jaques and Gilly Salmon
Oxford and Leicester
2006

INTRODUCTION

Increasingly over the last two decades, learning in small groups has become a regular part of student experience whether in the seminar room, the laboratory, in independent groups, in online form or even in the lecture theatre. Though not always given a central role, group discussion, whether face-to-face, purely electronic or a blend of the two, has a critical role to play in the all-round education of students. This is not merely on the grounds of economy with larger numbers but through a rapidly expanding recognition of the nature and levels of learning that take place through active participation in group processes. Group interaction allows students to negotiate meanings, to express themselves in the language of the subject and to establish a more intimate and dialectical contact with academic and teaching staff than more formal methods permit. It also develops the more instrumental skills of listening, careful reading, presenting ideas (both in speech or in writing), persuading, and teamwork, all qualities attractive to employers with their greater expectations of the graduates' ability to communicate; and this is further underlined by the high standards set by radio and television which make for more critical audiences. But perhaps most importantly, group discussion can or should give students the chance to monitor their own learning and thus gain a degree of self-direction and independence of the tutors in their studies. All these purposes are of excellent pedigree. Yet often they are not realised to a satisfactory level and both tutors and students may end up with a sense of frustration.

Leading a successful group discussion, on or offline, does not always come naturally to many otherwise gifted tutors who may too readily fall back on a reserve position of authority, expert and prime talker. Brown and Atkins (1999) report research evidence that the mean proportion of time tutors spent talking in discussion groups was 64 per cent and could reach 86 per cent. Ramsden (2003) describes the 'thoroughly predictable outcomes' of traditional group discussion as a theory of teaching which assumes the mode of telling and transmission as its basis.

The development of skills in group leadership, for both face-to-face and online situations are a constant theme throughout the book.

CONTENT, PROCESS AND STRUCTURE

In all human interactions there are three main ingredients – *content, process* and *structure*. Content relates to the subject matter or task on which people are working. Process refers to the dynamics (both emotional, intellectual and behavioural) of what is happening between those involved. Perhaps because content is more readily definable, or at least examinable, it commonly receives more attention from all concerned. Process, on the other hand, though rarely attended to, is usually what determines whether a group works effectively or not. Group members are often only half-aware of the ways in which factors like physical environment, size, cohesion, climate, norms, liaisons, organisational structure or group goals affect discussion an understanding of which should enhance a participant's worth to the group. For no one is this more true than the leader, e-convenor, e-moderator or tutor who has a crucial position in determining the 'success' or 'failure' of a discussion group.

Students too can benefit from training and consequent alertness, both in the group skills of discussion and project teams, much of which can be developed through the self and peer assessment of these skills. And assumptions that online groups, left to themselves, will naturally progress beyond the stages of low-level exchanges to achieve a level of knowledge development are unlikely to be realised. To achieve successful outcomes for students, tutors too need training in the arts of working online. Without such training, the sophisticated, off-the-shelf, integrated educational software packages nowadays provided in many universities will not in themselves achieve effective outcomes.

Our aim in this book is therefore not just to promote understanding of group methods but to develop group skills for tutors and students alike as well as widening the range of possible group experiences. The title 'Learning in Groups' is meant to suggest that groups are not merely a valuable vehicle for learning about the skills and concepts of a subject discipline, but are also a way of learning about groups: developing abilities in cooperative work for later life.

What you choose to accept and use from the book will reflect your own practice and philosophy of teaching. Therefore, as a starting point we shall state our own position on learning in groups.

Cooperation is a key word in learning groups: tutors need to develop a clear and coordinated strategy for teaching students how to work together and improve their cooperative skills. Cooperation also means each and every member of the group taking a part and sharing responsibility for its success and in some cases having a clear brief to support each other's learning. In sum, an effective group will have both common shared aims and differentiated individual aims.

Assessment too has an important part to play in drawing the attention of students to the importance of effective group work and their part in it and, where it is accompanied by self and peer assessment and team grades, provides strong motivation to take full part in, and learn about, peer learning and teamwork.

So much for the dynamics of groups; what of learning? Our approach to learning is based the following assumptions:

- We learn best when we are personally and actively involved in the learning experience.
- Knowledge of any kind has more significance when we learn it through our own initiative, insight and discovery.
- Learning is best when we are committed to aims that we have been involved in setting, when our participation with others is valued and when there is a supporting framework in which to learn.

Groups can provide a further level of experience, meta-learning, (Jackson 2004) as they view their own thinking and skills in relation to others, reflect on their own abilities and are thus motivated to regulate their actions and behaviour for mutual benefit. And given that interactive behaviour in groups is an inseparable aspect of the person's social repertoire there is potential for self learning for life in this (Priola and Smith 2004).

Other forms of group-centred learning have also became increasingly popular: Peer-Assisted Learning. Problem-Based Learning and Enquiry-Based Learning (PAL, PBL and EBL) have gained status and popularity, and the emergence of Team-Based Learning as a core strategy is emerging as yet another powerful challenge to the traditional design of courses. New and imaginative stratagems seem, quite rightly, to evolve every day, all in one way or another embodying principles of active and interactive learning.

We have tried to write a book that is both readable and practical; one which permits flexibility, yet covers most of the ingredients of this wondrous mix of human behaviours.

This edition includes several structural changes as well as updating, though it retains a similar basic structure and content. Examples of more recent theory and practice in groups both face-to-face and online have been incorporated; exercises based on the text appear in the Appendix; more exercises are accessible on the website www.learningingroups.com. New material on the fast-growing phenomenon of online learning groups, both synchronous and asynchronous and whether in its own right or as part of a blended course, has been incorporated where appropriate. We are also interested in the way that online communication has expanded and enriched opportunities in networking, both in and between groups, and consequently in the creation of communities for learning, practice and even therapy. The important difference, however, between the two modes is that the written word replaces speech and visual cues particularly in asynchronous online group interaction and leaves an audit trail or record of proceedings. And the time delay in asynchronous online group work which can sometimes run over a period of days or even weeks and across time zones is not usually conducive to instant feedback; but it does have the advantage of offering more time for reflection both in action and on action, particularly given the record of proceedings. (For a fuller treatment of working with groups online, see Salmon 2002b).

USING THE BOOK

Tutors and e-moderators

We hope that this book will be of use to practitioners working with groups in many fields, countries, domains both on and offline. In UK Higher Education, often the people in these role are called lecturers; in colleges of Further Education, they may be tutors, and in schools they are teachers. In the corporate domain, *trainer* is often the word. Worldwide there are other names – perhaps instructors, teaching assistants, professors and more. We don't mind at all what you call yourselves but on the whole we've chosen the word 'tutors' to mean those stalwart and talented humans working with face-to-face groups and the term 'e-moderator' to include both the familiar roles and newer skills that cover human intervention in the virtual world. We hope you'll consider yourself included.

Discussion and interaction

Discussion of some kind takes place in almost all groups; it is a form of interaction mainly, but not exclusively, located in education where the learning takes place mainly through talking about subject matter in order, among other things, to gain deeper levels of understanding. We use *interaction* as a more generic term for all sorts of group activity especially when we are looking at various communication behaviours.

Members, students, learners and participants

Where we are writing about interaction in a group in general terms we refer to those involved as *participants*; as *members* when considering composition and identity and as *students* when in an educational context engaging with learning with and through subject matter. When we focus on learning strategies we use the term *learners*. Confusing? We hope not: they all seem to fit in wherever they occur.

Groups and teams

We use the term *groups* for people who come together to share knowledge or to learn from each other through discussion. We use *team* when they are engaged in a task with a plan, product or decision as the end point.

Assessment and evaluation

When we refer to *assessment* we mean ways in which students' progress and achievement are measured and often graded. *Evaluation* refers to methods of monitoring and getting feedback on courses and teaching.

CHAPTER ONE

THEORY AND PRACTICE IN GROUP DYNAMICS

This chapter provides you with a background in the theory of learning in groups. We introduce a range of understandings of how groups work and their significance for learning. You can skip it if you wish, but we hope that if you move on, you'll come back later!

Group phenomena have been the focus of many interpretations and analyses through both research experiments and theoretical interpretations. While experimental evidence can produce and confirm the existence of many important aspects of group dynamics, the value of theories, especially where based on extensive observation and insight, is in their contribution to a richer understanding of some of the more complex phenomena evident in groups, and how to handle them. They can also help to illuminate and organise research evidence in a way which extends its meaning beyond the situations from which they were derived. So you will see that we try and weave them together. No doubt you will do your own testing and weaving too.

INDIVIDUAL AND GROUPS

In this book we consider the group from both individual and collective viewpoints, and most importantly, both together!

First we acknowledge that individual people are the raw material that go to make up groups; not all collections of individuals will have a sense of belonging to a group, though outsiders may perceive them as such; the collective identity, if it is to emerge, will require some form of recognition and response between the individuals who may have different perceptions of their situation vis-à-vis the group as a whole as well as their part in it.

As a group develops so they are likely to experience, and be affected by, whatever purposes, norms, roles and relationships are assumed alongside a shared identity. In that sense a group exists only in the minds of individuals functioning as a collection of people.

Groups

Here is our working definition of groups:

> Groups exist as *more than* a collection of people when they possess all of the following qualities to a greater or lesser degree.
>
> *Collective perception*: members are collectively conscious of their existence as a group.
>
> *Needs*: people join a group because they believe it will satisfy some needs or give them some rewards such as recognition or self understanding through feedback.
>
> *Shared aims*: members hold or quickly develop some shared aims or ideals which bind them together. The achievement of aims is may be one of the rewards.
>
> *Interdependence*: members are interdependent insofar as they are affected by and respond to any event that affects any of the group's members.
>
> *Social organisation*: it comprises a social unit with norms, roles, statuses, power and emotional relationships.
>
> *Interaction*: members influence and respond to each other in the process of communicating. The sense of group exists even when members are not collected in the same place, such as when they are part of an online group.
>
> *Cohesiveness*: members want to remain in the group, to contribute to its well-being and aims, and to join in its activities.
>
> *Membership*: two or more people interacting explicitly or implicitly for longer than a few minutes constitute a group if there is recognition of mutual bonds.
>
> We include the dyad or pair as a group in this book if it meets most of the characteristics above.

Teams and groups – do we regard them as the same? As we stated in the Preface, we use the term group for people who come together to share knowledge, for personal development or to learn from each other through discussion. We use team for groups that are engaged in a task or project geared towards an end product or decision. All teams can thus be viewed as groups, but not all groups as teams.

Now we introduce some key theories that we consider most important to explore to underpin our understanding and working with learning groups.

PSYCHODYNAMIC THEORY

Freud was the first to offer theoretical insights into group behaviour. In *Group Psychology and the Analysis of the Ego* (1921) he claimed that people are drawn into, and remain in, groups because of emotional ties between members, and that one of the principal mechanisms in the effecting of such ties is identification – the process whereby a person wants to be like his or her parent(s). The Freudian school saw the basic processes in a group as outward manifestations of the inner lives of its members: the intrapersonal expressed as the interpersonal. The Tavistock model arose from this approach and has developed one of the most powerful interpretations of group interaction.

Bion (1961), one of the Tavistock's key figures, proposed that a group operates simultaneously at two levels: the work group and the basic assumption group. The work group meets to perform a specific and overt task. However, this is frequently obstructed, or diverted by the powerful emotional drives of the basic assumption activity. The basic group behaves as if it shared the following tacit assumptions or motives.

Obtaining security and protection from one individual on whom it can depend. Security and protection can derive from the designated leader or any member who is accepted in the role. The group unconsciously assumes that some sort of magic resides in the leader. In learning groups, students frequently direct attention to the tutor's remarks, as if he or she were the source of all wisdom, to the exclusion of their colleagues' contributions. Even if they lose respect for a particular tutor there is a sense in which the position is endowed with authority or some external power.

Preserving the group from annihilation by either attacking something (fight) or avoiding the task (flight). Fight would typically involve the group in scapegoating some other person or group in order to avoid a difficult problem. Flight may involve withdrawal, passivity, dwelling in the past or jesting, and the group may seem happy to distract itself from its task by focusing on some other harmless and irrelevant issue. In either case, the group uses its energy to defend itself from its own internal fears and anxieties, such that it neither develops nor achieves an effective output (de Board 1978).

Engaging in pairing. Pairing has as its basic assumption that the purpose of the group is to bring two people together who will somehow save the group from its current predicament. Two individuals form a bond in which warmth, closeness and affection are shown. Frequently this happens when the group is bored, lost or resentful in its discussion and is unable to express or otherwise cope with these feelings. In learning groups pairing may take three possible forms.

1   Two students provide mutual respect and support for each other to the exclusion of other members who are thus rendered inactive.

▼

7

2 The pair engage in intellectual battle, each partner representing a different side of a conflict that has been preoccupying the group. Again the rest of the group are mere bystanders.

3 The tutor may pair with the group as a whole and collude with them in their wish to avoid the appropriate task.

The Tavistock theoretical concepts were developed through a wealth of experience of groups in therapeutic settings and at conferences in human relations training and the Tavistock Institute applied them with some degree of success to industrial and organisational settings. However, they are not always easy to accept and to identify without a certain amount of induction and it is sometimes said that their interpretations of group behaviour are probably 25 per cent right 25 per cent of the time. They may be less relevant to learning groups committed to the task of intellectual development, but we think that every tutor should at least be aware of them as a latent force as when issues surface they can be quite powerful.

Understanding Tavistock in your groups

Pairing is often characterised by a sense of unreal hope: 'Everything will be okay when we get a new room', 'It'll come all right in the New Year'. The need to face up to and work through disappointments and failures is conveniently avoided by this unreal but seductive promise of things to come. Pairing can also be likened to two cells coming together in order for the group to reproduce itself – that is to say, develop another task and direction for the group distinct from the agreed one.

The Tavistock approach has also brought into focus other issues of value in our understanding of group dynamics such as concepts of authority, responsibility, boundaries, projections, organisation and large group phenomena.

Authority in groups

Whenever decisions have to be made, as in a team or a project group, about tasks and process or about the allocation roles, authority problems are likely to occur. Whose job is it to decide? Can the group give any one person that sanction? Where a designated 'authority person' exists, a group may either find itself dependent on them, or counter-dependent (attacking authority). Sometimes an individual may become a repository for repressed or unexpressed feelings in a group, no matter how reasonable or unreasonable, and where these are about their perception of the leader may resolve into a conflict between the two as protagonists.

Many students who object to the authority of the teacher are not really seeking an alternative to the status quo. They may be avoiding the need to accept that learning is their own responsibility and that they have to face the consequences of the choices they make. It is important therefore for the teacher to create the conditions in which the students can make conscious choices of alternative courses of action, supportively but firmly bringing such issues out into the open (see contract, pages 90 and 93).

Responsibility

Often there is a feeling in groups that the ultimate responsibility for each person's action, and its consequences, resides in any figure of authority. In learning groups, students may not take responsibility for the role they play in contributing to a successful experience. Whether they are accustomed to challenging authority overtly, accepting it meekly, or tolerating it with resentment and bad grace, they may never have examined the consequences of such attitudes. Somehow the responsibility for what happens is assumed to lie firmly on the shoulders of the teacher who may find it difficult to shrug it off. Equally problematical may be the actions of a teacher who wants to keep everyone happy and meet all their needs. It may seem easier to respond to a student's sense of helplessness by offering to meet it and without questioning its provenance, to play the role of the compulsive helper, thus missing an opportunity to develop the student's capacity for self-growth into greater autonomy and responsibility.

Boundaries

All of us have a physical and psychological boundary in relation to others. Our own skin constitutes a physical boundary while the distinction between our private thoughts, feelings and fantasies, and the 'known' or assumed outside world constitutes another. The same can be said of the group; both in a subjective sense, and a more objective and symbolic way, boundaries can distinguish one group from another. The physical or virtual space occupied by the group and the time span it covers are obvious and objective boundaries. Both of these are typically under the control of the tutor or leader. Less tangible and more subjective are the task boundary, which determines what the group should or should not do, and the input boundary which requires members to undergo certain social procedures before membership is acquired. Evidence of the strength of subjective boundaries can be readily perceived if a stranger – perhaps a new student – arrives unannounced in an established group, or if the tutor invites a colleague to sit in on a seminar.

Projection

Sometimes the negative feelings we have towards other people are too dangerous to permit of conscious expression and, as a mechanism to defend us against the anxiety that this produces, we attribute these feelings, motives or qualities to the person or persons towards whom our feelings are really directed. We thus experience the feelings as coming 'at us' rather than 'from us'. This is the mechanism known as projection. Some students may for instance see the tutor as hostile when they are in fact feeling hostility to the tutor but unable to recognise it. They will usually hotly deny the existence of such a feeling if challenged.

Just as individuals can plant their own bad feelings on others in the group, so a group can spend a lot of time and energy in projecting its own conflicts or inadequacies onto another group or the institution. This is more usually more true of staff groups (discussed further in Chapter 8) and student political and union meetings than of learning groups.

Organisational structure

The power relationships in the group, whether determined by outside factors (e.g. the course, the tutor's position in the institutional hierarchy) or by internal concerns such as how clever or dominating other students are or appear to be, can have a profound effect on the work of a group. Structural relations of this kind may manifest themselves in who sits where, who takes initiatives, who defers to whom, and in the 'pecking order' of contributions. In general, structures which are not revealed and discussed lead to feelings of mistrust. The structure of a group does not automatically exist from the beginning but develops through a process of differentiation and sorting. It can also change according to the mood of members or the special requirements of the task in hand. The recognition of this problem had led some group leaders to allocate special roles and responsibilities in a group on a rotating basis.

Large groups

As the size of a group increases, so its characteristics change (see Figure 1.1). Many regard six as a critical number for groups in all sorts of situations. With six or less, the degree of intimacy, whether physical or virtual, offered by close proximity can somehow make it difficult for group members to register their feelings about the group. Leadership tends to be fluid and interchangeable. As the group size increases, the climate of the group changes. Individuals become less constrained by the norms of the group and become more aware of their feelings. In addition, leadership and other roles become more established. With numbers of 12 to 25 the likelihood of full face-to-face – indeed virtual – interaction decreases and sub-groups start to emerge. When the group is over 25 in number, effective interaction between everyone becomes almost impossible. When in a room, some people, because of the group's size, may have to sit behind others, and anyone speaking may fail to see, or be seen by, everyone in the group; in online groups, individual responses get overlooked in the welter of messages. When leadership occurs it is likely to take on a clear cut, 'external' role. (Chapter 7, pages 162–5 looks at some of the practicalities of working with larger groups)

Whereas in the small group it is easy to think but difficult to feel, in the large one the opposite is likely to be the case. It becomes difficult to mobilise the intellect, issues become polarised, splitting ('I all right/you all wrong') takes over as a defence against anxiety about chaos, and, in order to manage this, people are likely to stereotype each other. The leader or teacher, as someone who is evidently different, is likely to be subject to these perceptions more than most and the authority/dependency problem will almost certainly be sharper and more acute.

Leaders may be invested with all sorts of power and expertise. But as soon as they come up with something the group regards as 'inferior' their credibility will sag and they may be attacked for their inadequacy. Power is more sharply polarised; too sudden or big a change in the power relationship is likely to produce a flight/fight situation. If the group challenges the leader, and if in turn it is challenged back, it may retreat or withdraw. An example of this would be when a teacher, after playing a formal and omniscient role, invites the class informally to come up with some of their own ideas.

Another experience of people in large groups is that their identity becomes more fragile and their sense of reality is distorted. The mechanism of projection (see page 9) is likely to operate: unwanted

Number of members	Changing characteristics
2–6	Little structure or organisation required; leadership fluid
7–12	Structure and differentiation of roles begins; face-to-face interaction less frequent
13–25	Structure and role differentiation vital; sub-groups emerge; face-to-face interaction more difficult
26–?	Positive leadership vital to success; sub-groups form; greater anonymity; stereotyping, projections and 'flight/fight' occur

More cohesion (arrow pointing up, left side)

More tension (arrow pointing down, right side)

Figure 1.1 Changing characteristics of groups with increase in membership

parts of the self are pushed onto others, and fantasies about other people's motives, attitudes and intentions abound.

So much for the undercurrents! At the behavioural level, it becomes evident that the larger the group, the more formal and oratorical the spoken contributions become. In the educational context we can see that students have two kinds of relationship open to them: one is with small discussion or learning groups with which they already have some identity, and the other with the wider group membership, many of whom they know from social or sporting contacts, or even in another learning group. In training 'workshops' there is a constant alternation between small groups of different sizes and the large plenary group. In some ways this mixture can provide participants with a sense of a home base (their sub-group) amid the feeling of identity loss that the large group may create. The facilitator in workshops however is able to circulate round the sub-groups and is thus less likely to be on the receiving end of displaced or projected bad feeling through becoming more 'real' to participants.

The complex play of relationships in a large group and the emotional swirl that is likely to go with it is thus, at least potentially, fraught with confusion, inaction and frustration. Strong leadership is both needed and, usually, gratefully accepted.

GROUP ANALYSIS

Group analysis provides a more social view of interaction which it sees as taking place at four levels: Mirroring, Exchange, Social Integration and Collective Unconscious (Zinkin 1994). Mirroring implies a degree of sameness between members whereas Exchange arises through difference. The social nature of group members enables a network or matrix of discussion where each person can compare and contrast their own ways of thinking and behaving with that of the others and to change these as he or she thinks fit (Abercrombie 1969). Because perceptions are often based on assumptions which are non-rational and even unconscious, this process is capable of bringing to the surface a range of otherwise untested aspects of both personal and shared learning.

Such interactions contrast with those in the kind of seminars where individuality and competitiveness are the norm or where they are conducted as a sequence of questions and answers between the tutor and students; they are more typical of Associative Discussion (page 119) where the tutor takes a more recessive or even absent role. This free exchange of information and explanations between people who see one another as equals goes on to build up a common pool of knowledge, a specific culture and the sense of doing this together becomes of interest to the participants.

Each group will naturally, through a process of 'other-than-conscious' trial and error, sort out its social rules and thus acquire its distinctive culture. An anthropologist might approach groups in a similar way, asking questions about social rules and the system of exchange:

- What is the medium of the exchange?
- What are the rules governing the exchanges that are made?
- What is the function of the exchange and what purposes is it serving?
- Are there any exchanges taking place which are detrimental to the group's aims?
- Is everyone aware of the nature of the exchanges and of the rules governing them?

This theory also holds notions of 'fair play' in which group members can expect to get back what they have given in transactions. On the negative side this can mean that no one in the group wants to risk 'losing out'; a positive outcome could or should be that the totality of transactions is much greater that the sum of the parts and the groups as a whole thus reaps benefits. For this to happen there may also be a need for recognition among group members of a need to help the group and not just themselves.

GROUP APPROACHES FOR DIFFERENT PURPOSES

T-groups

This form of group training developed from the need of trainers to review their own problems in groups. The 'T' stands for training, not therapy. They are designed to help participants examine their own patterns of behaviour in a group setting and to become more sensitised to what goes on in the dynamics of a group. Typically they comprise 8 to 12 members who are strangers to each other and two trainers whose task is both to hold the boundaries of the group and to offer a commentary on what they observe happening. The group members will increasingly become able to learn from the trainers, to observe, comment and reflect on the process of the group as it develops. The task of the group is sometimes stated as 'To study the process of the group as it evolves and our own part in it'. The focus is therefore very much on the 'here and now' experience. The group is not structured in the sense that activities are not proposed by the trainers, and whatever happens becomes data for the group's learning. Much of the learning comes in the form of personal feedback from the group and one of the trainer's responsibilities can be seen as maintaining a balance between challenge and support (Smith 1980).

T-group courses or laboratories could well be residential extending over several days and usually include other forms of group experience such as large group and inter-group activity, all of them exploratory and experiential.

The value of learning from T-groups is reflected in Miller (1993) who derived the following set of guidelines for working with groups experientially:

A   Minimise/simplify structure
B   Use inter-group as well as interpersonal communication – in order to enable people to explore structural as well as individual similarities
C   Import (selected?) bits of the real world into the laboratory environment
D   In designing laboratories, keep in mind at all times how things work in 'real life'
E   Encourage intervention/confrontation (e.g. through the asking of questions as well as self-disclosure
F   Use metaphors to explore interpersonal behaviour
G   Remember that past and future are experienced in the present

The implications of Miller's guidelines are evident in later chapters of this book when we explore group activities, the tutor's role and groups in on and offline contexts.

Theme-centred Interaction

As much a method as a theory, theme-centred interaction (TCI) is concerned with three constituent factors, each of equal importance: the 'I', the 'We' and the 'It' of group interaction. For productive discussion to occur, the 'I' of individual interests must be balanced with the 'we' of group related-ness and the 'it' of the theme or topic. The theme is treated as common property to which the individuals (which include the 'I' of the leader) and the group as a whole relate and should include a gerund – as for instance 'observing accurately' – in order to create a momentum and a sense of participating.

These three elements are enveloped in a 'globe' (see Figure 1.2). The globe comprises the physical or virtual, social and temporal environment in which the group takes place. It includes the shape of the room or virtual space, the arrangement of the furniture or layout and the emotional climate of the group. Each member of the group is expected to act his or her own chairperson in charge of an inner 'committee' which comprises four members: 'what I want to do', 'what I ought to do', 'how that might affect others', and the chairperson, who has to decide which of these should have

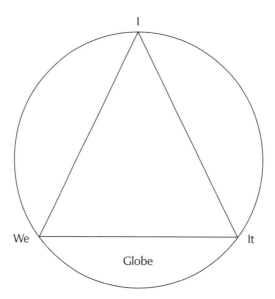

Figure 1.2 The theme-centred interaction triangle and globe

precedence. Such concepts can work equally well whether face-to-face or in the virtual group environment.

TCI includes two further principles: that thought and feeling should not be separated and that each person speak for themselves. This latter implies that no one can speak on behalf of others (either the group as a whole or any individual) without checking with them. But more importantly it encourages group members to speak in the first person rather than the generalised 'you'. For example the statement 'when you are in groups like this you can't think what to say' would be preferred as 'when I am in a group like this I can't think what to say'. The nature and tone of the statement usually changes dramatically with the change of personal pronoun.

This basic structure is supplemented by the ground rule 'disturbances take precedence': if a group member is unable to focus on the group task because of some distraction – being angry, bored, upset or excited, for example – they should say so. The emotional underlay is thus revealed in a personally responsible way. TCI has strong roots in both existentialism and psychoanalysis. It provides a framework for each individual to internalise and understand his or her own place and function in a group. It is also immensely practical and can be applied to a number of group settings to which other explanatory frameworks may not be suitable.

Many of these communication principles are useful reminders in online and offline groups and help to support students in speaking for themselves.

Shaffer and Galinsky (1974) give more extensive analysis of the nature of T-groups and TCI and compare them with other group methods like Tavistock groups.

theory and practice in group dynamics

'Informal education' groups

Informal education differs from formal education in that it is related to the space in which the contact takes place as well as the nature of the interaction (Trelfa and Féaviour 2002). Its main focus is on reducing interpersonal gaps, whether between the facilitator and those s/he is working with, between co-workers, between individuals in the group, between the group and those not in the group and the wider community. Its strength lies in 'the ability of educators to be participants, to involve themselves in the action without becoming an overwhelming point of reference'. Informal education regards itself as an oral culture, a profession based on conversation, a 'refinement of the processes we all go through', such as thinking about and learning from experiences (Smith 1994).

Exploration of the nature of informal and situated learning (Sharples et al. 2005, 2006; Kukularka-Hulme and Traxler 2005) has once more come to the fore with the advent of the use of portable devices, such as iPods, originally intended for entertainment, or Personal Digital Assistants (PDAs), originally intended for business use, and which are now being used as learning devices.

Boundaryless groups

New aspects of group process are developing through the boundaryless nature of online group communication which allows people the facility of meeting without the need to be in the same place and at the same time and location. Lisa Kimball (2001) has compared the various options.

Same Time, Same Place meetings

The most familiar mode, working with the notion that we need to see and be physically near each other in order to build up trust; the group sits in a circle such that everyone can see each other and where the facilitator's presence is always influential whether active or not. Sometimes extraverts dominate and some find little time to collect their thoughts.

Same Time, Same Place with Mediating Technology

Participants at a face-to-face meeting can take time out to communicate using linked computers which allows issues to be highlighted rather focus on the characteristics of the person. And audit or review can be made later, including by those not at the original meeting.

Same Time, Different Place

Same-time media such as audio or video-conferencing that allow the group to see or hear each other which can help the group feel 'together' or 'in synch'. The facilitator will need to ensure that turn taking occurs and that remote locations are not missed.

Asynchronous communication allows people to participate when and where it is more convenient for them. Messages can be reordered and reviewed in various ways. Participants have choice when and with what to engage, and then to review their contribution. In web-conferencing, despite geographical and time zone differences, contributions can be so organised to appear as a continuous stream, like the transcript of a play.

Online groups with various names and purposes are becoming increasingly popular: Learning Communities, Communities of Practice, Community Workshops all create possibilities for wider ranges and levels of communication. See this book's website for examples.

INTERACTION THEORY

Whereas psychodynamic theory emphasises the effect of unconscious processes in the group which exist beyond the awareness of the participant, the interaction approach is concerned with overt interpersonal behaviour between members of the group. This has contributed to our understanding of group work by providing categories for the observation and analysis of different kinds of behaviour in small groups. The categories include qualitative and quantitative considerations, and are designed to comprise all possible types of behaviour. McLeish et al. (1973) maintain that the interaction analysis system should include:

> - the affective or emotional components of behaviour;
> - the cognitive or intellectual components;
> - the non-verbal or 'meta-language' components;
> - content or message components;
> - sociological or personal network segments of behaviour.

Although originally designed as research tools, interaction analyses have been increasingly used for training purposes to provide feedback to teachers, trainee group participants and teams. In describing apparently straightforward and overt behaviour, an interaction analysis makes it possible to provide participants with increased personal insight through objective and largely non-evaluative feedback. They may also have opportunities to practise different skills and to test them against reactions from their colleagues. In producing a comprehensive analysis of a group discussion, interaction analysis provides information on the differences between participation, and the development of different phases in a group's existence. Online, where typically everything that has been 'said' is available for later review, such categories can be helpful in seeing patterns emerging.

The basis of interaction analysis is that everything which a group says or does, including non-verbal acts, may be coded – including items like body posture, facial expressions and tone of voice. The set of categories devised by Bales (1970) is shown in Figure 1.3. It forms a symmetrical pattern and describes different aspects of group functioning. The various categories form complementary relationships. The first three comprise the positive socio-emotional area and correspond to the last three in the negative socio-emotional area. Categories 4, 5 and 6, in the task area, comprise 'answers', while 7, 8 and 9 correspond as 'questions'. Individual categories can be paired off or 'nested'. Categories 6 and 7 focus on problems of communication; 5 and 8 on evaluation and 4 and 9 on problems of control. Categories 3 and 10 are concerned with decision-making in the group, 2 and 11 with reducing tension and 1 and 12 with reintegration, the settling of emotional issues. These combined pairs relate

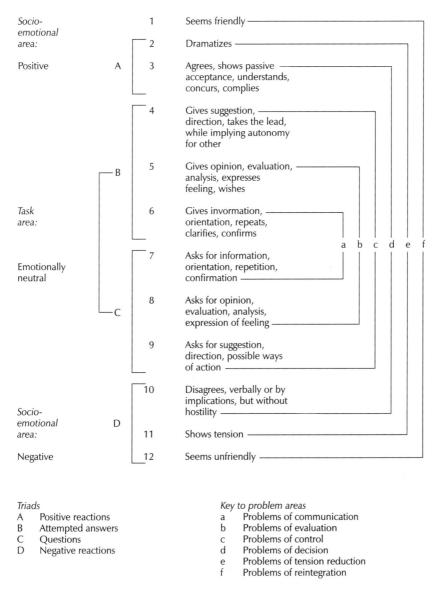

Figure 1.3 The verbal analysis of behaviour: Bales's system (1970)

to phases in the evolution of groups too, as they move outwards from communicating the task (6 and 7) through evaluation (5 and 8) to the making of decisions in 3 and 10. It also demonstrates that in the initial stages of a task, the group should be concerned with the instrumental or task components of the interaction, and then, as it moves towards making decisions and achieving agreement, so it becomes more clearly involved in the emotional side of the process.

Theoretically, this is how a group interaction evolves. However, events rarely follow this smooth path and whilst the sequence may be followed in a general sense, the actual group interaction is an unstable, ever changing process subject to all sorts of influences. The analysis assumes that members of the group are not radically affected by external factors such as previous animosities or extrinsic motives in their behaviour in the group.

Bales's position is that if we can outline behaviours in a group as objectively as possible, it will be easier for people to accept what happens and change accordingly to improve group process. It is our experience that group members are constantly surprised at the feedback they get from an interaction analysis in respect of both the quality and the quantity of what they contribute to discussion. However, it is not always so easy to categorise behaviours in the way indicated by Bales, more particularly in the socio-emotional area where people frequently keep their feelings to themselves or are trying somehow to compensate for various feelings they have towards other people or towards the whole group. Online, feelings may need to be checked in some way, or interpreted. The analysis makes no concession to the notion of a group culture but can be a valuable analytical tool for visible group interaction.

Six-category Intervention Analysis

Another form of behaviour analysis proposed by Heron (1976 and 1989), although based primarily on one-to-one interventions, can apply equally to a group learning environment and particularly to the tutor's role. Heron's six-category intervention analysis focuses on all 'desirable and worthwhile types of intervention: that is, they exclude only negative and destructive types of intervention'. The categories are devised in a form which contributes to self-assessment and self-monitoring for group leaders and members where the development of active participation is encouraged and rewarded.

The six categories fall into two main groups, authoritative and facilitative: authoritative when the leader is in a dominant or assertive role; facilitative where the role of the leader is seen to be less obstructive and more discreet.

Under the *authoritative* mode the tutor can be:

1   Directing
        Raising an issue for discussion, re-routing the discussion.
        Suggesting further work to be done.

theory and practice in group dynamics

2 Informing
    Summarising.
    Interrelating.
    Giving knowledge and information.

3 Confronting
    Challenging by direct question.
    Disagreeing with/correcting/critically evaluating student statement.
    Giving direct feedback.

Under the *facilitative* mode the tutor can be:

4 Releasing tension
    Arousing laughter.
    Allowing students to discharge unpleasant emotions such as embarrassment, irritation, confusion and sometimes even anger.

5 Eliciting
    Drawing out student opinions/knowledge/problem-solving ability.
    Facilitating student interaction.
    Enabling students to learn and develop by self-discovery and personal insight.

6 Supporting
    Approving/reinforcing/agreeing with/affirming the value of student contributions.

Two of these six categories – eliciting and informing – are of special importance for group work in that they form a spectrum from student-centred learning to tutor-centred learning (see Figure 1.4).

The details of both these categories indicate some of the particular skills the group leader should employ in performing the interventions. *Echoing* refers to the practice of repeating or rephrasing, without any special emphasis, the last few words a group member says before pausing, designed to encourage expand on his or her thoughts. Various open-ended questions can serve a similar purpose (see page 188–9). *Selective echoing* is the skill of picking out from a contribution a few words or phrases which seem to carry an implicit emotional charge, or which appeared to cause some sort of agitation in the student. *Empathic divining* is a way of sensing an implicit feeling, thought or intention that is not fully expressed and tentatively labelling it. *Logical marshalling* involves picking up the threads of a discussion, interrelating them and sometimes indicating where they might be leading and putting this back to the group in a succinct way. Online, participants should be encouraged to create coherent message pathways around a particular topic, to support weaving and summarising activities. The online bulletin board or forum that you are using will have a way of setting up specific 'streams' of replies to a starter message that we call 'threads'.

STUDENT-CENTERED

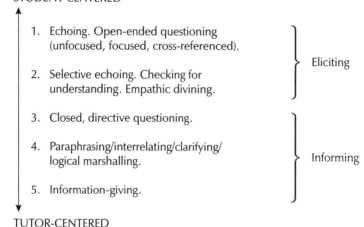

1. Echoing. Open-ended questioning (unfocused, focused, cross-referenced).

2. Selective echoing. Checking for understanding. Empathic divining.

   } Eliciting

3. Closed, directive questioning.

4. Paraphrasing/interrelating/clarifying/ logical marshalling.

   } Informing

5. Information-giving.

TUTOR-CENTERED

Figure 1.4 The spectrum from student-centred to tutor-centred learning

Various suggestions for the use of these categories, particularly those in the facilitative mode, are suggested in Chapter 7.

Online concepts

The way people relate to each other in the online world has different characteristics compared to the physical classroom world. Most people are much more familiar with being able to see and thus 'read' each other through body language, so online takes more effort and more 'getting used to' at first. This does not mean that it is deficient. Far from it. All the theories so far in this chapter are relevant but there are some additional understandings needed to interpret them for the online world and we have tried to weave them in and alert you to them throughout the book. In a nutshell, so long as each individual has time not only to become relaxed with the technology but also how to relate to other members of the group without meeting, there are many advantages. These include time for reflection and choice of when to respond. Agreed clock time does not limit individual participation. The common and difficult-to-avoid stereotypical responses related to looks or voice are absent and if the virtual group is appropriately structured (see page 43) , then the tutor's role can be one of joy in encouraging out-of-the-ordinary responses from all participants. And the tutor or group leader – the person we call the e-moderator – has the opportunity to apply the theory in asynchronous time.

THE ROLE OF EMOTIONS

In much of this chapter we have looked at aspects of groups that can help or hinder their progress, many of which involve conscious or unconscious dispositions and assumptions. It would be a mistake however to forget the influence of understandable emotions when there is a disjunction of aims or a clash of interests. Because in a learning group the topics, tasks and aims of the group may be largely intellectual or practical, tutors, especially those whose central concern is with the imparting of a body of knowledge, may lose touch with how the participants are feeling and the consequent impact of that on the group, such as poor attendance or under-performance, that may result. The case studies in Chapter 10 provide examples of group learning which focus on ways that learners can be engaged while still maintaining a clearly academic focus. Although styles of learning may vary from subject to subject, the majority of learners prize both the sense of belonging which small groups afford them and the chance to test their understandings with their peers. This is an area where research evidence and psychodynamic theory are in agreement. The importance of emotions and feelings in learning is now being emphasised by terms such as 'Emotional Intelligence' and 'Emotional Literacy' which imply a strong linkage between the way we think and the way we feel (Goleman 1995).

Moreover, intellectual growth, as we shall see later (pages 56–7), is closely linked to emotional development.

By the same token tutors/leaders/moderators need to recognise the part their own emotions may play in the process. This recognition is important not merely for the effective functioning of the group but for the more far-reaching educational aim of developing the student as a congruent person – one who is able to hold together the different levels at which he or she experiences life and to communicate responses genuinely.

Attending to students' emotional needs should not only benefit their intellectual powers but also develop their capacity to tackle the sort of relationships that are so familiar to the professional situations. Contemporary life places a premium on the ability of people to get on with each other, to be able to handle interpersonal problems rather than to avoid them, and to do so constructively and creatively. Nowhere is it more possible to practise these qualities than in small-group work when learning is not subject to purely academic limitations. And lest we consider the emotional side of learning to be about what lies beneath the surface of normal human interactions, let us remember the transformational effects of fun, enjoyment and play in learning, a theme we shall return to in Chapter 6.

DISCUSSION POINTS

- To what extent do you think that a theoretical approach constrains our understanding of group dynamics and to what extent does it provide a helpful structure for either face-to-face or online groups?
- To what extent do you think that the problems in groups that you have belonged to arose from some of the unconscious forces described in this chapter rather then an imbalance of behavioural qualities?
- Choose a problem incident in your group. Which aspects of theory seem to shed most light on what happened?
- Can you explain your experience of virtual groups in terms of theoretical approaches. If not why not?

CHAPTER 2

STUDIES OF GROUP BEHAVIOUR

Chapter two explores the essential characteristics of effective groups and a range of issues affecting group dynamics

Over the past 50 years a wealth of information has been compiled by social psychologists working with experimental groups in laboratory settings. Some have focused on individual behaviour, some on the individual as a group member or on the group as a whole and others on intergroup behaviour. They offer us special insights into group behaviour that can help us with learning in groups too. Group members and participants often find research-based concepts and principles helpful in understanding what's going on and what options there may be in dealing effectively with them.

However, a little word of warning for practitioners. Most of the work of social psychologist concentrates on the group performing practical tasks rather than developing learning or personal growth. The behaviours of long-established groups over a period of time in learning and teaching settings, compared to groups brought together for experimental purposes, may be rather different. Experiments rarely touch upon the complex phenomena of interaction which dominate many learning groups, including the expectations of future interactions, which develop *over time* over time or the awareness of roles and responsibilities *outside* the group meeting (Olivera and Strauss 2004; Galanes 2003, citing Stohl and Putnam 1990 and 1994). We now have online groups providing direct evidence over long periods of time without the physical presence of observers. Researchers gather evidence through transcripts of authentic processes with an ongoing group. Online group processes and be monitored through a structured developmental process or 'scaffold' (see page 277). So as a tutor or e-moderator you should to test the relevance and value of research evidence in your own contexts, by incorporating some of the principles into your teaching procedures. Everyone must be their own translator; evidence must be interpreted in the light of practical experience with and in everyday groups. However, we have given you some pointers and ideas throughout this chapter . . . questions to ask yourself!

The next section, developed from Knowles and Knowles (1972), deals with some of the factors derived from numerous sources and insights that are likely to influence the experience and the outcomes of groups of various kinds. The groups they refer to include families, committees and discussion groups; in other words the properties relate to all sorts of groups and situations. All of them are relevant to the learning group.

PROPERTIES OF GROUPS

Time boundaries

Past

Members of a new group bring with them sets of expectations arising out of what they know of the origins, history, or composition of the group – which significant people are to be in it; or perhaps they simply imagine the kind of group they would like it to be. They may build up expectations from any statements they have heard about the group's purpose and task. Members may also bring with them attitudes to other members born out of prior relationships outside the group, and the group itself may carry a reputation for a particular style, climate, or level of achievement. In education, students will probably have picked up comments about how well or badly the group went in the previous year.

The formation of a group requires that someone make decisions about place, resources, and the size and composition of the group. Whoever undertakes this task, for example the leader, will have considerable influence in the success of the group, at least in its initial stages.

In an established group, members may carry with them feelings derived from previous meetings; they may look forward to the resumption of an exciting interchange or may dread the re-enactment of conflicts and time-wasting tactics. They may have to do preparatory work, such as a paper or a report, and their anticipation of what will happen may cause them to approach or engage with the group in a predetermined way. New members may need careful briefing on the group's norms and procedures.

Present

While a meeting is in progress members may sometimes be taken up with thoughts about what may be happening concurrently elsewhere: an important external event, what is going on in another, possibly similar, group; why an absent member is not there, and so on.

The agreed duration of the meeting imposes another time boundary. Frequently the leader assumes the sole right to determine how long it should last and may even make arbitrary and idiosyncratic decisions about when it should end or break. The leader's awareness of time constraints in terms of the achievement of certain aims, the appropriateness of tasks, when to intervene, curtail, summarise, and so on, is of great importance and given the assumptions that are usually made about the leader's responsibility in this domain it seems appropriate that he or she should initiate and handle discussion about how long the meeting should last. Yet within the meeting conflicts may well arise between 'coverage' of topics and completion of tasks on the one hand and the need to finish on time on the other.

Future

Whatever matters are discussed, decisions made, or problems solved, the minds of group members will at some stage turn to what will happen when the meeting ends. They may be thinking of what they have to communicate and to whom, of resuming former roles and relationships outside the group. They may also have it in mind that they may be answerable later for what they said or did within the confines and culture of the meeting, especially to other members with whom they may have a less democratic relationship in the wider world. Finally, there will undoubtedly be an anticipation of the end of the meeting which will bring with it a sense of relief, if it has been tedious or tense, and of sadness if it has been exciting and involving.

Questions to ask about time boundaries are:

- What do members need to know beforehand – place, time, aims, membership, roles, prior tasks?
- What arrangements have been made for their meeting – physical setting resources, and the like?
- How well were the members prepared for joining the group?
- What expectations are they likely to have from previous meetings of the group and from group members?
- What prior experience of group discussion or teamwork might they have had?
- What external distractions might occur?
- Should there be any rules about openness and confidentiality?
- What are members expected to do after the meeting?
- How acceptable are these future tasks?

Physical environment

Several critical factors in group dynamics – flow of communication, perception of status, emergence of leadership, for example – are affected by things like the physical position of group members, their distance apart, and their body orientations. These in turn are strongly influenced by the shape and size of the room in which a group meets, and the spatial arrangement of chairs and tables. A long, narrow room will probably limit eye contact along its length and impel members to talk to others across the room, but not along it. Anyone who sits at the end of a long table or behind the only desk in the room is likely to be accorded leadership status. Dominant members will tend to choose the more central seats in any group situation, and reticent ones may even try to sit outside the group. The further apart members are, the less talkative and more formal is the interaction likely to be. Tables create a physical barrier which may be reassuring in groups where formality is of the essence, or where there is a wish to maintain personal distance or space. They may also be invaluable as a writing surface. A lack of tables may be threatening to some but it usually encourages openness and informality.

Personal space, the area around a person which he or she regards as private, will of course vary from individual to individual, but it is clear that people of higher status often prefer, or are accorded, greater distance between them and others. (The seats on either side of a leader in an otherwise undifferentiated circle of chairs are often the last to be filled by other group members.)

The location of a group meeting has its effect too. The leader's room is his or her territory and underlines the authority role. The members' union bar on the other hand could be a more egalitarian venue but has the drawback of invasion by others, not to mention licensing limitations. Just as groups may assume territorial rights over physical space and objects, so may members act territorially about positions in a room.

Questions to ask about physical arrangements:

- What associations does the room have in the minds of the group members?
- Is it the leader's room, a formal classroom, or some neutral area?
- Is the room to be a regular venue?
- Might discussion be vulnerable to noise or interruption?
- Can everyone be equally spaced?
- Is anyone (especially the leader) likely to have a special position e.g. behind a desk or at the head of a table?
- What can be done by moving furniture, to improve communication in the group?
- Can everyone make eye contact with each other?
- How possible is it to rearrange the grouping of chairs and tables?

Group size

Two contrasting features exist with regard to the number of people in a group. The larger the group, the greater is the pool of talent and experience available for solving problems or sharing the effort; on the other hand as the size increases, fewer members have the chance to participate, and indeed the differences in relative participation increase to the point where one or two members may well begin to dominate; it thus becomes more likely that reticent members will fail to contribute, though they may well enjoy the relative anonymity a large group affords them.

The smaller the group, as we have indicated on pages 10 and 11, the greater is the likelihood of close relationships, full participation, and consonance of aims. Whereas in a small group or team, leadership and other roles are likely to be shared or rotated, the formation of sub-groups, and the increasing differentiation of roles in a large group will ensure the emergence of a leader. Where there is an agreed leader (e.g. the teacher or chair) the need to counteract the above tendencies places special demands on his or her awareness of the problems and skills in coping with them. When does a group become 'large' and does it still have any merits? Most theorists, researchers and practitioners agree that five to seven members is the optimum for leaderless groups. In the case of led groups, as for academic discussion, the maximum for member satisfaction is 10 to 12.

The chart on page 35 of the chapter graphically illustrates the likely differences in participation patterns with different sizes of group.

Larger groups are an advantage when it requires the combining of individual efforts as in brain-storming. They are of less value when everyone must accomplish the task, which is the general situation in most discussion groups. If the group is small (i.e., two or three in number), the leader is likely to be dominant from the start. With a large group (eight or more) the divergence of aims and the need for role differentiation may push the leader into a dominant position. However, as we argue in Chapter 6, the use of sub-groups can overcome many of the difficulties in large group interaction.

Questions to ask about group size:

■ What size of group is appropriate to the aims?
■ How many people can be comfortably fitted into the room and still have good eye contact?
■ Will the leader take a leadership role or will participants take responsibility for the process?
■ Does the leader intend to split the group into sub-groups?
■ Will the group still be large enough if one or two members are absent or not contributing?

Group composition

As a general rule, a heterogeneous mix provides the best combination for interaction and achievement of task. Such qualities as age, sex, culture and personality may be taken into account, though one can never be sure what mixture will lead to effective participation. Individual members will contribute differently according to who they are grouped with, sometimes producing what is known as an 'assembly effect' – a convergence of needs and behaviours, which is often impossible to predict. Indeed the leader may be part of it, for example when a group of dependent participants is led by an authoritative or charismatic person.

Whether from the point of view of learning, problem-solving or decision-making, the mixing of quicker or more intelligent students with their slower counterparts can enable a teaching process between the students to take place. Yet often the most powerful influences are the personal likes and dislikes of fellow members. People tend to agree with individuals they like and disagree with those they dislike even though both may express the same opinion.

With project and task teams both the size of the group and its composition will need special attention. Small groups may lack the necessary range of expertise while larger groups may prove more difficult to hold together. Who should decide the membership and how? While self-chosen groups may have their merits they may lead to the kind of conformity of interests and abilities; teams of friends may collude in not challenging each other (see Norms, page 29). A carefully balanced group membership using Belbin's (1981) team roles (see page 153) can be followed by negotiated changes where individuals make a case.

In allocating students to groups, the leader may want to ask questions like:

■ What are the main differences between students?
■ How can the range and balance of roles and expertise be pre-determined?
■ What kinds of task are suitable?
■ Which students seem to identify with and support each other?
■ Which students are likely to be continually at loggerheads?

- What exclusive cliques do there seem to be?
- How might subsequent changes be legitimised?

Participation pattern

At any given moment every group has a particular participation pattern. For instance, it may be all one-way, with the leader talking to, or answering questions from, the members as in Figure 2.1; or it may be two-way, with the leader speaking to the members and the members responding; or it may be multidirectional, with all members speaking to one another and to the group as a whole. In a given group this pattern may tend to be quite consistent, or it may vary from time to time. The studies do not indicate that any one participation pattern is always best; it depends upon the requirements of a given situation. But many studies show that on the whole, the broader the participation among members of a group the deeper the interest and involvement will be. Some questions you may ask about a group to understand its participation pattern are:

- How much of the talking is done by the leader, how much by the other members?
- To whom are questions or comments usually addressed – the group as a whole, the leader, or particular members?
- How much non-verbal participation is evident particularly among members who don't talk much?
- Do some members look bored or uninterested?

It is very easy, and often useful to a group, to chart the participation pattern during periodic segments of time, thus providing objective data about this aspect of its dynamics, as in Figure 2.1. You may also be interested to compare these with a group seated in a circle without a rectangular table and thus with better eye-to-eye communication.

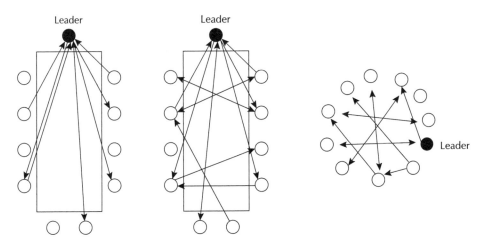

Figure 2.1 Patterns of participation

Communication

It is through communication that members of a group learn to understand one another and to influence, or be influenced by, each other. Yet communication is not just a matter of expressing ideas clearly. It is often suffused with unintended effects, fears and dislikes, and unconscious motives. Often the non-verbal part of communication is the most eloquent. A great deal is revealed about what a person is really thinking and feeling by their facial expression, posture, and gestures.

The content of communication is important too. In every subject area there is a specialised vocabulary which a newcomer may find off-putting. A clique within the group may sustain a private joke which intentionally excludes the rest.

For any communication to take place, speaking must be complemented by listening. Students may often, through preoccupation with their own thoughts or scorn for another's opinions, fail to hear what is being said. Ground rules in which each speaker in turn has to summarise what the previous one said can encourage more purposeful listening.

Questions about communication:

- How clearly do members express their ideas?
- To what extent do they appear to be listening to each other?
- Do they make connections to or build on each others' contributions?
- To what extent does the leader dominate discussion?
- Do they check for understanding or ask for clarification when they were not sure of what somebody else meant?
- Is there good eye contact round the group?
- Are feelings as well as thoughts communicated?

Cohesiveness

Cohesiveness is a measure of the attraction of the group to its members (and the resistance to leaving it), the sense of team spirit, and the willingness of its members to coordinate their efforts. Compared with members of a low-cohesive group, those in a high-cohesive group will, therefore, be keen to attend meetings, be satisfied with the group, use 'we' rather than 'I' in discussions, be cooperative and friendly with each other, and be more effective in achieving the aims they set for themselves. The low-cohesive group will be marked by absenteeism, the growth of cliques and factions, and a sense of frustration at the lack of attainment.

Questions to ask on group cohesiveness are:

- How satisfied are members with the group and their part in it?
- Did members seem glad to see each other again?
- Did there seem to be a sense of shared purpose or was everyone 'doing their own thing'?

- Did any sub-group or private conversations develop?
- Was the quality and quantity of communication high or low?
- Did members turn up on time and stay to the end without looking distracted?
- How much interest or lack of it was apparent in what was happening or where the group was going?
- Did members talk inclusively about the group – 'our group', 'we', and 'each one of us' rather then 'the group', 'I', or 'you'?

Norms

Every group tends to develop a code of ethics or set of norms about what is proper and acceptable behaviour which may vary and develop over time. Which subjects may be discussed, which are taboo; how openly members may express their feelings; the propriety of volunteering one's services; the length and frequency of statements considered allowable; whether or not interrupting is permitted, whether the tutor can be challenged – all of these, and many more do's and don'ts, are embodied in a group's norms. Some norms will be strictly adhered to while others allow for variation. It may be difficult for a new member to catch on to a group's norms if they differ from those of other groups he or she has experienced since these norms are usually implicit rather than openly stated. Indeed, a group may be confused about what its norms actually are, and this may lead to embarrassment, irritation and lost momentum over the first few meetings. It may be helpful to invite a group to break into sub-groups to discuss its norms and perhaps to discard some of those which seem counterproductive.

Questions about norms include:

- What evidence was there of a code of ethics regarding such matters as self-discipline, sense of responsibility, courtesy, tolerance of differences, freedom of expression, and the like?
- Are there any marked deviations from these norms by one or more members; how does the group respond and with what effect?
- Do these norms seem to be well understood by all members, or is there confusion about them?
- Are there 'meta-norms' about breaking or not breaking norms?
- Which of the group's norms seem to help, and which seem to hinder the group's progress?

Sociometric pattern

In every group the participants soon tend to identify certain individuals that they like more than other members, and others that they like less. These subtle relationships of friendship and antipathy – the sociometric patterns – have an important influence on the group's activities. Some research indicates that people tend to agree with people they like and to disagree with people they dislike, even though both express the same ideas. Questions which help to reveal the sociometric pattern are:

- Which members tend to identify with and support one another?
- Which members seem repeatedly at odds with others?
- Do some members act as 'triggers' to others, causing them to respond immediately after the first member's comments, either pro or con?

Procedures

Procedures are explicit rules or conventions for ensuring that what a group wants to happen, does in fact happen. They are the means of handling problematic events like making decisions, conflict, distribution of tasks, assessment and evaluation; and they may be invoked by, or applied to, any member or the whole group. Procedures may also be seen as devices for ensuring the smooth running of the group and the achievement of agreed aims. They may be formal and strictly codified, as in many committees, or informal and loose as for teams and working groups. The main virtue of a procedure is that it is usually set up before the event and this detaches discussions of how the group should handle problems in general from the problem-solving process itself.

Typical rules and procedures for groups may be:

- All decisions should be made by consensus.
- Anyone may call time-out at any stage in order to review progress.
- The group starts and finishes on time.
- The first five minutes of every meeting are spent milling around the room and chatting.
- The group follows an agenda.
- Members take on functional roles like timekeeper, summarizer, and so on.
- Each member has a maximum time-limit for contributions.

A very sophisticated group might also agree a meta-procedure which determines how any of the above rules or procedures might be changed. Rules and procedures may be invented in response to questions like these:

- How will the group decide on aims, tasks, and agendas?
- How is the group to make decisions?
- What regular process problems are likely to arise?
- How can it make best use of the resources of its members?
- How is it going to ensure full involvement in discussion?
- To what extent do the procedures incorporate the explicit norms or ground rules of the group?
- How will it monitor and evaluate its progress?
- How will it coordinate the various activities outside the group or in sub-groups?

Structure

When a group comes together for the first time and begins to interact, various differences between the members begin to appear: differences in status, influence, role, ability, and so on. The pattern of relationships that is thus established is known as the group structure. The pattern will, of course, change according to the nature of the task or the stage of discussion and the most influential person for one purpose may not be so for another. Where there is no appointed leader, as in tutorless groups, the leadership may, therefore, move round different members of the group. A structure that emerges in these ways is known as the invisible structure.

A visible structure exists when the group agrees a division of labour, roles, and responsibilities, in order to get essential tasks performed. You could for instance distribute a set of roles to the group: *initiating, giving and asking for information, giving and asking for reactions, restating and giving examples, confronting and reality-testing, clarifying, synthesising and summarising, gatekeeping and expediting, timekeeping, evaluating and diagnosing, standard-setting, sponsoring and encouraging.* Online these structures emerge more slowly, and most virtual groups need more help than face-to-face groups to achieve them.

Such a method, though it is valued by some students, maybe too socially demanding. A structure that encourages participation is pyramidding (page 122), a sequence of stages involving individual work, followed by discussion in pairs, then in fours, and a final session with the whole group or class. Several other structures are proposed in Chapter 6.

Questions to ask about structure include:

- What kind of pecking order(s) emerged among the participants?
- What kind of group roles or functions were missing, and what effect did this have?
- What role did the leader adopt – instructor, facilitator, chairperson, resource, consultant? Was it clear?
- Did participants have any specified roles?
- Was the assessment role of the leader clear to the participants?
- How did the invisible structure match any visible one?
- How was the invisible structure manifest? Who influences whom, who volunteers, defers to others, etc.?
- Was the group structure, visible or invisible, appropriate to the task?

Aims or goals

Aims are implicit in most, if not all, groups though they are not often thought about and even less often discussed. These aims may be intrinsic in nature: 'to discuss environmental pollution', or they may be extrinsic: 'to make decisions about the course' or 'to prepare for an examination'. Aims also have social and task dimensions. Social aims include 'to develop group loyalty and a sense of belonging' while task aims refer to qualities like judging ideas and checking progress. They are complementary. If the social dimension is not given due regard, participants may feel cool about the group and have no sense of commitment. If the task dimension is missing they may become dissatisfied and feel frustrated at not achieving anything worthwhile. The social dimension has an additional educational scope. It includes qualities like self-awareness, the ability to work independently yet cooperatively in a team – all important aspects of the participants' personal development. Online, clarity of purpose and reasons for continuing to take part need to be explicit for participants to consider it worthwhile.

Members of any group are likely to have their own personal and, sometimes, hidden aims and these may have little to do with the aims of the group as a whole, where these are known. Sometimes these personal aims, for example, impressing the leader, scoring off another member, wanting approval of the group, capitalising on other participants' ideas, may undermine the intended aims of the leader. It is the leader's job to somehow accommodate or mobilise the personal aims within the overall aims; and there is usually no better way to do this than through as open discussion as possible of all the aims arising from the group.

The issue of aims and their function in learning groups is discussed more fully in Chapter 5.

Questions about aims are:

- How involved were the members in the formulation of the group's aims or goals?
- Were these acceptable to them?
- To what extent did everyone inside (and outside) the group share the aims?
- What separate and independent aims did members have?
- Was the method/technique/interactions appropriate to the aims? How do you know?
- What unintended outcomes were there?
- Did the group evaluate progress during and at the end of the meeting/series of meetings?

SOCIAL AND TASK DIMENSIONS

It is easy to assume that groups differ substantially in their nature: informal social groups like coffee circles appear to have few rules or procedures and certainly no specific goals. Their members belong for the emotional satisfaction they get from being with people they like and enjoy. Membership in these groups is voluntary and tends to be fairly homogeneous. The success of the social group is measured in terms of how enjoyable it is.

Other groups, however, such as committees, working parties, staff meetings and discussion groups, usually have goals (though not always as shared and explicit as they might be), and more or less formal rules and procedures. The membership tends to be more heterogeneous – based on whatever is required to do the work – and sometimes brought together out of compulsion or sense of duty more than free choice. The success of the task group is measured in terms of how much work it achieves.

However further study of these apparently different kinds of group indicates that that they do more similarities than differences – the social or task dimensions exist for all groups though they may be in different proportions. As Knowles and Knowles (1972) observe:

[M]ost groups need the social dimension to provide emotional involvement, morale, interest, and loyalty; and the task dimension to provide stability, purpose, direction and a sense of accomplishment. Without the dimension of work, members may become dissatisfied and feel guilty because they are not accomplishing anything; without the dimension of friendship, members may feel that the group is cold, unfriendly, and not pleasant to be with.

Group maintenance and group task functions

Group functions have been classified thus:

1 *group-building and maintenance roles* – those which contribute to building relationships and cohesiveness among the membership (the social dimension);
2 *group task roles* – those which help the group to do its work (the task dimension).

The first set of functions is required for the group to maintain itself as a group; the second set, for the locomotion of the group toward its goals. For example, some *group-building functions* are:

- *encouraging* – being friendly, warm, responsive to others, praising others and their ideas, agreeing with and accepting the contributions of others.
- *mediating* – harmonising, conciliating differences in points of view, making compromises.
- *gate-keeping* – trying to make it possible for another member to make a contribution by saying, 'We haven't heard from Jim yet', or suggesting limited talking – time for everyone so that all will have a chance to be heard.
- *standard-setting* – expressing standards for the group to use in choosing its subject matter or procedures, rules of conduct, ethical values.
- *following* – going along with the group, somewhat passively accepting the ideas of others, serving as an audience during group discussion, being a good listener.
- *relieving tension* – draining off negative feeling by jesting or throwing oil on troubled waters, diverting attention from unpleasant to pleasant matters.

And the following are some *task functions*:

- *initiating* – suggesting new ideas or a changed way of looking at the group problem or goal, proposing new activities.
- *information-seeking* – asking for relevant facts or authoritative information.
- *information-giving* – providing relevant facts or authoritative information or relating personal experience pertinently to the group task.
- *opinion-giving* – stating a pertinent belief or opinion about something the group is considering.
- *clarifying* – probing for meaning and understanding, restating something the group is considering.
- *elaborating* – building on a previous comment, enlarging on it, giving examples.
- *coordinating* – showing or clarifying the relationships among various ideas, trying to pull ideas and suggestions together.

- *orienting* – defining the progress of the discussion in terms of the group's goals, raising questions about the direction the discussion is taking.
- *testing* – checking with the group to see if it is ready to make a decision or to take some action.
- *summarising* – reviewing the content of past discussion.

(Knowles and Knowles 1972, p. 54)

All the functions are clearly not needed in the same measure all the time and it can happen that any one of them used at the wrong time can interfere with the progress of the group. When a group is not functioning effectively, it will probably be because nobody is performing one or more of the functions listed above that is crucial at that point for the group to progress. It is also typical in any group that some of its members will tend to perform certain function more readily and effectively than others and there is a risk that they might become typecast in that role, rather than the various functions being shared and performed as and when the group needs them and individual members can recognise the need for them.

Group members may also exhibit behaviour which does not help the group to progress in achieving its goals. This 'non-functional role', as it is commonly called is likely to satisfy only the personal needs of the person in question. Non-functional roles might include:

- *blocking* – interfering with the progress of the group by going off on a tangent, citing personal experiences unrelated to the group's problem, arguing too much on a point the rest of the group has resolved, rejecting ideas without consideration, preventing a vote.
- *aggressing* – criticising or blaming others, showing hostility toward the group or some individual without relation to what has happened in the group, attacking the motives of others, deflating the ego or status of others.
- *seeking recognition* – attempting to call attention to oneself by excessive talking, extreme ideas, boasting, boisterousness.
- *special pleading* – introducing or supporting ideas related to one's own pet concerns or philosophies beyond reason, attempting to speak for 'the grass roots','the housewife', 'the common man', and so on.
- *withdrawing* – acting indifferent or passive, resorting to excessive formality, doodling, whispering to others.
- *dominating* – trying to assert authority in manipulating the group or certain members of it by 'pulling rank', giving directions authoritatively, interrupting contributions of others.

(Knowles and Knowles 1972, pp. 55–7)

Other members of the group will probably feel irritated or at least uncomfortable with such behaviours, and react with silence, hostility or rejection. Yet may of course be difficult to pinpoint some of the categories simply, because a non-functional behaviour may be seen in different ways by different members and almost certainly by the person themselves. But is is reasonable to assert that any group that is able to recognise these behaviours for what they are and sees them as a symptom of somebody's unmet personal needs, and to constructively deal with them, is going to be able to devote itself more effectively to the group-building functions.

The effects of group size

The tendency for many of the above behaviours to become dominant can increase with group size for reasons explained on page 25. Even in small discussion groups participants contribute unequally and there is little doubt that the scope for participation decreases exponentially as numbers increase as the following graphs clearly indicate.

In the first diagram which shows the percentage of contributions in a group of five, one member – the highest contributor – has made over 40 per cent of the contributions while another – the lowest contributor, has made only 7 per cent. In the second diagram, a group of eight, the difference becomes more marked. The highest contributor has maintained a similar level of contribution but

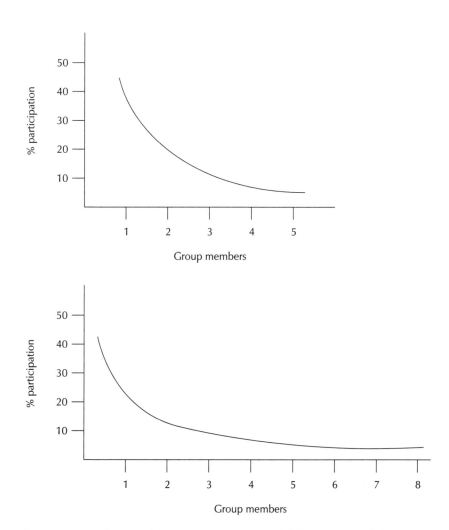

Figure 2.2 Distribution of participation in groups of different sizes (Bligh 2000)

the lowest six have each made only 3–8 per cent of the contributions. The implication of this is that larger groups need more structure organised for them if they are to function effectively within the usual time boundaries; either the leader will have to take a firmer hand and set up sub-groups with specified tasks, or some other form of leadership will emerge.

In online groups, size is a significant interaction variable in achieving discussion to enhance academic learning. Discussion in smaller groups of six to eight creates more evidence and experience of higher levels of knowledge construction compared to larger groups if there are effective task-centred e-tivities and structures in place (Schellens and Valcke 2004).

LEADERSHIP

Thus far, in looking at group functions, we have made little distinction between those relating to leaders compared with those of other members. Leadership can happen in different ways: a leader may be designated prior to the group's starting or may assume such a role because of his or her external position; such leaders may lack many of the qualities needed for handling the often complex dynamics of the group. Leaders may also emerge naturally or be elected by the group. What most commonly happens, whether or not the role is allocated is that some form of leadership rotates within the group according to task and personal interest at a particular time and is thus a function of the interaction such variables.

The style (real or perceived) of leadership can profoundly affect both the climate and the achievement of a group. In a classic series of laboratory-based experiments Kurt Lewin and others studied the influences of different leadership styles on group behaviour. They tested three types of leader behaviour: 'autocratic' , 'democratic' , and 'laissez-faire'. The effects were clear and dramatic:

- Autocratically led groups were more dependent on the leader and less considerate in their peer relationships, engaged in scapegoating, and even destroyed what they had, as a group, constructed. They were however quicker and more productive in the achievement of their task than the other groups.
- Democratically led groups, though slower in getting going, showed more initiative, friendliness and responsibility, supported each other, expressed greater satisfaction and continued the work in the absence of the leader.
- Laissez-faire groups produced less work than autocratically and democratically led groups, spent more time talking about what they should be doing, played around and experienced more aggression than the democratic group but less than the authoritarian.

The autocrat was the least liked of the leaders, with the democrat by far the most popular. This study has been substantiated by most of the research conducted over the past 50 years to the effect that, though some situations may require autocratic and others laissez-faire leadership, in most normal situations, groups thrive best when the leadership functions are democratically shared among the members of the group. However, under certain conditions, such as when urgent decisions are needed or when the group is large, autocratic leadership may be more effective. Where the commitment of members to a decision and its implementation is paramount, democratic groups are valued.

Such understandings are firmly substantiated in more recent work by Galanes (2003) who conducted interviews with of 23 'effective group leaders' and participants on what they believed was important in leading groups. The following five categories emerged from her research:

1   Establishing the intention for the overall project

   ■   Having vision and making it clear.
   ■   Making sure members know the ultimate goal.
   ■   Motivating members to want to be part of the group at the outset; helping people buy in to the project; inspiring members to support the vision, mission, goals.
   ■   Having a clear sense of purpose, knowing where you want the team to go.

2   Building the team and developing a positive group culture

   ■   Understanding group dynamics and using them to create a warm, supportive, inclusive climate.
   ■   Making sure people know each other; knowing that members need to get something out of the group and working to make sure individual needs are met.
   ■   Valuing people as individuals; selecting the members with the right kinds of skills and attitudes; making sure they feel valued, wanted and respected.
   ■   Creating an atmosphere where people feel safe to contribute, that the leader will support members in expressing themselves and stop behaviours that are counterproductive to this.
   ■   Having a meeting that is fun, light-hearted, enjoyable; having a good sense of humour.
   ■   Allowing a graceful way for non-productive members to leave the team.

3   Monitoring and managing the team's interactions during meetings

   ■   Trusting in the group process and the group's expertise.
   ■   Monitoring to check participation levels, checking in with members between meetings.
   ■   Building consensus.
   ■   Keeping members informed about things that affect them.
   ■   Supporting questioning, disagreement and conflict, but not personal attacks.
   ■   Asking the right kinds of questions.
   ■   Using the right kind of leadership for the situation.
   ■   Using appropriate techniques to achieve goals.

4   Managing the group's task and keeping the group focused

   ■   Agreeing and being committed to the leadership task.
   ■   Reducing any uncertainty in the group about the overall task, having a clear picture of it and communicating it to the group, constantly paying attention to the group's progress towards the goal.

- Keeping the group task-focused and moving towards its goal.
- Paying attention to process and structure.
- Preparing for meetings, getting ready for meetings.
- Organising the group's work, dividing up the tasks, making sure everyone has something to do, delegating, following up.
- Managing the group's time.
- Removing obstacles to the group's work and progress.
- Evaluating the group's process and progress, looking for ways to improve, asking members to do the same.

5   Communication behaviours and personal characteristics

- Modelling the behaviour s/he wants others to show; admitting mistakes, not dominating discussion; being less of a contributor than encourager of others.
- Inspiring confidence in others.
- Personal characteristics: self knowledge, self monitoring, passion, integrity, honesty, work ethic, knowledgeable about the issue.
- Exhibiting 'we' rather than 'I' behaviour, putting the team first.
- Listening and demonstrating the value of listening.
- Exhibiting effective interpersonal communication skills, making it easy for others to talk to her/him.
- Doing things to help themselves, e.g. calming affirmations, introduction.

GROUPS IN MOTION

Much of what we have been discussing so far has been concerned with the variables that make up a group – its properties and the membership and leadership functions. But groups are thriving and developing organisms which never stand still. Groups move both as a unit, and through the interaction of the various elements within them. A change in structure (as we shall see in Chapter 6) can affect participation which in turn may affect communication, norms, leadership and so on. Figure 2.3 from Guirdham (1990) shows a useful visual summary of the generic stages with the different emphases on individual, group and task needs indicated by the size of the circles.

Stages of group development

It may be informative nevertheless to look at one approach in more detail. Of the various schema that have been proposed, the following, based on Lawrence in Bligh (1986), probably best fits the psychodynamic orientations of Chapter 1.

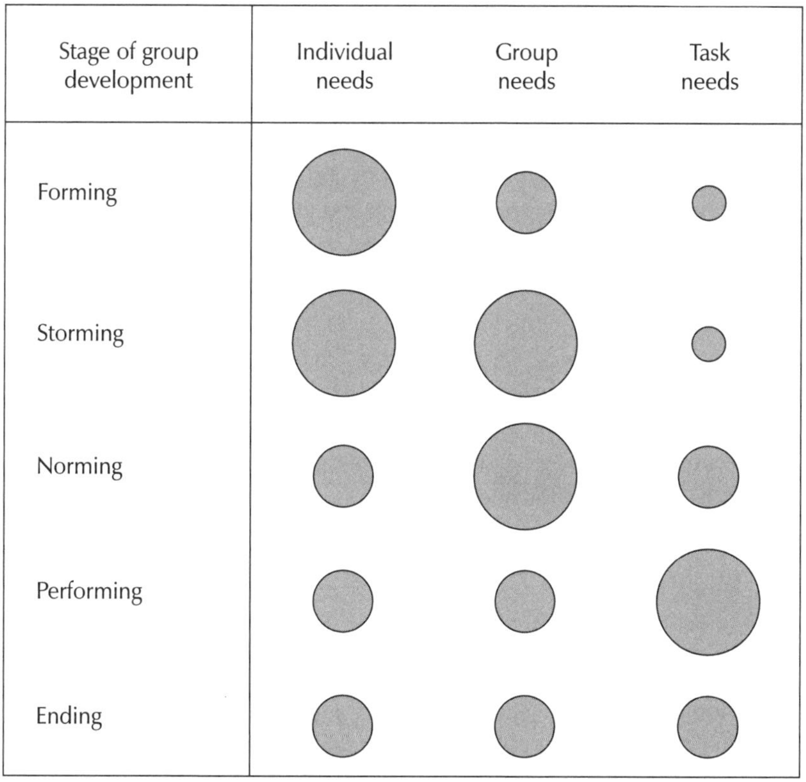

Stage of group development	Individual needs	Group needs	Task needs
Forming	●	●	●
Storming	●	●	●
Norming	●	●	●
Performing	●	●	●
Ending	●	●	●

Figure 2.3 Relative influence of individual, group and task needs on group members' behaviour at different stages of group development

Based on Guirdham (1990) *Interpersonal Skills at Work*, Prentice Hall

Forming

When a number of people come together for the first time to form a group there is an initial concern with the nature of the task: what has to be done and by what time and with what resources? Group members will equally be checking out what is appropriate behaviour and adjusting accordingly. There is also, at this stage, a strong dependence on any authority in the group as a form of counterbalance to the deeper question which is about 'Why am I here?' or 'Do I really want to be here'? This need to create a sense of self in the group is labelled 'self-lodging' by Denzin (1969): 'If valued portions of self are not lodged, recognised and reciprocated, a dissatisfaction concerning the encounter is likely to be sensed. If self-lodging doesn't take place successfully, the person may fail to take up a rational standpoint.' This supports the paradoxical hypothesis that a group cannot come together until each member has established her or his own separate individuality.

Storming

This stage typically includes conflict and an expression of interpersonal hostility within the group. It is as if any of the uncertainties and deeper emotions from the previous stage have become unfrozen and or projected onto other people of the group. Bennis, Benne and Chin (1985) describe it as a stage of counter-dependence on authority. Differences are asserted and seen as all or nothing, for or against. Issues of personal freedom versus the group authority and leaders of opposing arguments collect followers.

Norming

Emphasis is now placed on the mutual concerns and interrelationships. The freedom/authority conflict of storming has been resolved. Behaviours now turned to listening, asking opinions, building on others, etc. Personal norms are replaced by group norms, common goals are agreed, ground rules may be established and a sense of open collaboration is created, but not without some compromise on the freedom experienced in Stage 2, and some negotiation.

Performing

Now members settle into, and are reasonably satisfied with, functional roles. Schroder and Harvey (1963) called this positive interdependence with simultaneous autonomy and neutrality. The group acquires a distinct sense of itself as a culture. One role which the group will probably decide is that concerned with its continuity, which naturally leads to the fifth stage.

Informing

In this the final, and sometimes ignored, phase the group starts to give voice to the outside world, communicating, for instance, with other groups, and agreeing how it will further its work.

Lawrence points out that the above stages depend upon certain assumptions which may or may not exist: that the group manages to survive the *storming* stage and does in fact move from stage to stage until they achieve their goal without falling apart; and that problems of outside hierarchy, which might distort the sense of shared purpose, are not imported into the group.

A SEVEN-STAGE MODEL OF GROUP DEVELOPMENT

Many of the classic studies of group development have involved group leaders who took a passive or non-directive role and did not directly intervene in the group process (Johnson and Johnson 1987), and this contrasts with the typical tutor-led group in higher education. They propose the following seven-stage model for learning groups where there is a leader with clear responsibility for the effective functioning of the group.

1   *Defining and structuring procedures*
    At the first meeting the group will expect the tutor/leader to explain what is expected of them, what the plan and purpose of the meetings is and how the group is going to operate (whether or not this fulfilled is of course a matter of choice). Typically with a learning group, the tutor will clarify the task, explain procedures, and generally set up the group in readiness for its work together.

2   *Conforming to procedures and getting acquainted*
    As the group gets used to the procedures and norms of the group they also become more familiar and relaxed with each other. The group is still dependent on the tutor for direction and they are happy to conform according to the process norms of the group whether explicitly or implicitly expressed. They do not yet feel a personal commitment to the group's goals or to each other.

3   *Recognising mutuality and building trust*
    The group members begin to recognise their interdependence and to build a sense of cooperation and trust. They internalise the sense that group learning is a collaborative venture and participate actively in discussions. There is a feeling of mutual support and trust.

4   *Rebelling and differentiating*
    This stage represents a pulling back from the previous two as members start to resist the responsibilities they had apparently accepted and become counter-dependent, contravening many of the group-learning procedures. Sometimes this may mean returning to a more passive, minimal effort role and forgetting the previously held cooperative ethos. Despite its apparent negativity this stage is important for members in establishing interpersonal boundaries and a sense of autonomy which can lead to a stronger, because self-owned, collaboration. Johnson and Johnson suggest that tutors should regard this rebellion and conflict as a natural and 'deal with both in an open and accepting way'. They recommend:

    ■   Not tightening control and trying to force conformity: reasoning and negotiating.
    ■   Confronting and problem-solving.
    ■   Mediating conflicts while helping to underpin autonomy and individuality.
    ■   Working towards participants taking ownership of procedures and committing themselves to each other's success.

    'Coordinating a learning group is like teaching a child to ride a bicycle', they say. You have to run alongside to prevent the child from falling off, giving the child space and freedom to learn how to balance on his or her own.

5   *Committing to and taking ownership for the goals, procedures and other members*
    The group becomes 'our' group, not the tutor's. The group norms of cooperation become internalised and no longer have to be externally imposed: the member are no longer dependent on the tutor as the driving force and find support and help from each other. Friendships develop.

6 *Functioning maturely and productively*

A sense of collaborative identity develops as the group matures into an effective working unit. Group members learn to operate in different ways in order to achieve group goals and can readily alternate attention between task and maintenance concerns. At this stage they can usually cope with any problems that arise in the group without the help of the tutor who in turn takes on the role of a consultant and resource to the group. Labour is divided according to expertise, members ask for and accept help from each other and leadership is shared among the members.

Johnson and Johnson remark that many discussion groups do not reach this stage either because the tutor does not have the ability to establish cooperative interdependence or group members do not collectively possess the necessary skills to function in this way. Part of the tutor's job is therefore to ensure that group members are acquiring the skills they need to progress to this stage.

7 *Terminating*

Every group has to come to an end and its members have to move on. The more cohesive and mature a group has become, the more sadness will accompany its ending for both members and tutor. The last meeting must deal with this as a recognisable problem and not avoid it as they leave the group to move on to future experiences.

Most groups, if they are developing effectively, with move fairly quickly through the first five stages, devote most time and energy to the mature and productive stage, and then terminate quickly. The skill of the tutor in handing over the 'perceived ownership' of the group goals and procedures as it moves from the first two stages through the rebellion is of course critical.

THE FIVE-STAGE FRAMEWORK FOR E-GROUPS

Online learning has given specific attention to what the learners should contribute in order to participate effectively. For an online process to be successful, participants need to be supported through a structured developmental process. This involves designing in advance for their participants, and then leading them gently through, during the time the interaction is running. The Salmon five-stage model provides an example of how participants can benefit from increasing skill and comfort from working online and networking with each other, and what the e-moderator needs to do at each stage to help them achieve this success.

Paralleling Johnson and Johnson's seven-stage model, and specific to online computer conferencing, the model (Salmon 2003), is based on and developed from the experience of participants in early computer-mediated conferences (Salmon 2004). It shows how to motivate online participation, to build learning through appropriate online activities (e-tivities) and to pace e-learners through online courses.

Arranging gradually more demanding participative and interactive tasks provides the action base for the model. We call these 'E-tivities' as they are explained further in Chapter 6.

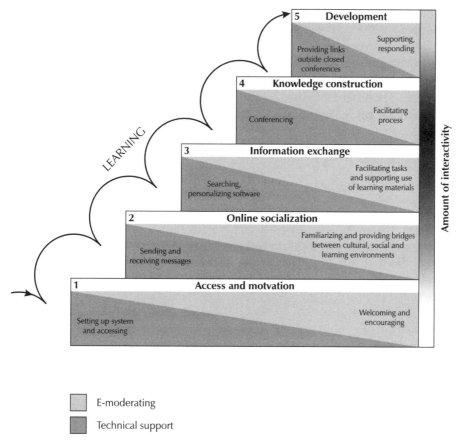

Figure 2.4 Model of teaching and learning online through online networking

Individual access and the induction of participants to online learning are essential prerequisites for online conference participation (stage 1 at the base of the flight of steps). Stage 2 involves individual participants establishing their online identities and then finding others with whom to interact. At stage 3, participants engage in mutual exchange of information. Up to and including stage 3 a form of of cooperation occurs whereby each person supports the others participants' goals. At stage 4, course related discussions develop and the interaction becomes more collaborative. At stage 5, participants look for more benefits from the system to help them achieve more personal goals and reflect on the learning processes.

Each stage requires the participants to master certain technical skills (shown in the bottom left of each step). Each stage calls for different e-moderator skills (shown in the right top of each step). The 'interactivity bar' running along the right of the flight of steps suggests the intensity of interactivity that you can expect between the participants at each stage. At first, at stage 1, they interact only with one or two others. After stage 2 the number of others with whom they interact, and the frequency, gradually increases, although stage 5 often returns to a return to more individual pursuits.

Given appropriate technical support, e-moderation and a purpose for taking part, nearly all participants will progress through these stages of use. There will however be very different responses to how much time they need at each stage before progressing. The model applies to all software. The chief benefit of using the model to design a learning process is that you know how participants are likely to exploit the system at each stage and you can avoid common pitfalls. The results should be higher participation rates and increased participant satisfaction. E-moderators who understand the model and apply it should enjoy their work and find that their work runs smoothly.

Note here that this model is one that is much more accessible to unobtrusive monitoring than might be achieved face-to-face.

FIELD STUDIES

Most of the research into group work in tertiary education is naturally centred on discussion groups. It is interesting therefore to draw comparisons between this and the more general research evidence described above. There is general agreement that some of the more important variables in discussion groups are:

- seating position;
- talkativeness;
- personality of the participants;
- kind of leadership.

In the online context, these variables may translate additionally as:

- Time of arrival in the conference (later arrivals may be joining a conference already in full swing) and habitual logging-in patterns (such as always joining in an active discussion later in the day because of other time demands or a differing time zone).
- Facility with the written word, including mastery of the software, keying skills and a willingness to see contributions 'on the record'.
- Fit between learning style and the online environment, particularly in asynchronous conferencing.
- Fit between the design of the learning tasks and the online platform in use.

Compare the foregoing with Deutsch (1949) who studied the effect of giving different information on the assessment of a group to members of different groups. He noted that where groups were to be assessed collectively, in cooperation, they showed more coordination of effort, diversity in amount of contribution, subdivision of activity, attentiveness to fellow members, mutual comprehension and communication, greater orientation, orderliness and productivity per unit time, as well as more favourable evaluation of the group and its products compared with groups who were informed that each individual would be assessed independently. Davey (1969) in an experiment with 800 groups of different sizes concluded that with up to approximately seven group members the permissive style of leadership seemed most productive, but above that a controlling style seemed to work better. This leads to consideration of the value of tutorless groups. Marris (1965) found that, when staff were absent from groups, participants felt far less inhibited and frequently discussed their work with each other. They felt that seeking help from staff was viewed as a confession of incompetence. Of course sub-groups within a larger group are a form of tutorless group and Beard and Hartley (1989) point to the success of discussion in pairs (buzz groups) before participants raise questions more formally with the teacher.

The presence of a tutor does not of course imply his or her active participation in discussion. Abercrombie (1979), for instance, developed a technique of group work in which the tutor played the part of an onlooker who asked the occasional question or made a comment, rather in the way that a group psychotherapist might do. In this case, the task was specific: to help participants consider evidence carefully and to make valid judgements on their observations. The objects of scrutiny were radiographs or an account of an experiment. Some participants were clearly unsettled by this procedure and others rejected it out of hand, though nearly all were amazed at the degree to which unconscious assumptions had appeared to influence their judgement. Upon testing at the end of the course, it was apparent that participants in this class were better able to distinguish between facts and inferences, made fewer false inferences, explicitly considered alternative hypotheses more frequently and were less often fixed in their view of the problem by dint of previous experience, than were a control group. This experience had apparently helped them become more objective in making assessments of scientific material.

It thus appears that groups are demonstrably valuable for many of the more sophisticated aims of higher education to do with critical thinking, making diagnoses or decisions, solving problems, and changing or maintaining attitudes to the subject under study. Indeed Bligh (1998), surveying the research evidence on different forms of teaching, concluded that discussion methods are more effective than didactic methods (e.g. the lecture) for stimulating thought, for personal and social adjustment, and for changes of attitude, and, more surprisingly perhaps, were no worse than the lecture for effectively transmitting information.

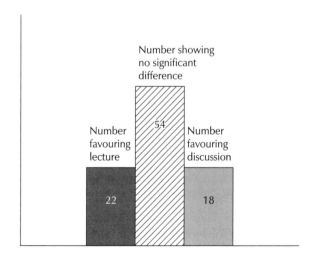

Figure 2.5(a) Lectures compared with discussion, with transmission of knowledge as the criterion

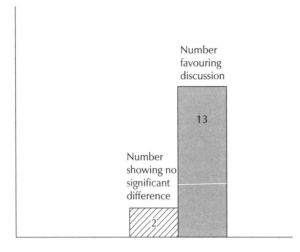

Figure 2.5(b) Lectures compared with discussion, with promotion of thinking as the criterion

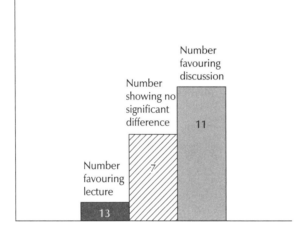

Figure 2.5(c) Lectures compared with discussion, with attitudes as the criterion

PREFERENCES AND PROBLEMS

The disposition of tutors and participants to learning in groups is of course another factor in their effectiveness and research into this would, as Neath (1998) states have to take into account whole learning environment, including the traditional culture of individualism and competition, as much as what skills and knowledge all involved have of working and learning in groups. This is especially an issue when participants are working in project teams and may suffer as a result of the inadequacies of one or more of their members or indeed the team as a whole. This commonly experienced problem is what makes books like *Learning in Teams* (Gibbs 1994) so important as training material for both tutors and participants. Luker (1987) in Brown and Atkins (1999) lists a number of student and tutor likes and dislikes on the subject of small group teaching, a selection of which are made here.

Why TUTORS like teaching small groups

- The informal atmosphere – opportunity to get to know students at a personal level and for them to get to know me.
- Feeling of informality and, when things go right, that students have learnt something and – even in statistics – enjoyed themselves.
- Seeing a student suddenly grasp an idea for the first time, which makes for him or her a number of other disjointed areas simultaneously fall into place.
- I can be stimulated by students' ideas.
- Opportunity for providing instantaneous, personal, feedback on their own thoughts and efforts.
- Being able to give praise.
- The educational goals are readily defined, almost as a contract between me and the group.

Why STUDENTS like learning in small groups

- I can personally have a greater influence on what is being discussed. I can actually remember, and feel I understand what we are discussing.
- I am able to participate and to find out other people's ideas.
- I like the flexibility of a small group. We aren't bound to a rigid schedule.
- It teaches you how to converse in a literate manner.
- It helps develop your power of analysing problems and arriving at solutions.
- By being in a smaller group, one feels part of a class rather than just another face in a sea of faces. I actually feel more part of the university.

What TUTORS find difficult and dislike in small groups

- Keeping my mouth shut.
- Getting a discussion going.
- It often requires considerable skill to direct discussion in fruitful directions.
- It requires considerably more mental alertness and flexibility than a formal lecture, and can be a bit of a strain.
- Getting students to see me as an equal, talk to me as they would to their peers, and lose their inhibitions about displaying ignorance in front of me and their peers.
- Very difficult to establish the kind of atmosphere in which students will begin to talk. They tend to be very much afraid of *not* saying the right thing.
- Shutting up the vociferous.
- Bringing in the meek.
- How to deal with a poor or irrelevant answer.

What STUDENTS find difficult or dislike in small groups

- A small group can easily be dominated by one person.
- When members of the group will not talk.
- Long silences.

- Being asked to contribute when you don't want to.
- Being directly asked vague questions.
- A feeling of being assessed by the lecturer through your answers to questions and your attitudes.
- Sometimes you feel threatened by the closeness of the lecturers.

In online groups, there is the additional demand of thorough training for the tutor and effective induction for the participants before the online discussion and the learning outcome can to be effective.

TUTOR AS RESEARCHER

The concept of a tutor as one who is putting into practice ideas developed by other does not carry universal appeal. Each teaching situation is governed by a unique set of variables which no general researcher could conceivably take into account: the personality of the tutor, the special characteristics of the participants, the effects of the learning milieu in that institution and the structure of the particular curriculum being taught, to name but a few. If tutors are to research their own teaching the question arises: how can the objectivity and rigour demanded by research be obtained? As Pring (1978) observes: 'being objective is opening to public scrutiny the basis upon which one's judgements are made so that counter-evidence and contrary arguments might, if they exist be levelled against what one says. I may be correct in declaring at the end of the lesson that things went well, but my judgement is subjective insofar as there is no evidence against which another might test the truth of what I say'.

In order to conduct classroom research one would need to formulate hypotheses and choose an appropriate test procedure. Such hypotheses would be unlikely to embrace all the variables, yet as long as they are regarded as provisional and are stated clearly, they can be very instructive. Among test procedures one might use, are:

- an interaction analysis (for example, the one on page 17);
- recording either with audio or video tape; online, the written record will serve;
- recording one's own comments in a diary;
- drawing out the participants' perceptions.

None of these would stand up on its own as reliable research evidence, but taken together they could be employed as a 'triangulation' technique in which each account of what happened is tested against the others. This proposal of the teacher as an activator in research, rather than as a recipient, is an exciting one in that it implies a greater sense of direction and self-autonomy for the teacher. It is firmly supported by Rowan and Reason (1981) who propose an interactive style of research in which the mutual influences of researcher and 'researched' are acknowledged.

Action research

Given the teacher's position of being both researcher and partner in the researched scenario at the same time, orthodox research practices make little sense, nor does it make professional sense to watch things going wrong and doing nothing to rectify them. In a practical and very accessible book, McNiff, Lomax and Whitehead (1996) describe action researchers, unlike orthodox researchers, as 'intent on describing, interpreting and explaining events while seeking to change them for the better'. They also claim that action research can lead to the researchers'

- own personal development;
- better professional practice;
- improvements in the institution in which they work;
- making a valuable contribution to the good order of society.

Action research unashamedly recognises and values the personal part that the researcher plays as both the 'subject and the object' of the study. The researcher therefore has to take a self-critical stance, admitting errors and taking full responsibility for mistakes. It demands the exercise of communication skills (listening in particular), management skills, quiet reflection and collaboration, all of which are agreeably congruent with the essence of good groupwork.

DISCUSSION POINTS

- Take the sets of questions on pages 24–32 and answer them for, or in, your group.
- How would you describe the balance between social and task dimensions in your group? What can you do to affect this?
- How would you characterise the role of leadership in the achievement of task goals compared with social goals in your group?
- To what extent do you feel any of the above concepts and principles apply to online groups only, offline groups or to combinations?
- How can you use the online process to understand your learning groups better?

CHAPTER THREE

APPROACHES TO LEARNING

This chapter focuses on the understandings drawn from research and experience and the various factors that characterise and affect the way learning takes place and their implications for groups.

FROM RESEARCH INTO PRACTICE

Over the past 25 years, the nature of learning, including through and with technology, has been the subject of much study and debate. Results of research have started to markedly influence teaching practices in education and training. The focus is shifting away from the activities of the teacher – the transmission model – and transferring to those of the learner.

The shift changes our beliefs about the tutor's role in learning from one of expert and figure of authority to one who encourages participation, dialogue and interaction by students with course materials and with each other. 'We must focus on what the student does while learning, what role the student adopts and how the student interacts not only with the learning input, but also how the student thinks and feels about learning and to how the social environment mediates and determines the quality of learning' (Nicol 1997: 1).

The tutor should function as a promoter of learning, intellectually critical, stimulating and challenging but within a context that emphasises support and mutual respect. Equally the climate has changed in the conception of what learning comprises. We should be concerned not with what learners take from what is available to them but with their approach to learning, the personal meaning they derive, the factors that motivate, and the social context and value system in which the learning occurs.

Studies have contributed helpful explanatory concepts that have become incorporated into practical ideas by trainers and developers and though much of it has been developed prior to the extensive use of learning technologies, deal with learning in whatever environment it takes place. The effect of the concepts may often be indirect but, when it coincides with the practical experiences of the group work and the basis of the training to teach methods for academics, it begins to acquire meaning and relevance. Action research on the relationships between learning and teaching can lead to outcomes that have more significance for, and effect on, those involved than 'pure' research evidence; yet they too provide a foundation for many applications which derive from their inspired interpretation by other than the original researcher.

Another major change of our expanded educational system in the twenty-first century is that learning groups are much more diverse than they were 25 years ago. Any approach to learning design needs to focus on a wider range of needs and styles of contribution; in other words a cross-cultural perspective. Three important elements become apparent in this:

- An understanding of one's own culture and its relationship to others.
- A meaningful way of gaining knowledge of the culture of others relevant to the learning task.
- A recognition that responding to diversity is not only a normal part of learning but also highly beneficial to acquiring knowledge.

(Mama 2001)

Approaches to learning vary systematically from one culture to another (Richardson 1994) and those students who may have little or no experience of discussion-based learning and of their role vis-à-vis the tutor in their own background may also need guidance in adapting to learning in groups both through careful use of inclusive methods in the group. The encouragement of collaborative study outside class time (Ryan 2000) can be very helpful, a strategy supported by Biggs (2003) in respect of particular groups of students who can be 'so demure and shy in the classroom (and) so noisy and boisterous outside'. The inference that online discussion may be of special value for less assertive students is borne out by Rainsbury and Malcolm (2003) who found that two groups of students who often lacked confidence in face-to-face situations – mature students and those of non-English backgrounds – found it easier to express an opinion on asynchronous discussion boards, and inferred that such online discussion could be used to develop their groupwork skills.

Where diversity includes such factors as wider differences of ability, low motivation or disillusionment, the task of supporting learning may extend to one of mitigating low performance or even reducing attrition rates, whether it be in respect of the group itself or the course as a whole. Here, the effectiveness of the tutor can be crucial in creating an inclusive climate which allows students to be themselves and which does not assume the learning and social styles of the more academic or younger students. This climate of learning can include an awareness of different previous educational experiences, the language of instruction and implied requirements, alternative learning styles and needs and other assumed norms (Thomas et al. 2003).

Explorations of learning styles challenge many assumptions and continue to suggest alternative solutions in the realm of student learning. They also present insights into the value of group work and the way in which groups may be organised and run to greater effect.

Our attention now focuses less on trying to change learners and more on changing the way they experience, perceive and conceptualise their learning in groups.

THE NATURE OF LEARNING

'Many theories and insights exist in respect of what learning in fact comprises. They depend as much on the orientation of the definer as on the nature of learning' (Brown 2004).

For a committed *behaviourist*, learning is the modification of behaviour brought about by experience. For most *cognitive psychologists*, learning is the study of how information is sensed, stored, elaborated and retrieved. Others stress the importance of *metacognition* – learning to learn – or reflection on action as well as experience *per se*. *Humanistic* psychologists are more likely to insist that personal growth and development are at the heart of learning, while *constructivists* argue that learning is primarily concerned with how people develop different conceptions and constructions of reality.

These different views of learning are themselves examples of constructivism at work, of how different people view learning. Each view leads to a different emphasis and consequent neglect of other features of learning.

Behaviourism led to the use of learning objectives and outcomes as a means of setting directions to learning. Mager (1984) asserted 'If you don't know where you are going, it is difficult to select a suitable means for getting there.' It focuses on what the learner is expected to be able to do as a result of their activity, how they should demonstrate their achievement, the conditions under which that will occur, and what the criteria will be for acceptable performance. It says little about the process of the journey, though it can help in creating and clarifying learning outcomes (see Chapter 5).

Constructivism on the other hand does not view knowledge as the pursuit of an external phenomenon but as one construed by individuals through their experience and with the support of their own cognitive frameworks. It sees learning as an active process in which learners engage with and build new ideas or concepts based upon their current and past knowledge. Such knowledge may include past experience, formal teaching, reading, sharing with peers and their creative endeavours. The learners select, transform, integrate and make choice informed by their unique mental models in developing their understandings. Constructivist approaches enables the individual to 'go beyond the information given'. Learners should therefore be encouraged to discover principles by themselves and to engage in active dialogue with their tutor and with each other, *as a learning strategy*. 'Good methods for structuring knowledge should result in simplifying, generating new propositions, and increasing the manipulation of new information' (Bruner 1977).

With constructivism as a basis, the task of the group tutor or e-moderator is to:

- gauge the students' readiness to learn;
- get the students to explore their own way forward;
- fill in any gaps;
- help to organise the knowledge so that it can be most readily grasped by the learner, by simplifying, generating new propositions, and increasing the manipulation of information.

The ideas around constructivism in teaching have arisen in the twenty-first century partly in response to the potential for more active student-led learning in online environments and away from passive teacher-led instruction. There are various versions of the theoretical underpinnings. One is an introspective view of knowledge as personally constructed and built on an individual's earlier internal mental models in the light of his or her new experiences (Stahl 2005). Another view is of knowledge as rather more external, and the group learning and teaching experience helps the students to internalise it. Taking part in a group of learners with sympathetic and supportive facilitation (or online e-moderation) is critically important to the construction of the knowledge. In practical terms, constructivism implies the need to promote discovery, dialogue, interaction, contextualisation and reflection, rather than delivery of content and information (Cooner 2005, Stahl 2005).

Group interaction involves learners in gauging their own viewpoints in relation to those of others and to construct and evaluate their knowledge and viewpoints through active dialogue.

LEARNING RESEARCH

Rather different aspects of the students' approach to learning were revealed through a series of seminal studies by Marton and Säljö (1976). They identified two distinctive approaches among students in the way they read texts:

Surface-level processing in which students take a passive approach and are concerned with:

- Covering the content.
- How much they have learned.
- Finding the 'right' answers.
- Assimilating unaltered chunks of knowledge.
- Learning verbatim.

Deep-level processing in which students take an active approach and are concerned with:

- The central point.
- What lies behind the argument.
- The whole picture.
- What it boils down to.
- What it is connected with.
- The logic of the argument.
- Points that are not clear.
- Questioning the conclusions.

The study of these two differing approaches leads to certain conclusions:

- People who process mainly at the surface level divert their attention to the 'sign': deep-level processors search for that which is 'signified'.

- Those who adopt a deep approach are more successful in exams: surface processors tend to pass only when they manage to overcome the tedium which that form of learning often induces.
- Deep processors are more versatile: they find it easier to tackle 'surface' questions than surface processors do 'deep' questions. Strong motivation increases the likelihood that deep-level processing will occur, while anxiety induces a hurried fact-grabbing strategy. Experienced tutors soon notice the increasing desperation among students to memorise 'facts' and know 'what is what' as exams approach!
- Surface and deep approaches are closely related to the level of satisfaction a student derives from the experience of learning: a surface approach can be painfully hard work while a deep approach is likely to increase motivation.

The most succinct summary of the dichotomy comes from Ramsden (1992): 'Surface is, at best, about quantity without quality; deep is about quality *and* quantity.'

In a parallel investigation, Pask (1976) drew a distinction between *holists* who adopted a broad perspective and looked for a variety of interrelationships and *serialists* who were typified by their attention to details and a pattern of learning by increments. Holists ask a different order of questions too, about broad relations, and form hypotheses about generalisations as opposed to serialists whose questions are 'about much narrower relations and (whose) hypotheses are specific'. Lest it be thought that holists are successful in all respects it should be added that they are likely to over-generalise and to make remote and often mistaken connections. Serialists, on the other hand, are often victims of their own caution, and their inability to make connections often makes integration of knowledge a difficult task for them. Pask also noted the versatile learner who is able to adopt the holist or serialist strategy according to the task at hand. He demonstrated, moreover, that holists are not good at learning serialist material; nor are serialists good with holist material, but students whose learning style matched the material learned it quickly and accurately. The parallels with surface and deep approaches to learning are apparent.

DEVELOPMENTAL PHASES IN LEARNING

Underlying the approach learners take is their understanding of what learning itself consists of: this understanding is influenced by the context they find themselves in and by the learning demands these contexts make. They are likely to change their approach to learning both through interaction with others and by gaining clearer understandings through feedback on what is expected of them. The following sequence indicates possible ways in which that development may take place. Gibbs (1990) identifies five stages in the development of students' understanding, with examples of the kinds of things that students who have these conceptions say.

Students who understand what learning is at levels 1, 2 and 3 have trouble comprehending what a deep approach consists of and are very unlikely to take a deep approach to learning tasks. Students who are at levels 4 or 5 can take either a deep or a surface approach, depending on the task and their perception of its demands. The connection between these underlying conceptions of learning and the approach students take to specific learning tasks is so strong that it is impossible to predict the quality of learning outcomes directly from students' conceptions of learning. All you need to know about a student is that she has a conception of learning at level 1, 2 or 3 and you can be fairly certain that she will only derive a superficial and fragmentary understanding from, for example, reading a chapter.

1   *Learning as an increase in knowledge.* The student will often see learning as something done to them by teachers rather than as something they do to or for themselves.

      To gain some knowledge is learning . . . We obviously want to learn more. I want to know as much as possible.

2   *Learning as memorising.* The students has an active role in memorising, but the information being memorised is not transformed in any way.

      Learning is about getting it into your head. You've just got to keep writing it out and eventually it will go in.

3   *Learning as acquiring facts or procedures which are to be used.* What you learn is seen to include skills, algorithms and formulae which you apply which you will need in order to do things at a later date, but there is still no transformation of what is learnt by the learner.

      Well it's about learning the thing so you can do it again when you are asked to, like in an exam.

4   *Learning as making sense.* The student makes active attempts to abstract meaning in the process of learning. This may only involve academic tasks.

      Learning is about trying to understand things so you can see what is going on.

      You've got to be able to explain things, not just remember them.

5   *Learning as understanding reality.* Learning enables you to perceive the world differently. This has also been termed 'personally meaningful learning'.

      When you have really learnt something you kind of see things you couldn't see before. Everything changes.

For some students, then, their limited understanding of what learning consists of prevents them from approaching learning tasks in a deep way and therefore from learning effectively. Two important questions about such crude and disabling conceptions of learning are: where do they come from? and can they be changed?

As well as being asked about what they think learning is, students have been asked what they think good teaching consists of. Some think that the teacher should do all the work and make all the decisions. The teacher should select the subject matter, present it in teacher-controlled classes, devise tests and mark students on how well they have learnt the material which has been presented. What is to be learnt and what learning outcomes should look like is completely defined by the teacher (a 'closed' conception of teaching). Others think that while the teacher has responsibility for setting the learning climate, for making learning resources available and for supporting students, all the responsibility lies with the student: responsibility for selecting learning goals, devising appropriate learning activities and for judging when learning outcomes are satisfactory (an 'open' conception of teaching). It will probably come as no surprise to learn that the former, 'closed' conception of teaching is held almost exclusively by students with conceptions of learning at levels 1, 2 or 3, while the latter, 'open' conception of teaching is held by students with conceptions of learning at levels 4 or 5. This relationship is summarised in the table below.

Table 3.1 Conceptions of learning and teaching

Conception of learning	Conception of teaching
Reproducing (Levels 1, 2 and 3)	Closed Teacher does all the work and makes all the decisions
Making sense (Levels 4 and 5)	Open Learner does most of the work and makes most of the decisions

INTELLECTUAL DEVELOPMENT

In post-compulsory education students are free, possibly for the first time, to learn in their preferred way, and to develop their own sense of what is worth learning. In groups their perception of this evolves as they encounter the exchange of views where each can compare and contrast their own ways of thinking and behaving with that of the others, including the tutor/moderator, and to change these as he or she thinks fit.

In an interview study of students at the Liberal Arts College at Harvard, Perry (1970) found a coherent progression in the manner in which students approached learning, experienced values and construed the world during their college experience. He identified a sequence of nine positions through which students appear to have progressed as they moved through college. Basically the sequence comprised a development from a dualistic, authority-accepting position, through a relativistic 'anything goes' phase to a final stage of open-minded commitment.

Position 1 – dualism. There are Right and Wrong Answers to everything. Authority, whose role is to teach the answers, knows what these are, and if I work hard, and learn the Right Answers, adding more and more to my stock of knowledge, all will be well.

Position 2. Diversity of opinion and uncertainty exist but that's only because Authority is confused or ill-qualified. They set us problems only to enable us to find the Right Answer by ourselves.

Position 3. Some uncertainties and differences in opinions are real and legitimate. But this is a temporary situation for Authorities who are still searching for the Right Answer.

Position 4a. Where Authorities don't know the Right Answers, everyone has a right to their own opinion; no one is Wrong!

Position 4b. Some Authorities are not asking for the Right Answer: they are grading us as they do because they want us to think about things in a certain way, supporting opinion with data and so on.

Position 5 – relativism. All knowledge and values are relative but equally valid. Everything has to be seen in its context. Dualistic, Right/Wrong thinking is a special case in context.

Position 6. I'm going to have to make up my own mind in an uncertain world with no one to tell me whether I'm right or wrong.

Position 7. I've made my first commitment!

Position 8. Now I've made several commitments, I've got to balance them in terms of priorities. Which do I feel really committed to and responsible for?

Position 9 – evolving commitments. This is how life will be. I must be wholehearted while tentative, fight for my values yet respect others, believe my deepest values to be right yet be ready to learn. I see that I shall be retracing this whole journey over and over – but, I hope, more wisely.

In Perry's view, a student moves into a new phase as the prior one becomes inadequate in coping with the uncertainties and complexities of the world and knowledge. The meanings and structurings attached to the old phase are not lost but contained within the new one to be used where appropriate, and each step is accompanied by a 'joy of realisation' but also a loss of certainty and an altered sense of self. The changes and progression appear to be applicable to all ages and to varied backgrounds and situations. Though they do not necessarily develop at the same rate in all aspects of a student's life he or she may well transfer more advanced forms of thinking to less developed areas.

One would hope that most students will enter colleges at a stage beyond position 1 and progress at least to position 5 by the end of a full-time course at tertiary level. However, fewer students appear to reach the stage of maturity implied by position 9. Even the acceptance of relativism as a perception of the world represents revolutionary change in thinking and values for many students and as such is a challenge to some of their fundamental beliefs. It is akin to the restructuring of scientific theory which takes place from time to time in the history of humankind (Kuhn 1973). Such a profound transformation is thus one of great significance in the intellectual development of the student, yet paradoxically it is one which is often the most quietly realised.

Perry also describes forms of 'deflection', or reversion in the process, which offer a way out at critical points. These are temporising, where a student bides his or her time in one position; escape, a sense of withdrawn disenchantment; and retreat, an entrenchment in the dualist, absolutist framework of positions 1 and 2.

Perry's study raises questions about structure and sequence in course design, about the presentation of knowledge and the ways in which students are grouped for teaching, about the techniques and skills that tutors bring to discussion, and about ways of assessing students. To what extent is it possible, particularly in group discussion, to assist students to growth points in their development, while allowing for the emotional dispositions to which intellectual forms are often wedded? Is Perry's scheme applicable only to the so-called liberal arts, or is it equally relevant to the learning of science and technology? Whatever the answers may be, and they will doubtless vary according to circumstances, there is little doubt that the studies of recent years stimulate thought on the nature of student learning even if they present a somewhat selective picture.

THE SOLO TAXONOMY

SOLO stands for the Structure of Observed Learning Outcomes and is a developmental schema for describing the way in which students' learning reveals stages of increasing complexity as they master an academic subject (Biggs 2003).

As students learn, so their ways of expressing and demonstrating what they have learned develop in structural complexity.

This schema, which is assumed to apply to any subject area, includes five stages:

▪ *Prestructural* refers to that stage where students can acquire information but make no coherent interpretation of it, or meaningful response to it. While the responses may appear quite sophisticated and elaborate they do not make any overall sense. It is the quantitative accumulation of knowledge.

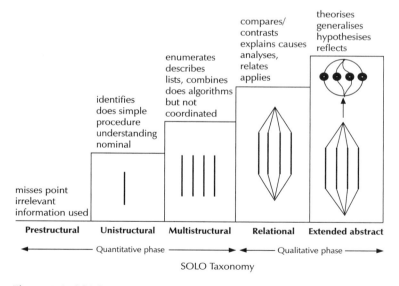

Figure 3.1 SOLO taxonomy

- *Unistructural* responses focus on one aspect adequately enough but fail to identify its significance.
- *Multistructural* responses focus on several relevant aspects but see them neither in relation to each other or the whole: 'seeing trees is a necessary preliminary to adequate understanding, but it should not be interpreted as comprehending the wood' (Biggs 2003: 40).
- At the *Relational* level the student is making sense of the various aspects of the topic or problem: 'the trees have become the wood' and points are made which pull together the whole and linked to a conclusion.
- At the *Extended Abstract* level, the student is able to extrapolate, to develop higher order principles and extend the topic to wider fields. Each level contains the lower level plus a bit more. As Biggs says: 'Each partial construction becomes the foundation on which further learning is built.'

The SOLO schema is useful for prioritising learning outcomes and objectives in the curriculum and for the development of learning in groups. A mode of progression in discussion from the pre-structural to the extended abstract is typically the direction aspired to in most learning groups, and this has clear implications for the styles of task and intervention which we address in Chapter 6. How it relates to what must be considered an equivalent sequence – the Perry stages of intellectual and ethical development – raises interesting questions about what connections exist between cognitive and affective changes in learning.

METACOGNITIVE LEARNING

Students who think outside and beyond what is given are able to understand more profoundly and learn more lastingly (Biggs 2003, Boud 1995). Metacognitive learning is about thinking beyond or transcending the immediate knowledge or skills through reflecting and acting on the processes involved in thinking and acquiring understanding. This involves thinking on at least two levels. A metacognitive strategy could include:

- *Forethought* – thinking about the tasks, problems and contexts for learning underpinned by task analysis and self-motivational beliefs.
- *Performance* – the capacities and attitudes to instruct self and seek help to learn, underpinned by self-observation (also called reflection in action).
- *Self-reflection* – self-evaluation in relation to own performance with criteria or goals including comparing own perceptions of performance with feedback from tutors and other students.

(Adapted from Jackson 2004)

Common examples of metacognition arise in activities such as learning about learning, problem-based learning, self and peer assessment, peer tutoring and the self and peer monitoring of group behaviour, all of which could be an integral part of a well-run group. Because group learning exposes students to multiple viewpoints it helps them to make connections between concepts and ideas; it provides opportunities for 'scaffolding' (students supporting each other's learning) as in peer-assisted learning and online networked approach (see page 43); and it often results in students teaching each other.

MOTIVATION

Motivation arises from a dynamic interaction between the student's goals and values and their experience and appraisal of the situations they encounter. The rewards of commitment and hard work backed by challenge and support are themselves motivating forces for further learning. It may take the form of:

- *Intrinsic motivation*, which derives from personal goals and interest in the subject, personal engagement with the tasks chosen, and a feeling of competence and confidence; or
- *Achievement motivation*, focusing on personal levels of attainment, more competitive and self-seeking, leading to a strategic and versatile approach to studying (Entwistle 1998).

But motivation can be as much an interpersonal process especially when experienced in an effective group:

> Cooperative learning methods can be an effective motivator. When students in groups share responsibility for achievement there is a decreased risk of personal failure and increased support for individual persistence . . . Group learning involves shared goals which leads to increases in students' sense of responsibility and self-efficacy; it provides a supportive atmosphere for learning.
>
> (Nicol 1997: 3)

Students' willingness to learn may also be affected by more subtle, social factors such as the kind of formal or informal feedback they get either verbally or non-verbally, spoken or written, intended or unintended from both tutors and fellow students. Some feedback is also likely to be self-referential – 'I'm not good enough'. Two factors prevail: the students' need to feel included and their desire to achieve. Students' desire to achieve can be enhanced where they feel accepted and valued by staff, and acquire a positive social network through effective collaborative learning activities.

IMPLICATIONS

Here are a few working hypotheses based on the above studies:

- Many courses, especially those with high student contact hours and heavy pressure of exams, are likely to inhibit deep, holistic, relativist thinking and encourage a reproductive, fact-grabbing strategy of learning.
- Deep, holistic, relativistic students are more likely to prefer the openness of small discussion groups to the more formal, distant relationships of highly structured lecture courses.
- With metacognitive awareness students can develop modes of thinking, arguing and behaviour which can enable higher levels of learning and better team performance.
- The teaching style of tutors will reflect their own way of thinking about knowledge.
- A blend of formal lectures, small group work, individual study and project group work may be

best for the majority of students and a course sequence which focuses increasingly on the latter methods will prove acceptable on several counts.

- Entirely online courses bring both benefits and challenges to designers and participants, so models based on research and previous practice should be used, rather than experiments.
- The most academically successful students will be able to recognise differences in teaching styles and learning tasks and adopt strategies of learning appropriate to them.
- There is a need to think about small and large group methods in relation to the development of particular intellectual skills, or cognitive styles along with the assessment tasks given to students in providing sufficient encouragement for deep-level processing.

Surface processing may be the only strategy possessed by many students when they arrive at university. It may be an aspect of a personality trait or previously acquired as a means to success in school and therefore easily shed. As students may find changes in their ways of thinking traumatic, tutors require sensitivity and skill in accommodating the variety of student styles within a climate of intellectual growth. Students too readily slip into disillusionment and consequent failure because the range of demands on them is too great. Tutors must help students understand what choices there are in approaches to learning in groups and give them opportunity and support in making their choices. Small groups provide the most suitable environment for this to occur.

Principles of good practice

Chickering and Gamson (1989), following a lengthy study of research into learning and teaching in the USA, produced a comprehensive set of principles of good practice for undergraduate education, all of which can be seen as supportive of, and informative about, appropriate group learning methods.

PRINCIPLES OF GOOD PRACTICE FOR UNDERGRADUATE EDUCATION

Good practice encourages student–teacher contact

Frequent contact between teachers and students, in and out of classes, is the most important factor in getting students motivated and involved. Teachers who demonstrate concern help students to get through rough times and to keep on working. Students' intellectual commitment is enhanced by knowing a few teachers well; it encourages them to think about their own values and future plans.

Good practice encourages cooperation among students

Learning is enhanced when it is more like a team effort than a solo race. Good learning, like good work, is collaborative and social, not competitive and isolated. Working with others often increases involvement in learning. Sharing one's own ideas and responding to others' reactions improves thinking and deepens understanding.

Good practice encourages active learning

Learning is not a spectator sport. Students do not learn much just sitting in classes listening to teachers, memorising pre-packaged assignments, and reproducing the expected answers. They must talk about what they are learning, write about it, relate it to past experiences, and apply it to their daily lives. They must make what they learn part of themselves.

Good practice gives prompt feedback

Knowing what you know, and don't know, focuses learning. Students need appropriate feedback on performance to benefit from courses. In getting started, students need help in assessing their existing knowledge and competence. In classes, students need frequent opportunities to perform and receive suggestions for improvement. At various points during their studies, and at the end, students need chances to reflect on what they have learned, what they still need to know, and how to assess themselves.

Good practice emphasises time on task

Time plus energy equals learning. Learning to use one's time well is critical for students and professionals alike. Students need help in learning effective time management. Allocating realistic amounts of time means effective learning for students and effective teaching for teachers. How an institution defines time expectations for students, faculty, administrators and other professional faculty can establish the basis for high performance for all.

Good practice communicates high expectations

Expect more and you will get it. High expectations are important for everyone – for the poorly prepared, for those unwilling to exert themselves, and for the bright and well-motivated. Expecting students to perform well becomes a self-fulfilling prophecy when teachers and institutions hold high expectations for themselves and make extra efforts.

Good practice respects diverse talents and ways of learning

There are many roads to learning. People bring different talents and styles of learning to college. Brilliant students in the seminar room may be awkward in the laboratory or art studio. Students rich in practical experience may not do so well with theory. Students need the opportunity to show their talents and learn in ways that work for them. Then they can be encouraged to learning in new ways that do not come so easily.

Based on: Chickering and Gamson (1989) *7 Principles for Good Practice in Undergraduate Education*.

THEORIES ABOUT LEARNING

Multiple Intelligences

Howard Gardner (1993) developed a theory of multiple intelligences which proposes a wider range of learning modalities that are important to human development. He defines intelligence as 'the capacity to solve problems or to fashion products that are valued in one or more cultural settings' (p. 60). His eight types (the last one added in 1997) give pointers to the need to accommodate variety in teaching and learning strategies and methods.

- *Linguistic intelligence* refers to a learner's capacity to absorb information best by saying, hearing and seeing words. Their strong ability to memorise names and places and their facility with words makes them valued in 'academic' writing.
- *Logical/mathematical intelligence* refers to a learner's capacity to excel at categorising and classifying. They work well with numbers and will enjoy exploring the logical patterns and relationships in what they learn.
- *Spatial intelligence* refers to a learner's capacity to learn by visualising and enjoy drawing and designing. They excel at puzzles, maps, and charts, and minds are best stimulated by the 'gestalt' of a visual image.
- *Kinaesthetic intelligence* refers to a learner's need to move and touch in order to learn effectively. This can apply to people or materials and may involve their recalling times when they were physically in a certain place.
- *Musical intelligence* refers to a learner's capacity to appreciate, respond emotionally to, and even create music. Certain kinds of music (mainly classical) can be used to stimulate this intelligence as well as others.
- *Interpersonal intelligence* refers to a learner's requirement for interaction and sharing with others. They benefit from the cooperative aspects of group work and other tasks that promote interpersonal relationships both in and out of the classroom.
- *Intrapersonal intelligence* refers to a learner's capacity to enjoy working alone on projects and pursuing their own interests. They would appreciate the individualised nature of reflecting quietly on their learning through diaries or logs.
- *Naturalistic intelligence* refers to a learner's capacity to make distinctions and relationships between natural phenomena without any necessary engagement of the other intelligences.

Academic work has traditionally given priority and emphasis to the first two intelligences, linguistic and logical mathematical, largely relegating the others to a secondary position, with a consequent exclusion of a great deal of talent. If teachers tend to design material and courses in their own dominant intelligence and assess students accordingly, students whose natural propensity is towards other intelligences will have their learning needs less than fully met. It also raises questions about the research into learning described described earlier in this chapter, conducted by academic researchers on students already in academic institutions. On a more positive note, Gardner's theory underlines the need to provide variety in the learning experience in order to accommodate not only the diversity of preferences in any one group of students but the range of intelligence available within each student.

Rogers's ten principles

Carl Rogers (1983), in his book *Freedom To Learn*, bases his principles of learning not merely on his work on *humanistic* psychology, but on many years' experience of university teaching. His principles still have much currency for learning in groups today:

- Human beings have a natural potential for learning.
- Significant learning takes place when the subject matter is perceived by the student as having relevance for his/her own purposes.
- Learning which involves a change in self-organisation – in the perception of oneself – is threatening and tends to be resisted.
- Those learnings which are threatening to the self are more easily perceived and assimilated when external threats are at a minimum.
- When threat to the self is low, experience can be perceived in differentiated fashion and learning can proceed.
- Much significant learning is acquired by doing.
- Learning is facilitated when the student participates responsibly in the learning process.
- Self-initiated learning, which involves the whole person of the learner (feelings as well as intellect), is the most lasting and pervasive.
- Independence, creativity and self-reliance are all facilitated when self-criticism and self-evaluation are basic and evaluation by others is of secondary importance.
- The most socially useful learning in the modern world is the learning of the process of learning, a continuous openness to experience and incorporation into oneself of the process of change.

Groups can provide a natural scenario for enabling the development of almost all the qualities proposed by Rogers, given the kind of design and leadership which values the presence and contribution of all participants.

Experiential learning

Rogers states above: 'Much significant learning is acquired by doing.' The experiential learning cycle sequence developed by Kolb (1984) has the underlying premise that learners learn best when they are active, take responsibility for their own learning, and can relate and apply it to their own context.

The rationale of experiential learning is as follows. We all learn from the *experience* of doing a task, and the results of that learning can be used constructively and even assessed. But it is not sufficient simply to have an experience in order to learn. Without *reflecting* on this experience, possibly through

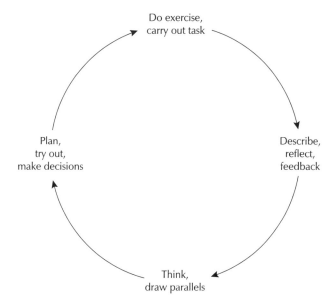

Do exercise,
carry out task

Describe,
reflect,
feedback

Think,
draw parallels

Plan,
try out,
make decisions

Figure 3.2 Experiential learning cycle

discussing it with others, it may be rapidly forgotten or its learning potential lost. The feelings and thoughts emerging out of this reflection can fit into a pattern that starts to make sense such that *generalisations and concepts* can be generated, and relationships made with existing theories. And it is generalisations and theories which give the learner the conceptual framework with which to *plan and tackle new situations* effectively. The experiential learning cycle may be represented by the above diagram.

Honey and Mumford (2005) have taken the cycle further by nominating four 'learning styles' corresponding to the above phases and developed a set of self-administered questionnaires which enable respondents to gauge their own preferred or most dominant style and to identify those which may need strengthening. These are labelled as follows:

- *Activists* who are open-minded and enthusiastic about new ideas but get bored with implementation, like to be involved in new experiences, problems and opportunities, but learn less well when listening to lectures or following precise instructions.
- *Reflectors* who like to stand back and observe from different perspectives, to review events and think about what they have learned, but function less well when put in leadership positions or have to work with tight deadlines.
- *Theorists* who tend to be more analytical and detached rather than subjective and emotive in their thinking and prefer a structured situation with a clear purpose, but learn less well when they have to do things without knowing the principles or concepts involved.
- *Pragmatists* who are keen to try things out, tend to be impatient with lengthy discussions and like to have a model they can copy, but learn less well when there is no immediate benefit they can recognise.

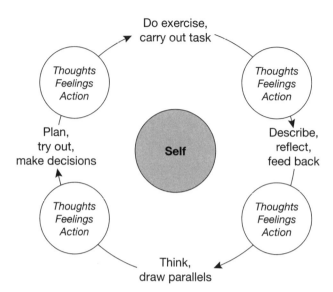

Figure 3.3 Experiential learning cycle modified

An added element that should be considered in this cycle is the effect of emotions on the learning that takes place. At every phase experiential learners are engaged in an interplay between thoughts, feelings and action (or behaviour), each or all of which can influence choices in progressing round the cycle: these are illustrated in Figure 3.3.

Such analysis can be helpful for not only project and task teams (see Chapter 6) but also to generate some meta-learning about personal preferences and their effects in group discussion. Not only may it be helpful to recognise and construct the cycle as a possible learning sequence in groups, but also to take account of the four learning styles in selecting members for a task or project group.

As an interesting footnote to this, reflectors, though often regarded as introverts in classroom situations, have demonstrated a higher satisfaction with online delivery; the additional time for reflection online leading to their behaving more like extraverts when online (Downing and Chim 2004). See also pages 138, 248, 265 and 266, in Chapter 6 on the process of reflection in e-tivities.

CONCLUSIONS

The knowledge and understanding of the way people learn that has blossomed over recent years has moved the debate about quality in learning and teaching a long way forward. Deeper approaches, metacognition and active learning are consonant with, and lead to, qualitatively superior learning outcomes. Group learning is a key to both the development and the achievement of these kinds of learning because it encourages learners to:

approaches to learning

- Articulate and test their thoughts and assumptions;
- Interpret and expose their ideas and values to alternative viewpoints;
- Think beyond what is given, to build and extrapolate;
- Make connections and integrate their ideas;
- Improve their communication and teamwork skills;
- Deepen their thinking;

and through these processes, to

- Develop and change their values and commitments, especially to learning.

Group learning also promotes practice in thinking and explaining:

> [i]t exposes students to multiple viewpoints which helps them to make connections amongst concepts and ideas; it provides opportunities for 'scaffolding' (students supporting each other's learning); it often results in students teaching each other; it involves shared goals which leads to increases in students' sense of responsibility and self-efficacy; [and] it provides a supportive atmosphere for learning.
>
> (Nicol 1997: 4)

We shall return to this theme in Chapters 6, 7 and 8.

DISCUSSION POINTS

- Describe in general terms what you or your group learns. How? In other words, what seem to be the effective processes?
- In what ways can a group leader encourage meta-learning, deep processing, holistic thinking and intellectual development? Where are you in all this?
- Do any of the students in your group appear to lack self-confidence? What do you attribute that to? Do you know what they attribute it to?
- How does the balance between different approaches to learning work out in your group and how does that affect the interaction?
- What are the similarities and differences in group behaviour, coherence or success depending on the blend between on and offline working?

CHAPTER FOUR

COMMUNICATING IN GROUPS

This chapter is about observing with greater accuracy and skill the processes of communication and your own part in it whether as a leader/facilitator or a participant.

THE PROCESS OF COMMUNICATION

It is through communication that people achieve an understanding of one another and are thus able to influence, and be influenced by, others. No amount of understanding of group behaviour is sufficient for successful participation in groups unless each person in the group has the capacity to communicate effectively. Communication occurs only when a message is appropriately received. Only when there is a predisposition to observe, listen and, in the online environment, read and watch and try to understand can clear communication take place – and this implies a degree of trust and openness between participants. Without these, mutual understanding and influences are liable to distortion: cooperation is unlikely.

Communication is often regarded as little more than the process of passing and receiving information. Concern for improving communication usually centres on the skills of writing, speaking, reading and, less frequently, listening. Typically, the emphasis will be on qualities like clarity, conciseness, precision and logical sequence. Yet many, and possibly most, errors in communication occur because of psychological rather than logical factors. The feelings, attitudes, behaviours and relationships of those involved in communication are more likely to determine whether it is effective or not. The addition of technology often deflects observers and participants alike away from feelings, though they are still paramount. The process of communication is therefore far from being a rational or mechanical exercise (see Figure 4.1).

Communication involves much more than person A saying something to person B and the latter hearing it, interpreting it and acting on it correctly; it is not merely about words said [or typed on a screen (Crystal 2001) where the recipient cannot respond until the whole message is received and

Figure 4.1 Model of communication 1

therefore cannot react to it as it is being formulated]. Face-to-face communication is of necessity a two-way process.

To paraphrase Kolb et al. (1984): A brings to the interaction with B not merely the content of the message he/she wishes to convey but much more. A brings her-himself as a person. A has a self-image and, to varying degrees also a set of attitudes and feelings towards B. The message to B, therefore, in addition to certain content, may well be loaded with cues as to who A feels her/himself to be as a person (e.g. confident and secure versus tentative and wary), how A feels about B as a person (e.g. warm and receptive versus cold and uncaring) and how A expects B to react to A's communication.

If the issue were even as simple as that we might have a reasonably easy task in communicating. The trouble is we are not always aware of what we are actually putting across. We convey things we do not intend. The message thus gets distorted so that the above picture is transformed into something like Figure 4.2. The online environment provides way of reviewing and considering the words of others. Even then, however, there is a strong possibility of being misunderstood. Irony, for example, rarely works without the accompanying wink.

In addition, we often have more than one intention when we communicate something: sometimes the secondary intention becomes the stronger one and, where this is at a less-than-conscious level, the message may well be distorted beyond recognition.

Every action, even (and sometimes especially) remaining silent, is a form of communication and is open to interpretation and response by others. Our body, face, gestures, physical proximity and eye contact all have a marked effect on what we are communicating and on how the other person feels about us and what we intend to communicate, yet are often ignored when we try to determine what goes right and wrong.

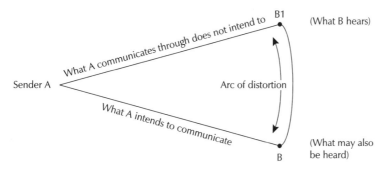

Figure 4.2 Model of communication 2

A tutor, for example, who looks stern or unresponsive when a particular student speaks, whilst saying 'Yes, that's really very interesting' is communicating a message beyond words and a confusing one at that. So, too, is the tutor who, though meticulously correct in exposition, shows no enthusiasm for subject or students, or who always sits behind a desk separate from the tutorial group. Online, an e-moderator who lurks but does not comment can be viewed with suspicion. Similar to one who, perhaps through lack of time or options offers cursory 'well done' messages to well-crafted and considered student responses may find the group dropping away. Distorting messages are conveyed by the tone of voice, facial expression, body posture, gesture or physical location. The problem is that the underlying feelings and thoughts which frequently emerge most powerfully through non-verbal cues are not usually amenable to discussion and action. Similarly, an online message that is cold and peremptory, that closes off discussion, that seems to exclude the original sender, that ignores significant parts of the sender's message or answers a different question – or ignores the message altogether – communicates more than just the words on the screen.

Those on the receiving end of a communication may also be party to the distortion. They have to listen or read and interpret appropriately and this is not at all easy when they are receiving contradictory messages simultaneously. A common problem in interpersonal communication is failure by the receiving party to attend fully to what is being said and thus miss the important points of a message. Sometimes this is because the receiver is preoccupied, or had a particular way of thinking about something (a mental set) which predetermines the interpretation. Online environments win here due to the possibility of review and revisiting.

Hearing or noticing only part of a message may also serve the receiver's purpose, especially when there are contradictory signals being expressed and he or she has a legitimate choice. The receiver's part in the hearing and interpreting of messages may be represented by a diagram complementary to Figure 4.2 (see Figure 4.3).

At times, we may consciously wish to convey more than one intention at a time. For instance when we express our thoughts in an interview we are usually trying to impress at the same time, to present

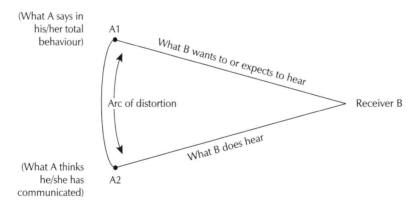

Figure 4.3 Model of communication 3

ourselves in a favourable light. A lot of classroom behaviour is to do with impression: students trying to demonstrate their knowledge, their interest, their regard for the teacher; tutors trying to maintain an aura of objective expertise and control. There is nothing wrong with trying to impress provided it is appropriate and one is aware of it.

We are also likely to distort what we hear because of our personal needs. The need to be liked or to have everything neatly categorised, for instance, may blur our perception of what we are being told. Rather than attending to the complete message, we may block a lot of otherwise important information. Our need to be liked may cause us to be over-sensitive to negative components in a communication: our need for order and neatness or control may predispose us to miss some excellent ideas from students or colleagues who find it difficult to express themselves clearly. What we intend to do with the information when we have it can also cause us to filter and select.

An added factor which may contribute to distorted reception is threat, whether it manifests itself in a direct personal challenge from a group or an individual or in a more general and ill-defined way. The distortion or denial that occurs as a result of threat derives from either the need to protect our self-esteem or from the anxiety which has its roots in early childhood experience. Fear of criticism, reproof, rejection or ridicule inevitably set up defensive barriers, yet because they are at a conscious level they are at least open to scrutiny and change should we wish. Not so amenable to change are the distortions resulting from childhood conflicts, repressed because of the danger they originally posed, and reawakened at a less-than-conscious level by particular people or events in adulthood. Both of these threats may be revived by a specific thing somebody does or says to us or by an environment which has a high degree of evaluation, control and competitiveness.

Many of the complexities and problems of communication can be tackled through the use of metacommunication: describing the communication that appears to be taking place. For example 'I didn't take in what you said then, could you repeat it?' or 'This seems to have developed into a question and answer session – I suggest you talk me through what you've written on the form for a while', or 'The messages have been coming thick and fast. Let's recap and see where we've got to.' These are critically important skills for the e-moderator too.

Online communication, interaction and participation

Working together online involves a hybrid of familiar forms of communication. It has some of the elements of writing and its associated thinking, and some of the permanence of publishing, but it also resembles fleeting verbal discussion. The discursive style of the typical participant lies somewhere between the formality of the written word and the informality of the spoken.

The shifting of time between log-ons is also important. Being able to reflect on messages and on the topic under discussion offers the opportunity for participants to reflect on issues raised online and then mould their own ideas through the process of composing replies.

The traditional view of the Internet is that it promotes openness, and participants expect freedom to express their opinions and to share their experiences and thoughts. Face-to-face identities become less important and the usual discriminators such as race, age and gender are less apparent. Successful participation in online communication does *not* depend on a high level of computer literacy and it often appeals to inexperienced computer users.

Research from educational environments shows that authority and control of the communication may shift at from teachers to students, trainer to trainee, the more frequently as the students become more competent and confident online. Existing hierarchies and relationships can change and even fade. The social and contextual cues that regulate and influence group behaviour are largely missing or can be invented during the life of the conference. It is easier to leave the conference unseen – and unembarrassed – than is possible in face-to-face contexts and synchronous chat sessions. It is also easy to 'lurk' or 'browse' – read conferences messages but without contributing.

The 'downside' of online communication is such that mistakes are rather public and recorded for all to see. Tardiness, rudeness or inconsistency in response to others tend to be forgiven less easily than in a more transient face-to-face setting. Minor complaints can escalate when several individuals in a forum agree with each other (Salmon 2002, 2004).

THE CONTENT OF COMMUNICATION

The words with which we choose to make our communication are important too, not just for the precision and clarity they offer but because they give colour and light to what we say. Students starting with a group are often at pains to learn how to handle the accepted vocabulary of the subject, and can easily gravitate towards the use of clichés and labels. 'Oh that's a case of X' can cut out the possibility of open discussion when X is a concept which has been invented mainly to box in uncertainty about a phenomenon. More commonly one might hear 'That's a mathematics problem' or whatever the subject in question is, as a way of foreclosing discussion on a topic.

Style and meaning are of relevance too in how people communicate. Statements which begin 'it is' or 'they are' have a more distancing effect than those starting with personal pronouns, especially 'I think' or 'I like'. A psychological distance is also established by the use of theoretical rather than personal understandings. Stanford and Roark (1974) divide the problem into five categories of meaning: theoretical, abstract, objective, personal cognitive and personal experiencing. Theoretical explanations are the fabric by which we write bits of experience into comprehensive explanations. Psychologically they are impersonal and distant. Theories, abstractions and objective referents can be verified by opinions of others and are thus open to consensual agreement. But personal meanings are open to our scrutiny only; we are the sole judge.

Online, an analysis of the nature and purpose of communication is more accessible than face-to-face. These nine ways of theming snippets of text to determine what is happening in a group exchange can be helpful to e-moderators who wish to better understand the nature of contributions.

INDIVIDUAL THINKING OFFERED AS A CONFERENCE MESSAGE

1   Offering up ideas or resources and inviting a critique of them.

2   Asking challenging questions.

3   Articulating, explaining and supporting positions on issues.

4   Exploring and supporting issues by adding explanations and examples.

5   Reflecting on and re-evaluating personal opinions.

INTERACTIVE OR RESPONSIVE THINKING POSTED AS A CONFERENCE MESSAGE

6   Offering a critique, challenging, discussing and expanding ideas of others.

7   Negotiating interpretations, definitions and meanings.

8   Summarising and modelling previous contributions.

9   Proposing actions based on ideas that have been developed.

(Salmon 2004)

Discussion, and even lectures, which focus entirely on 'what is' or 'what other people have said' may help students in jumping academic hurdles but have little personal impact on them. It is as if:

> subject matter has the only 'real' meaning and the students' personal meanings are irrelevant or secondary at best. The effect over a long period of time, especially for students with different experiential backgrounds from the teachers is to drive them away into a world where their meanings are never those of their environment and accepted as having worth.
>
> (Stanford and Roark 1974)

The online environment, with its time lags and text-on-screen, is believed to promote more personal and group 'reflection' in and on action (Salmon 2002). In the All Things in Moderation courses, we ask participants to 'reflect' at the end of each week, as a way of providing an indication that they should move on and of encouraging them to write their thoughts for others to comment on. Frequently, participants amaze themselves by producing analogies and metaphors from the offline world to help themselves both understand and communicate their experiences of working on line.

The effect on students is probably to encourage in their minds, and culture, a split between that which is acceptable for academic discussion and their more personal experience in the environment or institution as a community – a division, that is, between educational knowledge and everyday knowledge.

> This week I learnt about the key e-moderating skill of 'weaving'. I see myself as a little worm, wandering around in the rich soil (of the delegates' on-screen messages). Collecting up a little titbit here, a leaf there, an interesting stone here and valuable seed there and representing them in a new way to make a brand new, highly organic insight. CF

> The course is ending and I'm at the top of a mountain looking back. You bet it feels like I've climbed a mountain, and a steep one at that! (Apologies colleagues for the various times I let go the rope . . . I got a little scared by the altitude). But, now flag in hand, I've planted myself firmly whilst I look back at the journey. I've finally realised the importance of building easy pathways and steps up the e-mountain for my students, and that, although they may be somewhat fitter than I am, they still need my greater expertise in teaching to pull them upwards. BB

IMPROVING COMMUNICATION

As we have already seen, the lack of trust and the existence of threat in any interaction can have a distorting effect on communication. The establishment of honest and meaningful communication can be achieved through these precepts, simple to state but not so easy to practise:

1   Develop a sense of mutual trust and openness.
2   Correct distortions in communication through constructive feedback.
3   Engage in meta-communications: communicating about the process of communication.

The first point demands a willingness to be open to oneself (recognising and accepting one's own feelings), to others (being able to disclose these feelings discreetly) and to the world around us. The 'Johari window' (Luft 1970) is a helpful device for analysing and working on this problem.

The Johari window (Figure 4.4) is used for increasing personal and interpersonal awareness. It comprises four quadrants:

Quadrant 1: The free and open area refers to behaviour known to self and to others.
Quadrant 2: The blind area refers to things about us that others can see but of which we are unaware.

Quadrant 3: The avoided or hidden area indicates things we prefer to keep to ourselves (hidden agendas or personal feelings).

Quadrant 4: The area of unknown activity represents the sort of things that are accessible neither to us nor to others, but which may eventually be revealed. Such behaviours and motives could have affected our relationships, without our knowing it, all along.

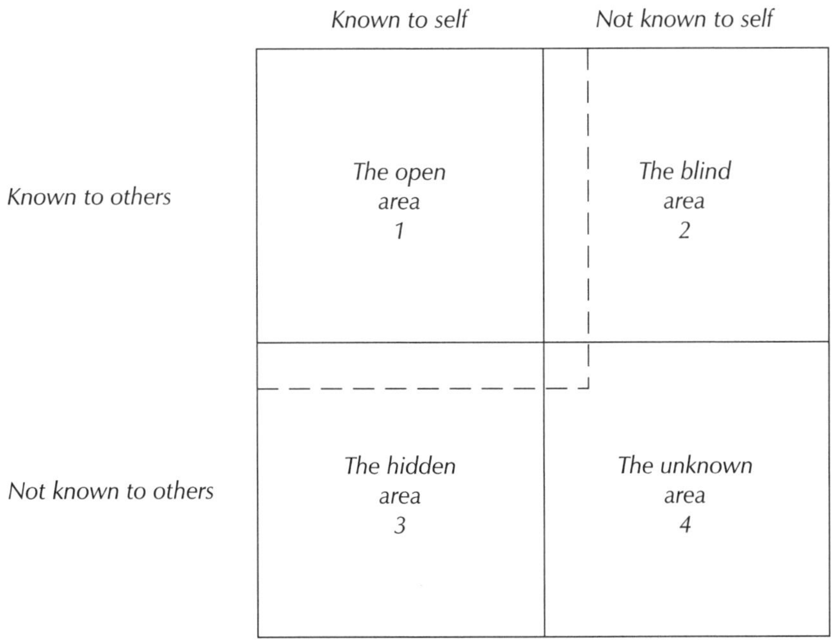

	Known to self	Not known to self
Known to others	The open area 1	The blind area 2
Not known to others	The hidden area 3	The unknown area 4

Figure 4.4 The Johari window

Luft suggests that a change in any one quadrant will affect all the other quadrants. By disclosing some of our own feelings or private experiences we expand quadrant 1 into quadrant 3. This makes it more possible for other people to let us know something about ourselves that we were unaware of, for example, 'You always smile when you're angry', which in turn expands quadrant 1 into quadrant 2. This leads to the more open form of communication indicated by the broken line in Figure 4.4. Exercises using the Johari window may be found in Pfeiffer and Jones (1974) and Kolb et al. (1984), but it is a simple enough tool to use in any group whose members have experienced or observed each other over even a short period of time. (There is also an exercise in the Appendix on pages 313 and 314.)

GIVING AND RECEIVING FEEDBACK

The following simple rules about this most sensitive area of communication are likely to promote action and change. The underlying principles are existential: 'I speak of my own experience; I cannot assume yours' and 'I own my feelings.'

GIVING FEEDBACK

- Feedback is usually better when invited rather than imposed.
- Be descriptive rather than evaluative. Describing what we actually see or hear reduces the need of the receiver to react defensively.
- Reveal your own position or feelings vis-à-vis the other person: For example, 'I get very confused by your questions.'
- Be specific rather than general: for example 'That's the third time you've said one thing to me privately and another publicly.'
- Take into account the receiver's needs as well as your own.
- Direct feedback towards behaviour the receiver can change or control.
- Timing is critical: it is usually better to give feedback as soon as possible after the particular behaviour, though one should always take into account the social situation, the receiver's vulnerability and their readiness to listen.
- Check that the receiver has understood; if you can, get them to rephrase the feedback to see if it's what you had in mind.
- When feedback is given in a group allow giver and receiver the opportunity to check with others in the group on its accuracy.

RECEIVING FEEDBACK

- Listen to the person who is giving the feedback; accept what they are saying as genuine and helpful; try to understand their feelings, what they are describing and what they are suggesting you do.
- Accept feedback as a gift.
- If there is a possibility, check the feedback with a third party.
- Give the feedback serious consideration, weigh up the consequences of changing or not changing, express your thoughts and feelings about alternatives.
- Communicate your decisions to the giver.
- Tell her/him what they could do which might help you to change.
- Thank the giver for their concern and help.
- Online, bear in mind that the receiver may read your words many times. Construct them a little more carefully.

If we accept that communication is inescapably a two-way process, then feedback is probably the best way of getting evidence on the effectiveness of our communication. It enables us to learn about how others see us and about how we affect them. It is thus a vital ingredient in the process of evaluation which we shall examine in more detail in Chapter 9.

Online monitoring and feedback

In online communication both the content and process of communication are, as we have already noted, amenable to both monitoring and review as the interaction progresses: feedback, or rather suggestions for improved communication, can be offered as part of the e-moderator's role in building the group collaboration and performance. An example of that process taking place can be found on the book website. It also demonstrates the moderator's role to which we return in Chapter 7.

TRANSACTIONAL ANALYSIS (TA)

TA is more commonly used by psychologists but we have found it most valuable for learners and tutors alike as a tool for understanding communication in learning groups.

The 'superstructure' of the communication process is likely to be accompanied by a substratum of emotional forces to do with the relationships involved, whether at a conscious or unconscious level. A simple but powerful model for analysing the processes of human interaction was devised by Eric Berne (1968) and later amplified by Thomas Harris (1973). Taking Freud's concept as a starting point, Berne proposes that each person comprises three basic 'selves' – the Parent, the Adult and the Child – each of which is capable of affecting the tone of communication.

These 'ego-states', as they are called, exist within each of us as a result of our early life experience. They are not – like Freud's superego, ego and id – elements of our inner world operating on each other at an unconscious level. Rather they are conscious experiences of everyday life imprinted in the person as a result of internal and external events encountered during the first few years of life. Transactional analysis addresses itself to the interaction between people, rather than to their inner psyche and is therefore more readily available for a study of relationships in teaching and learning.

The *Parent* in us acts according to how we perceived our mother, father or parental figure behaving. The Parent is often concerned with prescribing the limits of behaviour, issuing moral edicts, teaching 'how to', protecting, nurturing and fostering; and these functions are typically accompanied by the tones of voice and the non-verbal expressions which partnered them when we experienced them in their original form. For obvious reasons teaching frequently puts us in the position of behaving parentally or at least of being tempted to do so. Institutions provide a broadly parental function (and in view of this it is not surprising that young people often take it out on the physical fabric of schools and colleges). This is not to say that the functions or the Parent are intrinsically either good or bad. The important thing is that we be sufficiently aware of the Parent in ourselves so that we can use it or not (and in any case appropriately) according to our interpretation of what is happening in any transaction.

The *Adult* is that part of us which is concerned with the gathering and processing of information and with rational action in the 'real' world. It derives from the time in our childhood when we began to manipulate objects external to ourselves and to realise we could achieve something worthwhile through our own original thought. The Adult in us is ruled by reason rather than emotion; it is not however synonymous with 'mature'. The type of functions specific to the adult are therefore the acquiring and sorting of data (even about one's Parent, Adult and Child states) and the choosing of alternatives and the planning of decision-making processes. The Adult may thus manifest itself in a variety of ways and is the side of us most concerned with analysing the very transactions it is part of.

The *Child* in us is the residue of emotional responses experienced and recorded in early childhood. These responses are essentially internal reactions to external events. The re-creation of similar events in later life is likely to trigger the corresponding reactions. There are many different 'children' within us and they experience the same feelings now as they did when we were little. Where the feeling derives from parental impositions or restrictions it is likely to be that of frustration, anger, fear, rebelliousness or conformity. Where it comes from the glorious excitement of first discoveries it is likely to connect with curiosity, creative delight, desire to explore, spontaneity and trust. Other biographical traces may also include competitiveness (from sibling rivalry) and dependency.

Each of us comprises all three ego states. None of these states is better or more important than the others. 'Appropriate' behaviour is determined by the situation, the Adult's analysis of it, and the Adult's ability to handle the Parent and Child according to perceived circumstances.

Needless to say, the psychopathology of individual human beings is never as simple as this model proposes, but TA is nevertheless a convenient and, at times, telling way of analysing what goes right and wrong in human communication. It can be important for the tutor to acquire the ability to pick up the verbal and non-verbal cues signifying the existence of a particular ego state. In the world of teaching one might come across cues of the kind shown in Figure 4.5 on page 81.

Transactions

In diagrams of transactions, the ego states are commonly represented by their initial letter while communication is indicated by arrows in the appropriate direction. A transaction is complementary where the ego state of the responding person is the same ego state to which the communication was directed. It is crossed where this correspondence is not achieved and ulterior where one correspondence is intended but another conveyed. Crossed and ulterior transactions clearly lead to unsatisfied, frustrated or angry feelings. An example will illustrate these three kinds of transaction.

A student comes to see a tutor: 'I don't know, I feel like giving up the course – it's all just one big muddle.' This could be intended as a (C) —> (P) communication. For there to be a complementary transaction, i.e. (P) — > (C), the tutor might respond: 'I'm sorry to hear that. Here – take a seat while I make a cup of coffee' (Nurturing Parent) or 'Now come on, pull yourself together, nothing's that bad' (Admonishing Parent).

Alternatively, the tutor might say: 'I see, well it seems to me you've got the following alternatives.' Or 'OK, well what do you see as your choices?', which would be (A) — > (A) responses. This would constitute a crossed transaction, one in which the sought correspondence is denied. It is therefore likely to be inappropriate as an initial move.

If, on the other hand, the tutor responded: 'Oh, I thought you were going to go and see the counsellor', it might well sound like an Adult response with overtones of Critical Parent or even irresponsible Child. Either of these would constitute an ulterior transaction typically leading to a tangle of ill-feeling.

To quote another example from teaching; a student might say: 'I'm fed up, none of the articles is in the library like you said they would be', (C) —> (C), or (C) (P). The tutor could reply either: 'If you were a bit quicker off the mark there would be no problem', (P) — > (C). Or 'I've got a few copies here you can have', (A) — > (C). Or 'That's not my fault', (C) —> (C).

It is typical and proper that teaching should function a great deal at the Parent level. Education does after all involve the setting of standards, advising, guiding, fostering and so forth, but there is always the danger that teachers will direct such transactions indiscriminately to the student as 'Child' rather than providing open choices appropriate to a given situation. A generalised Parent-like posture can easily produce in students a corresponding Child-like response which in turn confirms the original Parental status.

Transactional analysis includes in its orbit several other useful ideas for teaching and learning. For example, Harris (1973) has expanded Berne's original scheme of transactions to include the following 'life positions':

> I'm not OK – You're OK
> I'm not OK – You're not OK
> I'm OK – You're not OK
> I'm OK – You're OK

and these are likely to determine the quality of the Parent–Adult–Child transactions. We may recognise people (including ourselves) who readily adopt the 'OK' and 'Not OK' positions though the situation can be as strong a determining factor as a predisposition. Clearly 'I'm OK, you're OK' is the most healthy and creative transaction and one we would all strive to achieve, at least for ourselves.

This scheme has been developed into a model called the 'OK Corral' (Stewart and Joines 1987) which provides some useful insights for working with groups. Any member of a group including the tutor may have a general disposition to any of the positions derived from childhood which can be triggered by a particular kind of social interaction.

If, unaware, we get drawn into one of these 'operations', we are likely to offer a predictable justification for them. But we also have the choice of adopting an 'Adult' awareness of what is happening and changing the outcomes. For a tutor, possible techniques for increasing the likelihood and frequency of I'm OK – You're OK transactions might be:

- Warmly welcoming group members to the first session – which translates 'virtually' into a warm opening announcement or sometimes individual e-mails.
- Smiling warmly when speaking to or being spoken to by a group member, making your messages warm and acknowledging senders.
- Making sure you know (and use) their names by using a seating/name plan/list of online students;
- Apologising if you forget one or get it wrong.
- Having an informal chat with likely antagonists beforehand or sending a welcoming e-mail.
- Thanking students.
- Showing that you value their contribution – even though you may not agree with the point being made.

The important thing, as Brookfield (1990) says, is to be and present yourself as authentic and credible, even if this takes a bit of practice. Online, try checking back at your messages and see for yourself how you 'came over'!

	I'm not OK	I'm OK
You're OK	Get away from Pass time 'I can't do it' Frustration Do it as a matter of duty Fears failure Gives up responsibility	Get on with Use time 'I can succeed' Challenge Collaborative approach Fears are appropriate Informs and shares responsibility
You're not OK	Get nowhere with Waste time 'I give up' Ignore it Defiance Fears loss of self Takes passive stance	Get rid of Kill time 'I don't care' Promotes compliance Control Fears loss of control Puts own needs first

Figure 4.5 The OK Corral

One of the strongest and boldest claims that TA brings to the world of human relationships is the belief that people, through self-awareness, are able to change themselves and develop their potential to change others. By recognising what can cause hurt, misunderstanding and frustration in relationships they are better able to break out of unproductive communication and bring more creativity, enjoyment and freedom into their social environment. This is a bold claim and one which needs careful examination. Nevertheless, TA provides a valuable explanatory framework for human interaction, one to which it is easy to relate, develop and apply to learning groups.

BARRIERS TO COMMUNICATION IN GROUPS

Much of what we have discussed so far in this chapter has been based more on a one-to-one relationship than on the more complex network of group interaction. Groups involve a level of awareness of self and others' perceptions that may hardly feature in a pair. Behaviour becomes more the object of scrutiny by those who are not directly engaged, the more so online where the history of the interaction is available for all to see.

Beneath the surface of what is evident through people's behaviour in groups lie several personal needs, wishes and behaviour traits which can lead to a climate that is less than open. For instance each individual has a personal need for survival, self-enhancement and recognition, all of which may militate against the goals of the group. Then there may be power games being played out in terms of the desire to influence and control certain members, some of the motivation for which may lie outside the actual meeting of the group. Thirdly there are often members for whom openness, trust and intimacy are felt to be risky or where the climate makes them feel a risk, and a spirit of defensiveness is created. Typical defensive strategies are:

- being concerned with self-image;
- stopping people from expressing their own ideas;
- trying to dominate the discussion, including ignoring others' online messages and merely adding one's own;
- trying constantly to change other people's opinions;
- always responding with certainty and force;
- being judgemental;
- implying superiority;
- avoiding the expression of feelings;
- worries about the use of technology.

Many of these can be circumvented through the promotion of ground rules, explicit codes of behaviour, which are discussed in Chapter 2.

The two greatest barriers to effective communication in a group are to do with the previous experience both of groups and of the particular group members, and of false and inappropriate assumptions about other members of the group based on this or indeed on an initial impression of them. As explained in Chapter 1 our first experience of groups (in our original family or equivalent social environment) does to a large extent determine the way we respond both to the individuals and to the group as a whole. If our experience of such groups has been painful or frustrating we may even go so far as to create the paradoxical situation in which we see the group in a similar way when it is far from being like this. In other words it becomes a self-fulfilling prophecy. There's a further danger, too, that we are liable to stereotype people who are similar in some way to those who have affected us, perhaps adversely, earlier in our life and we therefore behave towards them as if they were such people. An extension of this is what may be called 'longitudinal stereotyping' in which we believe that, because somebody has behaved in one way, perhaps in the early in the life of the group, they will behave in the same way thereafter. If, for instance, such a person has come across as muddled or arrogant in their contributions at one stage the assumption can easily be made that they will continue to be muddled or arrogant in the future.

Further assumptions may include believing that we know what others mean by what they say (even though *they* may often not know) or that everyone experiences phenomena in the same way. But the abiding meta-assumption is too often that communication is a simple and uncomplicated process: and that one can identify anybody's intentions from their behaviour simply because we know what *our* intentions would be were we to behave or speak like that.

By the same token our efforts to help, to offer suggestions, to take a leadership role in the group may equally be misinterpreted as attempts to control or to ride roughshod over the needs of other members. As Napier and Gershenfeld comment: 'These false assumptions greatly reduce our ability to communicate in a group, or even understand what seems to be happening around us.'

Communication is a primary ingredient of learning. Its various components of expressing, instructing, listening, giving feedback, verbal or non-verbal, are all essential elements in group learning. In this chapter we have looked at how various personal elements can both enhance and diminish its value and how so often we can fail to communicate what we intend. However the willingness to listen carefully, to share and negotiate, to give and receive constructive feedback, together with skills in the use of meta-communication can all help to build a climate of openness and trust which in turn generates a climate of responsible and responsive communication – the prerequisites of a shared experience of learning.

DISCUSSION POINTS

- What areas of communication do you find most rewarding in and productive (a) your everyday life; (b) your work generally; and (c) groups which you belong to or lead?
- What barriers to communication do you notice in these areas? How do they arise and how might you tackle them?
- What kind of transactions seem to govern your relationships in the various groups you belong to? How does this work out (a) for you; and (b) for the group?
- In other words, where do you feature in the OK Corral (a) in relation to the group as a whole and (b) in relation to individual members, especially the leader?

- To what extent do members really listen to each other in the group? Write down on a scale from 1 to 10 the extent to which you believe you listen to others. Are there members of the group who talk more to each other than the rest? Draw a diagram of the most typical flows of communication and compare yours with those of other group members.
- To what extent do you find technology helps or hinders communications in your groups?
- What kind of differences do you observe in your online groups compared to your face-to-face groups? For example, is there greater or faster evidence of self-disclosure? Do they discuss but not reach a conclusion so easily?

CHAPTER FIVE

AIMS AND PURPOSES OF GROUPS

This chapter focuses on a range of aims and learning outcomes for groups. The ideas can be used by tutors/leaders, and learners/participants to know what is expected of them, how well they are achieving, and ways to identify and produce aims and outcomes for practical purposes.

You may like to consider these significant questions as you read through:

- To what extent do learning groups have to involve a procession of knowledge from outside to inside and outside again?
- Does it have to be the tutor or e-moderator who controls the input, processing and output of knowledge?
- What can the learning group incorporate from the aims and purposes of other kinds of group?

GROUP PURPOSES: TASK AND MAINTENANCE

Groups in their wider contexts (see Chapter 2) form for many purposes including:

- learning from each other;
- pooling resources;
- making decisions;
- mutual support;
- sharing ideas;
- creating something.

Learning groups embody all these activities and functions and more. Their two major areas of aims are concerned with task and with maintenance. In the academic context task aims will usually be intellectual, such as:

- The exercise of critical judgement;
- The ability to analyse statements and cases;
- Questioning underlying assumptions and values.

Many people belong to social, political, interest or hobby groups on the Internet: online teaching and learning groups are more purposeful and require more focused behaviours and attention.

Task aims for tutors and e-moderators include those of a pastoral or remedial nature, such as:

- recognising when students are in difficulties;
- checking for misunderstandings in reading or lectures;
- reassuring and encouraging slower or less vocal learners.

Group maintenance includes aims like:

- creating a sense of belonging;
- generating a sense of trust and openness;
- handling conflict in a constructive way;
- establishing a spirit of cooperation;
- creating interest in, commitment to and enthusiasm for the subject and learning more about it, all of which contribute to a student's engagement and willingness to learn.

Maintenance aims facilitate or underpin task aims. However, maintenance also implies repeated attention and adjustment to the running of the group if the task is going to be achieved. Maintenance aims become increasingly more relevant as the size of the group increases (see pages 10–11). Small groups of three and four may work on a task without concern about who is doing what, or any formal leadership role being needed; where a class is divided into small sub-groups (see pages 120–30) the maintenance problem is very much subsumed to the task. However, to achieve task aims in a larger group, either members must be aware of the dynamic groups processes within it and be skilled in handling these, or the tutor must take on a firm leadership role. Online, structure is simply essential for success.

So, in larger groups of more than six, agreement should be made early about how to set about the task and the distribution of responsibilities within the group.

THE NATURE OF AIMS

Educational aims are a public statement of values: what teachers, and those who influence them, claim to prize in their courses. Some aims, such as those to do with key or transferable skills and intellectual rigour, may reach across many fields of study; others are more specific to a subject area and represent what is regarded as important in terms of the subject or forms of thinking ~~ ' specific to it.

Several writers have described the use of aims and learning outcomes as instruments of course design (Stenhouse 1975, Rowntree 1981, Ramsden 1993 and Toohey 1999). As group activity plays an important part in course design we need to ask questions such as:

- What are aims and learning outcomes specifically for learning in groups?
- How do we devise them?
- How can we make sense of learning in group aims in terms of classroom practice?
- How can we make sense of learning in groups aims in terms of online practice?
- To what extent must they match the students' conceptions of learning? (See Chapter 4).

Aims serve to focus attention on the direction of teaching and act as a reference point for choices of what is to be learned. Online they serve as a key motivator too. In the words of Dewey (1944), the aim as a 'foreseen end':

> [I]nvolves careful observation of the given conditions to see what means are available for reaching that end and to discover hindrances in the way; suggests the proper order or sequences in the use of means; makes choice of alternatives possible.

If we do not make such aims explicit, and therefore negotiable, then participants in a group discussion may be following their own hidden agendas and lacking any common frame of reference. The function of aims therefore may be not only to help establish a direction in learning but to clarify the opportunities offered by a situation.

Negotiating group aims

When aims are negotiated further levels of group engagement can result:

- Opportunities for intra-group discussion and agreement arise (Matthews 1996).
- Decisions about tasks *and* content can be made collaboratively.
- A better sense of collaboration develops among a group in achieving the aims.

A starting activity might be to ask students to generate a list of what they are most interested in learning in the course and the background information they bring to it. Such activities work well, if simply laid out, in virtual groups. Groups that have worked on the same content through different tasks learn from each other as each contributes their learning to the whole class.

AIMS, OBJECTIVES AND OUTCOMES

The distinction between these three concepts is not always made. Our view is that:

aims and purposes of groups

Aims

- indicate broad directions for teaching;
- are closely related to values and learning processes;
- are not intended to be pinned down in measurable form.

Objectives

- can be used as descriptions of what the learner should have done, experienced or completed by the end of a learning occasion.

Learning outcomes

- demonstrate what the student should have achieved or learned by the end of the learning process;
- should be measurable;
- bear a similarity to assessment questions;
- form part of a rational and systematic approach to the teaching and learning;
- form part of the process of sharing intentions with to students and colleagues.

Teaching, so the argument for specifying learning outcomes runs, is a rational activity. To satisfy the needs of a well-designed course, learning outcomes should be specified, the means of achieving them specified and measures applied to evaluate the effectiveness of the strategy (the principle of constructive alignment described on page 218).

The importance of groups in achieving outcomes is that through discussion, modelling and practice they can be demonstrated and assimilated in a mutual and purposeful way. Students can little by little learn what the skills and values specific to the subject and academic thinking are. Groups are, potentially at least, the market place for buying into the mores of the course. Learning outcomes, in these terms, constitute a translation of aims into specific qualities – knowledge (expressed in terms of a demonstrable product or behaviour) behaviours, skills and attitudes. Aims must necessarily precede learning outcomes even if only in an implicit sense, and serve to guide them. They provide the value system against which learning outcomes can be judged. Learning outcomes also give us some ideas for tasks with 'structured' groups (see pages 120–33 and Wilson 1980).

Here's how an online course for developing activities (e-tivities) introduced course aims and objectives.

Online groups can be used for a wide range of special purposes. These include:

- Logistical convenience: they reduce journeys of all kinds; participants have more freedom when they work together.
- Dramatically reduced costs associated with travel, catering, training facilities and meeting rooms time; and away from the office, though allowances must be made for setting up effective platforms and providing excellent 24/7 support.

- The exploitation of the benefits of asynchronous text-based communication: these include more open communication, reduction of hierarchies, reduction of discrimination based on appearance and accent.
- The appeal to individuals who may be unwilling or unable to travel to one location due to caring commitment or physical or mental disability.
- The appeal to individuals who fail to thrive in more regular learning groups, e.g. young people or excluded groups.
- The desire to maintain an audit or record of all postings for later review or analysis.
- The ability to create truly global and/or cross cultural groups.

In our online e-moderator courses, we give participants an early opportunity to explore purposefulness.

SETTING EVENT OBJECTIVES

Our experience of working online suggests that the most important part of designing any event is the early stages – particularly setting clear objectives.

Here are just a few questions to consider. As a result of their being involved in your event:

- What do you want your participants to know?
- What do you want them to be able to do?
- How do you want them to feel?

Here is your chance to set a compelling, exciting, and motivating objective. What you choose to write will set the tone of your event. Recall the resource in week one 'Motivating language'. Now is an opportunity to employ those exciting words to full effect.

The event objectives should be:

- **s**pecific enough so that their attainment can be **m**easured,
- **a**chievable with the resources at your command, and
- **r**elevant to the purpose of your event and the **t**ime available.

In short SMART!

One of the most important considerations is measurement. If you can't measure your participants' progress towards the attainment of your objectives, then you have little idea how well they are doing!

There are some tried and tested methods to help you to know how your participants are getting on.

Recall the means your teachers at school used: marked tests, assignments, exams, or portfolios.

Think about how businesses make judgements about customers: satisfaction surveys, after-sales telephone calls, in-depth interviews.

Note how organisations find out what their members of staff think: appraisals, suggestion boxes, staff surveys, one-to-one meetings.

Our approach is to count the number of lessons a course member participated in (quantity), review the shared reflections (quality), and analyse the end-of-course questionnaires (both quality and quantity).

What might you do? Here's an e-tivity to help you.

E-TIVITY

Purpose: to gather specific ideas on measuring participants' progress towards achieving your intended objectives.

Task: Post a message on the E-tivity board containing the key objective for your event and two ways in which you will measure its success.

Respond: by suggesting ways to improve one other participant's objective and another participant's methods of measurement.

Resource: Examples of objectives and methods of measuring progress.

Aims for group learning

By now, you will have realised that learning in groups has an important place in all levels of education, if used appropriately. However, group work can be wasteful without specific purposes and fit with the curriculum. Brookfield (1990) suggests we should consider carefully our reasons for group discussion before we prepare for it. He proposes the following (slightly adapted) aims:

Intellectual Aims

- To engage students in exploring a variety of perspectives.
- To help students in discovering new perspectives.
- To emphasise the complexity and ambiguity of issues, topics or themes.

- To help students recognise the assumptions behind many of their habitual ideas and behaviours.
- To increase intellectual agility.
- To encourage active listening/attention.

Emotional aims

- To increase students' emotional connection with a topic.
- To show students that their experiences, ideas and opinions are heard and valued.

Social aims

- To help develop a sense of group identity.
- To encourage democratic habits.

These aims recognise the mutuality of the task and the socio-emotional dimensions of group behaviour underlined in Chapter 2. Group tutors are 'uniquely placed', according to Forster (1995) 'to develop higher-order intellectual functions which are at the heart of undergraduate education'. They can achieve such aims:

- By drawing on the subject expertise, setting learning tasks for students, monitoring how they perform them and responding accordingly.
- Through skills of group management, encouraging students to take an active part in the group, so learning from the other students as well as a tutor.
- By exercising self-awareness, as a result of which they can judge the fine line that lies between, on the one hand, contributing their subject insights to the work of the group and, on the other, so dominating the group that students are denied the space to take responsibility for their own learning.
- By asking questions that promote and extend learning, and challenge assumptions.

A typical predicament for tutors is in establishing a balance between, on the one hand, their authority as subject expert and, on the other, as leader and facilitator of the learning group. This is highlighted when students have queries, when the natural desire to give a full and informative answer has to be set against challenging the students to think and be less dependent; and the balance becomes more tricky to sustain when a tutor has engaged in excessive preparation and feels compelled to justify this by controlling and dominating the discussion.

Problems such as these can be alleviated by the tutor orienting the students and presenting a shared purpose to the discussion and entering into a form of mutual contract by making explicit what the aims or outcomes of any group session are.

Table 5.1 presents a set of learning aims achievable in most learning groups, even where they are not all consciously pursued; it also presents related tasks and outcomes which make much more specific the kind of activity that makes the aims achievable. Many may feel that personal growth, teamwork skills and self-direction in learning have little to do with small group teaching, the essential purpose

Table 5.1 Learning aims for discussion groups

Aims	Related tasks/outcomes
1. *Understanding* Helping students to consolidate and enhance their understanding of a subject or discipline	▨ clarifying concepts, theories and procedures ▨ reflecting on interconnections ▨ testing their understanding through examples, cases, illustrations
2. *Critical thinking* Helping students to develop their capacity for thinking critically and analytically	▨ reviewing evidence in the light of theories ▨ learning how to 'set' and solve problems or approach questions and issues ▨ enhancing their capacity for logical reasoning and formal argument
3. *Personal growth* Helping students to develop and mature as individuals	▨ clarifying attitudes, articulating and reappraising values ▨ developing in self-confidence and self-esteem ▨ evolving a sense of responsibility and commitment
4. *Communication skills* Helping students to learn how to communicate effectively with others	▨ refining listening, questioning and explaining skills ▨ presenting and defending a position clearly and cogently ▨ giving and getting feedback
5. *Group and teamwork skills* Helping students to learn how to collaborate and work as an effective group or team	▨ setting, allocating and monitoring tasks ▨ supporting and encouraging other members of the group or team ▨ initiating, directing and leading tasks
6. *Self-direction in learning* Helping students to take progressively greater responsibility for their learning	▨ clarifying their own goals as learners ▨ managing their study time and effort and setting priorities, accepting responsibility for evaluating their own work and their progress as learners

Source: Forster et al. (1995) *Tutoring and Demonstrating: A handbook*, p. 13.

of which, they say, is to make sure that students have really understood what they have been trying to get across in lectures, or are able, through argument, to develop critical judgement. But most skills can only be achieved when there is a genuine sense of opportunity for self-expression and it feels safe to take risks.

Discussion in groups can help students to know enough about themselves and about others to enable them to work independently and yet cooperatively within a team. A paradigm of learning which incorporates this vision is that of Fink (2003) (see Figure 5.1).

Learning how to learn
enabling students to continue learning for the future and to do so with greater effectiveness

Caring
which gives students the energy they need for learning – maybe through feelings, interests or values

Human dimension
which reminds students of the human significance of what they are learning

Integration
which gives learners a new form of power especially intellectual power

Application
which allows other kinds of learning to become useful

Foundational knowledge
which provides the basic understanding necessary for other kinds of learning

Figure 5.1 Taxonomy of significant learning

Source: Fink 2003.

This paradigm propels teaching and learning in the direction of the arrow from the acquisition of knowledge into multiple dimensions of learning. Fink sees learning as a process of change. 'For learning to occur, there has to be some kind of change in the learner. No change, no learning. And significant learning requires that there be some kind of lasting change that is important in the learner's life', a view that relates to William Perry's findings on intellectual and ethical development (Chapter 3, pages 56–7).

Seen in relation to such aims, Bloom's taxonomy (see pages 101–2) with its main focus on the purely cognitive aspects of learning can be seen to be lacking in many of the learning requirements required by twenty-first century society, employers and the world at large, such as learning how to learn, leadership and interpersonal skills, ethics, communication skills, character tolerance and the ability to adapt to change.

Team-based learning (TBL) (see Chapter 8, page 213) gives a much sharper focus to the group as a transformative medium, one in which problem-solving and teamwork skills are both an end in themselves and a means to higher (deeper?) levels of learning. Fink (2004) claims that, when used properly it:

- transforms 'small groups' into 'teams';
- transforms a technique into a strategy;
- transforms the quality of student learning;
- for many teachers, transforms (or restores) the joy of teaching.

TBL differs fundamentally from other group work in that, rather than being an adjunct to the central (possibly lecture-based) thrust of a course, as are many discussion groups, it involves a fundamental change in the overall structure of the course.

When students learn to play a variety of roles in the process of learning and achieve a degree of freedom from dependency they can become more sensitive to different points of view and ways of thinking and learn to work cooperatively with others using the varied skills of the group. They may also develop a surer sense of social identity, and a feeling of belonging and commitment.

PROJECT AIMS AND OUTCOMES

There are two further circumstances in which the specification of learning outcomes may be particularly valuable for group work. One is where the students undertake a personal or peer responsibility for the conduct of their own work. In some cases this can lead to their assessing their own work. Knowles (1986) described a study of personal learning contract in which students decide their own learning needs, strategies for achieving them, evidence of their accomplishment, and criteria and means of evaluating them. The development of the contract is facilitated by the tutor who encourages the students to use various combinations of teamwork in pursuit of their goals.

The other circumstance is in projects or other self-directed work where students may be encouraged to develop their own individual learning outcomes in groups and thereafter pursue them with group support. In both these cases, the specification of learning outcomes may be seen as a way of investing the authority of the absent tutor in a set of guidelines and standards.

Typical aims for projects (Jaques 1988) may include the following:

Individual skills

- Develop a personal interest and expertise in an area of the subject.
- Demonstrate an ability to handle new problems.
- Form independent judgements.
- Collect and interpret unfamiliar information.
- Show initiative.
- Encounter facts, views and situations from unfamiliar perspectives.
- Integrate knowledge from a range of sources.

Group skills

- Learn to work cooperatively.
- Share in a decision-making process.
- Exercise leadership, chair meetings.
- Be flexible in adopting roles to suit the changing needs of the group.

Personal Awareness

■ Learn about own strengths and weaknesses in respect of the above.
■ Make a realistic appraisal of ability in relation to the complexities of the task.
■ Gain a sense of satisfaction through personal achievement.
■ Gain a sense of autonomy and freedom within the constraints of the task.

Communication skills

■ Communicate work in a clear and effective manner in discussion and in writing.
■ Develop questioning and listening techniques in seeking and making sense of information.
■ Develop skills of logical and persuasive argument.
■ Write a coherent and readable account of the work done.

Though some tutors may object to the idea of promoting personal skills and values, in project work it can be extremely helpful for students to know what new team and problem-solving skills they need to develop in order to tackle the project and even to assess their development. Wellington (1998) describes a multi-disciplinary project in which students were given the following outcomes/objectives. The students were to:

■ Formulate, through group interactions, solutions to business problems which require the integration of design, manufacturing and marketing solutions.
■ Separate engineering, accounting and marketing problems into solvable elements; explore solutions mindful of the influence each discipline had on the other.
■ Demonstrate understanding of manufacturing design and the possible need for redesign.
■ Exhibit committee chairperson, secretarial and recording skills.
■ Negotiate responsibilities within a group to ensure effective project management.
■ Compile, present and defend a syndicate report on the project.
■ Assess personal and peer performance in achieving individual and group objectives.
■ Value the complexity of issues and range of people affected by the introduction of new products and technology.
■ Appreciate the degree of involvement necessary in the decision-making process in a typical industrial situation from disciplines including planning, marketing, finance, processing, quality, legal and human resource management.

Wellington (p. 145) quotes research which concludes that group motivation is optimised when students have clear goals to attain, feel confident about performing well, have positive outcome expectations, attribute success to ability, effort and strategy, and receive relevant and prompt feedback. Further research evidence indicates that the following factors are among those regarded as significant in group projects:

■ *Goal activation* – projects encouraging students to achieve their own goals.
■ *Goal salience* – goals being clear so that students know what is expected.
■ *Multiple goals* – lead to greater success.

- *Goal alignment* – goals aligned with each other and not in conflict.
- *Optimal challenge* – tasks being difficult and challenging but not excessively so.

He also cites the evidence of the importance of tasks being structured so as to highlight short-term goals which help students to feel confident, and for the need for assessment to be relevant to the objectives.

DEVISING LEARNING OUTCOMES

> Aims and objectives (outcomes in particular) must be connected quite forcefully to the learning activities that are designed to enable the student to achieve them; they must be embodied in the actions and words of the teacher who professes them; they must be continually presented to students in order to provide a clear framework in which they can work. The most compelling reason for using [learning outcomes] is that it forces us as teachers to make our intentions for student learning explicit.
>
> (Ramsden 1993)

As already explained, one value of learning outcomes is the way in which they enable a sharing of intentions by making them more explicit and checkable. But they also provide a useful check on the tendency to fail to provide diversity in assessment methods and questions and, in describing what the student should be able to do by the end of an event, they make it possible for the students to make choices and not be held back by uncertainty and confusion about what will be assessed.

So, a clear learning outcome should say what the students should be able to do, the conditions under which they should be able to do it, and how well they should be able to do it. It should therefore contain (if we are to follow the rubric) *an active verb, an object* and a *qualifying clause* which specifies a context or condition. Clearly it should also identify important learning requirements, be achievable and assessable, and use language that the students can understand. So verbs like 'know' and 'be aware of' do not conform to this rubric. Let us look at a few learning outcomes and how they might be derived.

The verb in learning outcomes

It is important, especially when matching the learning outcome to an appropriate assessment, to select the most suitable verb. A useful tool is Bloom's Taxonomy of Educational Objectives which describes the objectives relating to knowledge, intellectual abilities and skills in the form of a hierarchy of six categories: *knowledge, comprehension, application, analysis, synthesis and evaluation*. Following are some examples of verbs listed under the appropriate category:

Knowledge and Cognitive Skills

Collection and use of information: find; extract; organise; present, etc.

Knowledge of facts: know; be aware of; list; name; recount; define, etc.

Interpretation of knowledge: understand; describe; restate; explain, etc.

Application of knowledge: solve; give examples; apply; draw (up), etc.

Analysis of knowledge: compare; contrast; distinguish; appraise; debate; analyse; examine, etc.

Synthesis of knowledge: formulate; teach; design; develop; redefine; propose, etc.

Evaluation of knowledge: assess; criticise; evaluate; appraise; judge; discriminate, etc.

Key Skills

Learn; operate; manipulate; change; present; listen; intervene; lead; collaborate.

Attitudes and Values

Connect; appreciate; value; care; support; be willing; interested; committed; enthusiastic; be creative; enterprising.

Problems of clarity

It is worth noting that some verbs commonly used in learning outcomes can be confusing and vague – especially those related to knowledge outcomes. 'Know', 'understand', 'have a knowledge of', 'be acquainted with', 'have a grasp of', 'develop a working knowledge of' etc. give no indication of what is expected either in process or testable product if that is what is required.

Stating learning outcomes

Here are some examples of learning outcomes derived from aims. Note the inclusion of terms in some of them that can help the student to understand what counts for quality in assessment.

HISTORY

Course Content: Historical perspectives

Aim: To understand the importance of historical perspectives

Learning outcome: By the end of the course you should expect to: be able to communicate knowledge and present arguments in a way which conforms in terms of style, organisation and scholarly approach to the standards and conventions prevailing within the discipline of History, and to be committed to it as a way of thinking

LITERATURE

Course content: Gender and ethnicity in language, literature and culture

Aim: Make students aware of gender and ethnicity in language, literature and culture

Learning outcome: By the end of the course you should expect to: recognise and challenge ways in which power relations (e.g. in terms of gender, ethnicity and class) are constructed and perpetuated in language, literature and culture

POLITICS

Course content: Trends in post-communist politics

Aim: To compare and contrast developments in the different countries after 1990

Learning outcome: By the end of the course you should expect to: have compared at least 3 contrasting developments in post-communist countries and assessed critically the impact of them on each other

LAW

Content: Rules and principles of law

Aim: To become more critical of established rules and principles in law

Learning outcome: By the end of the course you should expect to: have developed a commitment to looking critically at rules and principles in law, and propose reforms in the law, within an explicit value system

ENGINEERING

Content: The creation of hydraulic jumps and breaking waves

Aim: To understand the nature of energy loss and its implications

Learning outcome: By the end of the course you should expect to: be able to describe the components of energy and the manner in which they are dissipated; solve simple problems from practical examples; demonstrate critical interest in the phenomenon and the forms of its occurrence in the world

While it is perfectly logical to prepare and communicate learning outcomes, human activity does not always follow such a rational pattern. People tend to act on inspiration, on intuitive shifts and changes, and to respond spontaneously to the immediate situation. Nowhere are these unpredictable factors more evident than in discussion groups. The pursuit of a specific learning outcome in a group discussion could also destroy the possibility of achieving many other equally valuable aims such as those to do with creative thinking, autonomy or democratic learning. In other words, for the educational experience in a group to be valuable, the student must enjoy the freedom to question, to disagree and to make interpretations, and this may take the individual and the group in a direction other than that which was intended by the tutor or the course planner – or the examiner. In the experience of many tutors, what continually happens is that, to quote Pring (1973), 'one's conception of the enquiry or activity is altered in the very pursuit of it . . . the ends in view are constantly changing as one gets nearer them.'

Group discussion is more of a conversation than a one-way programme. What is more, there are few rational connections between means and ends, except where, as previously indicated, the two are coincident. Even if it were possible to select a method to achieve a particular learning outcome, other concomitants such as the group mood, tutor–student relationships or contextual issues like the proximity of examinations could frustrate the intentions of the tutor. This is part of the problem of selecting learning outcomes as if they existed prior to and independent of the students and, more importantly, of the group upon whose very existence and energy their achievement rests.

Nevertheless the articulation of outcomes can achieve at least three important goals: to clarify not only to tutors what they are trying to achieve and hence what they might have to do to these ends; to make the same information available to colleagues working in collaboration with them; and to make clear to students what they are expected to achieve, thus establishing a form of learning contract with consequent freedom to pursue learning in alternative ways.

Some have got round the problems of prior specification of outcomes by describing them after the learning event has taken place, agreeing what these were as part of a learning process for the students. *Unintended* and unpredictable outcomes can thus be revealed and, dare one say, celebrated.

So, the specifying of aims and outcomes need not be restrictive: it can provide an intentional framework in which intuitive and spontaneous changes can be made thus enabling tutors and students both separately and together to discuss the desirability of their aims (and their hidden values). All this can contribute to a sense of shared responsibility for learning, particularly because it focuses attention on what the student learns rather than what the tutor knows, but also because it releases the students from an over-reliance on the tutor's agenda. In these ways, the expressing, sharing and negotiating of aims in group teaching help to achieve a further aim – that of creating a sense of self-direction in learning. Nowhere is this more important than in some science and technology courses where mastery of content is often stressed as an end in itself, and little is done to help the student relate to personal goals and frames of reference. If and when choice is exercised in the curriculum it is usually by the tutor. The students are deemed unqualified to select what is to be learned – or how. It may well be, as Entwistle (1981) suggests, that students tend to specialise in subjects where the teachers suit their own personality and patterns of abilities (as we discussed on page 98). Yet, as we have seen on page 172, there is a contradiction in students being presented with an implacable intellectual authority in subject areas (e.g. science and technology) where our understanding of the world and the techniques for harnessing its forces are in a constant state of evolution and even revolution (see Kuhn 1973), where change is the only stable factor.

Learning outcomes can be designed not only to clarify and indicate what is expected in relation to skill areas, but also at progressive levels of attainment. The following example of generic academic outcomes with indicative levels was devised for Education Studies at the University of Wolverhampton.

GENERIC OUTCOMES WITH INDICATIVE LEVELS

A Make use of information

level 1   supplement notes with appropriate reading;
              reference correctly;
level 2   select and use relevant references and quotation to support the points you are making;
level 3   use specialist texts and journals to substantiate your arguments;
              draw together material from a variety of sources into a coherent argument;
level 4   present an overview of an area of concern;
              give a comparative and critical review of key authors, rival theories and major debates.

B Analyse

level 1   identify ideas, concepts and that underpin theories in your subjects;
level 2   explain the relationship between different elements of a theory;
              distinguish between evidence and argument and hypothesis;
              evaluate ideas and concepts;
level 3   recognise the difference between assertion and argument;
              recognise and acknowledge inconsistencies in arguments;
level 4   identify discrepancies and movements in positions over time;
              check the consistency of hypotheses with given information and assumptions.

C Think critically

level 1   examine problems from a number of perspectives;
level 2   question and challenge viewpoints, ideas and concepts;
              make judgements about the value of evidence, concepts and ideas;

level 3 ◻ develop and be able to justify your own opinions on significant ideas and concepts in your own subject;

level 4 ◻ justify and substantiate the choice of a particular approach or model.

D Synthesise ideas and information

level 1 ◻ relate new ideas and concepts to previous ones;

level 2 ◻ relate theoretical ideas to practical tasks;

◻ integrate learning from different modules you have studied;

◻ organise and structure ideas, concepts and theories into a coherent whole;

level 3 ◻ synthesise clearly theoretical perspectives and practical application within a given professional context.

(Allan (1994))

Another source of aims and learning outcomes for the group tutor can be found in educational theory. Bloom, in what became a classic educational text (1956, 1964), classified learning outcomes into two basic divisions: the *cognitive* (knowledge and intellectual skills); and the *affective* (development of attitudes and values). Clearly, in the process of learning, it is impossible to discriminate between these categories of behaviour. Skill is required to learn a piece of knowledge, to apply it or to write about it, and our attitude to both knowledge and its application in a particular environment is important in determining how well we perform these operations or indeed whether we do them at all.

These words are also invaluable for use in designing engaging learning activities in text-based online environments (Salmon 2002).

VERBS APPLICABLE TO THE COGNITIVE DOMAIN

1 Knowledge

arrange	order
define	recall
duplicate	relate
label	recognise
list	repeat
memorise	reproduce
name	state

2 Comprehension

classify	indicate
describe	locate
discuss	report
explain	restate
express	review
extend	select
identify	translate

3 Application

apply	operate
choose	practice
demonstrate	schedule
dramatise	sketch
employ	solve
illustrate	use
interpret	write

4 Analysis

analyse	differentiate
appraise	discriminate
calculate	distinguish
categorise	examine
compare	experiment
contrast	question
criticise	test

5 Synthesis

arrange	formulate
assemble	manage
collect	organise
compose	predict
construct	plan
create	prepare
design	propose
develop	rearrange
devise	set up
express	write

6 Evaluation

appraise	evaluate
argue	judge
assess	rate
attach	reframe
compare	score
conclude	select
contrast	summarise
critique	support
defend	test
estimate	value

Verbs applicable to the Affective Domain

These are concerned with **attitudes, emotions, values, commitment, and interpersonal relations**:

accept	praise
challenge	question
contribute	share
join	support
offer	try

Although the specification of desired behaviour can be a constraint on the democratic processes of group discussion, a list such as this could provide tutors with a useful focus on two counts: first, each could form an operative verb in the instructions for a group task; second, a tutor could develop a repertoire of questions based on these verbs to have 'up his/her sleeve' and draw out as spontaneously as possible during the progress of a discussion. For instance the verb 'summarise' might suggest an intervention from the tutor like, 'Would anyone like to put all that together now?' (See pages 188–90 onwards for further proposals on tutor interventions).

There is also the question of how precise we can, or should, make the outcomes of discussion, especially in social sciences and humanities where learning may emerge naturally in unpredictable ways and be all the better for that. Hussey and Smith (2002) argue that clarity and explicitness in learning outcomes are 'largely spurious', that their use can be restrictive and that what they attempt to clarify in anticipation is largely determined by the experience rather than a predetermined criterion of quality. The processes of group discussion may thus be seen to be of paramount concern in the pursuit of quality.

REALISING AIMS AND OUTCOMES

Whatever hopes and good intentions we may have for group work, there is always the risk for all concerned of 'losing the plot' – becoming distracted by unforeseen issues and problems or being unable to deal even with predictable problems. Though group discussion clearly has the potential to provide the opportunities for students not merely to engage in intellectual discourse but also to create a social 'family' to which they can belong and with which they can identify, it can equally become a source of frustration despite the best intentions. Clearly, the role of the tutor in settling the atmosphere in the group will determine whether aims to do with open and cooperative styles of behaviour as opposed to closed and competitive ones is significant, as is careful preparation for students engaged in group projects.

In both discussion groups and group projects the importance of taking the risk of making mistakes and learning from them cannot be understated. To achieve this state of affairs, the tutor has to balance a concern for academic standards with a capacity to understand and deal with the workings of group process as well as an attitude of generosity and praise for new solutions to old problems. The students may correspondingly applaud their tutor's resourcefulness in introducing them to new experiences in group learning.

If, finally, we return to the question posed at the start of the chapter, it will be evident that learning groups are amenable to a much wider range of aims and outcomes than is commonly supposed and that many of these bear a similarity to the aims and outcomes of groups in the wider world. Insofar as learning groups comprise a meeting of human beings with some shared goals, it seems probable that processes like pooling resources, making decisions, gaining mutual support, sharing ideas, creating something and so on would always exist in the process, at least subliminally. Yet if they could be made more explicit, may be by doing just that and by negotiating them and perhaps by incorporating them into more practical, real-world tasks, not only might they create more stimulation and variety of opportunity in learning for students, but also develop their awareness of group and teamwork concerns for their future careers.

The conversion of aims and outcomes into acceptable and realistic activities in the classroom is the central concern of the next chapter.

■ What kinds of discrepancies appear to exist between the express aims of groups you belong to, or lead, and what actually happens? How do they arise?

■ Draw up a chart like Figure 5.1 for the aims of your own group(s). To what extent do they vary within the group or between groups? What values and assumptions lie behind the aims?

■ How do you think the aims of your group relate to:

  ■ The broader aims of your course?
  ■ What is actually assessed on the course?

■ Do you find that your online groups stick to given objectives or do they tend to explore wider aims?

CHAPTER 6

ACTIVITIES FOR GROUPS

> This chapter addresses a wide repertoire of activities that help you to plan and achieve a range of learning outcomes for groups, whether face-to-face or online.

The activities in this chapter:

- can be used in entirely face-to-face group situations;
- can be run synchronously or asynchronously in entirely online situations;
- can be 'blended' in a programme where participants meet and work online.

There is an infinite number of sets of combinations.

Of course, before you can blend, you need to have a sense of the flavours of each contribution. For example, where most of the provision is face-to-face, e-tivities can extend precious contact time, by early provision of information to work on before a session or as reflection on action or to gather feedback. The asynchronous mode can free the tutor from the constraints of time and place where an extended activity does not require intervention at a specific time. If most of the work is online, an occasional meeting can provide fun and reinforcement to the group. In this situation it is best to establish the online group first, and meet half way or towards the end of the programme.

RANGE AND FORMAT OF ACTIVITIES

E-tivities

- Structured participative group work online.
- Based on one key topic, activity or question to make participation and e-moderating easy and effective.
- Motivating, engaging and purposeful.

- Based on interaction between learners/students and active contributions.
- Designed and led by an e-moderator (online teacher, tutor, trainer).
- Usually asynchronous (i.e. over time).
- Based on simple text-based bulletin boards.
- On or offsite, blended or online only.
- One-off or built into a programme.

E-tivities are important for online groups because:

- They're cheap.
- They're in the hands of the e-moderators.
- They're easily changeable.
- They utilise local, corporate, discipline-sensitive and tacit knowledge.
- They are focused on the application of learning.
- They are customisable and personalisable.
- They help to build communities of practice.
- They use any platform with a bulletin board.
- Evaluation for quality and effectiveness can be built into process.
- You can use them for any topic, any level.

If you are designing for entirely online groups, or any kind of blend, we suggest you start by using the structured 'e-tivity' framework. You have seen some examples of these throughout the book. E-tivities should be designed and prepared prior to the groups' arrival online.

Key features of e-tivities

- Illustrative title.
- Small piece of information, stimulus or challenge (the 'spark').
- Online action which includes individual participants posting a response (the 'invitation').
- Interactive or participative element – such as responding to the postings of others (the action and interaction).
- Elapsed time allowed, posting times required.
- Summary, feedback or critique from e-moderator.

On the bulletin board or forum aim to provide just one instructional message, which contains everything a student will need to take part. Include:

- The purpose of the e-tivity (why the participants are doing it). If the e-tivity is assessed, indicate what might indicate success and how they can achieve it.
- What participants should do and how they can go about doing it.

- How long it should or could take in minutes or hours as well as when the e-tivity starts and when it should finish.
- How the participants should work together.
- What the e-moderator's role is and when s/he will post.

Large groups, equality and inclusion

In large groups, though the pool of talent and experience available potentially provides a wide range of views and a greater sharing of effort, the incentive to take an active part may be less. In face-to-face discussion differences in relative participation increase to the point where one or two members may well begin to dominate and reticent members may fail to contribute (though they may enjoy relative anonymity). Where there is an agreed leader the need to counteract fragmentation places special demands on his or her awareness of the problems and skills in coping with them.

The smaller the group, the greater is the likelihood of close relationships, full participation and consonance of aims. In a small group, roles are likely to be shared or rotated. Five to seven members is generally regarded as the optimum for leaderless groups. In the case of led groups, and for discussion purposes, groups of 15 tend to be the largest size that allows for reasonably full participation. Online, 15 is certainly the largest for full participation. By dividing and arranging larger groups into smaller units, however, we can make the tasks of learning and its management both less demanding and less problematical.

Differentiation and equality

Because of the natural tendency of larger groups to differentiate roles, equality is harder to achieve than in small groups, a factor that is as likely to apply to both online and face-to-face situations. Using structured activities breaks larger groups into smaller ones while still maintaining a sense of the whole group. Groups do not find it easy to work virtually (Rossen 2001), so without careful structuring, and the use of active and interactive e-tivities, it is unlikely that discussion will move beyond sharing

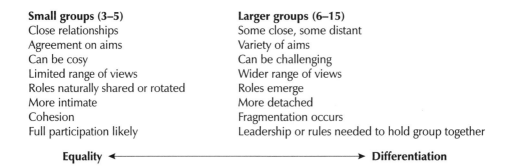

Small groups (3–5)	Larger groups (6–15)
Close relationships	Some close, some distant
Agreement on aims	Variety of aims
Can be cosy	Can be challenging
Limited range of views	Wider range of views
Roles naturally shared or rotated	Roles emerge
More intimate	More detached
Cohesion	Fragmentation occurs
Full participation likely	Leadership or rules needed to hold group together

Equality ←——————————————————→ Differentiation

Figure 6.1 How the experience of large groups is likely to differ from that of small groups

information, support and encouragement. E-tivities are based largely on participants 'making sense' of material through interaction with their peers and with their e-moderators. Online equalness is usually easier to achieve as no one has to wait a turn and shy people sometimes blossom. Be careful with humour and irony, though: it doesn't work so well until participants are very comfortable, and offence can be taken.

There are perceived differences, too, in the ways men and women approach discussion. Tannen (1991) agues that many women approach a group as an individual in a network of connections; in which 'conversations are negotiations for closeness in which people try to give confirmation and support, and to reach consensus . . . Life [for them] is a community, a struggle to maintain intimacy and avoid isolation' (p. 25). Where men may assume, and seek, hierarchies of power and accomplishment, women look for hierarchies of friendship. While men and women may have similar aims of learning and achievement, women are likely to pursue them through connection and men through opposition (ibid.). Also, in the view of Brookfield and Preskill (2005), men 'tend to adopt a "report" form of speech that serves to maintain their independence and helps them negotiate status . . . When men and women join in discussion, the norms of report speech, if not challenged, usually prevail' (p. 153). And where sub-groups are formed, men tend to be the ones who take on the role of reporting back to the whole class.

Brookfield and Preskill suggest four approaches to inclusion:

1   *Begin discussion with some form of personal disclosure* such as individual experiences, enthusiasms and fears so that the students feel they know each other. Group rounds (page 121) and paired introductions (interviewing and introducing a partner) are useful devices here.
2   *Encourage ground rules that make it OK for everyone to stumble in conversation*, miss the point and so on without feeling discredited; teachers (tutors) can help by modelling this.
3   *Call time-outs* to allow students to review and connect points that have been made with their experiences.
4   *Introduce periods of women-only discussion*, possibly alternating with men-only periods, and comparing the two.

They also suggest that a brief analysis of ways in which gender appears to influence discussion, both from the student's and your (the tutor's) point of view, could provide valuable insights.

And as you will see later in this chapter (page 117 et seq.), we have indicated those activities that are more likely to secure equal opportunities in discussion.

Lewis and Habeshaw (1995) provide a set of tasks and exercises for the promotion of equal opportunities in courses.

Seminars

'Seminar' is a generic title for group discussion with fairly intellectual aims, led formally or informally by the tutor or e-moderator and focused on issues arising from the subject matter, rather than student difficulties. Seminars usually run with 8–20 participants. One student typically will be asked to present a critical analysis to introduce the discussion.

Ideally, seminars provide an intellectual stimulus that is difficult to match, though unsettling group dynamics along with a lack of tutor skill sometimes create an unsatisfactory experience for students. The success of a seminar depends on the skills of the tutor or e-moderator and the ability of the students to work with whatever evolves in the group. When seminars go well, they can be a most exhilarating experience. An effective seminar discussion demands patience from the tutor, preparation by the students, and a suitable mix of personal qualities. The exceptional tutor may succeed in elevating a seminar to a memorable level of intellectual ferment.

Treadaway (1975) describes seminar types:

- The *monologue* or 'sitting at-the-feet of the master'.
- The *highly structured* or 'I know what you want to say'.
- The *duologue or 'wrestling match'* (one bright or forceful student wants to impress the tutor and a duologue ensues on areas which no one else knows about).
- The *anecdotal* or 'Did I ever tell you?'.
- The *essay-reading* or Oxbridge type.
- The *article summary* or 'We've all read this anyway' (the discussion can become sterile).
- The *examination-cramming* (the focus on passing the test).
- The '*I don't believe in structured discussion*'.

Treadaway also offers key pointers for successful seminars:

- Prepare the structure in advance of the start.
- No more than ten participants if everyone is to contribute, sub-group if necessary to reduce size.
- If use of English or lack of confidence may inhibit discussion, sub-groups may help.
- Use question and answer style if tutor must convey information.
- Ensure participants have a good view of each other and a comfortable room (or good regular access online and a fast bulletin board).
- Whether tutor, e-moderator or students lead, ensure the leaders have skills of stimulating discussion in others.
- The tutor or e-moderator may need to leave the discussion for a while.
- Insist prior reading or preparation is achieved and allow plenty of time.

An ideal seminar structure is prepared by a small group of people who discussed the topic in advance and distributed any necessary material to the whole group. They present the topic to the group who had already read something about it and emphasise points for discussion rather than just summarise. There is then discussion by the whole group or by sub-groups with the tutor or e-moderator moving from group to group and guiding rather than leading the discussion. There is a short summary at the end by the leader and encouragement for those particularly interested in the topic, or with any difficulties, to get together for further discussion later. Such a seminar can also blend on and offline.

Online seminars

Seminars can work effectively online, or aid the effectiveness of a face-to-face seminar: the easy provision of material for all to work on beforehand, with suitable guidance, will encourage purposeful discussion; the distribution of seminar notes or summaries and follow-up material afterwards will aid reflection and reinforce learning; and the collection of feedback will be facilitated. An entirely online seminar can take the form of a brief posting of a topic for discussion, either by the tutor or a student, with subsequent online whole-group discussion or in small groups leading to a plenary.

However, the common problems may still occur. The e-moderator or one or two students may dominate or students may not have prepared beforehand and the result may be desultory exchanges. However, in an online environment the e-moderator's presence is less and power relationships are more neutral. And by summarising at intervals from the extant written record, the tutor can attempt to keep the discussion on track – or perhaps better still as learning reinforcement encourage a student to provide the summary. If the seminar is run over an extended period, more reflective students will have greater opportunity to 'think before they write', especially given the written record of proceedings – and those who are slower at keying will be less disadvantaged. Those whose language skills are not up to the fast pace of a class-based seminar will be able to follow the written record.

Tutorials

The tutorial, whether face-to-face or online, is concerned with the development of the student's powers of thought.

Tutorials serve two main functions:

- As a regular meeting ground for the checking of student progress, locating misunderstandings in lectures and an opportunity to give special scrutiny to a piece of the student's work.
- As the setting for the pastoral role for the tutor.

In science and engineering the word 'tutorial' is often used to describe an exercise class of up to 30 in which students work individually on set problems while the tutor circulates. The tutor has a chance to check how students are progressing, though some students are wary of admitting mistakes or lack of effort to the tutor, and acquire stratagems for avoiding him or her during the class period. More on problem-solving classes can be found in Forster et al. (1995) and on problem-based learning on and off line (Savin-Baden and Wilkie 2006).

One-to-one tutorials can provide a highly focused exploration of ideas and their expression between tutor and student, although sometimes the power relationship between tutor and student may militate against a really interactive discussion. One-to-one tutorials are also extravagant in the use of tutors' time if they focus attention entirely on work prepared by the student. When a group tutorial is held, even though less time may be focused on individual concerns, more time can be spent on the less threatening process of comparing and contrasting ideas between peers.

ADVANTAGES	DISADVANTAGES
■ *they can focus attention on individual student work and ways of thinking* ■ *they help the tutor keep an eye on student progress* ■ *they provide continuity in tutor/student relationship*	■ *they can be expensive in terms of tutor time* ■ *the tutor is typically in a dominant role*

GROUP TASKS

Tasks specify what the students individually or collectively are asked to think about, whether a process like 'observe the behaviour of a white rat' or an end-product like 'list ten issues that strike you as important, and rank them'. Specific roles may be allocated too.

Activities can be viewed as a mix of task, roles, rules and procedures which comprise an educational experience. The coherence and effectiveness of an activity requires clear communication of its structure, monitoring what is happening, gently applying rules or adjusting them to advantage, and avoiding the risk of being drawn into interactions with the group that might detract from the intended outcomes.

There is an example of how these elements might fit together:

Outcome: You are expected to identify and competently use three different strategies for solving problems.

Tasks (for example):

■ Solve a given problem.
■ Monitor the strategies involved.
■ Share the findings and compare them with research evidence.
■ Draw up a classification of the findings.

Activities: might be organised in the following sequence:

individual work on the problem > pairs comparing methods and results > the whole group passing sheets of solutions round to each other to draw comparisons > group produces a flip chart sheet with their results.

Setting tasks

Students are often unsure about what to do in groups and may well take up the pursuit of separate individual goals while ostensibly engaged in collaborative discussion. Stenhouse (1972) even suggests that students may evolve a secondary task to study the tutor's behaviour! If such situations are to be avoided, the tutor should make the task, and her/his role in relation to it, explicit. The task must be carefully worded and produced as text – the instructions may be continuously posted in the Virtual Learning Environment and always available.

By placing the emphasis on task, the tutor can partly sidestep the ever-present problem of authority and dependency in the group. In setting a task for a group the tutor assumes authority in order to delegate it to the group in getting on with the task. The tutor may organise any structuring of sub-groups, set time limits, confine his or her authority to a position which is set by agreed rules and procedures, monitor what is happening and make consequent adjustments.

Having set the task the tutor can then monitor the work of the sub-groups to check that it is making sense to them and be ready to change or adjust the task to one which is more relevant to the immediate concerns of the group. Sometimes ideas for such changes occur spontaneously with remarkable results.

Boredom in a group can often be relieved by a change of task and with remarkable results. A break or a change of group composition can often restore energy levels; but just as importantly, it may help just to find out why it is failing to capture the desired enthusiasm and often that is because it is too abstract or remote from the interests of the students.

Equally, the tasks selected should be challenging. If they are too easy, one person may do it on their own; too difficult and it may result in disruptive interpersonal conflict. They should be significant to the group members in terms of both their interests and values.

The challenge of how to relate group discussion to personal experience or real-life processes is discussed by Parker and Rubin (1966), who argue strongly for the introduction of real-world experiences, rather than academic artefacts. They suggest a four-stage model:

1   *Creating and acquiring knowledge*: students observe phenomena, read expository material, collect evidence and listen to presentations.
2   *Interpreting knowledge*: students derive meaning from what they have learned; they relate new knowledge to old. The necessary skills include analysing, reorganising and experimenting with information and relating it together.
3   *Attaching significance and communicating knowledge*: students infer generalisations, relate information to new situations and learn or reorganise the information in new ways. These activities precede communication.
4   *Applying knowledge*: students use information to recognise, clarify and solve problems.

At a more practical level the following are equally important in preparing and communicating group tasks:

- An estimate of how long the activity will take.
- Whether the available room arrangement or online environment or media choice is suitable.
- The availability of resource materials.
- Whether it requires the tutor's involvement, and if so, when and in what roles.
- Whether the method it involves will assist continued building of a supportive learning climate – for example activities which provide opportunities for individual work followed by sharing in pairs or threes are useful for this purpose.

Forster et al. (1995)

You will note that online e-tivities follow similar patterns and moderators should equally aim for clarity of instruction in their 'invitation' to take part.

Here's an example of an e-tivity which exemplifies the care needed to make a task crystal clear. It is taken from an early stage of an online course for training tutors to construct effective e-tivities and forms part of a sequence of activities (All Things in Moderation Ltd):

ICEBREAKERS

In our experience there are four main types of participants:

- Innovators (who start things off first);
- Responders (who respond to messages that others post);
- Latecomers (who arrive late and are often breathless!);
- And finally non-attenders (who sometimes don't even know that they were booked on the course!).

Icebreakers tend to be completed by the first two groups, contributed to (eventually) by the third group – and never seen by the last group.

Therefore aim to design icebreakers that will work for participants arriving over a one-week period: ones that can be completed quickly using only what the participants can see or remember – icebreakers that they can complete without leaving their PCs.

Here is an example of an icebreaker:

Task: Post a message stating your favourite commercial brand (e.g. food, clothes, car) and why you have chosen it.

Respond: to others' messages by saying why you like or dislike their chosen brand.

Despite the simplicity of the example, some participants will answer a different question – and may even include their CV!

E-tivity Wield your E-Ice Pick

Purpose: to practise designing an e-tivity.

Task: design a short e-tivity icebreaker of your own that encourages the participants to reveal something about themselves. Post it in E-tivity 1.2 using the button below.

Respond: as if you were a participant to another participant's icebreaker.

Summary: will happen on Friday – make sure you've posted and responded by then please.

Typology of tasks for groups

There are some broad categories and specific examples from a potentially very wide range. Consider the merits of working online where a written record or audit trail would be beneficial.

Tasks for groups as a whole, or sub-groups

- Argue with tutor/students – disputation, debate
- Discuss a presentation
- Discuss misunderstandings
- Draw up a list of similarities and differences
- List items from experience
- List ideas, difficulties, preferences from reading
- List items from observation in group
- List items from reading
- Establish principles embodied in a text
- Mark own or each other's essays
- Set criteria for essay marking
- Generate ideas
- Pool information – for example from different readings, interpretations, data, useful websites
- Put items in rank order, rate them
- Make categories

- Make a list of relevant experiences
- Clarify problem/solve it/evaluate it
- Enact
- Agree a question or a statement worth making about a text
- Discuss critically
- Diagnose
- Mark each other's work
- Try to fill gaps in a solution or a text (e.g. a poem with a missing line)
- Report back on previous session (see pages 143 and 244)
- Argue relative merits
- Share anxieties
- Evaluate a case study with various possible answers and compare the results between groups
- Solve a problem and compare results between groups
- Compare and contrast items
- Identify the origins or purpose of something
- Share essay plans

- Share study methods
- Watch video sequence (with prepared focal questions or tasks)
- Read and evaluate text

Tasks for individuals followed by discussion in groups

- Mark off checklist
- Rank or rate and compare values
- Make decisions/proposals about case
- Construct model, etc.
- Observe group process
- Make choices
- Analyse text
- Allocate individual tasks – project work
- Suggest thesis and argue it
- Solve problem

Tasks for peer tutoring (see page 247)

- Teach
- Question to check learning
- Prepare questions
- Prepare tasks
- Counsel

Any tutor wishing to devise a new task may find it useful to apply some of the principles underlying these tasks:

- Consider the ways in which knowledge in their subject is created, interpreted, communicated and applied;
- Create situations in which social comparison and cognitive dissonance can take place;
- Incorporate and vary the use of different roles and functions described in Chapter 2.

Structuring tasks

When it is important to mobilise a sense of commitment and immediate purpose among a largish group of students, it makes sense to divide into smaller units by 'doing what comes naturally'. For example,

- Invite the students first to work individually to make a list for five minutes (online one day);
- Share their ideas in pairs for ten minutes (online one day);
- In groups of four to six, write up categories on a large sheet of paper (post a joint message, two days);
- Followed by 25 minutes of open discussion between groups. (three to four days).

The tutor or e-moderator 'wanders round' to check that everyone understands and accepts the task, and to help students in formulating categories. As you can see, such a series of activities could work well asynchronously online.

Game tasks

Games are essentially tasks with added rules and roles. Though games are most commonly associated with face-to-face activity, they are equally suited to online working.

For example, an engineering laboratory can be enlivened without any loss of standards by encouraging students to adopt a professional role in problem-solving as the following three examples demonstrate.

A   Dear Sirs,

I am designing a series of submerged pipelines to cross rivers in different parts of the UK (details given). I am in urgent need of a reliable check on the forces I might expect them to withstand and would be most grateful if you could test various models in a wind tunnel in order to give me some working data. Please send me your report within three weeks from this date.

Yours, etc.

B   The first-year students are currently studying the differences between static and dynamic forces. Could you please conduct the following experiment to check on the nature and magnitude of these differences and, having undertaken suitable rewording, write out a set of explanatory notes for the first-year students?

C   The valley of Erehwon (map and relevant data enclosed) is being considered as the site of a huge new dam and reservoir. You are to divide into three professional groups: engineers, technicians and journalists. The engineers must conduct a feasibility study on

(a)   dam structure;
(b)   water supply; and
(c)   hydroelectric power.

The technicians must determine measuring techniques for [a list of purposes given] and the journalists must compile a public relations brochure on the study. Your written reports should be submitted two days before the meeting of the study commission where they will be formally introduced and discussed.

In these three cases, and especially the last one, the rules and procedures, though not very explicit, are no longer embedded in the teacher/student relationship but in an understanding of everyday life outside the educational system, to do with the consultant/client relationship, students in a teaching role and feasibility studies respectively. Approaches like this are admirably suited to group teaching in professional subject areas or those which have low intrinsic interest and need some imaginative boost to get them going. Games and simulations are indeed most valuable in this regard.

Roles do not have to be imagined ones, however: they can be practical and purposeful in the context of a course. As students begin to engage with experimental work and have to learn all the new techniques and skills that they need, it may make sense to introduce them gradually, in stages, to the various aspects of their experimental work. This can be done by, for example, limiting the variables at the start so as to focus on factors like observation, errors, cross-referencing, before moving into more open-ended experiments.

In one chemistry practical (Exley and Moore 1993) a clearly structured sequence had each group of eight students in four pairs doing four experiments:

Task	Expt 1	Expt 2	Expt 3	Expt 4
Week 1	Pair 1	Pair 2	Pair 3	Pair 4
Week 2	Pair 4	Pair 1	Pair 2	Pair 3
Week 3	Pair 3	Pair 4	Pair 1	Pair 2
Week 4	Pair 2	Pair 3	Pair 4	Pair 1

The experiment allocated to each group in week 1 became their experiment and they had responsibility thereafter for the progress of that experiment throughout the following four weeks. They were responsible for:

■ Learning the aims, theoretical principles, calculations and techniques associated with that experiment;
■ Carrying out the first week's work on the experiment;
■ Instructing and directing the work of the other pairs in subsequent weeks;
■ Collecting and collating the results from the other pairs in the subsequent weeks;
■ Writing the final report of their experiment including the calculations and results of the other pairs;
■ Presenting an oral report of the investigation to all the students.

The output of each week's work was assessed by the students leading the experiment, the final report assessed by the teacher and the oral presentation by both class and teacher. This method involved an initial briefing of all the students on the operation of the scheme and with each group on their own experiment, weekly meetings between the student groups to brief and debrief and a training session on presentation skills with the whole class. An advantage of this scheme is that the students' learning is sharpened by their having to instruct other students with great care because the results contributed to the final presentation. Other advantages are that each pair of students has to write up only one report each and the staff have less repetitive marking.

Another approach to the sequencing of laboratory work set out to desegregate theory and practice. Rather than keeping lectures, reading, practicals and writing all separate, the different activities can be mixed (which is what usually happens in practice). For example you could:

- Design the experimental work during lectures.
- Introduce a bit of theory or send students off to the library in the middle of the practical.
- Allocate the first half hour of a laboratory to the completion, and handing in, of the previous week's report.
- Hold a seminar on the ethics of a particular practice or experiment during the laboratory session.

The case studies in Chapter 10 include further examples of group tasks in the context of the curriculum.

GROUP STRUCTURES AND ACTIVITIES

This section is designed to help you to:

- Gain a wider recognition, and use of, the range of variations and alternative activities or methods you can use in working with groups.
- Employ techniques which are less frustrating, more enjoyable, which challenge and stimulate the minds of students and which give credit to that under-used faculty of mind – the imagination.

Many of these less-than-familiar activities may be included within the bounds of what is a timetabled discussion group or 'seminar'. Others may need to be pursued in their own right, whether entirely face-to-face, blended or entirely online.

The activities are roughly grouped into the following patterns:

- Those structured either in terms of an explicit pattern of interaction, a change in the use of space or time sequence.
- Those designed to stimulate creative thinking.
- Those that stimulate the imagination by importing an external scenario.
- Those that students can operate on their own.

A further classification indicates those activities especially, but not exclusively, suited for:

observing or promoting equal opportunities

international groups

larger groups

online groups

We indicate which of these groupings the activities may be most suitable for, though with skill in handling the process and variations in structure or organisation of the groups, a much wider range of options is possible.

We start by looking at the variations of whole group discussion that are possible. Then from pages 120–33, we examine in detail a range of ideas for structured group discussion. On pages 133–9 we consider techniques for developing creative thinking in groups, namely brainstorming and synectics. Pages 139–47 are devoted to ideas for learning through games, role play and case study, and then, on pages 147–54, comes an exploration of independent learning in groups which covers peer tutoring and project work. We conclude the section by offering tips for designing e-tivities for use with groups, on pages 154–7.

The first three methods below involve the group as a whole remaining as one unit. The first two are of particular relevance for larger groups where the communication of knowledge is directed through the tutor.

Whole group discussion

Controlled discussion

. . . used for checking for knowledge and understanding of presented material. Discussion is controlled by the tutor; either students ask questions or make comments; or the tutor fires questions at students in the manner of a Socratic dialogue. Handled well with a large group, this approach can be effective provided the tutor has a level of self assurance.

ADVANTAGES	DISADVANTAGES
▪ *convenient to organise at the end of (or as a follow-up – possibly online) to a lecture* ▪ *quick feedback* ▪ *large and economical number of students*	▪ *inhibiting to open communication* ▪ *reticent students not heard, less of a problem online* ▪ *little peer discussion*

Step-by-step discussion

. . . based on a prepared text or audio-visual material that provides a sequence of subject matter. In leading the students through the sequence, the tutor draws out and guides the students' developing knowledge in discussion and, by using open-ended questioning skills (see pages 183–7), allows students some freedom to explore the realism of their own knowledge. The input for step-by-step discussion may be a sheet of notes, or a text shared by tutor and students alike, or even audio-visual material, where a 'stop-start' procedure can be employed (see page 247). This technique brings together several of the qualities of the lecture and the seminar and works online.

ADVANTAGES	DISADVANTAGES
▨ *economical use of large groups* ▨ *'authority' can be invested in shared text audio-visual material – students not dependent on tutor for content* ▨ *combines information-giving, processing and feedback aims*	▨ *as for controlled discussion, but to a lesser extent* ▨ *sequence and structure of discussion pre-ordained – may not correspond with students' needs*

Associative discussion

. . . used for giving people freedom in a controlled environment to talk about whatever comes to mind. Common in psychoanalysis and group therapy but also used to develop a particular form of learning.

The model of group therapy is that of the therapist who is trained to listen and refrain from comment while the patient 'freely associates', thus revealing underlying patterns of thought and feeling. Associative discussion operates on a similar principle. The tutor says very little but encourages spontaneity of speech among the students. What the tutor does say is by way of directing students' attention to anomalies and inconsistencies in what they have said, pointing out patterns and relevance in what might otherwise seem a vague and rambling discussion, and helping them 'to see themselves as capable of change' (Abercrombie 1979).

Students may discover, in the course of discussion, that they have highly specific, even idiosyncratic reactions to problems, to situations, to individuals; that they always slow down their ability to solve problems. In associative discussion, an understanding of the nature of knowledge, and self-insight can be realised in a manner no other teaching method can provide. It is first-hand, personal experience of the shifting nature of experience, the ambiguity of evidence, the tenuous nature of our most profound convictions. In these senses, free discussion is a means to intellectual growth – the sort of personal development that Perry (1970) describes as students move from the dualistic to the relativistic phases, and even onward to commitment (see pages 56–7).

The tutor's job is not to correct mistakes (other participants quickly pick up this task) but, with a good sense of timing, to inject comment on the nature of the argument; otherwise to listen attentively. By clearly specifying the aims and by intermittently restating them in the context of what is being said, the tutor sets a direction. By occasionally expressing feelings such as 'I don't know what I've done to shut you all up' the tutor encourages a recognition of the important part that emotions play in our thinking; by referring to his or her own habits when students are talking about theirs, and encouraging 'oscillation of attention between different contexts', e.g. from the present group to the whole class or profession, the tutor promotes the transfer of learning and a reflexive understanding of problems. The tutor's role is therefore to clarify the field of discourse and set its boundaries as well as to draw associations within the general aim.

A variation of this model was used on a basic Biology course in Sydney. The tutor was originally placed outside the group and the students were told she was present only as a resource and would not enter discussion unless the whole group agreed it was necessary. Later, a five-minute limit for 'non-intervention' by the tutor was introduced. Tasks ranged from the arrangement of specimens, diagrams or cards to intriguing questions such as 'Was Jack's Beanstalk possible?' Two of the themes that come through strongly in all the literature on these groups are the somewhat painful silences as it progresses from a state of dependency into one of responsibility, and the need for training for tutors in what is a very unnatural role for most.

The authority/dependency conflict is deeply rooted in the culture of teaching and learning. It takes a lot of courage, care and personal insight to handle it successfully. To an extent, the relatively novel nature of the virtual world can make such a transition easier for both tutor and students.

ADVANTAGES	DISADVANTAGES
■ *promotes intellectual growth greater student responsibility for learning* ■ *encourages flexibility* ■ *has long-term value*	■ *may seem a rambling kind of discussion* ■ *time needed for adjustment to process* ■ *learning difficult to assess by traditional means as often very internal* ■ *difficult role for many tutors*

Structured group discussion

The next set of group activities specifically involve direction by the tutor for the students to follow a sequence or a spatial pattern which can enable not only greater freedom to express ideas but also a focus on specific skills at different stages and from various positions. You will spot that these all work well in the online environment.

Milling

The class is asked to get up and mill around in the room, open space or synchronous online environment with a simple task like asking a question of each person they meet, or exchanging difficulties in understanding the topic – they must spend no more than (say) 30 seconds in each encounter. Milling can be followed by inviting general discussion of salient points.

ADVANTAGES	DISADVANTAGES
■ *physical movement; a break which can help free up thinking* ■ *brief one-on-one encounters allow safe expression of ideas* ■ *encourages social mixing*	■ *no control over what is discussed in encounters (could be an advantage!)* ■ *students see it as time-wasting*

Rounds

Each person has a brief time – 20 seconds or one minute, for example – to say something in turn round the group. This can go clockwise or anticlockwise, the direction can be decided by the first contributor, or members can speak in a random order as the spirit takes them. More interest and energy is usually generated however if the person starting the 'round' chooses who should go second, the second person who should go third and so on.

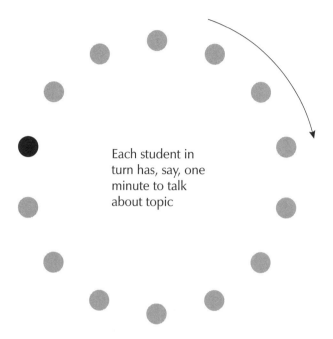

Each student in turn has, say, one minute to talk about topic

Figure 6.2 Group 'rounds'

Rounds are particularly useful at the beginning of any group meeting in order to bring everyone in from the start and, depending on what the group is asked to address in the round, as a way of checking in on learning issues. Such an activity – suitably organised by for instance by numbering off students or asking them to contribute alphabetically – could be a fruitful icebreaker for an online sequence of activities.

ADVANTAGES	DISADVANTAGES
■ *everyone contributes and can therefore feel included in the group* ■ *the tutor gets a sense of everyone* ■ *can be used as a gentle check on work done in preparation*	■ *as with all 'rule-bound' activities, natural spontaneity is curbed* ■ *if done in a circular sequence the last few can become quite anxious*

Buzz groups

Frequently, where the group is large, there is a need for a break in the more formal proceedings in order:

■ to provide a stimulating change in the locus of attention;
■ for the tutor to gain some idea of what the students know;
■ for the students to check their own understanding.

If, during the course of a lecture or other one-directional communication, students are asked to turn to their neighbours to discuss for just a few minutes any difficulties in understanding, to answer a prepared question, or to speculate on what they think will happen next in the proceedings, a sense of participation and some lively feedback is quickly achieved. It can also be achieved through e-mails or bulletin boards.

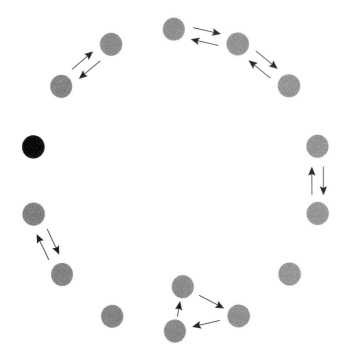

Figure 6.3 Buzz groups in a seminar

Buzz groups enable students to express difficulties they would have been unwilling to reveal to the whole class without the initial push of being obliged to say something to their neighbours. Taken by itself, the buzz group technique has little meaning and yet in the context of a lecture it can rekindle all sorts of dying embers. Its incorporation into a pattern of teaching events is described on pages 209–10.

ADVANTAGES	DISADVANTAGES
◼ can be used in any teaching situation for as short or as long as desirable ◼ helps students and teacher check on misunder-standings ◼ creates a stimulating break ◼ in face-to-face situations it can give the tutor a break to reflect	◼ can disrupt intellectual and social cohesion if timed wrongly

Three minutes each way

A variation of the buzz group, this allows each partner in turn to take a listening role for three minutes (or five) and to give unconditional attention to what the other is saying. The tutor has to be quite firm in making sure that the students know that this is not a conversation or discussion but a disciplined and focused opportunity for each person in to explore their experience without interruption. The only intervention the listener may make is if the speaker drifts too far from the topic to bring them back.

One particularly valuable use of this method is with 'learning partners' where, at specific times, pairs form to explain in turn what they have learned, how well and what they will do to maintain or improve that learning. It can also be very useful at the end of a workshop in presenting action plans.

ADVANTAGES	DISADVANTAGES
◼ simple and easily repeated once understood ◼ develops reflective mode of learning	◼ none if timed right – but difficult online and no obvious advantage over the delays between responses in e-mails

Snowball groups (Pyramids)

Buzz groups can be extended into a progressive doubling in which pairs join up to form fours, then fours to eights which finally report back to plenary session. This developing pattern of group interaction is known as a 'snowball'. It is amazingly effective in ensuring comprehensive participation, especially when it starts with individuals writing their ideas in the first stage before sharing them. Lest students become bored with repeated discussion of the same points, a sequence of increasingly sophisticated tasks is often desirable (see Figure 6.4).

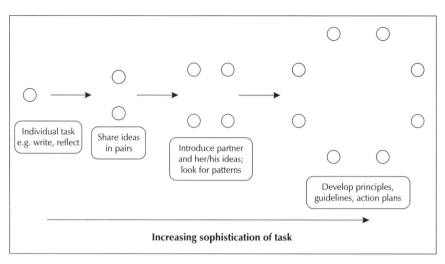

Increasing sophistication of task

Figure 6.4 Snowball or pyramid groups

ADVANTAGES	DISADVANTAGES
■ good for encouraging the creation of well-integrated ideas ■ allows students to think for themselves before discussing ■ generates full and lively participation in plenary discussion	■ breaks up cohesive feeling in some groups; takes time to unfold

Fishbowls

Fishbowls incorporate many of the best processes and structures of group practice. The concept of a fishbowl group springs from an obvious metaphor: a group of sentient beings observing another group of sentient beings who are swimming around in a less rarefied medium, and are aware of being studied while behaving in their usual manner. The observer feels at once detached and envious; superior and wanting to be part of the action.

Fishbowls differ from other methods as there is a mutual process and a differentiation of task: the inner group in a cognitive and the outer group in a metacognitive activity.

The normal fishbowl configuration has the inner group discussing an issue or topic while the outer one looks for themes, patterns, soundness of argument, etc. or uses a group behaviour checklist to give feedback to the group on its functioning; and the roles are then or at a later date reversed. They can of course be reversed without any feedback discussion. The tasks and the structure of fishbowls can be varied in many creative ways.

The sequence that follows would be difficult to replicate entirely online – role play, five-minute theatre and 'outward facing' in particular – but would lend itself to blending.

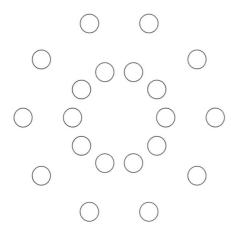

Figure 6.5 Fishbowls

ADVANTAGES	DISADVANTAGES
■ useful for generating and examining divergent views, and for cross-cultural or intergroup understanding ■ can add a new dimension to problem solving ■ a reasonably safe way to learn and get feedback on group behaviour ■ can be used to set agendas and objectives, for assessment and evaluation and to energise a group	■ the ground rules for the outer group may be difficult to maintain ■ if their task is not clearly explained and understood the outer group may become bored ■ the inner group may find the presence of observers inhibiting

Intergroup meeting
The outer group could be another seminar group who are there either to observe how a parallel group discusses a topic and give them a commentary, or to conduct a peer group assessment.

Empty chair
The inner group includes an 'empty chair' which enables anyone in the outer group to move to the inner group and ask a question or to make a brief statement before returning to the outer position.

Alter ego
Here, any outer person has permission to tap an inner person on the shoulder, either to take their place or, standing behind them, to put their point in a different way. This can be combined with the empty chair method. Alter ego can be used to advantage in evaluating a group where two people start with a prompt like a sentence completion, and talk about the group/workshop/course. Anyone can take the place of either person in the middle, even the tutor, and two useful ground rules are that everyone must have contributed by the end and that anyone in the middle who wants to come out can invite a replacement.

Role plays

Provided sufficiently confident students are selected, role play can be done 'in the round'. Alternatively, parallel role plays (say A interviews B) can be done in a number of small groups and then all the As come together to discuss the experience with the Bs observing, and vice versa.

Five-Minute theatre

A special and very effective version of the above is 'Five-minute theatre'. Groups of three to six select a problem which concerns them and they prepare to present it to their fellow-students as a short five-minute drama. They have 20 minutes to prepare and are advised to do a 'dry run' privately before the performance. The enactment is usually given without any 'prologue' to the others 'in the round'; the task of the outer group is to report what they have observed and particularly any insights and interpretations which may not have been transparent to the 'actors' or could have been revealed only through the drama.

Paired feedback

Less commonly, pairs are matched between the inner and outer group, members of the former briefing the latter acting as 'consultant' to their partner. who then observes the inner group discussion and after an period of time gives confidential feedback to their 'client'. The inner group then resumes discussion integrating the comments from 'outer' colleagues into a new round of discussion.

Representatives observed

When a number of sub-groups are first asked to make a decision like putting a list of items in rank order, all the groups could then elect a leaders/spokespersons who sit in an inner circle to make a final, agreed, decision observed by the others. After reaching the decision they could then 'face the music' back in the first groups.

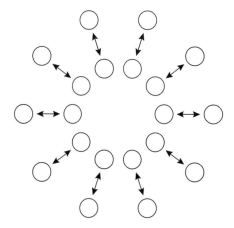

Figure 6.6 Fishbowl with paired feedback

Mix-up

After a round of normal fishbowl activity (discussion and observations), you could sub-divide each group: half the inner with half the outer to form two new groups who either work independently of each other or form a fishbowl relationship.

Hot seat

This was a method devised by some students for me after an experiential course I had run. They put a rotating chair in the middle, asked me to sit in it and proceeded to ask me questions about the course as I swivelled.

Outward facing

A fairly bizarre but interesting way to organise a fishbowl is to have the members of either group facing outwards. If the inner group face outwards, they may have problems in picking up non-verbal cues but they may find themselves listening more carefully and able to pick up cues from the outer group, especially if they are paired for the purpose. Alternatively the outer group can face outwards in order to fine tune their listening skills.

Crossover groups

The activity is designed both to make reporting back from sub-groups more exciting and to give all participants an active and responsible role. In the first phase they are divided into groups of approximately equal number to discuss a topic or work on a task – four groups of five, for instance. For the second phase, after a suitable time in discussion, they are asked in each group to number themselves from (in this case) 1 to 4 and told 'now form new groups – all the 1s together over here, all the 2s together there'. Alternatively, a colour coding rather than a numerical one can be employed as shown in Figure 6.7.

The task of each group member as he or she moves into the new group can be to report what happened in the phase 1 group following which a new discussion will naturally evolve. This technique is helpful in mixing a new group of students, on part-time courses where the circulation of ideas is never very rapid (Bligh, 1981), and with cross-cultural groups where there may be equal opportunities problems to do with language or culture or both.

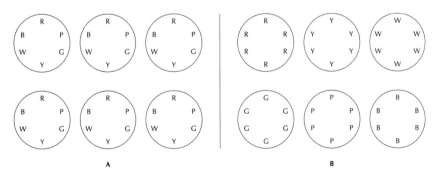

Figure 6.7 Crossover groups

A variation on the crossover groups model, the Jigsaw method, is described by Brookfield and Preskill (2005), based on Slavin (1990). In this, the students are asked to study topics independently in preparation for a discussion in which they will feature as 'experts', in conjunction with other 'experts'. The topics, chosen by the students for their own interest within the course outcomes, are distributed on a 'square root' basis – sixteen students in a group means four topics, four for each student. The students individually undertake the necessary study to become experts and, on return, meet in groups with the experts concerned with the same topic to share and upgrade their expertise. That done, they split into crossover groups, each group containing an expert from each topic who has to lead the discussion. This phase ends when all the groups have expressed reasonable satisfaction that the expertise has been shared and understood. Finally the whole group may reassemble for an open discussion.

ADVANTAGES	DISADVANTAGES
■ *excellent for mixing people and information* ■ *simple to organise and students enjoy it* ■ *avoids plenary discussion* ■ *everyone has to contribute and present a view not necessarily their own*	■ *can lead to confusion about learning outcomes* ■ *can break up absorbing discussions*

Circular questioning

One method of engaging the whole group from the start is to conduct a 'round' of questions. In its simplest version one group member formulates a question relevant to the theme or problem and puts it to the person opposite them who has a specified time (one or two minutes) in which to answer it; follow-up questions can be put if time permits. The questioning and answering continues clockwise round the group until everyone has contributed, at which time a review of questions and answers can

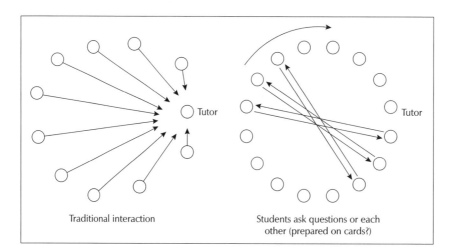

Figure 6.8 Circular questioning

take place; this could of course include answers that other would like to have given. Online, the use of names, numbers or colours would serve to designate the person to whom a question is addressed.

Questions thought up spontaneously can sometimes be a little facile and shallow so to encourage deeper levels of learning the tutor can ask students to prepare their questions on cards and then insert some of her/his own or simply ask students to prepare their questions by e-mail. The tutor can add some if necessary. These can be returned to the originator or selected from a pile at random to get discussion started. Circular questioning can also be used to advantage in problem-solving and decision-making groups.

ADVANTAGES	DISADVANTAGES
■ *a simple and quickly understood process* ■ *it ensures everyone is engaged in and has contributed to the topic in the first 10 or 20 minutes*	■ *the questions can be facile* ■ *it can be frustrating for those wanting to contribute when it is not their turn* ■ *it can stifle a natural wish for open discussion*

Line-ups

In line-ups the students are asked to adopt a position in a line which represents their view on an issue; a series of tick boxes could serve online.

Line-ups serve two valuable purposes: to get members of a group to tease out opinions values or attitudes which might otherwise remain obscure; and as a means of organising sub-groups.

The line in which the students are asked to stand denotes a range from one pre-defined polarity to another and they are asked to negotiate their position in it with others in order to establish they are in the correct place. For example:

Method A is the best approach to the problem

Method B is the best approach to the problem

Figure 6.9 Line-up 1

It is useful to place two chairs to represent the extremes. If, as is quite common, nobody feels strongly enough to stand at one end you can stretch the scale by asking the person who feels nearest to that value to take the physically extreme position. When used in this way a line-up can form a sort of opinion poll which enables both tutor and students to see what the balance of opinion is and make whatever relevant decisions are necessary.

I'm doing this course reluctantly

I'm doing this course because I really want to

Figure 6.10 Line-up 2

It can also help when there is a sense of simmering hostility or resistance in that, by having it brought out into the open, its 'owners' can lose a lot of their negative energy.

Figure 6.11 Line-up 3

If the intention is to form sub-groups, then by organising a mix of value positions in the sub-groups drawn from the line-up you are less likely to get cliques and splits in the group or workshop. The simplest way to effect this is to ask them to number off, according to the number of sub-groups you want, from one end to the other and ask all the 1s to form one group, the 2s another the 3s another and so on. You will thus achieve a membership in each group that is heterogeneous in opinion. (See page 26 on the importance of heterogeneity in groups.)

The criteria can be more arbitrary, for example: according to height, shade of hair, length of little fingers or any other visible criterion.

ADVANTAGES	DISADVANTAGES
■ *a quick way of getting a survey or 'straw poll' of opinion in a group* ■ *a visible and fair way of dividing into hetero-geneous sub-groups* ■ *create physical movement and informal negotiation*	■ *can bring out opinion differences too early in the proceedings* ■ *sometimes students are afraid to admit to any extremes and so cluster in the middle*

Horseshoe groups

This describes a way of organising a class so that it can alternate with ease between the lecture and discussion group formats. Rather than the students facing the front in serried ranks, they are arranged around tables in a horseshoe formation with the open end facing the front as in Figure 6.11.

A tutor can thus alternate between instructive talks and giving the groups a task such as a problem or an interpretation; the task should of course be one demanding collaboration among the students. The horseshoe format can be of great benefit in science and engineering exercise classes if students are given problems at the start and then the tutor circulates round the groups, listening and asking or answering questions. Should any general problem emerge, an explanation can be offered by the tutor or indeed by any student to the whole class.

Whether the groups are given identical, similar, or entirely separate problems there is always the opportunity to open up discussion on a sticky point or to ask groups to explain their solutions or

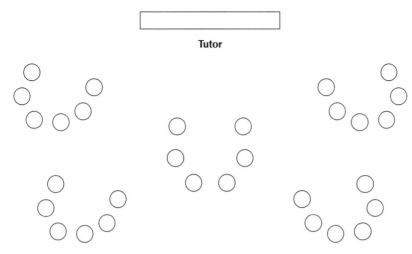

Tutor

Figure 6.12 Horseshoe groups

decisions to each other. To give each group a different role in relation to the task can also add energy and interest.

The plenary session can be run in several ways apart from the traditional one of a reporter presenting from each group. Written reports could be circulated for comment, groups can interview each other (A to B on C, etc.) or one member of each group could circulate; groups could produce and display posters, everyone can be given a number and the tutor picks a group and number at random (A3, D5, etc.). The tutor could pick up the necessary information from each group and present a unified report her or himself (Bligh 2000) or simply change the room layout to form one large group and let discussion emerge naturally without any structure. This is also an occasion where two other methods can be used to great effect. Reporters can form the inner group of a *fishbowl* or everyone can be involved in reporting using the *crossover* method (see above).

The horseshoe group format may also be used for syndicate meetings (see page 130) and could be run online, though the 'horseshoe' format would be irrelevant – it would become the more usual and straightforward 'groups > intervention > groups > plenary' type of e-tivity.

ADVANTAGES	DISADVANTAGES
■ *students can clear up misunderstandings, share uncertainties and teach each other*	■ *some students manage to avoid doing anything*
■ *tutor has flexibility of talking or listening*	■ *tutor cannot easily identify students in difficulty (unless 'remedial' exercise set up)*
■ *students help each other*	■ *many 'problem' tasks not suited to group work*

Delphi and nominal group technique

Two group methods that do not involve discussion in the normal sense are the Delphi technique and the nominal group technique. In each of these the interchange takes place through the processing of written statements or ideas and they are therefore useful tools when a group cannot meet face-to-face or there is a risk of a quiet minority being submerged by a more vocal majority. They work well online.

Delphi

Delphi is a method for reaching consensus on issues, or collecting opinions. Information is separately collected from all those contributing and then analysed and summarised, before being fed back to everyone. Each person then has the chance to reconsider their view in the light of the summary before sending in a further, more developed, contribution. This cycle can be repeated as many times as is practicable and effective.

Variations may include feeding back opinions which differ from the majority and asking them to justify their viewpoint and then to note and inform the group of any resulting changes in their opinion.

A form of the Delphi technique can be used in a face-to-face situation, where group members are asked to write their comments or problem solutions on Post-it stickers and place them on the wall before agreeing how the cards should be clustered and reorganising them into theme areas.

ADVANTAGES	DISADVANTAGES
■ *each person can put forward their own view anonymously without evident influence from the others*	■ *it can be time-consuming to organise*
■ *when the group cannot easily meet in the same place it makes consensus achievable*	■ *it can take much longer than face-to-face discussion*
■ *contributors do not have to spend travel time getting to a meeting place*	■ *participants do not get the stimulus of face-to-face contact*
■ *they are likely to give more considered thought to the issues*	■ *as it is not a public discussion, the integrity of the collators is critical*
■ *there is a clear and safe framework in which to express opinions*	
■ *it lends itself to e-mail as the medium of communication*	

Nominal group technique (NGT)

This differs from the Delphi method in that ideas are collected in a face-to-face situation and pooled publicly. The collation and sorting of ideas can be done by one or two members of the group, which thus delegates more responsibility for learning.

Typically a problem or theme is proposed and individuals are given a sheet of paper on which silently to respond with short written phrases. They are then invited, in turn going round the group, to read out one idea and this is recorded as presented on a board or flipchart. If anyone is stimulated with a new idea by that of someone else they can add that to their sheet. The tutor/facilitator continues to elicit one idea per person for a second or third round until all ideas have been gathered.

In the next stage the ideas are labelled, usually with a letter of the alphabet, in order to make reference to them easier and the subsequent ranking of solutions (if it is a problem-solving session) to be achieved.

Time is then allocated to clarification of the ideas in open discussion; members are invited to ask for the meaning of words and phrases and the thoughts behind them.

The final phase is a process for deciding the relative importance of the ideas. Each member has a set number of cards (no more than five) on which to write the items recorded on the flipchart that have the highest priority for them and to write a number on the card to indicate its rank order in their preference. The cards are collected and the numbers processed on a master sheet.

ADVANTAGES	DISADVANTAGES
■ *ideas can be expressed freely without pressure to conform* ■ *a wider range of ideas is usually produced within a shorter space of time than in traditional discussion and debate* ■ *everybody's ideas are given due and balanced consideration* ■ *NGT can be used to determine and promote interest in topics for a course*	■ *the restriction on free and open discussion can cause irritation among those who enjoy (but sometimes dominate) free discussion* ■ *the tutor/facilitator has to take a dominant role in maintaining the proper process and pooling the results – though the latter could be delegated*

Creative thinking methods

Though creativity does not always fit comfortably within the academic paradigm, with the possible exception of the visual arts, it has been a popular source of original ideas and change in the commercial world for more than half a century. However recent publications such as the CASE (Creativity in Art, Science and Engineering) project (Dewulf and Baillie 1999) have signalled its growing recognition across higher education in the UK, and offer a stimulating mix of principles, techniques and case studies as well as ideas for implementation in courses. Gilly Salmon's on book e-tivities addresses further ideas for working in asynchronous mode.

Here we consider traditional techniques for creative thinking in groups: brainstorming and synectics. Both of them introduce ground rules and special roles for the leader which, by limiting the scope of communication, can paradoxically release a great deal of creative energy. Both work well online.

Brainstorming

This is the best-known and most frequently employed procedure to stimulate creative thinking. It was devised by Osborn in 1938 in reaction to much of the cramped thinking he saw being applied to the solution of problems at business meetings. It is only one part of a creative problem-solving procedure: that designed to generate ideas.

The full procedure includes the stages of fact-finding, idea-finding and solution-finding.

- *Fact-finding* involves the definition and preparation of problems; definition in the picking out and refining of the problem; preparation in the gathering and analysis of relevant data.
- *Idea-finding* deals with the production and development of ideas through brainstorming.
- *Solution-finding* relates to the evaluation of tentative solutions and the choosing and implementation of the agreed one.

Online, brainstorming will work most effectively in the synchronous mode; using a real-time 'chat' tool would be ideal.

The two main principles of brainstorming are the 'deferment of judgement' – evaluation and criticism inhibit the freedom of creative thinking – and 'quantity breeds quality', based on the premise that we have to work through conventional ideas before we can get to original ones.

During brainstorming sessions four rules operate:

- *Criticism is ruled out* – any attempt at evaluation must quickly be ruled out of order; this also includes discussion as it usually raises doubts and qualifications.
- *Free-wheeling ' is welcomed* – the wilder the idea the better because it is more likely to 'break the mould'.
- *Quantity is wanted* – the more ideas suggested, the greater the likelihood of an original one coming up.
- *Combination and improvement are sought* – participants are encouraged to build on and improve each other's ideas and combine them to form new ideas.

The participants in a brainstorming session should ideally have knowledge of the problem areas though not be too close to the problem, and be of such a mix as to provide a variety of experience and personal style. Osborn (1963) regards the ideal size of group as 'about a dozen' and this is the experience of most practitioners. The leader must be both alert and pushing yet be able to maintain a friendly and informal atmosphere. A typical session might proceed as follows:

---

1   The leader makes sure that the problem has been properly defined and background information prepared.

---

2   Having arranged everyone so that open communication can take place, the leader runs a warm-up session (especially for novitiates). For this purpose, the leader may place an object, e.g. a plastic beaker, brick, paper clip into the middle of the floor and invite a quick generation of ideas on possible uses of the object. Alternatively have it passed round the group with an idea from each person as they hold the object. Online, a verbal description or link to a picture would suffice. In order to free members from the usual inhibitions the leader might throw in some less conventional ideas, especially comical or humorous ones.

3   The leader reminds everyone of the rules and principles and prepares to write up on a board or large sheet a title for each of the contributions (online messages would aid the generation of the record); constantly pushes for more, proposing own ideas where necessary, stimulates further lines of thought by asking how the 'thing' could be changed in terms of colour, shape, motion, etc.

In a brainstorming session on the problem of 'How to remove oil slicks from the surface of the sea' the dialogue might go as follows:

–   *Burn it* (write 'burn it').
–   *Let it get washed ashore and scrape it off the beaches* (write up 'scrape beaches').
–   *Sink it with sand* (write 'sink with sand').
–   *Blow it out to sea* (write 'blow out to sea').
–   *That won't get rid of it* (reprimand for evaluating).
–   *Soak it up with seagulls* (write 'soak with seagulls').
–   *Harness it to seagulls* (write 'harness to seagulls').
–   *Train seagulls to dive down and suck it up into straws and drop these into a waiting tanker* (what shall we write down for that? – sucking gulls!).

And so on.

5   The ideas may then be evaluated by the same group, a completely different one, or a mixture of the two. As a first step it is often fruitful to ask 'What is the wildest idea on the list?' and try to translate this into a practical proposal. The above list might, for example, throw up 'sucking gulls' as the idea to develop, and this could lead to the more practical proposal of helicopters holding the suction end of a pipe onto the slick with the delivery end held in an adjacent tanker.

6   Finally, discussion focuses on the implementation of the chosen solution(s).

Reverse, or negative, brainstorming can be a productive variant: if we turn a situation or a problem around and look at it differently, we often raise fresh and interesting new perspectives and ideas. We can move from divergent to convergent thinking by completing the process through a re-reversal. For instance, in thinking about how to create exciting online activities, Gilly Salmon (2002: 142) in a section on 'Creativity and e-tivities' asks, 'How can we make group e-tivities more boring?' She suggests:

- always lecture, don't involve others in activities;
- never make your objectives clear;
- single individuals out and demand answers to your questions;
- don't virus-check;
- talk endlessly about your own experience without relating it back to the concepts of the course;
- intervene regularly and answer your own messages.

Now take the list and reverse the ideas – you have a simple list of good practice. For example:

- plan activities and involvement of everyone;
- ensure the online environment is suitable and have plenty of pacing and breaks;
- be clear about outcomes expected, timings and process;
- support the group process as a whole, avoiding unnecessary interventions;
- use only appropriate and clear teaching sparks, links and references;
- plan examples and illustrations carefully.

Brainstorming has been well tried and successfully proved in the production of creative solutions to all manner of real-life problems. In education, the very simplicity and quickness of this technique makes it well worth a try, especially in design, project work or other areas where open-ended problems are of consequence.

ADVANTAGES	DISADVANTAGES
- *simple, easy to learn* - *good fun* - *can easily be generalised to include many aspects of life*	- *can be facile and unproductive* - *some people unable to function in it* - *would work better in synchronous mode*

Synectics

A more structured and thorough scheme for creative-problem solving was developed by Gordon (1968) and Prince (1972). Synectics is built around many of the psychological states known to be helpful in overcoming blocks to creative thinking. It uses analogues and metaphors, encourages a wide range of ideas, and pays particular attention to the role of the leader. Synectics is both a problem-solving technique and a means of training people to be more creative. In utilising so many of the conscious, preconscious and even unconscious psychological mechanisms of human ability it appears to stimulate hard work, spontaneity and a happy connection between the rational and the emotional.

The psychological states are:

- Involvement and detachment – an oscillation between close personal resonance with the problem and detachment from it.
- Deferment – avoiding the danger of the quick and superficial solution.
- Speculation – the freedom to let ideas flow easily.
- Hedonistic response – a recognition that the feeling aroused, as a solution is approached, is an indication of where the discussion should go.

These psychological states are induced through a series of 'operational mechanisms' which serve to 'make the familiar strange' – people are distanced from the problem in order to free them from their prior concepts of it – or 'making the strange familiar' in order to bring them closer to it. For instance, one participant in an online course to develop e-moderating (online tutoring) skills used the analogy of the circulation of the blood to describe knowledge circulation:

> I find it helps to picture knowledge as a circulatory system. The components of blood are many and varied and derive from a number of sources. Some of these are internal, such as hormones (contributions from other participants), some of them external, such as food (spark and Web site). Knowledge enters into the bloodstream in a similar way. If things are not going well, attempts may be made to inject the knowledge (give additional information, assess). It circulates around with pumps to help (the e-moderator!) and serves a critical life-giving purpose for the person concerned . . .

The operational mechanisms are as follows.

Personal analogy
Each person is invited to imagine him/herself to be the object under consideration, to merge him/herself with its physical existence. In the case of a concrete object such as a spring, or an oil slick (the problem being considered) the individual would attempt to feel the tension, the glutinousness, or whatever. With personal and social problems, role play may do the same thing. In personal analogy, group members are asked first to describe the facts about their identified-with object, its everyday experience and how it feels about its existence.

Direct analogy
Now the group thinks of instances where comparable modes of operation, function or movement exist. The oft-cited case is that of Brunel getting his idea for the design of caissons (river bridge foundations) from seeing shipworms tunnelling into wood.

Symbolic analogy
Here the emphasis is on finding a visual or metaphorical image which helps to free the mind from the constraints of literal thinking. One group used the Indian rope trick as a symbolic analogy for the design of a jacking device to fit into a box 4 inches square.

Fantasy analogy

The value of fantasy is in the way it can act as a releasing mechanism for unconscious motives and wishes. Fantasy analogy is based on Freud's notion that creative work is the result of 'wish fulfilment'. It is an effective way of making the familiar strange. The group is asked to abolish their rational understanding of the object or problem and indulge in daydreaming. For instance, members might be asked, in tackling the problem of inventing a vapour-proof closure for space-suits, 'How in your wildest fantasies do you want the closure to operate?' Alternatively, the group may be led into a story fantasy based on how the initiator of the concern senses the problem. The 'hedonistic' responses (see page 137) are picked out to see what they reveal.

In a synectics session on how to design a training workshop for administrators, a fantasy story conducted as a group round led into the notion of poodle dogs floating down from the sky by parachute. This was quickly forced into the somewhat more practical proposal that random individual tasks be showered upon participants at the beginning of each day.

The online environment, with its time lags and text-on-screen, is believed to promote more personal and group 'reflection' in and on action (Salmon 2002). In the All Things in Moderation courses, we ask participants to 'reflect' at the end of each week, as a way of providing an indication that they should move on and of encouraging them to write their thoughts for others to comment on. Frequently, participants amaze themselves by producing analogies and metaphors from the offline world to help themselves both understand and communicate their experiences of working on line:

> This week I learnt about the key e-moderating skill of 'weaving'. I see myself as a little worm, wandering around in the rich soil (of the delegates on screen messages). Collecting up a little titbit here, a leaf there, an interesting stone here and valuable seed there and representing them in a new way to make a brand new, highly organic insight.

> The course is ending and I'm at the top of a mountain looking back. You bet it feels like I've climbed a mountain, and a steep one at that! (Apologies colleagues for the various times I let go the rope . . . I got a little scared by the altitude). But, now flag in hand, I've planted myself firmly whilst I look back at the journey. I've finally realised the importance of building easy pathways and steps up the e-mountain for my students, and that, although they may be somewhat fitter than I am, they still need my greater expertise in teaching to pull them upwards.

> (Salmon 2002a)

Unusual techniques abound in synectics. Because creative thinking is essentially a free-flowing and undisciplined process, structure has been built in to help clarify and emphasise what is happening. Gordon (1980) and Prince (1972) give more detail on techniques.

The role of the synectics leader in facilitating the creative process is illuminating to a host of group-dynamic problems. It is most important to avoid prematurely evaluating ideas in a problem-solving group or for the leader to indulg in comments on their negative aspects.

Prince (1972) gives the following advice to leaders of organisational teams:

- *'Never go into competition with your team'* – everyone else's ideas have precedence over the leader's.
- *'Be a 200 per cent listener to your team members'* – in order to understand someone's view the leader may paraphrase or build on it.
- *'Do not permit anyone to be put on the defensive'* – there is value in what everyone offers and the leader's job is to find it; those seeking negative aspects should be asked what it is they like or would prefer.
- *'Keep the energy level high'* – the leader should be alert, interested, involved and demonstrate this with body movements or encouraging messages; he or she should use humour, challenge and surprise.
- *'Use every member of your team'* – verbose members should be thanked rather quickly after a contribution, their eyes avoided (or the online equivalent) when inviting a response and if all else fails, talked to frankly; quiet members should be brought in.
- *'Do not manipulate your team'* – whatever ideas of his or her own the leader may want to have adopted he or she should work towards the group over solutions being reached; the leader's job is to keep them informed on their stage in the synectics process.
- *'Keep your eye on the client'* – the person presenting the problem should be constantly referred to: copying an extract from a message into your reply is an appropriate online technique.
- *'Keep in mind that you are not permanent'* – the leader is the servant of the group, and must keep lines of communication open and emphasise imagination and flexibility; assuming that power accrues to traditional leaders and that everyone wants the role, the leadership should be rotated.

ADVANTAGES	DISADVANTAGES
■ *taps subconscious mental processes, stimulates the imagination, people work hard and intensively* ■ *provides clear procedures*	■ *demands considerable skill and time* ■ *is unfamiliar in many academic environments*

Games, simulations, role plays and case studies

At all stages of education our challenge is to enable students to act out the problems and issues under discussion and make decisions about them based on a more personal understanding of their nature and implications. Tutors' interest in games may result from a recognition that enactment of issues can serve to integrate knowledge into the framework of values, beliefs and personal behaviour of students. The tendency to 'fun' and a more relaxed approach online may fuel the move towards more games. The medium for this 'gestalt' is the imagination, that faculty of mind so often written off because of its association with fun and the supposedly childish connotations that holds.

In the twenty-first century, online individual and collective games are normal everyday activities from early childhood to adulthood. However the assumptions which underpin the use of games as educational tools were exposed nearly a century ago by Dewey (1916):

The difference between play and what is regarded as serious employment should not be a difference between the presence and absence of imagination, but a difference in the material with which the imagination is occupied. The result (of overlooking this) is an unwholesome exaggeration of the fantastic and 'unreal' phases of childish play and a deadly reduction of serious occupation to a routine efficiency prized simply for its external tangible results.

(Dewey 1916: 236)

There are versions of games, simulations and role play that can used online. Indeed many work extremely well.

Games and simulations and their debriefing provide an excellent example of the experiential learning cycle (shown on page 65) in action. However, those students who get most out of games and simulations are those who are able to maintain a delicate balance between play and reality. They commit themselves wholeheartedly to what they are continuously aware is an exploratory device, and the energy seems to be released through the creative interplay between fantasy and reality. The experience of games and simulations brings a further meta-dimension to the experiential cycle, that of play, a factor that in a successful game with suitable players is likely to suffuse all parts of the cycle. It allows people to imitate and experiment safely with new behaviour in the context of a prepared situation and to gain instructive feedback on it in the knowledge that the boundaries between the imagined world and the real one are safe.

Here are our definitions of games and simulations for educational purposes:

■ *Games* describe a group exercise in which players cooperate or compete towards a given end within a regime of explicit rules. Players behave as themselves (even if they do display exceptional behaviour at times). Cricket, chess and charades are obvious examples of popular games; educational games include 'The Colour Game' (six people with hidden agendas have to agree on a colour), 'Back to Back' (where a drawing is described so that a back-to-back partner can draw a copy) and 'Starpower' (players trade tokens to acquire power). Games are generally given no real-life context and people act as themselves.

■ *Simulations* are working representations of reality; they may be an abstracted, simplified or accelerated model of the process. They allow students to explore social or physical systems where the real things are too expensive, complex, dangerous, fast or slow for teaching purposes. A game may be transformed into a simulation by the addition of a specific context or scenario which could vary from the highly complex ('virtual reality') to the outline that allows players space to invent their own details.

■ *Role play* involves people imagining that they are either themselves or someone else in a particular situation. They are asked to behave as they feel that person would, and to try behaviours that may not normally be part of their repertoire in order to broaden their sensitivity to, and understanding of, interpersonal problems. The role may be prescribed:

> 'You are the leader of a pressure group opposed to the siting of a new youth club on land adjacent to an old people's home.'

or self-defined where individuals are invited to enact a situation as themselves. Sometimes roles are written in the form of aims, e.g.

'Your aim is, without revealing it, to become chair of this committee.'

- *Exercises* are games, simulations and role plays stripped of their roles and scenarios: participants work either in groups or individually on a task e.g. devising a set of guidelines on how to write essays based on the pooled experience of the students. The source of information could be the participants themselves or resource material. In design and build exercises the participants typically have the task of constructing something with a given set of materials, e.g. a number of index cards or Lego pieces. In-Tray exercises have participants working independently through a sequence of papers, each requiring a decision, and then comparing the results with what others have done.
- *Case studies* are descriptions of a real-life event presented in order to illustrate special and/or general characteristics of a problem. They allow students to study quite complex problems that include elements which could not be contrived in a classroom simulation. Case studies have the advantage of depth and complexity, but involve a more distanced, second-hand style of learning. They can however incorporate role play where the problem is one that requires exploration of the dynamics of a human interaction rather than armchair speculation.

Games and simulations

A game becomes a simulation when a scenario is provided – it constitutes a simplified representation of life. Many younger people are most familiar with roles and aims from online games. The scenario might be a public meeting, a classroom or a radio station. If play is not prescribed by rules then it is usually shaped by roles, and the roles may be fixed – such as 'You are the city architect who has been fighting a losing battle over the provision of pedestrian precincts' – or free, where people act themselves in a given situation. Sometimes roles are written as aims: 'Your aim is to become chair of this committee.' What is described as role play is often therefore an exercise in which interpersonal encounters can be explored with some degree of freedom. Whereas in games the interplay occurs within a pattern of clear and often artificial rules, in role play what happens is governed by the implicit rules of everyday life in a defined situation.

All of these definitions are a matter of degree and balance – combinations abound. It is possible for instance to have a simulation in which communication between groups is governed by rules, where the activity in the groups is determined by roles and where each group has a singular objective to fulfil in competition with the others. Most simulations are depicted in the diagrammatic model shown in Figure 6.13.

The model in Figure 6.13 may be contracted or expanded to suit. As depicted here it comprises a number of groups – A, B, C and D – each with a goal and possibly a shared role (e.g. a pressure group). The inter-group communication may replicate what happens in real life (e.g. if there is a hierarchical relationship there may be more communication channels available 'downwards' than 'upwards'). The relations between each group may be ordained by roles. Each group's attention is focused on a model which may be a concrete object (e.g. a 'Lego' town), or map, or an imagined problem scenario. The task of the tutor in a simulation/game is usually that of referee (though this may be delegated) who

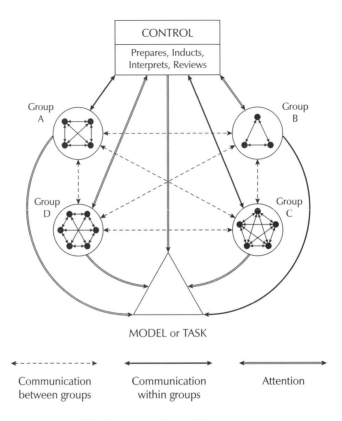

Figure 6.13 Diagrammatic model of games and simulations

plays a benign 'God', and who supervises the setting up, smooth running and debriefing of the exercise. All of these operations require qualities often ascribed to a deity – prediction, an element of mystery, apparent control of the elements, the creation of ad hoc roles and rules, and a tendency to ignore requests.

Debriefing, the review of a game or simulation, is the most important part of the task educationally and should last for at least half the duration of the exercise itself in most cases. Abstract games often require double or triple this amount. This reflective discussion helps students to generalise from their particular experience and to think beyond the immediate experience. The following pattern for debriefing is one which seems to put the students' learning into perspective.

- How are you feeling right now? (Often this needs to be asked in order to tap some of the emotional charge of the exercise.)
- What was going on in the simulation? Who achieved what? What different perceptions were there of what happened? (These are particularly important questions to put when, by accident or design, a lot of intense feelings have been aroused).
- What did players learn about themselves, each other, social groups, social systems, limitations of science and so forth?

- What did the simulation tell them about the 'real world'?
- How did it parallel the 'real world'?
- How could the simulation be improved?
- How is everyone feeling now?
- What might you do differently as a result of your experience in the simulation?

The debriefing discussion, though typically conducted as a plenary, on-or offline, can often be enlivened by dividing the class into sub-groups, especially ones whose membership cuts across the grouping in the simulation. Following the debriefing the often loose and variable learning can be better tied up and consolidated with students in syndicates or task-orientated groups with tasks like:

- Discuss and report back on generalised insights.
- Make links with learning from more traditional sources: lectures, reading, for instance.

A range of facilitation skills special to games and simulations can be found in Jaques, 2005.

Games and simulations are considered to be particularly valuable in promoting social and professional skills such as communicating, role-taking, problem-solving, leading, decision-making, and so on, not to speak of their less academic but more affecting function in opening the eyes of participants to what it feels like to be in someone else's position. Games and simulations are also claimed, with good justification, to increase the level of motivation and interest in the subject matter, develop a greater sense of self-awareness and personal power, and create a freer and more democratic climate. As for cognitive learning, apart from the impact of all the above in energising the learning process, games and simulations can facilitate the understanding of relationships between separate areas of subject matter, particularly those where personal action is demanded. Nevertheless, without the consolidating effect of debriefing and further tasks a lot of this learning may remain only half-realised.

ADVANTAGES	DISADVANTAGES
- *experience is first hand and concentrated* - *motivation intrinsic to activity, learning well retained; high level of interest* - *removes tutor/student polarisation* - *learning occurs at various levels*	- *time-consuming, can demand a lot of preparation* - *some students don't or won't participate, colleagues regard games as trivial* - *materials often expensive, learning unpredictable and difficult to evaluate* - *dangers of hurtful stress in some, especially where not carefully handled by tutor*

Role play

Role play is usually taken to mean the enactment of an encounter or relationship, often within an agreed scenario, in order to get inside the human experience of a case or problem, and to practise some of the interpersonal skills required for its solution. It can illuminate and clarify at both the level of the original problem and what the particular 'players' bring of themselves into it: in other words to provide personal feedback. For role play is not just about acting: it reveals much about the real feelings and skills of those involved, and it is possibly this which makes it so threatening to some. But, run effectively, it is capable of realising a set of rather special aims:

- Developing sensitivity and awareness from first-hand experience.
- Understanding and empathising with other's perspectives.
- Trying out new skills and behaviours.
- Providing 'live' material for study by observers.
- Integrating thought and feeling.
- Testing out a model.

In the example below, taken from an online course for training e-moderators (www.atimod.com) to understand the student perspective, at times course members must respond to activities as if they were themselves students; at other times they must respond as if they were the e-moderator. An example of the latter would be:

This is how the various roles in the course are explained to participants:

Your roles on this course

It is important to keep in mind your roles as you work your way through the course. You will take the roles in this course of:

1   A participant in an online course
2   A developing e-moderator and
3   A member of a sub group of course participants

The roles may each have different objectives:

- A participant aims to to learn the skills of the e-moderator by doing the e-tivities.
- An e-moderator aims to enable participants to gain from the online interactions.
- A group member aims to work with others to draw key insights from the course.

In many of the e-tivities you will contribute initially as a participant and then resp.nd as an e-moderator.

So keep three hats by your PC to remind you of what role you are in!

Role plays in context

It may be useful to view role plays as a part of a spectrum of simulated reality, bound less by rules than games, and with more freedom to explore personal feelings and behaviour. Games are played when one or more players compete or cooperate for payoffs, according to an agreed set of rules. Players behave as themselves (no roles) though they may well display exceptional behaviour. Games are designed so that success is achieved by the use of the materials to be learnt. Many games are abstract in that the materials are shapes, colours or numbers which have to be manipulated in some way. As a result the players can ascribe all sorts of meanings to the activity, so the games are capable of a rich variety of application.

Devising a role play

Ready-made role play exercises do exist and can be found through Google on 'Role Play' and 'Role Play Exercises'. However you may have to create your own exercise to suit particular purposes and consequently take the risk of improvising with groups of trainees. A list of options can be found on our website www.learningingroups.com.

We are sometimes asked whether using the potential full anonymity of online supports role play and teaching and learning. In our view, there is little value in allowing participants in a teaching and learning environment to become truly anonymous and participants tend to reveal themselves as much online as offline, perhaps more. However there is evidence that many students find role play easier online because they have time to compose a response and are spared the stress of thinking on their feet and this is extremely helpful for those students who are not native speakers. In addition with extra time to reflect, students produce better responses (Knight 2004).

Scenario-based learning

Located somewhere between a simulation and a case study, Scenario-Based Learning (SBL) involves a real-world story and context in which students are asked to draw on and integrate their prior learning in adopting a role specific to that scenario or even creating their own role. It presents them with issues, challenges and dilemmas and asks them to apply knowledge and practice skills relevant to the situation. Students are invited to make choices from various options and receive feedback based upon their choice. Scenarios can be skill-based, problem-based, issue-based, or speculative-based (where students postulate aspects of the future). SBL can be applied online where decisions about chosen paths in a scenario can be gauged and reviewed according to preset criteria. Errington (2005) gives more detailed insights into, and applications of, the face-to-face method, as does Kindley (2002) on what he calls SBeL.

Simulations in context

Games simulations and role plays may be used within a scheduled group learning meeting or class, or at a specially convened session. Alternatively, they may be used to bind together the separate elements of a course either in the form of a grand finale or by constructing the whole course as a 'partial' simulation in which students participate only at certain scheduled times and otherwise work on tasks demanded by or related to the simulation. For the imaginative teacher there is no end to the possible variations in the style and scope of games, role plays and simulations.

Case study

A standard technique of teaching in management and business studies, the case study is a simulation of a real-life situation in which the experience is second-hand and condensed. Case studies allow problems to be studied in a complex form, including elements of real-life events perhaps impossible to reproduce in the classroom. The main virtue of case studies is the way in which they can efficiently integrate a wide diversity of subject matter. They are mainly used in applied social sciences but there is no reason why they should not be used to advantage in science and engineering. Short case studies are often used as in assessment to test students' ability to synthesise.

Typically the students are provided with case notes in advance or on their virtual learning environment and are expected to prepare their own solution to the problem or problems presented. Case studies open up opportunities for role play (see page 143) where it becomes necessary to shed light on particular encounters rather than general issues. Case studies have the edge on simulations as a learning tool, as students are not tempted to trivialise; there is, however, little of the sense of risk-free competition and personal involvement which is an inherent part of games and simulations.

Case studies particularly benefit by being in the online environment. We find that having four to six participants works well with a structured framework lasting three to four weeks. We suggest that you send out short texts or other multi media information through the VLE but with a clear timetable and framework for exploring and analysing the case. Students will also benefit from a document sharing area and a blog or wiki (see page 206) so they can work on documents collaboratively. You can use the asynchronous nature of the environment to gradually release texts, video or other information if you wish.

The most intensive e-moderation is needed in the first week or two when students are exploring the case, particularly to ensure deepening discussion and full group participation. Encourage students to undertake roles that they are good at, such as resource investigation, as well as those with which they are less familiar, such as suggesting concepts and models to support analysis. When choices and judgements need to be made, the e-moderator should avoid too much intervention. If possible encourage the output to be a jointly produced product or report, which should include transferable models and ideas. If appropriate they can comment and learn from exploring how the team worked together as well as the content of the case – online an audit and review is easy to undertake. Ensure really good feedback is offered on a planned day through the online environment so that the team come back to receive it.

You can see a worked example of a business case online in Gilly Salmon's *E-moderating* (2004), pages 12–15.

In problem-based learning (see page 211), case studies are the driving force behind students' independent study: their learning is to a large extent dependent on the quality of cases presented to them. Dolmans et al. (1997) propose seven principles for the design of case studies.

- The contents of the case should adapt well to the students' prior knowledge.
- A case should contain at several cues that stimulate students to elaborate.
- If possible the case should provide a context that is relevant to the future profession of the students.
- Present irrelevant basic sciences concepts in the context or a clinical problem to encourage integration of knowledge.
- A case should stimulate self-directed learning by encouraging students to generate learning issues and conduct literature searches.
- A case should enhance students' interest in the subject matter, by sustaining discussion about possible solutions and facilitating students to explore alternatives.
- A case should match one or all of the course objectives.

ADVANTAGES	DISADVANTAGES
integrative – encourages a 'broad view' *develops a sense of objectivity* *demands tolerance of several points of view*	*requires some maturity and prior experience of students* *makes heavy demands on the tutor in holding the discussion together* *can be time-consuming*

Independent learning in groups

Independent learning is a process, a method and a philosophy of education through which learners acquire knowledge by their efforts and develop the ability for enquiry and critical evaluation. Independent learning can be a goal and a process: a method of learning and a characteristic of learners. Dimensions of independent learning include the ability to think and act autonomously, and to realistically appraise one's own shortcomings and approaches to self-management (Candy 1991).

Many of the early uses of e-learning were based on ideas of independence resulting in hundreds of self-paced CD-ROMS being produced. We soon realised though that interaction through groups and access to responsive teachers, on or offline, results in more fun and deeper learning. In practice collaborative learning and independent learning are not different animals. Working in groups not only improves students' understanding of topics in their courses but also develops their strategic-thinking skills, enhances their confidence and their ability to work and learn independently (Yazici 2004).

A dilemma which commonly faces tutors in seminars is how to exercise a degree of control over the content while at the same time giving students room to express their ideas in their own terms; to a great extent this is resolved in syndicate learning. The technique is described by Collier (1983). The students in small tutorless groups (five to six members in each) are given joint assignments which require reading, discussion and written work.

- The tutor's first task is to prepare the assignments; these may cover the same ground as a lecture course and comprise a developing sequence of questions and references.

- Some assignments may be considered sufficiently important to be worked on by all the syndicates on behalf of the class as a whole. The students distribute the reading, discussing and writing tasks among themselves with the groups, and meet to work on the tasks while the tutor circulates among them. Plenary discussions are held at various points during the course.
- The collection of student views emerges in either a written or an oral report; dissenting opinions, where they arise, are included.
- The tutor summarises the reports in a formal lecture suggesting any changes and improvements in the work produced and extending ideas beyond the students' material where appropriate.
- A final plenary session follows.

The students are thus given both the security of specific content and a clear task, and the freedom to exercise their own skills and judgement in critically analysing and synthesising information. Collier claims that syndicate learning cuts across any of the fundamental assumptions about teaching and learning which the educational system may have established in the students. Thus the students are placed in a situation where, in the first instance, they form views derived from their reading and experience and from discussion with their peers, rather than from the tutor; the students form bonds within their syndicates which give them some support in the face of the tutor's authority; the relations are no longer controlled by the naked confrontation of the tutor with a number of separate individuals and can thus become more easily personal and informal.

Many successful online discussions can be structured in a similar way and have the advantage of using online and freely available 'content' to help develop students search, evaluation and discrimination skills in Internet resources.

Some students may find it difficult to function in groups without the guiding hand of a tutor, but it is equally liberating to those students who have problems in expressing themselves freely in the presence of a tutor. Online it is easy and economical in terms of time for the tutor to keep a quiet eye on the progress of the different groups without being intrusive – and to take quiet remedial action where necessary. Syndicate learning also combines the two ingredients of high motivation – competition between groups with the consequent cohesion and purpose within them. There is nevertheless a tight prescription of task, and the boundaries of knowledge are firmly controlled.

In a more recent development recognition of the interplay between content and process in task-oriented groups is embodied in course structure known as Team-Based Learning (Michaelsen et al. 2004) where students learn and are tested individually on the relevant material to bring them to a starting level of competence before they join their teams. They are thus better able to apply their understanding when they join their teams, at which point there begins a programme of progressive monitoring and feedback on the teamwork which enables the creation of cohesive 'learning teams' which are capable of challenging levels of achievement.

ADVANTAGES	DISADVANTAGES
▪ *combines control of content with freedom in discussion* ▪ *authority is clearly delegated* ▪ *groups take pride in achievement and work harder* ▪ *disparate knowledge is integrated*	▪ *not all students able to cope in tutorless groups* ▪ *discrepancy between kind of learning and assessment methods* ▪ *overall control of what is learned tends to be non-negotiable*

Peer tutoring

It is clear that a lot of teaching is done in courses by the students themselves – perhaps more than many teachers would wish to recognise. In laboratory groups for example it is quite common to see students explaining points to each other and helping one another over basic misconceptions and more advanced problems. Not quite so apparent is the mutual help and support which exist outside the curriculum, in the refectory, the halls of residence, in the library and through e-mail and text messages.

Peer tutoring is a way of harnessing these valuable processes within the bounds of the curriculum. Peer tutoring offers benefits such as:

▪ Socio-psychological – close personal contact in an otherwise remote environment.
▪ Pedagogical – students are active as learners, teaching enhances learning for the 'student tutor'.
▪ Increased cooperation, motivation and self-esteem.
▪ Economic – a saving on staff time and energy.
▪ Political – it helps students effectively adjust to the curriculum as a 'system'.

Examples of different models of peer tutoring are:

▪ Senior students acting as regular seminar leaders.
▪ 'Proctors' who help test and guide more junior students through a programme of individualised instruction.
▪ Self-help groups.
▪ The learning cell, in which students in pairs alternately ask and answer questions on commonly read material.
▪ Sponsorship, where experienced students counsel new students firstly over practical matters to do with settling in, and later over study problems.
▪ Peer-assisted learning (PAL) where more senior students are trained to lead groups on learning problems (see page 196 for a fuller description).

To overcome the tendency to practise passive 'reception of information' and to look for 'success through competition' students may need to be inducted to the academic and social skills necessary for peer tutoring. Not all students will be suited to the role of peer tutor and some care should be exercised in both role choice and training. In others, everyone can be involved in the operation. For further reading on peer tutoring see Cornwall (1979) and Boud (1981).

Students can also practise a form of peer tutoring in learning teams – groups of four to six which have the following tasks, to:

- Maximise the learning of its members.
- Provide the incentive, the opportunity and the ability for its members to learn.
- Learn about teamwork through the conscious experience of working in a team.
- Develop the ability of its members to work in a team.
- Organise tasks and roles for each learning activity within an agreed set of rules.
- Rotate tasks and roles so that each member has a range of experiences.
- Monitor, and report on, their individual and collective progress.

The role of the teacher with learning teams is to negotiate appropriate rules to provide team training for the sharing of group tasks and opportunities. The activity of learning from each other does not, of course, have to be initiated by a tutor. Donaldson and Topping (1996) have written a do-it yourself manual for students who do not have, or do not want 'peer-assisted learning' to be organised for them, but are interested in the benefits of it in an informal, self-managed way. Peer support is increasingly offered and promoted in online conferences and forums.

ADVANTAGES	DISADVANTAGES
- *students actively involved – learn by teaching* - *integration of students into course facilitated* - *inexpensive*	- *students require training – needs regular monitoring* - *not all students good at it* - *may demand constant staff supervision for success – but this may be less of a problem online*

Projects

Projects are learning tasks in which the students have a choice of topic and direction and whose outcomes are unpredictable. They demand initiative, creativity and organising skills: they require that students produce a report, plan or design which comprises the solution to a problem. In pursuit of this goal the students have a considerable amount of time to develop their own learning strategies according to where the project takes them and generally rely on a supportive relationship with a tutor/supervisor. The kind of learning that can be achieved in project work, given commitment, energy and imagination from all concerned, is potentially vast in both variety and depth. Projects with joint outcomes work well in the online environment and promote effective working, though often considerable time is needed.

Group projects involve a different philosophy of learning from that of traditional group discussion methods. Students are responsible, to a greater or lesser extent, for the direction and range of the work they undertake, which may carry them beyond the tutor's or e-moderator's own area of subject expertise either in breadth or depth; much of the group activity may also be inaccessible to monitoring by the tutor. Consequently projects are likely to create all manner of anxieties as to direction, progress and personal competence. Key issues are:

- Students should be actively involved in the choice of the subject; this increases their involvement with the task.
- Students should be encouraged to discover for themselves the implications of the constraints, the availability of resources or institutional arrangements.
- Tutor needs to to strike a balance between over-direction of a students' work and under-direction.
- Students' enthusiasm is closely related to the production of documents – high at the beginning (when an outline and bibliography are being prepared) and at the end (when the final presentation is being fabricated), but low to the point of despair during the period of gestation. Arrange an input of teaching (presentation of ideas at a seminar, brainstorming sessions, simulations, discussion of the rough draft, or a face-to-face or synchronous meeting if working mainly online) in the middle of the lifespan of a project.

(Adapted from Goodlad 1978)

It is not unusual to find a group project resolving itself into a collection of individual, if related, tasks. A procedure for tackling this problem was operated at the City University, in electrical engineering where groups are selected and organised as follows:

1. Topics of interest to the class are listed.
2. The topics are whittled down, through discussion, to a small number.
3. Each student ranks the topics in order of personal preference.
4. The course tutor then allocates topics to students according to these preferences: the groups are thus constituted.
5. Tutors' names are not revealed or allocated till the groups are established.

(Edwards 1980)

Where on the other hand the approach is to allow the project to emerge as an expression of the combined interests of pre-selected groups, the teacher may form the groups, give or post online a set of papers covering a range of issues and then assist them in the formulation of a problem to be solved. Either the sub-grouping must be done arbitrarily according to some principle, e.g. random selection or heterogeneous mix, or the students take part in a team-building exercise.

Students can learn much through monitoring the group process, not merely about the personal and collective problems of teamwork, but about their priorities as individual learners. Various checklists and exercises (see pages 231 and 235 et seq.) should be of help in this respect.

Gibbs (1994), in three manuals entitled *Learning in Teams*, provides a stack of useful exercises and guidelines for both tutors and students involved in project teams. He particularly emphasises the importance of team building, organising the schedules, allocating tasks, monitoring progress and leading students to accept that teamwork is never easy. The section headings pretty well summarise all that needs to happen in effective group projects:

What it's all for
Forming a team

Developing a team
Sharing and organising the work
Making meetings work
Being creative
Spotting and sorting out problems
Reporting
Planning your next team

How the group organises itself and how it communicates with the tutor has been addressed by Yamane (1997), who tackles problems in project groups by assigning members one of four possible roles:

- *President/discussion leader* (see also page 153) keeps the group on task by developing an agenda and using it to structure meetings.
- *Scribe/recorder* who keeps minutes of each meeting (paying particular attention to work assigned to members) and distributes the record to the rest of the group.
- *Meeting coordinator* who considers each student's submitted work and 'class share' deals, as well as ongoing conversation with them to identify regular meeting times and places.
- *Intermediary* who periodically meets one-on-one with the tutor to report on his/her group's progress and to answer the tutor's questions about how the group is working as a team.

Belbin's (1981) team roles are helpful to students in selecting members of a suitably balanced team (Table 6.1). Given that no member will fit any role exactly, and there will be many overlaps, we suggest using the task to determine the strengths and weaknesses of any group to encourage reflection and adjustments of contribution. Gibbs (1994) suggests that students identify their own primary and secondary strengths and preferences as a potential team member. The table can be used for review of how well the group is functioning as it progresses.

The keeping of a group diary, logbook, online blog or wiki could also help in forming the basis of a commentary on the work of the project, to be submitted, but not assessed, with the project report. If, on the other hand, the students are being asked to learn about teamwork issues through experience, you may wish to give them some help with their programming of the work – it is all a matter of time and priorities.

Projects offer students a unique chance to develop skills and capacities that might never be apparent in other kinds of learning; such an opportunity is very important in our age of employability. They give students feedback on their ability to handle freedom in relation to the constraints of the outside world, to cope with real problems and to build up a continuing interest in them beyond the completion of their studies. The learning potential of projects is therefore enormous. Group projects add the further benefits of pooling resources, division of labour and the enjoyment of interpersonal learning. However, not all students are happy with the experience of group projects as such:

> When I encounter students who have had courses where small groups were used in a substantial way, I ask them whether they felt the experience overall had been a positive or

Table 6.1 Team roles for project teams

Team roles	Strengths	Potential drawbacks
Innovator	Produces ideas, ready to challenge inertia and complacency	Ignores details, can be impatient, over-sensitive
Resource investigator	Can find people, brings new information to the team, responds to challenge, enthusiastic	Can be too optimistic, may lose interest once initial interest has passed
Chair/coordinator	Self-confident, positive, good at guiding team, promotes decision-making	Can be bossy or manipulative Can be inflexible
Implementer/shaper	Makes things happen, changes ideas into plans, careful and efficient, needs to succeed	May be impatient if things don't go the 'right' way
Monitor/Evaluator	Careful, looks at all options, tests out ideas, thinks strategically	Can be distant, over-critical, doesn't inspire others
Team worker	Shows and interest in others' ideas, listens, concerned with social interaction, places team above personal concerns	May be indecisive when most needed, e.g. when urgent action required
Plant	Creative and imaginative, unorthodox	Ignores practical details
Completer/finisher	Follows through, conscientious, works hard to finish things properly	Can be over-anxious about detail, and perfectionist, doesn't like to delegate

Source: Based on Belbin (1981).

a negative one. Almost half the time they say it was a negative experience. When I ask why, they report a number of familiar problems. Perhaps the most common one is: 'I had to do most of the work and yet all of us got the same grade' (i.e., it was unfair). Somewhat related but different is: 'Several of the students in my group simply didn't care what grade they got (but I do), and they therefore didn't put much time in on the project.' Also frequently heard is the lament: 'We were supposed to meet outside of class, but our group never found a good time to do that. So we didn't have many meetings where most of the group was there.'

(Fink 2004: 5)

The role of monitoring and assessment in creating a rewarding experience for students in project groups is critical. A group project should be assessed according to criteria that demand a cooperative effort clearly negotiated with the group near the start of the project or, at the very least, before irrevocable decisions are made. This is addressed more fully in Chapter 9.

Heron (1981) proposes a scheme for self-monitoring and assessment where one of the critical aims is for students to learn about themselves as learners. The tutor's role in promoting group experiences in project work is considerable. If students are to gain full benefit from working together there must be

■ A demand in the project design for collective effort.
■ Training opportunities for the students in teamwork.
■ A clear monitoring of the students' team dynamics.
■ An assessment that emphasises group effort.

Each of these features requires leadership from the tutor, but external to the group: in other words a clear definition of authority and boundaries (see Chapter 1).

Further reading on the role of the project tutor may be found in Jaques 1988 and 1989.

ADVANTAGES	DISADVANTAGES
■ *freedom to study in depth and breadth* ■ *chance to tackle real problems, provide solutions that can be tested in 'real world'* ■ *learning-active; comprehensive challenge to students*	■ *things can go radically wrong* ■ *challenge and freedom may prove too much for some students* ■ some tutors not able to function in non-directive role or outside area of subject expertise ■ *assessment may be a problem*

Designing e-tivities for groups

Working in the online environment demands prior design and posting of instructions. Once done however, the instructions can be modified and reused for many groups over time. E-tivities were developed to ensure the best use of low-cost networked techniques in the interests of successful group work of all kinds online. Because of these special features, we call them 'e-tivities'. They can be adapted and used for almost all the techniques described in this book.

The key features of an e-tivity are described below. Each one should be developed into one clear on-screen message, which we call the 'invitation'.

1   *The spark*: A small piece of information, stimulus or challenge. This can be a short reading, a quote, a picture or whatever you wish. But ensure that it is highly accessible through the online environment.
2   *The individual action*: Request a clear response from each participant, and show them where to post their response message.
3   *Response to others (the dialogue commences)*: Indicate clearly how they should answer, develop and help others.

Getting a group to work together

E-tivities need to be clear and simple to follow. They should give a reason to participate that is motivating and emphasises the purpose for the group's activity. Group activities will often be about gathering and assembling information, such as building a list of websites associated with a topic or a list of aspects of a topic of particular interest to participants.

The process and roles must be considered too. Here are a few of the questions to think through:

- What is the purpose of the group?
- How will the group interact?
- What separate streams or threads will the group need to have set up on the bulletin board?
- How long will the e-tivity last – calendar time, online time, offline time?
- Who will take the lead, summarise and chase up the latecomers?
- What form do you want the output to be in and where do you want the output to be placed?
- How will the contributions be assessed?

The acid test for the quality of the instructions for setting up a successful group e-tivity is that no one needs to ask any questions to clarify the instructions. However, do ask a naïve user to check your own e-tivities before you go live – such people have an uncanny knack of asking penetrating questions!

An example of an invitation from an All Things in Moderation e-tivities course in 2005

E-tivity 3.2: Group working *<number and title essential!>*

Purpose: to practise writing instructions for a group task. *<always tell them why it's worth taking part>*

Task: Design a motivating e-tivity before Wednesday at noon, and post it in *E-tivity 3.2*, to get your online group to perform a simple exchange of information on a topic of your choice and produce a summary of the issues they consider to be most important. *<indication of what they should do, by when and where to post their message>*

Respond: by returning to the forum from Wednesday afternoon and commenting on the 'sparks' – things that excite you – in other participants' e-tivities. *<indication of what to do next>*

Plenary: I will summarise on Saturday – please make sure you have contributed by then and come in over the weekend to pick up the summary. Key points from this e-tivity will be used as a spark for our next one. – Good luck! Terry, your e-convenor.

<indication of time scale and how output will be used>

Planning an e-tivity of your own to try

Name of e-tivity (choose an enticing one)	
Purpose Really sell this to your participants.	
Check that you can use it too to evaluate for quality and outcome	
How many participants? Suggest 6–15 maximum first time	
Structure? Design: 3 days on this, 4 days on that, 4 days for summary & feedback etc.	
E-lapsed time needed i.e. Calendar time, usually at least a week!	
E-moderator's time Estimate your time (Then double . . .)	
E-moderator actions What you'll do and when . . . most important part is keeping participants going and providing summary & feedback	
Student time Asynchronous working needs plenty of time to work	
Student actions What will they DO, (don't forget to include responses to others)	
How evaluated? Against what criteria will you judge success, and how will you get that information?	

VARIETY AND BLEND

The value of acquiring a repertoire of tasks, group activities and a blend of online and offline is compelling. Reasons include:

- Students' learning styles vary, and implicit in each of the activities described is a different approach to learning (Ramsden 1984, Gardner 1993).
- Knowledge is constructed by individuals through their own experience and with the support of their own cognitive framework.
- Most students need a variety of stimulus and experience because of variable spans of concentration as well as activating the various learning modalities in each.
- Variation of experience, perspective and skills employed can enhance learning (Fazey and Marton 2002).
- As students develop intellectually and emotionally, a change in their relationship to knowledge and its 'agent', the tutor, is necessary (Perry 1970).
- It is possible to cast the teaching and learning net over a wider range of learning outcomes than would otherwise be feasible.
- Students who have experienced a variety of approaches to learning and to human interaction are more likely to achieve increased choice and awareness in ways of working in later life.
- It is impossible to fully predict the way any teaching and grouping interaction will go: a tutor therefore needs to be adaptable and resourceful to maintain interest and momentum.
- By making choices and exercising a wider range of skills the tutor becomes more alert.
- Evaluative feedback is easier: students can make critical remarks with less embarrassment when the tutor is not too closely identified with any one procedure.

Many of the various methods and media can be combined, embedded or linked with each other. In order to make such combinations work tutors and students have to both be 'planful' and flexible: ready with the resources and techniques to ensure an activity is possible and flexible enough to introduce it at a different stage than intended or to modify it to suit the occasion. If you are unfamiliar with working online you need some experience to make choices successfully. Becoming skilled in a variety of tasks and learning activities is as important as being resourceful in any specific situation and that involves a few process skills. How do we handle the knotty problems? Can we recognise the part we are playing in any interaction? Are we able to find time, space and a clear head to make decisions about what to do and when to do it? The next chapter tackles some of the issues.

DISCUSSION POINTS

- List as many group tasks as you can that will encourage people to understand and apply the ideas in this book.
- Draw up a chart of the various learning activities described in this chapter according to aims, tutor's role, special skills, etc.
- What would you look for as evidence of success for each of the techniques described? Why?

- Take the group methods described on pages 120–32 and list the principles of group behaviour that each seems to embody.
- Take three or four activities and indicate how you might adapt them for an online environment. Draw up two columns: in the left hand column, indicate the stages of the activity and in the right hand column the necessary adaptations you would envisage. Write (and ask for comments from others) the text of the activity as an e-tivity 'invitation'.
- Take one technique that appeals to you or your group and your topic and explore how you could start it face-to-face and extend it online.

CHAPTER SEVEN

ENABLING GROUP INTERACTION

The role of tutor and e-moderator

This chapter is written for group leaders. It includes the skills and tasks involved in promoting lively group interaction and achievement, whether face-to-face or online. We use the term tutor for face-to-face discussions and e-moderators for online discussions. In blended learning situations, these roles may be taken by the same or by different persons. We offer you some specific ideas about what tutors and e-moderators, and in turn the students and participants, can do to enhance the effectiveness of group learning through discussion.

TACTICAL AND STRATEGIC APPROACHES

In some cases tutors and e-moderators may choose to keep a low profile and merely respond to the ferment of interaction at suitable times. We call initiatives of this kind 'tactical'. There are some variables that a tutor or e-moderator can influence, if not control, by decisions taken before the group actually convenes. We call this kind of action 'strategic'.

So strategic refers to planning the overall structure and content of group teaching where, tactical, refers to the handling of events as the discussion itself evolves. In acting strategically, knowledge and understanding of group dynamics and of the characteristics of the particular group may suffice. For tactical purposes, however, the more elusive qualities of skill and sensitivity are demanded and these cannot be acquired without some training, practice and reflection. Online, the design of e-tivities are strategic, the facilitation of the group is tactical. Explicitly, we design for participation and motivation and e-moderate for the promotion of learning. Online, e-moderators must prepare well in advance since it is more difficult than in face-to-face situations to recover if discussions go wrong.

PREPARATION: STRATEGIC ISSUES

The tutor or e-moderator has an opportunity to influence the course of a learning group event in at least four areas of decision:

- group size;
- group membership;
- life-span;
- physical conditions or virtual environment in which the group interacts.

You may also wish to plan for possible exigencies and prepare a small list of self-questions to ask such as 'What am I trying to achieve and what do I have to do to achieve it?' (see Chapter 5) and 'What courses of action should I be prepared for?' (see Chapter 6 for some possibilities).

Though we often tend to make such decisions alone, there is a lot to be said for drawing on a friendly colleague's help to check out our thoughts. In virtual environments some technical help may be necessary. Care taken in the preparatory work can reap many later rewards and pre-empt several of the common problems of learning groups.

Similarities and differences between online and face-to-face learning groups

Where groups work mainly online, we expect to see most of the usual behaviours occurring, though some may manifest themselves slightly differently. E-moderators can use their usual understanding of groups and the behaviours of individuals within them to interpret what is happening (Alpay 2005).

However, many of the problems in online groups occur because of delayed or muddled discussions or time management. It is important to enable participants to log on not only once but many many times and to establish a pattern of taking part over time. To achieve this, online groups need good design of their tasks, good facilitation and support. Therefore, we need to *design for* – you might even say 'mimic' – the processes that face-to-face groups go through. In addition it is even more important in virtual groups to make members aware of ways of achieving successful team formation and allocation of roles and responsibilities, since these are unlikely to merely 'emerge'.

If you are working with groups used to mainly face-to-face communication, it may be helpful to encourage them to think about the similarities and differences. Here is an exercise Gilly has found successful in training e-moderators:

Imagine being in a room with other people, every one armed with a pad of Post-it notes and a pen. There is a wall with a space for each person with their name on it (let's call it a Mailbox) and a large space on the wall, called a Conference. Notes can be placed in the Conference space where everyone can read them and in individual's private Mailboxes. The only way of communicating is by placing Post-It notes on the Conference wall or in mailboxes. No one must talk to each other. (We try to stop any body language, but this is really hard to achieve! Participants can be very inventive!)

Many participants in this activity get very frustrated if their communication is ignored and they fail to get a reply. Some can get really annoyed if other people's messages get replied to before theirs!

The key issue is that people want a response. Silence is deafening. We know that the main motivation for logging on a second time in online courses is to establish whether someone else has responded to a posted message.

E-tivity: Building Bridges.

Purpose: getting the feel of online interactive communication.

Task: try the exercise described in the spark above, with a small face-to-face group. If you can only find one person, it is worth a try. About 30 minutes is enough time. Report back in one concise paragraph on how you and colleagues *felt* about it. Invite others online to offer you explanations and examples from their experiences.

Respond: to the messages that you find interesting. Comment on how your understanding will enable you to work more successfully online with others.

Your e-moderator will summarise and comment after 7 days.

Setting up groups

Size

The number of participants in each group has a profound influence on the kind of interaction that can be attained. The smaller the size, the greater is the likelihood of trust, close relationships and consonance of aims among members; these advantages may however be offset by the lack of variety, and the greater probability of a 'poor mix'. In online groups, 'no shows', lurkers or drop-outs can have an even more deadening effect on smaller-sized groups.

In the larger group, although a better mix and a more favourable student/staff ratio may be achieved, a sense of competition and a greater differentiation of role might be expected to occur. Not only does the opportunity for each member to contribute diminish in inverse ratio to the number of people in the group, but the discrepancy in level of participation between high contributors and low contributors is disproportionately greater. There are thus quite significant differences too in the style, frequency and length of spoken or written contributions, not to speak of non-verbal behaviour, in groups of three to six compared with those of 12 to 15 students.

In online groups we consider that up to 15 people is a viable number for one e-moderator to handle. Many processes can of course be divided into smaller groups, such as groups of five, with an online plenary. More than 15, and you cannot expect full participation from anyone – there is just too much time involved in opening and reading messages. Less than six and there is a risk that time lapses will result in feelings of non-responsiveness from the group.

In many ways the size of total group most amenable to a variety of aims and techniques is 20 to 30 (10 to 15 in asynchronous online groups). In recent years this sort of number has achieved popularity in management and teacher training as the most suitable for workshops. Workshop formats allow a variety of group techniques to be practised. Apart from the universal facility of organising dyads, they provide for a number of equal-sized small groups, with or without a tutor, or plenary sessions; workshops thus combine the advantages of small and large group experience. In online groups, size is a significant interaction variable in achieving discussion to enhance academic learning. Discussion in smaller groups of six to eight creates more evidence and experience of higher levels of knowledge construction compared to larger groups if there are effective task-centered e-tivities and structures in place (Schellens and Valcke 2004).

If timetablers and course leaders have not already determined the size of group for us, we might ask ourselves the following questions:

- What is the optimum range of group size socially and educationally for a given set of aims and tasks (assuming we can predict these)?
- What, apart from learning outcomes, do I hope the groups will achieve socially?
- What mix of sex, nationality, age, etc. do I want to have?
- Do I intend or need to be present as tutor with all the groups all the time?
- What limitations does the meeting room(s) or virtual environment impose on the total group size and the kinds of activities possible?
- How does it all fit into the scheme for the whole course?

Figure 7.1 presents some of the dimensions to be taken into account in choosing sizes for face-to-face groups.

Although decisions about group size may be predicated upon several variable factors, more often than not the tutor or e-moderator will be stuck with two fixed ones: the total number of students and the room or virtual environment in which they meet. However, with a little initiative, we can, whether with six students or 96, create a variety of group sizes for different purposes. The following are typical problems cited by Habeshaw et al. (1992) and some practical solutions based on themes in the book.

Large groups – typical problems and some solutions

STUDENTS FEEL ANONYMOUS

Use name labels written with marker pens so they can be seen from a distance; require everyone (including you) to say their names when they speak; eye contact – pause for a few seconds in making eye contact with each at different points in the discussion as you look round the group.

Online participants should be encouraged to say early in the process what name they would like used and to take part in access and socialisation e-tivities.

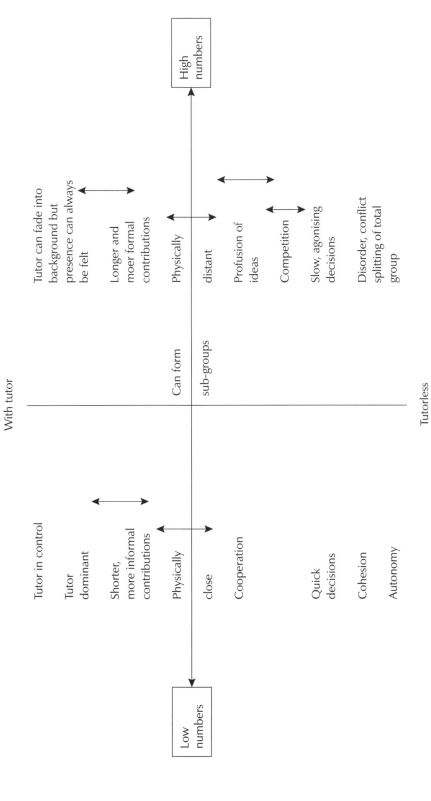

Figure 7.1 Characteristics of groups in relation to size and tutor's influence

Note: The short arrows indicate possible variations of that characteristic on the chart

There are too many to sit in a circle

Set up the chairs (without tables) for smaller groups and allocate them to seats, possibly with a card system. Or try one of the structures such as a Fishbowl, or Pyramids, or Circular Questioning from Chapter 6. Not a problem online!

Students find it hard to prepare

Draw up a programme of sessions with an agenda for each one. Ask for students to present in pairs and introduce self and peer feedback, if not assessment. Brainstorm a creative list of roles and scenarios for them to play in presenting. Tell the group the contract is is that everyone has to prepare for the seminar and it is the task of one person in turn each week to present a summary of the contributions. Online, develop clear processes and time scales in advance of their arrival

The group easily loses direction

Have a clear printed plan for each session with topics and questions that should be addressed. Use self-explanatory phrases rather than single words or titles. Or invite the students to work collaboratively with you in proposing agenda items, listing them on the board and having them rated in order of importance. Online, make sure instructions for e-tivities are clear and indicate when the e-moderator will be around.

There's too much inconsistency between parallel groups

Prepare a set of notes to include learning outcomes, programme, deadlines and assessment criteria. Draw up a schedule of meetings in consultation with all members of the staff team including any part-time tutors keep an overview and deal with difficulties and queries that have arisen. Circulate notes of all decisions taken. Online, everything is there. It's best to keep a record of any synchronous chat sessions to share with those who could not attend

Groups are too big for everyone to participate

Use structures and sub-groups such as those in Chapter 6. Introduce thinking time. Ask students to write notes on their questions and thoughts, whether or not they have expressed them orally, and collect these at the end in order to give them a written response at the start of the next session. Online weave and summarise. Encourage participants to as well.

Tutors feel unsure about what to do

Be ready to be more assertive in organising the session its group tasks and activities. Where they are in sub-groups, move around from group to group, joining each one unobtrusively (preferably sitting on a chair placed just outside each group) and listen so that you understand what is happening before intervening, if at all. You can play the role process consultant or subject expert with any of the groups. Online there's usually time to get help. Never disappear though!

THERE ARE TOO MANY STUDENTS TO MEET WITH THEM ONCE A WEEK

Split the whole group down the middle and alternate from one week to the next between tutor-led and student-led groups. Spend a clear amount of time in the tutor-led sessions setting tasks and responsibilities for the following week and checking progress at the previous one. Make sure there is a clearly-designated meeting space for the students. Use the 24/7 opportunities of online. Plan it carefully though.

STUDENTS CAN'T BE EXPECTED TO GIVE SEMINAR PAPERS TO LARGE GROUPS

Get students to present in pairs with peer assessment from the group for both individual and paired performance. Invite them, instead of presenting, to prepare a set of questions to promote discussion and assess the quality of the questions. Put them in sub-groups with peer assessment and circulate to see fair play. Online, use blogs and wikis.

STUDENTS LACK GROUPWORK SKILLS

Give them a questionnaire such as on page 231 and ask them to complete it before, during and after the series of meetings. Either give them, say 10 per cent of the total marks for it or make its completion a prerequisite for whatever final mark they get. Agree a set of ground rules. Online, use stage 2, socialisation, to establish ways of relating and working together

THERE AREN'T ENOUGH CLASSROOMS FOR ALL THE GROUPS

Meet at less popular times when classrooms are underused; meet in whatever places are available; book the rooms officially and seriously at an earlier stage; complain and request action! Blend with online e-tivities.

Group membership

The way in which participants are assigned to groups depends on the educational and social purposes of the group. As a general rule, a heterogeneous mix of students in each group provides the best chemistry for interaction and achievement of task. Such qualities as age, sex, nationality and personality can be taken into account. One procedure for accomplishing effective mixes is as follows:

■ Divide the total number of students by the possible number of groups to estimate the rough size of each group.

- Decide on criteria which might be used to differentiate one student from another, e.g. sex, age, background, expressed interest, exam results, nationality.
- Go through all the notes you have made to the above categories and assign a code to each according to these criteria A, B, C, etc.
- Then, starting with group 1, take one person from each of A, B, C, etc. until this group's complement is made up. Repeat this if the complement is more than the number of qualities. Do the same for the other groups. Finally, check that each group has a similar mix and adjust if not.
- Online, we find it often works best to use the 'leaving bus' approach – form groups up to a number required as they arrive, so they set off together.

There can be a problem in assigning students to asynchronous groups where participants log in over a period of time. Some groups may get off to a flying start, whereas others may struggle because of late arrivals. Active e-moderator monitoring of the setting-up phase is essential, together with encouragement of latecomers to log in as soon as possible and summaries of earlier messages.

Intellectual differences may also be taken into account. If the main purpose of the group is to solve problems or to clarify or elaborate matters which have already received attention, then there are both commonsense and research reasons why it may be wise to mix the better-progressed or more quick-thinking students with those who are either behind with their work or slower thinking (Amaria et al. 1969). Provided the given task demands cooperation, the former will find themselves teaching the latter we can kill two birds with one stone: the quicker students learn the subject matter themselves and the slower ones are provided with the opportunity to query misconceptions without embarrassment. Suddenly there are as many 'tutors' as students, an insight perhaps leading to the creation of Peer Assisted Learning (q.v.).

The sociometry, or likely pattern of emotional links among the members, is as important as individual qualities. In every group, personal likes and dislikes for fellow members soon begin to grow and can have an important influence on the way the group functions: people tend to agree with the individuals they like and disagree with those they dislike, even though both might express the same opinion.

Cliques may present another problem. There are good reasons for separating groups of students who have such close affinity with each other that they form exclusive sub-groups which could easily destroy the cohesive fabric of the larger group. On the other hand there may be pairs or threesomes who somehow trigger or inspire each other in more productive ways. You need considerable skill and sensitivity in watching out for cliques and taking appropriate action, which, though an extra chore, can avoid so many subsequent problems.

If the choice of group partners is to be left to the students, as happens often with projects, it is advisable to adopt a scheme which allows them to find partners with whom they prefer to work yet avoids the risk of some feeling left out or not chosen. A sociometric device suggested by Stanford and Roark (1974) is as follows:

> Give each student a card and ask them to write their name in the upper left hand corner. Then ask each to list two members of the class with whom they would like to work. If a

student can think of only one or wants to list more than two, that is perfectly acceptable. The cards are then handed in to the tutor who uses the information on the cards to assign students into groups containing at least one colleague for whom they expressed preference.

In online groups, this could be accomplished by e-mails to the tutor.

Even with preparation like this you need to be alert to the dangers of friends falling out or of exclusive cliques developing as the life of the group develops. What you might subsequently do about such happenings is suggested later (page 284).

The elegance of the workshop format described on page 162 is the facility it offers for varying the mix of people and affinities in groups while still allowing for planned changes of group membership, both for the sake of variety and in order to monitor the progress of each group. However, any such decision must be tempered by knowledge of the disruptive effect of breaking up groups.

Physical conditions for face-to-face groups

The physical arrangement of furniture often has a key influence on group interaction. Who sits where and at what distance from whom will affect the social roles and relationships pursued by members. Who holds the pen and stands by the white board is important too. The cardinal rule is, if you want full and democratic participation, play down any prior differences of role and reduce the likelihood of their becoming firmly established. A closer sense of shared purpose is more readily achieved.

A starting point in organising the physical arrangements is to ask yourself:

- What associations does the room have in the minds of the students?
- Is it the tutor's room, a classroom, a 'neutral' room?
- Is the room a regular venue, is discussion vulnerable to noise or interruption?

Then it may be sensible to consider the seating arrangements:

- Is everyone equally spaced?
- Does anyone have a special position, e.g. behind a big desk; at the head of a table?
- Can everyone make eye contact?
- How possible is it to rearrange the groupings of chairs and tables?

Watch out for the common practice of maintaining an evidently dominant position for yourself by sitting behind your desk, with students grouped round in front, without being conscious of the effect it has on participation. Figure 7.2 indicates some of the layouts commonly used in tutor-centred discussion groups. We leave you to make judgements on the level of participation and the sort of communication pattern likely to occur in each case.

Although an awareness of the effects of the physical position of students and tutor may be highly desirable, there is often a limit to the amount of self-conscious juggling of furniture that a group of students will be prepared to undertake. Sometimes there is a sense of 'Why can't we just stay as we

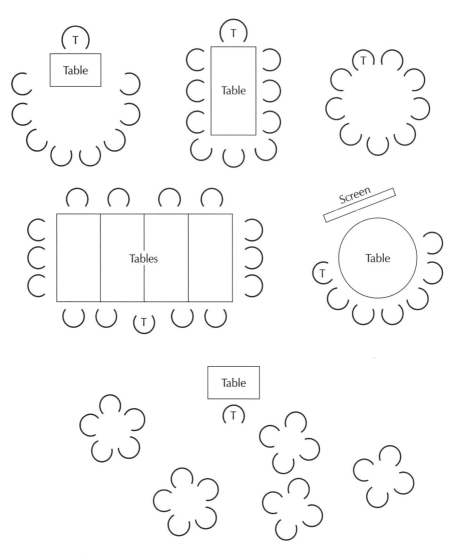

Figure 7.2 Optional arrangements of furniture in the classroom

are?', and perhaps the tutor should bow to this feeling rather than make a huge efforts to 'structure the environment'. If the configuration of chairs and tables is strange to the students, the tutor may have to explain the rationale, since revealing reasons and being attuned to the resulting feelings can not only make things easier but be of unforeseen benefit to the learning process.

Virtual conditions for groups
In the online environment, there are a range of characteristics and affordances that can support group learning if understood and worked with, but will certainly get in the way of it ignored or abused. These include:

- The way individuals relate to each other has an element of anonymity, even if names and descriptions are offered. The nature of the remoteness means that they are often willing to self-disclose sooner, more frequently and more deeply than in a face-to-face group. Encourage this.
- Feelings can often run high online and be more visible. At stages one or two, an individual may be angry about a lost password or downtime on the computer and say so. Others may join in the game of 'ain't it awful'. By the time an e-moderator arrives online (perhaps not till the next day), a mini-riot has ensued. It's best to intervene and soothe fast and often.

Humour, always a little risky, is hard to use online, where it is difficult to judge someone else's response. It can return when groups are more comfortable and familiar with working together.

Encouraging self-managing e-groups

E-moderating large groups can be time-consuming and participants benefit from becoming self-managing (Salmon and Lawless 2005). The basic framework of small groups is similar to the face-to-face version, for example:

- Invite larger groups into smaller work teams. Give them good time to complete an e-tivity and then report back to the larger group.
- Offer clarification about the task, the timescale, and the form of presentation, if necessary.
- Leave them to get on with the task, only intervening if they fail to post their contribution to the plenary on time.
- Start a discussion on the results of the plenary contributions but do not dominate it.
- Summarize the discussion or ask an experienced participant to do this.

However there are some special characteristics that will help groups to self-manage online:

- *Ask individuals to confirm when they have joined in*: A simple joining activity in the thread will leave a trace to indicate that participants arrived. A cross check against a list of participants will reveal who is late. Designate a participant from each work team to follow up less visible contributors.
- *State the purpose of the task*: The task will motivate the participants. Offer clarification, if necessary, but allow opportunities for flexible interpretations.
- *Describe how groups will be formed*: An element of self selection helps to maintain interest, but ensure that the method is simply described and incapable of being misunderstood.
- *Set up a thread for each group and let the group know where to locate the thread*: If you don't they'll only ask you!
- *Describe the form and type of content that the group should produce and where they should post it*: Aim to be prescriptive without being too restrictive. Indicate the main issues that must be addressed.
- *Set out the plenary process in the plenary thread*: This can be part of your welcoming message.
- *Ask the participants to review both content (their main focus) and the process*: Include setting up the group, the degree to which they found the task motivating, how they collaborated, their

approach to feeding back as part of the learning points – so it becomes 'natural and normal' to reflect not just their outputs but how they worked together.

Learning design

It is not always easy to predict what will catch the imagination of a group of learners or to anticipate which way the learning might go in a one- or two-hour face-to-face or extended online session: so plan for flexibility. Both the evolving dynamic of a group and the intellectual growth of students require that the sophistication and the spectrum of aims and tasks should change and develop both within each meeting of the group and as the group progresses through a course (see for instance the five-stage model in Chapter 2).

The choice of aims and tasks will be largely predetermined by what is feasible for a particular group and its physical or virtual environment, and also by its state of preparedness. The fate of 'prior reading' ('sparks' online) is an example. If participants do not prepare, then it's tempting for the tutor to lapse into a mini-lecture. If this is likely to happen, you need to have some tactics available will have some alternative strategy in readiness. Here are three possibilities:

- Have copies of a few seminal paragraphs, discussion points or critiques related to the text which the students can quickly read in the group (for the tutor to talk through what the students have not read puts the tutor in a lecturing role). Online, they can take the form of hot-linked resources.
- Discuss with the students why the work has not been done and perhaps agree a firm contract henceforward on preparatory work.
- Cancel the face-to-face meeting, or extend the virtual deadline, on the grounds that nothing useful can take place until the students have fulfilled their part of the (implied) contract.

As we saw in Chapter 5, specifying aims in group teaching carries with it several hazards, mainly because of the unpredictability of the outcome. Nevertheless, depending on the overall purpose of the group meeting, there are good reasons for improving our capacity to understand the tutor's job better through a process like the one shown in Figure 7.3. It indicates how we as tutors might take time out to anticipate, monitor, reflect and revise procedures.

As with all cycles, one can engage in the process at any point, though logically one might be expected to start at 'BEFORE'. The proposed activities under each stage are:

- *Before*
    - consider what you want to achieve (aims);
    - decide on how you might do so (techniques/tasks);
    - write some notes on these to refer to afterwards (read up any notes on previous sessions);
    - try to anticipate incidents or developments which might occur (start with 'the worst thing that could happen is . . .';
    - imagine what you might do to meet such eventualities;
    - decide how you might monitor what happens in the group during its progress.

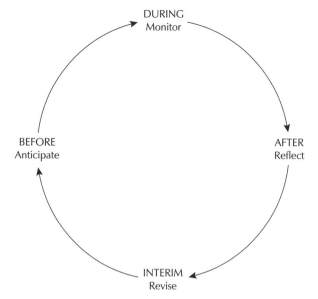

Figure 7.3 Monitoring strategy for group tutors

■ *During*

  – monitor what is happening; this will at the very least require you to set yourself slightly apart from the discussion at times, even when you are directly involved;
  – ask yourself how your intentions compare with what you observe happening and what that implies;
  – whenever the opportunity occurs take 'time out' either by yourself or collectively to take stock of progress.

■ *After*

  – check back with the notes you wrote before the session;
  – review the session – if possible with a colleague – and in any case jot down further notes on what you want to do differently next time;
  – look at any other information you have gleaned, e.g. video or audiotape, questionnaire, informal chats with students, transcripts, or 'a live recording'.

■ *Interim*

  – mull it over;
  – read books, chat to colleagues, check web, for new ideas;
  – revise as you see fit;
  – prepare new material.

While this model can be viewed as a 'macro' cycle of thought processes and experiences, most reflective tutors will be carrying out a series of 'mini' cycles in which the processes of anticipation, decision, action and assessment are quickly, if not subliminally, rehearsed during the group session.

This whole procedure may strike the busy tutor as far too self-conscious and elaborate for practical purposes. Yet it is merely making explicit a process of thinking that commonly exists at a subliminal level and which requires the tutor to make honest checks against first-hand experience. A 'meta' cycle might therefore be added – a check on the whole procedure and its revision or replacement according to personal needs.

The simplest adaptation might be to reduce the 'catechism' to two simple questions which, though self-evident, are most helpful to ask oneself prior to each meeting with a group of students:

■ What do I want to achieve?
■ What do I need to do in order for that to happen?

It is to the second of those two questions that we now turn in looking at the tactical aspect of tutoring.

DURING DISCUSSION: TACTICAL ISSUES

As soon as tutor and participants encounter each other at any face-to-face or virtual meeting, mutual sets of expectations about personal behaviour begin to hold sway. As explained in Chapter 6, the tutor, like it or not, is invested with some of the authority of the institution as an organisation inasmuch as it defines the rules and requirements of courses for the students, and this is compounded by the tutor's authority as judge and assessor of the students. In this sense the tutor will be an authority figure no matter how he or she may try to minimise it.

However, we need to distinguish between being 'in authority', being 'an authority' and being 'authoritarian'. As tutors and e-moderators we are in authority for the reasons described above and because we have ultimate responsibility for the time and space boundaries in the meeting: that is, we are (usually) deferred to over questions of starting and finishing, and who may join or leave. We will also be perceived as an authority in respect of our expertise in the subject matter. When either of these aspects of authority is challenged there is a possibility that we will fall into an authoritarian style of leadership in order to preserve the only image or role we are able to conceive of ourselves. What sort of threat such a challenge poses depends on either our point of view or on how we personally experience the problem. Fears of losing control or (at the level of unconscious fantasy) of being destroyed, are common in such situations. Online, the expectations are frequently of the 'flattening' of hierarchies and authoritarian e-moderators are rarely welcomed.

Roles in the group

The virtue of acquiring a repertoire of options is again evident. The authority role is not the only one available to us. We can adopt one or more of several roles according to how we define the need and the educational aims. The following set of leadership roles present some options for the versatile tutor.

Leader/instructor

This is the traditional role which is easily adopted through the preconceptions of both tutor and students though it frequently leads to dissatisfaction on the part of both. Typically, you initiate proceedings and demonstrate control over content and process with a short statement or summary and then try to draw out students' thoughts, periodically linking them together and redirecting the content of discussions as appropriate. Your task in providing the initial stimulus may be taken by a student, but in a sense only as an 'alter ego' for the tutor. There is a great danger with this role that the students may become over-dependent and feel constrained by what you demonstrate as acceptable knowledge, ways of thinking and academic standards. In educational terms, at least, you may thus establish an authoritarian or autocratic atmosphere.

Neutral chair

This is a variation of the leader/instructor role in which you control procedure but do not contribute to the content in any determining way. It is thus possible for you to create a 'democratic' atmosphere (see pages 36–8).

Facilitator

This is a difficult role for the 'traditional' teacher in that it involves careful listening and eliciting rather than giving of one's own knowledge. Both you and the students may find this regime difficult and even painful to adapt to. Don't suppose that the facilitator role represents a 'laissez-faire' style of leadership: rather there is a sense of shared or developed responsibility for learning. It usually requires that you be student-centred, helping students to express what they understand by respecting them for what they are, rather than for what they 'should' be.

Counsellor

If the personal or social needs of the students demand it, or if a tutorial is designated for such purposes, you may wish to draw out some of the students' emotional problems on the grounds that sharing anxieties can be both relieving and reassuring, and it may provide valuable feedback for you. You may also have some tentative suggestions for tackling the problems. Small, more 'intimate' groups are of course preferable for these purposes.

Commentator

Here, you sit outside the perimeter of the group and comment from time to time on the dynamic of the group interaction or on the kinds of arguments being used by members. In this way, though students may be aware of your presence and influence, they are not constantly using you as a reference point or focus of attention in discussion.

Wanderer

Where the total group is split into sub-groups (as in a workshop) who are working on a set task, you can helpfully infuse influence by circulating round the groups: to check their adherence to the task and identify any teething problems; to help them out of any unproductive patterns of thinking or interaction they have got into; to pick up trends in the discussions for use at any subsequent plenary discussion. In this way you can perform several roles in your travels according to what is currently taking place in any group you happen to drop in on. Here again, your authority is in general evidence but should not be obtrusive within the groups.

Absent friend

Many of the best virtues arise from necessity: tutors who find it necessary to absent themselves from the group for reasons of nature or administration are often surprised at the intense buzz of conversation or flood of messages which greets them on their return. It is an interesting test of the effect of one's authority to make a recording before, during and after one's temporary absence from a group. The essence of this 'role' is physical withdrawal from the room or analysing the online record of interaction, and this applies equally to situations where sub-groups have been formed as to the integral group. For instance, it is not unusual for a tutor to sense that her or his presence is causing some sort of 'stuckness' in the group, especially where students are being asked to make a decision which requires them to reveal some of their doubts and uncertainties. There is a danger nevertheless of the group(s) disintegrating unless a task (implicit or explicit) is generally agreed for the duration of the tutor's absence.

Your choice of role may be determined by:

- the declared aims and objectives of the meeting or the course;
- the kind of task undertaken; or
- a summary assessment of the dynamic of the group.

If you clarify the role this can help polarise activities more purposefully than is typically the case when the relationship between students and tutor is tacit and obscure. Several of the roles could be combined and varied over time. With a project group, for example, you may first act as a chair, then as a facilitator, followed by 'consultant and, because of the students' withdrawal to work on their project, an absent friend.

It is arguable that, as competent tutors, we are in and out of these roles continually and the above discussion merely confirms established modes. That is possibly so, but the muddled and often uneasy nature of some teaching relationships may need sorting out at times in order to make the transactions more straightforward and explicit. Students can thus reorient themselves to what you offer and respond accordingly.

While the spelling out of roles may seem in general to be valuable there may be occasions when, for good reasons, you may wish not to clarify your role: when for instance, your aim is to examine the students' response to the traditional leader role in order to dig out some of the deep-seated assumptions they may have about teaching and learning. Richardson (1967) describes the resounding silence which frequently followed her proposal to a group of students that they decide for themselves the form and content of the discussion. She claims it is important to discuss this reaction on the road to achieving a better comprehension of crucial relationships in the group and particularly the most problematical one, that of authority.

Authority and leadership in the group, can of course be devolved among the group members such that:

- Learning can be accepted as a cooperative exercise and as the aim of discussion.
- Everyone is committed to participate and help others to take part.
- Leadership functions can be shared or distributed.
- Participants attend or log in regularly and are prepared for the discussion.
- Assessment is accepted as an integral part of the discussion group.

Though a lack of satisfactory experience of democratic discussion may make it difficult for students to adopt such roles readily, with suitable preparation and practice including ground rules and modelling such a change can be achieved. The value of sharing them round the group can be immense as then students are able to learn the skills for lifelong participation in groups. These positive or helping functions would, however, be of little use if due recognition were not also given to some of the 'negative' behaviours, which Hill (1977) lists as:

- Aggressing (being aggressive).
- Blocking.
- Self-confessing.
- Seeking sympathy.
- Special interest pleading.
- Playing around.
- Status-seeking.
- Withdrawing.
- Dominating.

In order to achieve the positive functions group members will need to access a range of behavioural skills, when the occasion seems to demand it, in order to assist group process:

- Initiating – starting the discussion, proposing new ideas, activities, resuming it after a lull.
- Giving and asking for information.
- Giving and asking for reactions.
- Restating and giving examples.
- Confronting and reality-testing – restating others' messages and checking their examples.
- Clarifying, synthesising and summarising.
- Timekeeping and holding groups to discussion plan.
- Encouraging participation by others.

You will notice the similarities with the list of functions for group maintenance and task (on page 33), though here the maintenance roles are somewhat underplayed. Obviously, these functions are not required at all times or equal measure in a group. Indeed, as Knowles remarks, if a function is performed inappropriately it may interfere with the group's operation. But it can be helpful when a group is working unsatisfactorily to pause and consider which of these functions might be lacking and to remedy the situation before moving on.

Whether the functions should be allocated to individuals or shared and used as necessary by the group as a whole will depend on the skill of its members. What is fairly certain is that members should be discouraged from playing continually just one role, lest they become stereotyped in it. If possible, roles should be reallocated as and when individuals feel able to perform them adequately.

The following table spells out the competencies expected of the e-moderator.

Norms or rules

Whereas roles describe the positions taken by individuals in a given context, norms or rules define the context. Norms, except in particularly formal settings (e.g. committees) are internalised, implicit and generally unstated. Nevertheless, it is usually clear when they are broken: if disapproval is not openly expressed the 'offender' may feel a sense of exclusion.

In general, the norms of everyday interaction work for groups as long as they appear to be productive, or evidently maintain stability. Yet from our understanding of some of the unconscious processes to which groups regularly fall victim, it is apparent that this is not always the case. In some cases the unexpressed needs of members may be satisfied only through somewhat destructive behaviours which may stem from problems or circumstances outside the group.

Many of the problems that students feel in expressing themselves in groups stem from either uncertainty about what the 'rules of the seminar game' are, or from their feeling overly constrained by rules that they assume about authority and competition. For instance, it is frequently assumed that it is the tutor's job to fulfil most of the roles listed on pages 172–4 and it is not for the students to propose objectives, topics, changes of direction, or procedures. Often there is also a norm against expressing one's inner feelings or against interrupting anyone making a presentation in a face-to-face group. It is sometimes important therefore for a tutor to formulate with the group members some explicit ground rules which, though they may appear more constricting in some ways, can generate a sense of freedom as students begin to understand what is and is not 'OK', with the added knowledge that they are free to propose changes if they wish. It is the very fact that such ambiguities and confusions are hidden that leads some tutors, and more especially 'growth group' facilitators, to propose ground rules for discussion.

Ground rules

An agreed set of rules about how a group should work and how its members should behave can be of great benefit in setting a standard of mutual purpose and associated behaviours in groups, or as a reference when the process otherwise becomes unproductive.

There are some which the you can introduce and from the very start, for example:

- The group will always start of the agreed time (even if not everybody is there) and will finish at the agreed time, or will log in x times a week.
- Anyone has the right to suggest what the group should do next.
- Our shared aim is to listen and understand each other.
- When anyone 'speaks' they are addressing the whole group and not just the tutor.
- Everyone has some responsibility for the process; therefore it is up to every member of the group to bring in other members and not just the tutor's responsibility.

After one of two meetings of the group, or a week or so online, you can invite members to propose their own ground rules. This is best done by asking students to work in pairs to discuss what problems they have experienced in the group and for each to develop a list of rules which would improve group communication. These rules should embody both *rights* and *responsibilities*. Brookfield and Preskill (1999) gives a full account of the generation of ground rules.

Leadership interventions

> Of a good leader, when his task is finished, his goal achieved, they say, 'We did it ourselves.'
>
> (Lao-tse)

Encouraging interaction

For several of the reasons already described, students are often strangely inhibited in discussion and at best seem prepared to make only rather formal contributions. As one student remarked:

> People ask questions and this stimulates the group. I feel we don't mind if a friend asks a question, but if a lecturer asks you, you dry up. A member of staff will always have the answer at his fingertips. I've always resented making an idiot of myself.

Students who are remarkably talkative outside classes are often reluctant to contribute to group discussion when a tutor is present physically or virtually, and we have already noted how a tutor's leaving the room quickly stimulates a resurgence in conversation among the group, even on academic topics. What can a tutor do while present to induce a similar sense of open discussion among students without abdicating a leadership role? The necessary skills or behaviours are not difficult to acquire, though you may not find it easy to produce them always when most wanted. They are nonetheless worth including in our repertoire even if we do need to perform them self-consciously in the first instance. In the virtual world, as we show, text may have to substitute for visual cues in this phase.

Glancing round the group: It is generally considered rude not to look at somebody when they are talking to you. Yet to do so as a group leader will quickly create the sort of communication pattern illustrated in Figure 2.1(a) (see page 27). You may not find it easy to acquire the habit of scanning the group when students are contributing. Though you will want to catch the eye of a student as he or she talks from time to time you can, by looking around, encourage them to do the same thus causing the whole group to give that person more attention, so as to avoid a tendency for discussion to drift

Table 7.1 E-moderator's online competencies

Quality/ Characteristic	RECRUIT		TRAIN		DEVELOP	
	1 Confident	2 Constructive	3 Developmental	4 Facilitating	5 Knowledge sharing	6 Creative
Understanding of online process A	Personal experience as an online learner, flexibility in approaches to teaching and learning Empathy with the challenges of becoming an online learner	Able to build online trust and purpose for others Understand the potential of online learning and groups	Ability to develop and enable others, act as catalyst, foster discussion, summarise, restate, challenge, monitor understanding and misunderstanding, take feedback	Know when to control groups, when to let go, how to bring in non-participants, know how to pace discussion and use time on line, understand the 5-stage scaffolding process and how to use it	Able to explore ideas, develop arguments, promote valuable threads, close off unproductive threads, choose when to archive	Able to use a range of approaches from structured activities (e-tivities) to free wheeling discussions, and to evaluate and judge success of these
Technical skills B	Operational understanding of software in use reasonable keyboard skills Able to read fairly comfortably on screen Good, regular, mobile access to the Internet	Able to appreciate the basic structures of bullet boards, forums, and the WWW and Internet's potential for learning	Know how to use special features of software for e-moderators, e.g. controlling, weaving, archiving Know how to 'scale up' without consuming in ordinate amounts of personal time, by using the software productively	Able to use special features of software to explore learner's use e.g. message history	Able to create links between online and other features of learning programmes	Able to use software facilities to create and manipulate conferences and to generate an online learning environment, able to use alternative software and platforms

Online communication skills C	Courteous and respectful in online (written) communication Able to pace and use time appropriately	Able to write concise, energising, personable online messages	Able to engage with people online (not the machine or the software), respond to messages appropriately Be appropriately 'visible' online, elicit and manage students' expectations	Able to interact through e mail and conferencing and achieve interaction between others, be a role model Able to gradually increase the number of learners dealt with successfully online, without huge amounts of extra personal time	Able to value diversity with cultural sensitivity, explore differences and meanings	Able to communicate comfortably without visual cues, able to diagnose and solve problems and opportunities online, use humour online, use and work with emotion online, handle conflict constructively
Content expertise D	Knowledge and experience to share, willingness to add own contributions	Able to encourage sound contributions from others, know of useful online resources for their topic	Able to trigger debates by posing intriguing questions	Carry authority by awarding marks fairly to students for their participation and contributions	Know about valuable resources (e.g. on the WWW) and refer participants to them, and use them as sparks for participation	Able to enliven conferences through use of multi media and electronic resources, able to give creative feedback and build on participants' ideas
Personal Characteristics	Determination and motivation to become expert as an e-moderator	Able to establish an online identity as e-moderator	Able to adapt to new teaching contexts, methods, audiences and roles	Show sensitivity to online relationships and communication	Show a positive attitude, commitment and enthusiasm for online learning	Know how to create and sustain a useful, relevant online learning community

into a series of one-to-one duologues. The online equivalent is the open question, such as, 'Thanks for that helpful contribution, X. Thoughts/responses/reactions, people?'

Looking for signals: As you glance round the group, you will find yourself picking up cues from others who are puzzled, or anxious to check something. As the contribution ends, you will be in a better position to draw in some of the less vocal students.

Often the cues are not more than an in-drawn breath, a snort of frustration, a shifting of position, or a puzzled frown. To have noted them and to be seen to have done so, is usually helpful in deciding what to do or what not to do at the next stage in the proceedings. You will also be better apprised of the group climate. In fact the very act of glancing round may even be contributing to a more positive climate. It may not be so immediately apparent that online students are puzzled or frustrated. Again, an open question such as 'Is that OK, everyone?' will invite responses – providing the ground rules have been well set!

Using non-verbal communication: Sometimes it may be difficult to interrupt a discussion without sounding critical or punitive. A non-verbal intervention can work wonders in this situation. It may consist of catching a student's eye and giving an encouraging smile or an invitation to speak by raising your eyebrows. On others, the connection may be through gestures – an extended palm to suggest 'Would you like to come in now?' or using two hands to indicate 'What does everyone else think?' Of course, these non-verbal signals are natural partners to verbal invitations but are generally less intrusive and just as productive. Again, judicious open questions online will often do the trick, including where appropriate sometimes naming a student as an invitation, along the lines of: 'X, you made an interesting observation earlier about . . . Anything to add to that?'

Two non-verbal gestures which are often used and seem to work effectively are the 'traffic cop' signals designed to bring students into a discussion and to block them out (see Figure 7.4).

Bringing in and shutting out: The gestures in Figure 7.4 highlight two complementary purposes. In order to encourage a student to talk, it may be necessary for you to invite him or her into the discussion, either verbally or non-verbally. And it may be equally necessary to exclude more vocal members or to stop them before, as often happens, both their less vocal colleagues have become fed up with what they are saying. This becomes a sort of 'rescue operation'.

Sometimes an added verbal stimulus helps. For example, when a student silently smiles, looks puzzled, rolls their eyes you could say 'What are you thinking, Liz?' or 'You smiled, John'. This usually has the desired effect of drawing a student into discussion. Again, in the virtual world open questions to the group may have to serve. They show that you are there and that you genuinely wish to encourage responses.

However, the opposite problem may prevail: how to shut out someone who constantly talks or interrupts. Provided we can do it supportively and straightforwardly – 'Could you just hold it there Brian, it would be interesting to know how the others respond to that', or 'Let's put that on ice for the moment, Gill, while we hear what everyone else has to say' – the student should not feel unduly put out. The problem is rather on the tutor's side, as it can feel extremely awkward consciously to interrupt someone in the sure (but often erroneous) belief that one could be hurting their feelings,

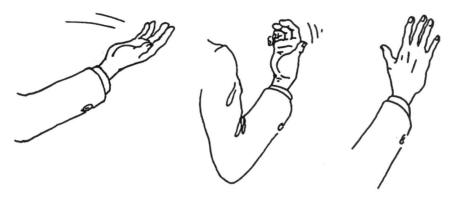

Figure 7.4 Hand signals for bringing in and shutting out

and you may well feel that the risk is too great to take in a group of students. Should this be so, the solution might be to practise these skills within the safer company of colleagues in a training group.

Online, careful use of language, and sometimes symbols such as emoticons can indicate humour, lighten moods.

Turning questions back: Of the many temptations open to the unsuspecting tutor, one is the supplicant question from students which places us on our authority pedestal: 'Can you tell us what you know about . . .?' or 'What should the answer be?' for example. You can simply turn the question back: 'Well, what do *you* think?' on the grounds that: the student probably has an vague idea of the answer anyway or would not have asked the question; and it is usually better to get students to formulate their own ideas in the first instance.

This is not to say that there are not many occasions when you may be the only person present who could possibly know the answer to a particular question or where a refusal to answer could slow down proceedings. The judgement in all these situations must be based on a recognition of the dynamic and the learning needs of the group.

Redirecting: A very useful and more comfortable variation of 'turning questions back' is to redirect or deflect them. For instance the question from a student: 'I don't understand what the author is trying to say. What does it all mean?' could be met with 'Well, what does anybody else think?' or 'Does everyone else have the same problem?' or 'Do you have any ideas about what it means?'

Supporting and valuing: Thus far we have considered some very quickfire, though not always easy, tactics for the tutor in a leadership role. However, it is easy to overlook an important ingredient of effective group discussion: the creation of a feeling of security and belonging; an atmosphere of trust and openness where people are valued for what they are and have no need to fear making a fool of themselves. Now this is easily said, but not so easily done in the thick of a hectic term's work where teaching and assessing become an almost undifferentiated continuum. The temptation to correct discussion contributions in the same way as one might write comments to an assignment is great. Perry (1970) describes how tutors typically view the discussion as 'an opportunity to develop initiative and scope in their own thinking', at least initially.

No sooner do the students get started, however, and some error or inexactness is voiced, than the older form of responsibilities imposes on the tutor the imperative of 'correcting'. In the time where this tendency gets in motion, three to five corrections of this kind appear sufficient to defeat the students' initiative for search and flow of their exploration ; over-frequent interventions from the online tutor having a similar deadening effect. The initiative for conversation then falls back on the instructor who then finds himself in a monologue or lecture or keying a long message as the online equivalent, with the sensation of being somehow trapped, compelled, by powerful forces, in himself and the students, to do what he had never intended to do.

It is of course OK to correct errors. The question is not one of 'whether' but rather of 'when' and 'how'. To reject or correct the first contribution a student makes would generally be counter-productive. Apart from inhibiting expression, as in the above quotation, it is likely to lock the students into the first four stages of Perry's scale of intellectual development (see pages 56–7). If you feel that some kind of corrective action may be called for, you can do this in a less inhibiting and intellectually more elevating way:

> Is that really so?
> Could you think about that again?
> Let's just look at that more carefully.
> How does that tally with what you said before?
> Would anyone else like to comment on what George just said?
> Uh-huh!
> OK, so what does everybody else think?

and so on.

Students will doubtless pick up that they have said something irrelevant or inconsistent but be encouraged to discover their own way out.

Checking and building: Students (not to mention tutors) are not always as lucid as they would wish to be when formulating ideas for the first time. Some of the most imaginative contributors to a discussion may find it difficult to express their half-formed ideas clearly at first. Lest the whole group continue in a state of confusion you can quickly check for understanding by simply asking: 'Let me check that I understand you. Are you saying . . .?' The student is often grateful for the clarification.

Ideally, it would be preferable if the students were left to make the interpretation for themselves: 'How does that connect with what you said before?' or 'Is Rita being consistent there?'

Sometimes you may go further in putting several emerging themes together and formulating a new coherent picture of the topic under discussion. But again – how much better it would be to allow the students to do so for themselves.

Re-directing: Again it is a matter of knowing when it is important to act and when the prevailing climate is too good to destroy. It is never easy, especially when the tutor has a planned schedule of discussion, to decide whether students would be glad of a change in the direction of the discussion or would feel cheated of a rewarding line of interest. Yet sometimes it is necessary to take command and say: 'Hang on to that but let's switch our attention to another aspect . . .' or 'I think we've reached the point where we could turn our attention to . . .'.

More often than not, it is difficult to be sure of the climate and also of one's own motives. A safer way of approaching the problem may once again be to test the group: 'Are you ready now to . . .?' or 'Do you think we've worked on that one for long enough now?'

It may be even more valuable to check the process as well as content: 'Could we stop at this point and check whether we're going about this the right way?' This intervention is almost identical with the basketball term 'time out' in which teams take a break from the game to review progress and discuss tactics.

There is nothing unusual about all these leadership interventions. They are practised quite frequently in everyday life but are somehow forgotten in the culture of a discussion group. We must, however, use them with discretion, not in pursuit of our own needs, but in response to what our growing awareness of the group process tells us.

Asking questions

Questions serve at least three purposes in discussion: to test the students' knowledge, to clarify information, and to stimulate students into expressing ideas and constructing arguments. Very often the same question can satisfy all these purposes, though that will depend on the group climate and any underlying message in the question.

There is perhaps a further purpose served by questions: the opportunity they give the tutor, or anyone else in the group, to make a link between what they and the others are thinking. The choice of question will depend very much on when it is put and the purpose of the discussion. If, however, we take the above three purposes of questioning, we can look at the different types of questions which relate to each and leave the decision as to their practical application to the reader.

Supposing you were to open a discussion with a question like this:

> Do you think the assassination of Archduke Francis Ferdinand was designed as a precipitating factor for World War I, even though none of the schemers, if schemers they were, could have had any notion of the consequences in terms of both the extent of hostilities and the degree of suffering that resulted?

Pause. Ten seconds' silence.

> Let me put it another way. On the evidence we have, was the war a typical example of intentional cause in international conflict? Or was World War II a better one?

Pause. Another ten seconds' silence.

> Did nobody read the papers I asked you to look at last week?

What, if anything, went wrong here? Were the questions too complicated? Did you wait long enough for an answer? What sort of answer was expected? This imaginary dialogue (based on two real transcripts) is intended to demonstrate at least one of the common traps in asking questions: posing a multi-part, highly academic and leading question at the start of a session, not waiting long enough for a response and then rephrasing it as another question. We all do this sort of thing from time to time and we usually wish we could 'unask' the question rather than become more deeply enmeshed through our own wish to appear clever. Yet having got ourselves into this fix perhaps we could learn from this tutor by waiting a little longer for a response, using our 'third ear' to reflect on the way the question came out, and possibly checking with students: 'Do you want me to rephrase that?' or 'Was that question too complex/obscure/involved to answer?'

Testing questions: These will mainly begin with words like 'what', 'where', 'when', 'which' – and will therefore be essentially convergent as they are intended to elicit specific information. They are concerned with:

- Checking knowledge – 'What is the best catalyst for . . .?' 'Which critics have described Godot as a comedy?'
- Comprehension – 'How do you justify that . . .?'
- Application – 'How do you predict that would work in . . .?' 'What relevance does that have in . . .?
- Analysis – 'What qualities do these have in common?' 'What would happen if . . .?'
- Synthesis – 'How does that connect with . . .? 'Could you summarise what we've discussed so far?'
- Evaluation – 'Which do you think is best?' 'How do you feel about that?'

Such questions are clearly linked with Bloom's taxonomy (see pages 100–1) and the accompanying list of verbs might prove a helpful reference. However, they can, as part of a probing exercise (Hedley and Wood 1978) be combined in a way which is searching and vigorous.

Clarifying questions: Whether a question is defined as a clarifying or as an elaborating one will often depend on the expression on the questioner's face and what has preceded the question. However, you could use these sorts of questions to clarify:

'Can you rephrase that?'
'What did you mean by . . .?'
'Can you give me an example?'

Where the last question fails you might follow it up with: 'Might this be an example of . . .? and provide one of our own.

Elaborating: Elaborating questions are essentially a gentler way of enquiring than the other questions we have discussed. They are concerned with helping students express themselves more fully, both in thought and feeling:

'Can you tell me more?'
'Could you elaborate on that?'

'Uh-huh, what else?'
'How does that make you feel?'

Echoing and selective echoing (see page 20), while not strictly a form of question, have an important place here. For example:

> Student: 'I've been thinking that, if you take the phenomenological argument to its limits then you end up with nobody helping others to make sense of their own world. There would be no point in teaching, for a start.'
> You: 'No point in teaching.' (Echoing)

> or

> You: 'Take the argument to its limits.' (Selective echoing)

In both these instances, the insertion of the word 'yes' in front of the echoes would serve online, if an appropriate opportunity were to arise.

It is easy to see how, with a little inflexion, these 'echoes' could sound like quite threatening questions. It is essential therefore that you say them in a neutral tone as though one was ruminating over the particular phrase. The responses to them can often be more effective and rewarding than those to 'ordinary' questions.

There are also questions which are intended to rouse the curiosity or the imagination. For example: 'I wonder if that really would happen?' or 'If you were in that position, what would you do?' Often questions like these are best kept ambiguous, though this could be very threatening for a new group.

Let us not forget, too, the principle of personal relevance mentioned already in the section on communications. A question like: 'How did it seem to you?' or 'What did you like about it?' is much more acceptable as a starter than: 'What is your assessment of Y's theory?'

It is clearly not in the best interest of discussion that you should spend most of the time asking questions: this would quickly set up a focal pattern of communication. The more students can competently take over the task of asking each other questions the more responsibility they will be taking for their own learning. However, it is quite properly the tutor's job to explore and probe further into students' understanding of issues.

Opening questions

In the case of large groups (say 20 to 40 in number) the importance of questioning as a spur to discussion becomes much more evident because of the increasing level of tension and sense of risk described on page 11. Huston (1995), in an article in the *Teaching Professor*, outlines how he manages the opening minutes of discussion in large classes:

> I first go over the material assigned, trying to identify the ideas and passages that seem most important, both for me and the students,

and begins to select clusters and themes on the basis of which he prepares opening questions for each area.

He then asks himself:

'Do I want to open with a shocking question designed to surprise the students into really imaginative thinking? Or should I choose instead a much more predictable beginning like: "How is this work like . . .?" or "What in this work did you find confusing, important, or notable?"'

'Should I perhaps open the discussion in a low-key way by simply asking what issues the students want to talk about, what questions they want answered?'

'Should I focus on a particular moment in the text or use it as a way of discussing crucial themes or problems?'

'Should I begin with a context-specific question that has important sub-textual ramifications?'

As we have noted, the group or class teacher must give more attention to the process than the lecturer, in order constantly to 'monitor the ebb and flow of ideas'. In focusing on the process, the tutor might have ready, or might be asking themselves, Huston suggests, an ongoing subtext of questions:

- Who is prepared?
- Is the material interesting most of them?
- Do they understand the reading?
- Who wants to participate?
- Who's carrying the discussion?
- Should I call on one of my best 'tunes' to give the class a lift? Or can the person shine on this issue?
- Am I attending to all parts of the room /all participants?
- Should I try the topic from a different angle?

It is thus a constant balancing act (as the article reminds us) between the content being discussed and the processes being used to discuss it.

For Huston, this attention to questioning is well worth the effort:

[T]eaching an effective discussion class is for me, a deeply human and humanising activity, a process built both on community and on communication, in which all of us work together – questioning, listening, examining, qualifying, challenging, explaining, and elaborating – to build something more imaginative, more interesting, more satisfying, and ultimately more enduring than any of us could build alone.

Effective questioning technique

Several research-based recommendations for effective questioning in discussion have been noted by Wilen (1986, quoted in Bonwell and Eison 1991). All of these questions are useful to build into online e-tivities or to finish an e-moderator weave, feedback or summary message. However, online, introduce only one in each message to enable participants to respond in coherent threads.

- *Plan key questions to provide structure and direction to the lesson*, whether face-to-face or synchronous/asynchronous online. A useful sequence might be:

  What are the essential features and conditions of this situation?
  Given this situation . . . what do you think will happen next?
  What facts and generalisations support your prediction?
  What other things might happen as a result of this situation?
  If the predicted situation occurs, what will happen next?
  Based on the information and predictions before us, what are the probable consequences you now see?
  What will lead us from the current situation to the one you've predicted?

In using this approach, some spontaneous questions will naturally evolve from students' responses, but the overall direction of the discussion has largely been planned.

- *Phrase questions clearly and specifically*: adapt questions to the level of students' abilities using vocabulary that is appropriate for the students in the class.
- *Ask questions logically and sequentially*: random questions confuse.
- *Ask questions at various levels*: (for) cognitive memory to establish an initial base; higher level questions can then be posed to illustrate the objectives.
- *Follow up on student responses*: Teachers can elicit longer and more meaningful statements from students if they simply maintain a 'deliberative silence' after an initial response. Too often teachers ask rapid-fire questions, one after another, a circumstance more like an interrogation than a discussion. . . . Invite the student to elaborate, make a reflective statement giving a sense of what the student has said, declare perplexity over the response, invite the student to elaborate, encourage other students to raise questions about the issue at hand, or encourage students to ask questions if they are having trouble.
- *Give students time to think when responding*: the single most important action a teacher can take after asking a question is simply to keep quiet. An analysis of the patterns of interaction between teachers and student in hundreds of classrooms found that teachers averaged less than one second of silence before repeating or re-emphasising material, or asking a second question. Under such circumstances it is no wonder that students remain silent. Training teachers to wait silently for three to five seconds after a question achieved significant benefits: the length and number of appropriate but unsolicited responses, exchanges between students, questions from students and higher-level responses all increased, while the number of students' failures to respond decreased.

- *Use questions (and techniques) that encourage wide participation from students*: frequent individual successes will ultimately empower even the most hesitant students to jump in.
- *Encourage questions from students*: create a supportive environment that allows risk taking and then encourage student to ask questions. They will respond.

The central task of the tutor is to model the behaviour and demonstrate the techniques that will enable students to be more productive members of the group. These principles are exemplified in a US college catalogue: Tutors should:

> . . . be good questioners, able to raise important issues that will engage the intellectual and imaginative powers of their students. Next, they must be good listeners, able to determine the difficulties of their students and to help them to reformulate their observations and examine their opinions. The tutors should be ready to supply helpful examples and to encourage students to examine the implications of their first attempt at understanding. In summary , the role of the tutors is to question, to listen and to help but first of all the tutors will call on the students to try to help themselves.
>
> (Myers 1988 cited in Bonwell and Eison, 1991)

A sequence of interventions

For any meeting or online session of a group there is usually a sequence during which the group settles in, starts to participate, explores questions and pulls ideas together. Here is a sample of face-to-face tasks and interventions to match them.

OPENING UP

Focusing attention	Doing introductions; stating aims, handing out or explaining task; reminding where last session ended.
Asking exploratory questions	*'Does anyone have any ideas on . . .?' 'What else?' 'Can you say a bit more?'*
Tapping into personal experiences	*'Does anyone have any experience of . . .?'*
Highlighting main question(s)	*'So what do you think about this?' 'Is that a useful way of understanding the problem?'*
Allowing for silent reflection	*'Let's just stop there and jot down anything that comes into our heads.'*

▼

ENCOURAGING PARTICIPATION

Listening attentively and holistically	Taking in the whole person, and the group responses; picking out what may be unsaid; being aware of any feelings or values which may lie behind what they say.
Looking round the group	Keeping an eye and ear open for others who may want to say something, thus helping anyone speaking to address the whole group, not just you.
Opening questions to whole group	*'Does everyone agree with that?'*
Bringing in and shutting out	Using hand signals; *'I had the sense that you wanted to say something . . .'; 'Hang on a minute Jo, let's come back to that in a minute.'*
Describing individual and group behaviour	*'You were frowning . . .'; 'You smiled . . .'*
Supporting, valuing, encouraging	*'This is side of the group hasn't said anything yet.' 'I liked the way you put that'; 'I thought you had some interesting things to say on this . . .'*

EXPLORING

Checking for understanding	*'Let me see if I understand what you were saying . . .'*
Making links	*'So how does that connect with . . .?'*
Re-directing attention	*'How about we look at this from another point of view?'*
Identifying differences of opinion	*'So how do you reconcile that with . . .?'*
Pointing out issues behind examples	*'That may be so, but how about. . . .?'*

PROBING

Questioning relevance	*'How does that fit in with . . .?'*
Questioning evidence	*'How can you be sure about that?'*
Looking for alternatives	*'Are there any other possibilities?'*
Checking assumptions	*'What are you assuming here?'*

Weaving and summarizing: the key e-moderating skills

Online, the key skill is more responsive than making proactive interventions. In other words, with well designed e-tivities, the e-moderator has a rich source of participants responses with which to work. This means that weaving, archiving and summarising are key tasks for e-moderators and add much value to online discussions.

Students can also usefully acquire and contribute these skills. Or the role of summariser can usefully be taken by two or three people working collaboratively (however, this takes up more time). Whoever undertakes the summary should always invite comment on the sufficiency and interpretation by the original contributors.

The purpose of *summarising* is:

- To weave and acknowledge the variety of ideas and contributions.
- To refocus discussion and activity when postings are too numerous. Summarise after each 20 messages, at a pre-agreed time or at regular intervals, e.g. every three days. In a large or busy e-tivity, this can be done daily.
- To refocus discussion and activity when postings have strayed from the topic.
- To refocus discussion and promote activity when e-tivities are going well.
- To refocus discussion and revive activity when postings are flagging.
- To signal closure of the e-tivity.
- To take the outcomes of an e-tivity to present or work on offline.
- To provide fresh starting points for broadening and deepening discussion.
- To remind students of the journey they have travelled.
- To reinforce and 'imprint' new information and knowledge.
- To provide a 'spark' for a new e-tivity.
- To provide a 'footprint' as a spark for a new group.

How to summarise:

- Collect all the relevant messages up into one document.
- Thank and praise the participants who contributed.
- Look for three or four key themes from the contributions and precis them in a sentence or three (maximum).

- If you wish, highlight individual participant's contributions that add fresh ideas or look at the topic in an interesting way.
- Add your teaching comments or critique, point out omissions, other perspectives or applications, make reference to further literature or ideas.
- Add a short further example of your own if necessary.
- Shorten the sentences, delete all unnecessary material.
- End with congratulations, praise or a positive note of some kind.
- Add a question or reflection for further consideration, if appropriate.
- Add further reading or follow up if appropriate (preferably electronic).
- Post message on the message forum with a really good, short title.

The purpose of weaving

- To emphasize and extend a point from a participant's message – to show wider or more generic application.
- To collect three or four snippets from different messages together and represent them in a new light.
- To highlight an issue or topic from one discussion that links with others.
- To agree or disagree with reasons in order to refocus the discussion.
- To highlight key issues to encourage two or three final contributions before summarising.

Real examples of summarising by group members

Here Keith weaves his summary into a text message:

Dear All,

I found it tough to summarize this week because of the diverging discussions that emerged. Oh well, here it goes:

On the topic of 'How to collaborate online' the group got off to a slow start but once Anita offered the question of 'Why collaborate online?', things really took off and group members entered into the knowledge construction phase.

Regarding the initial question, some useful tips were presented. Fiona spoke of the headache when technology fails and the importance of having students backup files. Keith agreed and reflected on the importance of good file management for all.

Now onto the real knowledge construction! Anita's question got the group going, but T and Anita were debating our shared understanding of online collaboration. Fiona had a eureka moment and stated that collaborating in knowledge construction is what we are really talking about. Although Fiona later referred back to a link from Anita that went against this understanding i.e. she suggested that the developmental process that the group went through to

▼

reach these shared conclusions was what mattered most. It also tied in nicely to an early posting which mentioned the importance of the group knowing very clearly what is expected of them.

We got there . . . any comments team?

Keith

Or they may be done as a list:

How to summarise the so many threads? And in 10 lines of text! I thought that it might be useful to make a listy sort of summary, especially since we've gone all over a bit.

We've discussed a number of issues about online collaboration. Here are some of the key points and opinions (with name checks!) to come out of our online collaborating about online collaboration . . .

Firstly, what is online collaboration? (Tina and Anita) We think it can be either collaborating in knowledge construction, or a group working together to achieve a certain task.

Just as with f2f group work, the group needs to know what is expected of them (Keith)

And if the group is not clear, then it is useful if one or more of them asks questions to clarify what they are doing and wish to achieve (as with Anita, in our case!)

Sometimes synchronous work is better for decision making (Keith)

Back up your work, in case of crashes (Fiona)

It can take time to get things done online (Keith)

The Group Pages feature with our online platform can be useful for online collaboration (Fiona)

Taking part in online collaboration can boost learners confidence with f2f work (Fiona)

Stages 1 and 2 may not be essential when students already have f2f contact (Anita)

Stages 1 and 2 are essential regardless, for establishing the environment in which meaningful Stage 3 and 4 work can be done (Keith and Fiona)

To conclude, I think we've established what is meant by online collaboration, and have worked together to build some ideas of how to successfully collaborate. We may know more by the end of next week!? Peta

Leadership and group development

In the context of the stages of group development (page 41), Johnson and Johnson (1987) propose a sequence which pull together many of the themes of this chapter. The leader's job, in relation to the seven successive stages, is to:

- Introduce, define and structure the group.
- Clarify procedures, reinforce members as they assimilate the rules and procedures, and help them become better acquainted.
- Stress and help model the need for cooperative interdependence and encourage the development of mutual trust.
- Accept the rebellion and differentiation between members as a natural developmental stage and use constructive confrontation and negotiation to affirm their right to independence from each other and the prescribed procedures.
- Enable the group members to commit themselves to take ownership of the group goals and procedures, as well as for other members.
- Act as a consultant and resource to enable the group to function effectively.
- Signal termination and help members to move on to a future group.

The tasks of the e-moderator in a developing online group, delineated in Figure 2.4 on page 43, are based on the five-stage model shown in Chapter 2.

Successful e-moderators:

1 Visualise success for individuals and their online groups, and engage with them in achieving the vision.
2 Turn apparent threats into challenges to be tackled as worthwhile tasks in themselves.
3 Create focus for the group by offering short-term goals and give a lot of constructive feedback.
4 Give very close attention to group processes, but avoid constant interventions and redirections.
5 From stage 4 onwards, promote the experience of 'going with the flow'. Most people have some sense of what this might mean.
6 Encourage participants to articulate feelings of engagement with the online opportunities to take part (e-tivities).

E-moderators have the added task of balancing time:

- The better structured the interaction is, the more time the e-moderator will have for giving feedback and offering weaving and summaries.
- Do not respond to each message yourself. Let students know you will read them and give feedback as to when.
- Estimate one minute to read simple messages, twice as long for longer ones.
- Doing an effective summary from 30 or more messages takes an hour.

Time estimates

E-moderators:

- Think out the e-tivity, explore it with others and plan it well in advance. Estimate: 3 hours for the first time, 1 hour second and subsequent times.
- If you plan to issue resources that are copyrighted, leave time to get permission. Try to use easily accessed non-copyrighted material whenever possible.
- Write, quality-check and put instructional messages in place online. Estimate: 2 hours first time, 1 hour second and subsequent times. Pilot by asking others to read instructions and respond 1 hour.
- Set up the bulletin board and resources, 1 hour first time, half an hour after that.
- Respond to any e mails and questions from participants or groups. Estimate half an hour.
- Brief any team leaders if necessary. Estimate half an hour.
- E-moderate the e-tivity: 2–3 hours per week.
- Summarise and plenarise, extra 1–2 hours to close off.
- Evaluation and feed forward to next time, 1 hour.

Technical support:

- Depends on platform and E-moderator's experience but may need 1–2 hours per e-tivity especially for the first time.
- Provide technical support and help to participants as necessary, 2 hours if participants are inexperienced, much less at stages 3–5.

Very discursive e-tivities such as those sometimes used in social sciences or humanities courses may need longer for e-moderators and e-tivities. Slow bulletin boards and forums may add to operational times.

DISCUSSION POINTS

- What prior planning is done in order that the groups to which you belong run successfully?
- What assumptions lie behind the various interactions, roles and rules described in this chapter? To what extent might students employ them?
- Write one or two ground rules that might improve interaction in your group.
- Invite the group to try them out in order to gauge their value.
- Make a note of the number of times you exercise the functions on pages 188–91 in your group. Invite others to do the same and compare notes.
- What skills are critically important for you (and your team) to enable you to work effectively, efficiently and happily in the online environment, and how will you acquire them?
- What elements and functions of your chosen online platform help you to discharge your e-moderating role successfully, and what get in the way? What can you do about these?

enabling group interaction

CHAPTER EIGHT

LEARNING GROUPS IN CONTEXT

This chapter describes how different aspects of the teaching and learning environment relate to each other and can be designed to inter-relate whether face-to-face, online or blended.

Groups do not exist in a vacuum; they are part of a social network and a physical or virtual environment in which the learners exchange experiences and share values at different levels. The physical environment embraces schedules, buildings, rooms and furniture and the virtual environment includes procedures for logging on, navigation, ease of use and accessibility. Both include the components and process of the course and programme. These components have an effect on:

- The feelings of group members.
- Their capacity to work effectively together.
- The availability and disposition of their tutors and e-moderators.

In Chapter 2 we drew attention to the effects of time and physical boundaries on group process and how these may affect attitudes to collaborating and learning, such as those that develop outside the learning group itself and create conflicts with the avowed intent of the group or the course. Even inside the group, pressures of imminent assessment can strongly affect the desire for exploratory or creative interaction. Such occasions may demand some 'thinking outside the box' to explore alternative options. Two of the case studies (pages 256 and 257) provide excellent examples of this in practice.

The social context of the institution can be an important influence on what happens in learning groups too. Different understandings of what constitutes learning, and the importance of group interaction in this, may well exist and these can form what we call a 'culture' – an outsider's view of what the insider does and what the insiders assume differentiates them from 'the others'.

Among the staff there are also likely to be such dispositions both towards students as a whole and between their own groupings. Disciplines are each likely to have, and support, their own 'tribal' culture and provide a further area of difference that may impact on the student's experience of learning:

> . . . attitudes, activities and cognitive styles of groups of academics representing a particular discipline are closely bound up with the characteristics and structures of the knowledge domains with which such groups are professionally concerned
>
> (Becher 1989: 20)

Almost every aspect of teaching and learning in universities (except eating and drinking in bars) has its online equivalent (Salmon 2005).

Students draw comparisons between experiences of different groups and between the prevailing learning culture in different departments at university. Department cultures which promote values and principles of openness, and tolerance of differences, prove more effective in the quality of teaching and learning they provide, and in the operation of group structure and processes (Massy et al. 1994).

BRIDGING LEARNING CULTURES

Cultural differences can be viewed as both 'vertical' as between teachers and students, and 'horizontal' as between different subject areas. While such differences are important to their members as a focus for special purposes they can equally hinder the sharing of what could, or should, be common interests and concerns between the groupings involved.

The following five schemes, each in their own way, are aimed at opening some of the doors that block communication and enable the pooling of shared interests and values.

Peer-assisted learning (PAL)

Underperformance, and even withdrawal and failure, can result from students' reluctance to admit inadequacies to tutors, and some students prefer to turn for support to groups staffed by their peers. Peer Assisted Learning (PAL, also known as Supplemental Instruction) has become increasingly popular in recent years as an organised form of face-to-face peer tutoring. There are now online groups offering peer support in the context of peer tutoring. In this, a specific role is taken by a trained student leader from a more advanced stage of the course or, for online support, a group member who has received special training in such a role (McLuckie and Topping 2004).

The aims of student-led support groups are to help students adjust more quickly to university life and to develop their recognition of competent performance, improve their study skills, enhance their understanding of the subject content of their course and prepare better for assignments and exams. The motivation to learn and to succeed is a complex issue to do with students' self-regard, comparison with others and untested assumptions about their own abilities, but poor motivation and self-doubt can be reinforced by the mismatches in course delivery. PAL aims to enable the doubts and problems of students to be expressed openly and to establish a safe environment of cooperative learning and mutual support, a value designed to transfer to the students' other learning activities. Patterns and rules for PAL vary considerably in different institutions, although attendance is usually voluntary; the sessions may be timetabled and supported by the related member of staff or course contact.

At Bournemouth University a one-hour PAL session is timetabled each week, where students work together as a group on course material or on another topic agreed by the group. The PAL leaders are prepared for their role during an intensive, two-day initial training course with follow-up training sessions. They have available to them extensive training materials and resources to use in their PAL sessions. They are specifically encouraged to use activities like those described in Chapter 6 with their groups and to focus on eliciting problems and misunderstandings rather than teaching, even if requested to do so by the group: 'Please remember that the PAL Leaders are not lecturers, so they're not allowed to teach – please do not ask them to!' (Fleming 2004).

Face-to-face PAL 'leaders' are often students who have just completed the first year of the course, and are therefore uniquely placed to help the new first-year students. They are viewed as 'experts' in surviving the first year, receive training in how to run PAL sessions effectively, and manage group discussion. The emphasis is on everyone in the group working cooperatively to develop their understanding of course topics and improve their study habits. PAL is not specifically aimed at weak students – *everyone* can benefit because it is intended to help students understand the more difficult subject topics on their course. The sessions are interactive and demand of the leader a range of organisational skills in setting and handling group processes.

The monitoring process (at Bournemouth) includes supervision from within the course by:

- A 'Course PAL Contact', a nominated member of the teaching team who meets with them regularly to review and plan PAL sessions.
- Central PAL Coordinators who observe PAL Leaders in their sessions on two occasions during the course of the academic year, and give them feedback on their techniques and group management.
- The same PAL Coordinators who operate an open-access policy in support of PAL Leaders.

PAL leaders are thus able to benefit not only by reinforcing their own knowledge foundations but in the range of leadership, group and management skills they develop. Further, PAL may be seen as a scheme which is learner-centred, clearly embedded in the system, and which promotes reliability, openness and collaboration across boundaries and which creates what Palmer (1998) would call a win-win situation.

McLuckie and Topping (2004) compare peer learning interactions in face-to-face and online situations and argue that the skills necessary for building effective online discourse need to be recognised, even assessed. Online interactions are likely to be more peer-oriented so one of the trained participants can take on a focus of 'interactive process management' by:

- Initiating discussion and topics.
- Setting the agenda.
- Setting norms.
- Offering recognition to contributors.

- Prompting responses.
- Comparing and contrasting, in order to identify agreement and disagreement.
- Weaving unifying threads.
- Crystalising consensus.
- Meta-commenting.

Student management teams

Cross-cultural group dynamics can also operate in the sphere of course management. Nuhfer (1995) describes a scheme in which, mimicking industrial Total Quality Management philosophies, he set up Student Management Teams – 'a partnership between students and professors that are formed for the improvement of the classroom community'. The team comprises about four students and a tutor who have a managerial role and take on part of the responsibility for the success of the course. The students meet each week to monitor progress and discuss possible improvements, and the tutor joins them every other week. All meetings are held in a 'neutral' area and a written log of suggestions and related progress is maintained. Students receive compensation for their time, a clear indication that their work and the improvement of teaching is institutionally approved. Nufher claims that the teams can improve the classroom learning environment by considering:

- How the course might be improved (sequence of material presented, designating areas of students' difficulty, removing students' misconceptions, preventing absenteeism, dealing with irritating behaviour by consensus and preventing observed problems).
- How the delivery of material might be improved (with the permission of the tutor in question).

Teams were also drafted for special purposes. An engineering professor wanted to know why engineering courses appeared unpopular with women and recruited an ad hoc team of female students to find out why. A foreign professor who had low evaluations because of his thick accent asked for help from the team with his communication; they helped him with his pronunciation, suggested more overhead transparencies and handouts with lecture outlines, as well as a glossary of terms that were difficult to understand. Another professor who was troubled by a hostile cluster of hecklers in a race and gender class was advised by the team to tell them to 'Shut up!', which worked for a time, When the hecklers resumed their activity the team turned on them, and eventually 80 per cent of the class confronted them with a concerted 'SHUT UP!'.

Student management teams offer a less threatening scenario for the admission of shortcomings and the collaborative search for solutions than that which exists in the more confrontational climate of student representatives and staff-student committees. The model defines students as colleagues and represents an astute use of group dynamics within an organisational system which traditionally regards students as receivers rather than creators of courses.

Action learning sets

Action learning sets are about solving problems and getting things done. They work well for staff or students as forums within or outside course processes. Action learning sets show that learning can be achieved, and practical problems solved, in modes other than discussion groups, agenda-based meetings and one-to-one counselling. Learning sets include a mutually agreed set of rules and procedures, to deal with issues and problems of their members and to ensure a clear focus on their needs. Individuals bring their own problems and the action results from the structured attention and support given by the group. Most problems have an inner and an outer domain: the inner feelings and thoughts about an event or a decision, and the outer world of the environment in which it occurs. The set is less concerned with personal development and discovery than with learning and action (Beaty and McGill 1992).

Time is allocated evenly to each member within meetings, within the usual three hours, although the set may decide that one member needs more time and reallocate time accordingly. The responsibility of the timekeeping role is paramount and the meetings need to be kept free of interruptions.

One of the paradoxes of groups is that until everyone has a sense of their own separate identity the group cannot cohere. In action learning sets this can be achieved by processes like group rounds at the start, although the continuing effectiveness of the set will be enhanced if it can interact in a free and unstructured way. A cycle proposed by Beaty and McGill is:

> *Connecting*: e.g. saying hello, shaking hands, hugging etc.
> *Nurturing*: e.g. having coffee ready, asking 'How are you?'
> *Energising*: e.g. sharing latest events, short interesting game/story/joke.
> *Working*: e.g. individual time slots.
> *Rewarding*: e.g. thanking and offering support outside the set.
> *Leave taking*: e.g. checking on action points, next dates, saying 'Goodbye'.

Attention to these stages can make all the difference between a formal and purely functional meeting and one which conveys a sense of wholeness and enjoyment.

One of the principles of action learning is that the set should formulate its own ground rules at the beginning of the process, and these are to last for the duration of the set, subject to agreed amendments and additions. There are usually ground rules about confidentiality but others concerning attendance, punctuality, communication and behaviour may emerge. Ground rules may be generated by brainstorming.

Rounds are a good way of starting a meeting. Each person in turn has, say, a minute to relate 'what's on top' (something that's occupying their mind at the moment) while the others listen silently. Another popular theme for a round is Joys, Trauma and Trivia (see Appendix) in which each member in turn describes something joyful, something traumatic and something trivial that has happened to them recently. Other useful processes include buzz groups, circular interviewing and brainstorming. At the end of a meeting the set will typically record and circulate the agreed actions and review the meeting in order to improve the process for subsequent ones and to decide who is doing what.

A facilitator may be a valuable factor to the success of action learning sets, especially in the early stages when there can be a tendency to revert to unfocused discussion or conventional processes. The main task of the facilitator is to model many of the skills so that they can become integrated into the regular practice of the set. For this to work effectively the facilitator may herself find feedback from the set a valuable asset. A truly effective active learning set can thus serve as a model for a learning culture in the wider context of the organisation.

Learning communities

> If we want to develop and deepen the capacity for connectedness at the heart of good teaching, we must understand – and resist – the perverse but powerful draw of the 'disconnected life' . . . We are distanced by a grading system that separates teachers from students, by departments that fragment fields of knowledge, by competition that makes students and teachers alike wary of their peers . . . Educational institutions are full of divisive structures.
>
> (Palmer 1998)

There has existed, until recently, an inherent irony in the encouragement of students to work in groups and teams by academics who make little effort to collaborate with each other in similar ways, especially in their own institutions. Yet in many senses of the term, they are part of a community, whether across subjects within the institution, or in the same subjects globally. In some institutions:

> For a sustained period of time – a quarter or a semester or even a year – teaching teams commit themselves to a course or program with a common group of students. Sailing together requires teamwork, collaborative skills, and collective responsibility that are less familiar to those of us in the habit of sailing solo.
>
> (MacGregor 2000)

Since the advent of the Internet, ideas and aspirations of professionals working in virtual communities have abounded. Most knowledge develops at the boundary between professional groups – what Etienne Wenger calls the 'wellspring for innovation'. Wenger considers the mode of creating the community (face-to-face or virtual) to be irrelevant. Although many online communities spring up through their own energies, they can, for educational purposes, be nurtured. Even then, there needs to be a lot of respect and understanding so that the deep process of mutual engagement and the 'chemistry' of communities of practice is not interfered with (Wenger 2005).

Learning communities can generate a range of benefits for specialists and generalists alike in:

- ◼ Capturing knowledge.
- ◼ Sharing best practices.

- Solving problems quickly.
- Driving innovation.
- Enabling professional development.
- Reducing costs.

You can find further discussion of the practice of the learning community on page 276.

Teaching teams

While the individualist culture of so much teaching in tertiary education may be advantageous to students in providing a variety of perspectives there are also compelling reasons for making public what may normally be a private activity, not merely through regular communication, but by ongoing collaboration in the delivery of a course.

> When a team of teachers form a learning community in order to focus on course design, delivery, assessment and so on, teaching ceases to be an isolated activity. Team teaching requires faculty members to change how they teach . . . Team teaching requires team building, collaborative skills, and collective responsibility.
>
> (Laufgraben and Tompkins 2004)

> Where the outcome of the teamwork is interdisciplinary students can see models of different teaching styles in the same classroom . . . Students have good models of collaborative learning when they see professors working together in and out of the classroom. Working with new people and learning more about another discipline is very stimulating for the faculty members and their enthusiasm makes the classes more interesting. Team teaching gets faculty members into other buildings to get better acquainted with colleagues we often have little contact with, and more familiar with their programs. The level of classroom discussion is improved when another professor is there asking questions and asking for clarification. This interaction provides good examples of how to ask questions and participate in class discussion, which is beneficial for students who might have trouble articulating their questions or may lack the confidence to question the professor who is the expert. Students see evidence that faculty members in different departments really do have consistent educational and intellectual goals, that becoming an educated person does not just involve learning information about separate disciplines.
>
> (Hanlon and Thomas 2002)

Online, it is helpful to have more than one e-moderator for larger groups. However, the e-moderating team should clearly work out what each will contribute and when they take responsibility for weaving and summarising. An e-moderator with well-developed online skills can often transfer understanding to one with more expertise in the topic.

TIMETABLES ON CAMPUS

The constraints of a timetable are significant factors in determining the pattern of communication and relationships in an institution that relies heavily on face-to-face teaching. Where the desire to learn is a less powerful drive than it might be, physical proximity and frequency of encounter may have a marked effect. To some extent the need for friendship and personal contact can mitigate many of the barriers of time and space determined by course schedules and dispersed buildings. The nearer one lives to somebody, the greater the likelihood that chance meetings will occur and even where they do not, their likelihood may also exert a strong influence. Of course, the very fact of meeting does not ensure that effective communication will occur; nor does the lack of meeting mean that it will not. Students whose rooms are relatively inaccessible may have fewer friends than those whose rooms are more accessible. Thomas (2002) alerts us also to the value of social facilities in the form of a special common room for those not living on or near the campus where they can meet up and spend time between classes and to the need to encourage such students to meet up there.

A similar situation exists where the proximity of a 'significant' person or object causes a person to attend to them more readily than another at a greater distance. People are always more alert to immediate demands. It is likely, therefore, that frequent casual encounters with tutors and group colleagues will serve as a regular reminder of agreed tasks and a spur for new ideas for the group. The frequency of group meetings will also determine the extent to which the group ethos will prevail over other priorities.

In the same way, the physical shape of the environment may well affect the nature of casual interaction. A building designed as a set of rooms leading off long corridors can limit encounters to hasty exchanges in the corridor or to specially arranged meetings in designated places, neither of which promotes spontaneous communication. A conveniently situated open area or refreshment facility can offset this sort of environmental drawback to some extent.

The problems of communication and relationships in the environment appear to echo those experienced in the learning group. Size, physical layout, personal proximity all play their part. The style of interaction present in a learning group could also be influenced to a large extent by its general environment. The implication of these considerations is that whether one is thinking of the learning group or its environment, physical arrangements must be taken into consideration if the kind of educational and social relationships we desire are to occur.

Many campus-based universities are now using virtual learning environments for resources and interactions just as much for students who come to campus as for distance learners. For example the University of Leicester podcasting (Edirisingha et al. 2006) and wiki projects (Dence et al. 2006) are aimed at enabling campus-based learners to get to know others outside their immediate location-based groups through working together online, motivated by short mps files on the Blackboard Learning Environment.

MOVING COLLABORATION INTO THE ONLINE ENVIRONMENT

The components that impact on the success or failure of online collaboration, though in many ways different from the issues relating to the physical environment, are just as complex and varied. Some of these are within the influence of human intervention through his or her design for participation and appropriate interventions.

Technology

Most participants and e-moderators work with asynchronous bulletin boards and forums provided in commercial VLEs such as Blackboard and WebCt, or sometimes open source versions such as Moodle. The more popular VLEs are focused on ease of posting materials for teachers rather than on providing collaborative tools. Therefore at present there are no readily available collaboration tools embedded in the technology, and so collaboration must be designed for and supported during the process by human intervention.

Basic problems do still happen with technology:

- Breakdowns in personal computers (PCs).
- Server and software upgrades.
- Slow modems in locations beyond the reach of broadband services.

A novice or a nervous participant will be unable to diagnose which bit of the system – hardware, software, connection and so on – is at fault and is likely to become exceptionally upset in the early days. Thus responsive and available helplines are critically important for the first couple of weeks.

As one participant put it:

> I started off with a bang and thought I was lost because I couldn't find anyone, then I thought I was going crazy because I couldn't find the right place to post the activities . . . so after completing a couple of the weekly e-tivities, I find myself unable to access the site (and the Internet) and spent hours on the phone complaining to anyone who would listen . . . hopefully now, I am back on track and wow have I missed heaps – where did all of these people come from??? This experience has given me a real insight into the problems course participants may encounter with Internet access, new technology and 'life getting in the way'.
> (Participant on All Things in Moderation E-moderating course, E-tivities Course 2004)

In the face-to-face environment the participants know the general approach to collaboration and what is expected of them. The technology in use is low level and familiar. Participants are naturally constrained by being in the same time and place.

Online, the constraints of time and place are relaxed (except perhaps during assessment deadlines), but so is the focus and discipline that encourages activities to be completed. This relaxation, which is hard enough for solitary private study, is especially important to generate when working with online and remote groups. Many participants are unused to taking part in such online forums – the experience is very different from handling individual e-mails.

Thus the freedom that online working gives with one hand is taken away with the other. The processes, so familiar in face-to-face groups, no longer apply in the same way, and additional problems occur. Participants need to learn how to collaborate all over again.

Frameworks for online collaboration

Much progress has been made in increasing online participation and collaboration as e-moderators have developed their skills in encouraging and supporting groups.

Threads

Forums with many threads and many messages present e-moderators with a significant demand on their time in summarising. Some VLEs include features to gather together selected messages – but none can yet provide intelligent editing. The skills of summarising and weaving have helped many e-moderators to encourage information exchange and knowledge-building, enabling genuine collaboration to occur in forums. Increased participation results from enthusiastic e-moderation and well-designed motivating activities. Activities can be designed to restrict participant messages to a single thread – easing the tasks of summarising and archiving.

The structure of e-tivities (Chapter 6, page 104) has enabled designers to set out simple-to-use and easy-to-understand activities. The method for collaboration is spelt out as well, particularly for tasks with several steps, and should include instructions such as where to post messages and the timetable for collaboration.

Collaboration methods need to be clearly described so that participants become familiar with them and can apply them by themselves at other times and on other courses. The aim is shown at the start, and once used, the collaboration method should become part of the participants' skills enabling online groups to self-start on the next occasion almost without prompting from the e-moderator.

Tables

The e-moderator can set up a table in Word which may have a number of questions within it and a space for answers. Participants are invited to answer each question, adding to the answers of others. Summarising becomes much easier as responses to each question are in a single cell. Participants soon pick up this idea.

Where the participants themselves can drive group activity the involvement of the e-moderator lessens.

Actions to improve online collaboration

The challenge for the online designer is to anticipate the needs not only of the participants but also of the e-moderator. Every participant wants a response but, in courses with over 100 students, it is impractical for the e-moderator to respond to every individual. Enabling the participants to collaborate effectively becomes essential for the well-being of the e-moderator!

Design starts long before any participant engages with the course. Preparing for the participants' needs is a demanding task. Feedback shows it is worthwhile for designers and e-moderators to experience courses from the participants' perspective, enabling needs to be properly anticipated and prepared for as part of the course design. Clear objectives, well-written process descriptions and supportive facilitation will provide greater participation in spite of VLEs that are weak in collaboration tools.

Collaboration tasks need to be identified early in the design stage and be an integral part of courses rather than last-minute after-thoughts. Within the development of a course there may be a number of excellent opportunities where sharing information among group members, brainstorming ideas or even role play can contribute to the participants' experience.

Some regularity of online activity is recommended so that participants get into a habit of accessing the online element of a course. For example, activities could be interspersed weekly with assignments and revision practice for exams. This can bring back discipline which is greatly needed by many participants.

Collaboration tasks and methods when described with great clarity save much time. Based on the many errors that we have trapped in the development stages of our own courses we recommend designers to collaborate with colleagues to proof-read to ensure ambiguities are edited out. We are currently experimenting with web access to editable text pages where developers can collaborate on a single document.

In summary, the problems groups have in collaborating online are:

1   Little software is appropriate for collaboration.
2   Participants are unfamiliar with collaborating methods.
3   Large groups demand much e-moderator time.

To address these issues, in the courses we run using the five-stage model and e-tivities we adopt the following approaches:

■   Make the collaboration process explicit.
■   Encourage participants to summarise.
■   Work hard to achieve clarity of activity description.
■   Try out new methods of collaborating.
■   Seek feedback from participants.

VIRTUAL LEARNING ENVIRONMENTS: THEIR FUNCTIONS AND RELATIONSHIP WITH GROUP LEARNING

As with all communication processes a reasonable degree of clarity is essential for understanding; message boards in VLEs are a case in point – what they cry out for is some separation. There must be a facility for easily weaving, summarising and archiving messages frequently. This one facility dramatically improves navigation and hence participation. Also, as a very minimum, task organisation messages should be in one place, there should be a place for discussions and a place for 'reflections' and feedback. Each activity (e-tivity) should have its own thread for replying. Participants must learn fast the conventions and their importance of posting coherent messages, with good clear titles, to their team *in the right places*. A search facility also helps.

When using a bulletin board (i.e. asynchronous online forum) it is very important to have ways of sorting and classifying messages. Otherwise, the board ends up with an enormous string of undifferentiated messages: there is no week-by-week organisation of the message board, and no obvious way of sifting out the threads, no possibility of changing the 'view' to earliest date, author topic, etc. If there is no easy way to go back through the messages to find particular ones, reflection is made more difficult. Without such a feature (and knowledge by all participants and e-moderators on how to use it), some people will always miss out.

An example is an initial explanatory message from a researcher (KG) about a request for first feedback thoughts from the online group – in the Creative Waves project (you can read more about it on pages 257–9). It appeared in the middle of a run of messages discussing how the next task was to be organised. (KG hesitated to even send it because he thought it perhaps intrusive, given the current flow of messages was about the task.) So it got in the way – and was ignored because it broke into the flow of task-oriented messages. KG's announcement of his presence as observer met more or less the same fate. The e-moderator similarly put a message in giving his reflections on week 1, but that was as equally ignored as KG's in evoking no response because it came in the middle of the task messages.

There also needs to be a systematic tracking and monitoring system to provide support and encouragement for lurkers, laggards and drop-outs. Of course this can be achieved in small groups by e-moderators but it is much better to have software provided and a clickable resource.

Blogs and wikis

Blogs (or web-logs) have for many people become one of the most important ways of learning about new and relevant information about a field of interest or study. Blogs began as an extension of personal home pages on the web. They include a series of dated entries and are listed with the most recent at the top of the web page. Of course, as they are online, they can include links and pictures as well as static text. The author can make them freely available by giving people the web address (URL) or they can be password-protected.

Blogs offer an e-finger on the pulse of an industry or field of study. What's more they are a way of finding out in a timely manner about the most important developments of almost any arena. News of articles, papers, applications and disputes appear in blogs long before they are captured by search services such as Google, and much longer before these *same* ideas appear in printed media such as books and published articles.

Although bloggers write as individuals, each blog attracts a relatively small number of readers. However, the readers are typically in strong online social networks and so information is shared and examined quickly, by larger numbers of people, from a variety of perspectives. Hence specialist interests are served and some blogs are highly political. Although commentators worry about the quality of knowledge on blogs, the openness of the circulation of views and the extensive linking ensures that nothing totally outrageous stands without some comment. Similarly blogs bring to the surface important issues that might otherwise be ignored, characteristically with a personal perspective and interpretation.

Educators soon caught on to the value of blogs, both for keeping up to date themselves and for use in teaching and learning. You can see how blogs might encourage self-expression – 'their own voice'- and student writing. You can also see how important they can be for learning if they promote self-expression through writing and perhaps critical thinking. Learners at all levels have caught on to blogs, usually with the encouragement of their teachers, from young school children to Harvard and Stanford!

A wiki is an online application on the web that allows everyone to add and edit the content. The process simplifies sharing of content and is a very effective way to exchange information through collaborative effort.

Blogs and wikis tap into some of the Web's greatest strengths such as personal authoring and publishing. They facilitate the sharing of deep rooted, examined, filtered and classified knowledge in a way we've not seen the like of ever before.

GROUPS IN COURSES

The amount of time and physical space available for face-to-face discussion groups can have a profound effect on the kind of learning which takes place. There is the world of difference, for instance, between the small group of eight students working intensively with a tutor for three hours, with a 20-minute coffee break included, and a science 'tutorial' in which 20 students assemble for one hour in a room with fixed benches or large tables arranged in rows, and extended asynchronous online groups.

In physical sciences, for example, traditionally there has been a tendency to view small group work as an added extra, a means of improving students' understanding of lecture material for instance, rather than as a coherent mode of learning in its own right. Part of the problem is the enormous load of information in the syllabus which many science and engineering lecturers have often believed must be transmitted.

Knowledge, to be acquired effectively, must be processed, its meaning incorporated into the students' patterns of thinking, and ultimately communicated by the student in a coherent and acceptable form. If the syllabus is taught as an accumulating sequence where each stage of learning is dependent on the previous one, then it is essential that the students learn progressively and not terminally (that is, not just in exam revision): they must integrate their understanding as they go along. Group discussion is an invaluable aid to this kind of continuous learning. If it is to be used, the course must be tailored to accommodate it as an integral feature.

Scheduling group discussion

Several frameworks are possible for the inclusion of group work in the formal timetable, perhaps advantageously for both staff and students blending in asynchronous online group work. Some of the groups are planned to occur within lecture periods, some between; yet others are linked to practical classes. Whether or not several groups can operate concurrently will depend upon the number of students, tutors and available facilities. For example, within a large hall with moveable furniture, any number of small groups could be formed before, during or after a lecture. In a terraced lecture theatre, however, any sustained small group discussion would probably have to be left till after the lecture.

One simple arrangement for the use of group discussion in a lecture is shown in Figure 8.1. A succession of more elaborate practices such as described in Chapter 6 can also be used while maintaining a sense of continuity and momentum through a whole lecture period. The session might begin with the display on the OHP, while the students are still assembling, of a set of headings which review the previous lecture(s), thus making effective use of what is normally 'dead' time. The lecturer then could then go on to address the outline on the OHP, thus pulling together ideas and topics dealt with in prior reading, seminars and lectures. No new material is added at this stage. Note that this is the longest formal input in the session – only nine minutes!

For Stage 3, a new transparency poses a question which directs students to work in twos or threes in making an application of their previous work. The lecturer moves round the class listening, helping and clarifying where necessary.

Stage 4 comprises a further short lecture with explicitly new material: students add new points to their handouts. This is followed by students discussing these new points in pairs while the lecturer moves round to check for understanding. A review of the students' responses is given by the lecturer in Stage 6. In Stage 7 the lecturer poses more difficult questions to the pairs concerning interpretation; this stimulates a buzz of activity at a point when one would typically expect a trough in the level of attention.

The lecturer then answers part of the question in Stage 8 and leads students to more advanced issues. The pattern of lecturer–student interaction continues till the last few minutes when students are asked to write a brief summary of the lecture.

This style of presentation requires not merely a considerable amount of assertiveness on the part of the lecturer in making sure that events move on crisply, but also sensitivity to the time needed to carry out each activity. However, a central ingredient for success in this approach is a very clear and explicit statement to the students on why one is lecturing in this way.

This sort of structure suggested in Figure 8.1 for a lecture session requires both careful planning and firm but sensitive direction by the tutor, particularly in making decisions about when to change the

			Time
			10.00 am
Stage	1	Revision OHP displayed	10.05 am
Stage	2	Revision talk on last lectures	10.14 am
Stage	3	Task: discuss in pairs	10.19 am
Stage	4	Talk	10.26 am
Stage	5	Task: discuss in pairs	10.30 am
Stage	6	Lecturer summarizes student answers. 10.33 starts lecturing again.	10.36 am
Stage	7	Task: specific questions on a map; discuss in pairs	10.42 am
Stage	8	Lecturer answers first two questions	10.43 am
Stage	9	Continued discussion in pairs	10.45 am
Stage	10	Talk: lcturer gives answers, and lectures (using OHPs)	10.48 am
Stage	11	30-second task: in pairs	
Stage	12	Lecturer refers to handout not covered in lecture	10.54 am
Stage	13	Students summarize lecture for themselves	10.56 am

End

Total lecturer talk	:	31 mins _____
Total student work	:	25 mins _____
Longest lecturer talk	:	9 mins
Longest student task	:	6 mins
Number of 'segments' of lecture	:	13

Figure 8.1 Integrating group discussion into the lecture

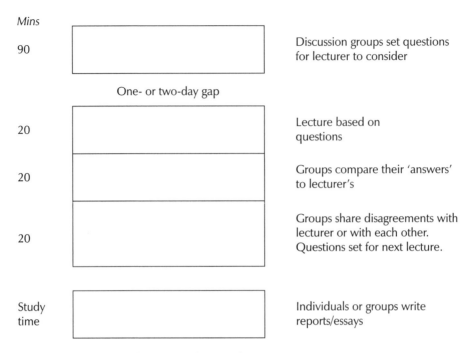

Mins		
90		Discussion groups set questions for lecturer to consider
	One- or two-day gap	
20		Lecture based on questions
20		Groups compare their 'answers' to lecturer's
20		Groups share disagreements with lecturer or with each other. Questions set for next lecture.
Study time		Individuals or groups write reports/essays

Figure 8.2 Sequencing lectures and group discussion

learning activity. A more extended version of the above scheme is shown in Figure 8.2. Sequencing lectures and group discussion would also work well in an asynchronous online format.

Figure 8.3 demonstrates a combination of group and individual work for practicals which carries over the distilled learning from one session to the next.

2nd part of 1st practical		*Study time*	*1st part of 2nd practical*
90 minutes	*45 minutes*		*45 minutes*
Groups do experiments	Paired groups share findings and discuss critically	Individuals write up reports	Paired groups appraise reports in dyads and discuss as a whole

Figure 8.3 Combining group and individual work in practicals

This arrangement primes students for a collective encounter with the lecturer. It makes a clear contrast to the kind of lecture that typically ends in a throwaway comment like: 'Oh, next week we shall be looking at . . .', or with the distribution of a lengthy and unannotated booklist.

The permutations of these arrangements are considerable and each tutor would have to work out a plan according to the aims and logistics of the course. In some cases, alternation and linking of lecture and discussion can be tightly organised as a total strategy for the whole course, perhaps incorporating blended online work. In others, given some leeway, it can be incorporated within an otherwise standard timetable.

One example of a successful exercise used in a lecture situation comes from Chemical Engineering. Felder and Brent (2003) describe the use of a TAPPS ('thinking-aloud pair problem solving') exercise in which the students work in pairs through a complex derivation or worked-out problem solution in the text or on a handout, with one of them explaining the solution step-by-step and the other questioning anything unclear and giving hints when necessary.

> Periodically I stop them, and ask them for explanations, providing my own when necessary, and have the students reverse roles in their pairs and proceed from a common starting point. It may take most or all of a class period to work through the entire solution, but the students will end with a depth of understanding they would be unlikely to get any other way. 90 per cent of the students are actively engaged with the material and getting practice in the skills you're trying to teach them, and 10 per cent are out to lunch. On the other hand, at any given moment in a traditional lecture, if as many as 10 per cent of your students are actively involved with the lecture material you're doing very well.

One further consideration relates to the problem addressed in Chapter 6 of coping with increasing class sizes to the point where the group becomes too large to comfortably achieve the aims prescribed for it. There is no reason, as we have already seen, why groups should not work independently on alternate weeks, provided rooms and appropriate tasks are organised. For example, when meeting without a tutor students could prepare questions and reports, pool their reading, solve problems set by the tutor or act as a peer tutoring group by answering for each other the questions they would normally ask of the tutor. When they meet with the tutor they would present the work they had discussed, interact as usual with the tutor and receive further briefing. Some of the options for timetabling these meetings are shown overleaf in Figure 8.4 (Gibbs 1995).

In looking at ways in which sequences of group work may be organised let's not forget that there are many courses, or parts of courses, which organise groups with varying degrees of self-direction whether face-to-face or online. You can find some specific examples of these later in this chapter but for the sake of contrast here are two generic approaches.

Problem-based learning

There continues to be debate at both local and global levels about what counts as problem-based learning and what does not. In comparison with many other pedagogical approaches, problem-based

Model 1 Pre- and post meetings

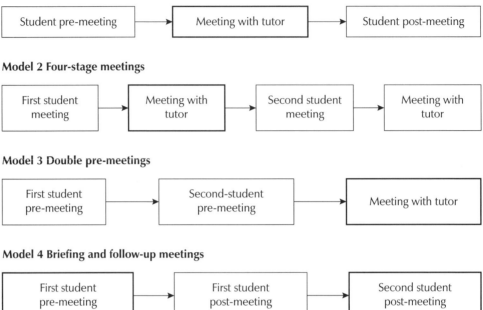

| Student pre-meeting | → | Meeting with tutor | → | Student post-meeting |

Model 2 Four-stage meetings

| First student meeting | → | Meeting with tutor | → | Second student meeting | → | Meeting with tutor |

Model 3 Double pre-meetings

| First student pre-meeting | → | Second-student pre-meeting | → | Meeting with tutor |

Model 4 Briefing and follow-up meetings

| First student pre-meeting | → | First student post-meeting | → | Second student post-meeting |

Figure 8.4 Alternative patterns of group meetings

learning has emerged relatively recently, being popularised by Barrows and Tamblyn (1980) following their research into the reasoning abilities of medical students at McMaster Medical School, Canada. Problem-based learning is an approach to learning where curricula are designed with problem scenarios central to student learning in each curricular component (modules/units). Students working in small teams examine a problem situation and, through this exploration, are expected to locate the gaps in their own knowledge and skills in order to decide what information they needed to acquire in order to resolve or manage the situation. They receive more or less guidance from tutors (acting as facilitators rather than subject experts). The problem itself does not need to be solved: the learning occurs in the quest. A typical set of stages for the group to work through on the problem situation is:

- What issues, topics and systems appear to contribute to this?
- What do we already know about these?
- What hypotheses do we have?
- What resources do we need to find in order to learn?
- How will we access the resources?
- How will we integrate our learning into the group task?
- How will we present our outcomes?

Lectures, seminars, workshops or laboratories may support the enquiry process rather than transmit subject-based knowledge. The starting point should be a set of problem scenarios regardless of whether a module or a whole programme is being designed. The scenarios enable students to become independent enquirers and help them to see learning and knowledge as flexible entities. Often these scenarios are described as messy, confusing or incomplete on the grounds that real life is like that and it presents a more open-ended and creative task. Problem-based learning has expanded worldwide since the 1960s and, as it has spread, the concepts associated with it have changed and become more flexible and fluid.

PBLonline, defined here as students working in teams of eight to ten on a series of problem scenarios that combine to make up a module, needs a collaborative online environment such as a VLE as described elsewhere in this book. It is a most appropriate model for working online for teams and for discussion leading to knowledge building. Real-time or asynchronous modes can be used, but what is important is that students work together to engage with the problem situation. Synchronous collaboration tools are vital for the effective use of PBLonline because tools such as Chat, Shared Whiteboards, Video Conferencing and Group Browsing are central to ensuring collaboration within the problem-based learning team. Students may be working at a distance or on campus, but they will begin by working out what they need to learn in order to engage with the problem situation. This may take place through a shared whiteboard, conferring, or an e-mail discussion group. What is also important is that students have both access to the objectives of the module and the ability to negotiate their own learning needs in the context of the given outcomes. The e-moderator can have continuous access to the text of the ongoing discussions without necessarily participating in all of them (Savin-Baden and Wilkie 2006). This conception of problem-based learning places it pedagogically in a collaborative online environment and thus it has a number of advantages over models mentioned earlier. Whilst many of the current models of online education focus on teacher-centred learning, PBLonline needs to be focused on a team-orientated knowledge-building discourse.

Team-based learning

A more strategic schema described by Fink (2003) is 'team-based learning' (TBL) where students, through an initial sequence of individual and group tasks, tests and feedback on their performance, develop into cohesive teams who then undertake challenging learning activities. Not only do the team members become very committed to the work of their team but, TBL exponents claim, demonstrate deeper levels of learning at an individual level.

> Team-based learning represents an . . . intense use of small groups in that it changes the structure of the course in order to develop and then take advantage of the special capabilities of high-performance learning teams. Such teams have two features that offer major advantages in an educational situation. As members of a team, individuals become willing to commit to a very high level of effort in their learning, and learning teams are capable of solving problems that are beyond the capability of even their most talented members.
>
> (Michaelsen et al. 2004)

The TBL group performance is founded on four essential principles:

■ Groups must be properly formed and managed.
■ Students must be made accountable for their individual and group work.

- Covering a 2–3-week block of time
- Covering one major topic within the course

Three phases of team learning

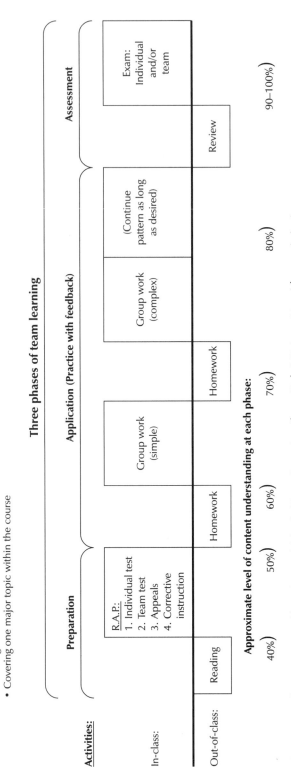

Activities: Preparation Application (Practice with feedback) Assessment

In-class:

R.A.P:
1. Individual test
2. Team test
3. Appeals
4. Corrective instruction

Group work (simple)

Group work (complex)

(Continue pattern as long as desired)

Review

Exam: Individual and/or team

Out-of-class: Reading Homework Homework

Approximate level of content understanding at each phase:

40% 50% 60% 70% 80% 90–100%

Figure 8.5 The sequence of learning activities in Team Learning (from Fink 2004, p. 11, with permission)

- Group assignments must promote both learning and team development.
- Students must have frequent and timely performance feedback.

Figure 8.5 indicates the organised progression of team building and group learning in a TBL course (reprinted by kind permission of L. Dee Fink).

Fink regards TBL as distinct from PBL in at least one respect: PBL relies on tutors to keep the groups functioning effectively, whereas TBL trains the groups to work as independent teams.

Within any curriculum, some aims may have priority over others at different times, and an important but often neglected job of the course tutor is to organise and monitor the teaching and learning so that some sort of coherent experience may emerge. Alert group tutors can plan their own unfolding patterns with the group but there may be wider considerations to be dealt with. One of these occurs on the modular or unit system of course design, where students can often experience a sense of 'bittiness' in their studies (Parlett et al. 1988), though today a departmental site may help students to keep track of the 'bittiness'. Some institutions have attempted to achieve a degree of integration across the modules by scheduling a 'synoptic study' session into the timetable. In the synoptic study students might discuss relationships between the elements, apply the separate knowledge to a particular focus (e.g. science and society) or solve integrative problems. A somewhat less conventional but nevertheless valuable task would be to discuss the experience of learning in each module and to explore ways of enhancing it.

Nevertheless, some sort of integrative small group experience would seem valuable in the unit or modular system to give students the possibility of developing a sense of social identity and a feeling of belonging and commitment to the intellectual life of the institution. Parlett and King (1971) report an attempt to overcome many of the fragmenting effects of an orthodox timetable in which students of physics worked on 'concentrated study' – the full-time study of a single subject for a month with no competing academic demands. This curricular innovation provided enormous scope and freedom for varied and spontaneous group work. At Worcester Polytechnic Institute in the USA (ASEE 1976), students take part in a project-based unit of seven weeks' duration in which they work exclusively on their project.

One aspect of student experience of higher education which does not appear to have received much attention is that of multiple group membership, often coupled with a complex of tasks. What looks on paper a well-coordinated and reasonably demanding course can be experienced by the individual in a very different way. Unfortunately, the day-to-day (not to speak of the hour-to-hour) experience of the student is rarely studied by course designers. The constant need in a traditional course programme for students to switch attention across specialisms, and to align themselves to different groups of people, can be either an inspiring stimulus or a muddling burden, depending on the individual student's capacity to cope with a variety of demands or, in less fortunate cases, their ability to defend against increasing bewilderment and anxiety by opting out and possibly failing.

Whatever kinds of group activity are formally organised, informal peer grouping will inevitably, and quite properly, occur and contribute to a greater amount of learning than commonly recognised. The effects of peer-group membership will vary with such motives and with the degree to which they find satisfaction through affiliation.

It is clearly not the task of tutors to become involved in maximising or otherwise determining peer-group affiliation and influence; to do so would be intrusive and could deprive students of essential freedom to learn in ways not available to them in the organised curriculum. It can, however, be enormously helpful for tutors to understand something of the nature of students' extra-curricular concerns and their motives for such involvement. Information of this kind could be quite valuable in forming judgements about what the course may be failing to offer any student, particularly when most of his or her energies appear to be diverted from the educational programme. Where the in-course learning groups lack an inclusive climate, either because of large numbers or a lack of concern for the students at a personal level, some students may feel alienated and gain solace from peer groups of a similar disposition. If this is so, it serves to underline the worth of aims in learning groups directed to personal development, self-esteem and a sense of belonging.

The social and organisational context in which groups exist can have a marked effect on the effectiveness of group learning and on the value placed on it by all concerned. The assumptions that learners and teachers share outside group sessions can have a profound influence on the culture that develops within them. Attitudes about particular methods, subject areas and even teachers can affect the desire to collaborate in solving problems and creating valuable innovations. In this chapter we have described ways in which all those involved can contribute to a more fruitful culture of learning in groups, whether online or face-to-face, by effectively employing group processes that transcend and provide vision beyond traditional, or otherwise supposed, social and academic boundaries.

DISCUSSION POINTS

- What external influences are there on the work of groups you belong to? In what ways do they affect what happens?
- What differences do you notice between the ways members of your group relate to each other inside as opposed to outside the seminar/meeting. What seems to determine these differences?
- How does technology as a mediator, barrier or enabler impact on the working of some of these examples? How could it have helped?
- To what extent does the physical location and timing of various groups you belong to affect the liveliness and the level of participation in them?

CHAPTER NINE

ASSESSING AND EVALUATING WITH GROUPS

This chapter examines methods that are capable of encouraging not only learning about subject knowledge but also the development of skills and a disposition to group and teamwork which can be of lifelong value – another aspect of metacognitive learning.

The linking of assessment of students and evaluation of groups[1] in the same chapter may seem unusual, but is intentional because of their close relationship where group learning is concerned. The performance and contribution of individual group members will to a large extent determine the overall success of the group. The contribution of a tutor (where there is one) will of course be an additional factor when it comes to evaluation, but where the major responsibility for a group's achievement lies in a collaborative model of learning the distinction between assessment and evaluation may be an unnecessary one.

One hears many arguments against the assessment of students in groups, some ethical and some practical. Some say that it is not the job of tutors to make judgements of personal qualities and skills, let alone develop them (though perhaps that is fear of the unfamiliar); others would claim that it is impossible to do so in a valid and reliable way, or that students would merely engage in 'faking good' – a false performance of the requisite behaviours in order to gain marks. Yet these issues are, to a greater or lesser degree, relevant to all areas of assessment. What makes assessment in group work so valuable and exciting is that in tackling the above as problems it can open students and staff to a more shared and democratic level of awareness about what is going on, what is being learned and what skills are needed to achieve that learning. Even more worrying is the tendency to try and 'force' motivation or participation in the online environment by making marks dependent on message contribution. We hope that throughout this book we have shown there are many more effective and successful ways of encouraging successful virtual group working.

---

1 North American readers please note that in the UK *assessment* refers to any measure of student achievement; *evaluation* refers to the process of getting feedback on teaching or courses.

Specifically, Biggs (2003) draws attention to what he calls the need for 'constructive alignment' of outcomes processes and assessment. He quotes Shuell (1986): 'If the students are to learn desired outcomes in a reasonably effective manner, then the teacher's fundamental task is to get the students engaged in learning activities that are likely to result in their achieving those outcomes'. Given the strong motivation that derives from assessment as attested by several contributors in Brown et al. (1998) the need to assess students' contributions to groups appears quite compelling.

Yet the problems of fairness and the ability to make valid judgements are often used to reject the idea that one can do nothing except assess individuals and then only on activities that are observable and judgeable by a teacher. In some cases they may also relieve the teacher, through the unaccustomed practice of delegation, of a considerable amount of work in marking and giving feedback. Assessment at a tacit level is going on in groups all the time, by tutor of student, student of student, student of tutor, and (as we have seen on page 59) each of these can affect others in terms of what they think the others are making of them. Better then, many would argue, to make the activity of assessment more explicit and beneficial by opening it to informed scrutiny and participation.

The idea of group assessment raises questions not normally considered which are perhaps all the more important:

- Are we assessing learning, contribution of ideas and contribution to group process, and how does the fact of assessment affect the natural flow of discussion?
- In what ways can the assessment aid the learning process?
- What method or process is used?
- At what stage does the assessment take place?
- Who actually does the assessment and of whom?
- Who decides on the criteria?
- Does the method require skills that need practice for both tutor and students?
- How is feedback given: written or spoken, written and spoken, positive before negative openly, anonymously?
- Are the rules of feedback (see page 77) respected; can it be regarded by the receiver as a 'gift'?
- Is feedback in itself all that is needed?
- What triangulation (self-peer-tutor) can be achieved bearing in mind the feedback rules on checking with a third party?
- What is the impact of assessment on relationships in the group?
- Are the necessary time and resources available to do it effectively?

THE PURPOSES OF ASSESSMENT

Assessment has many purposes, some of them not always made explicit to students. It encourages students to achieve, it allows tutors to diagnose strengths and weaknesses, it provides a profile of what students have learned, gives feedback to all parties, it reminds students about what is important, and it helps to predict success for future work and for accreditation. It can also be about building a profile as to what each member of a group has learned or contributed. But, when used to assess work in progress, it can also serve to clarify:

- Key concepts.
- Criteria and standards.
- The extent to which the overall aims are being achieved.

The Wingspread Principles of Good Practice for Assessing Student Learning (Chickering and Gamson 1989) provide substantial support for the use of assessment of group work as an integral part of the students' learning experience but also as a contribution to their personal and professional development:

PRINCIPLES OF GOOD PRACTICE FOR ASSESSING STUDENT LEARNING

The assessment of student learning begins with educational values

Assessment is not an end in itself but a vehicle for educational improvement. Its effective practice, then, begins with and enacts a vision of the kind of learning we most value for students and strive to help them achieve. Educational values should drive not only *what* we choose to assess but *how*. Where questions about educational mission and values are skipped over, assessment threatens to be an exercise in measuring what's easy, rather than a process of improving what we really care about.

Assessment is most effective when it reflects an understanding of learning as multidimensional, integrated, and revealed in performance over time

Learning is a complex process. It entails not only what students know but what they can do with what they know; it involves not only knowledge and abilities but values, attitudes and habits of mind that affect both academic success and performance beyond the classroom. Assessment should reflect these understandings by employing a diverse array of methods including those that call for actual performance, and using them over time so as to reveal change, growth and increasing degrees of integration. Such an approach aims for a more complete and accurate picture of learning and therefore firmer bases for improving our students' educational performance.

Assessment works best when the programmes it seeks to improve have clear, explicitly stated purposes

Assessment is a goal-oriented process. It entails comparing educational performance with educational purposes and expectations – these derived from the institution's mission, from faculty intentions in programme and course design, and from knowledge of students' own goals. Where programme purposes lack specificity or agreement, assessment as a process pushes a campus towards clarity about where to aim and what standards to apply; assessment also prompts attention to where and how programme goals will be taught and learned. Clear, shared, implementable goals are the cornerstone for assessment that is focused and useful.

Assessment requires attention to outcomes but also and equally to the experiences that lead to those outcomes

Information about outcomes is of high importance: where students end up matters greatly. But to improve outcomes, we need to know about student experience along the way – about the curricula, teaching and kind of student effort that lead to particular outcomes. Assessment can help us understand which students learn best under what conditions; with such knowledge comes the capacity to improve the whole of their learning.

Assessment works best when it is ongoing, not episodic

Assessment is a process whose power is cumulative. Although isolated, 'one-shot' assessment can better than none, improvement is best fostered when assessment entails a linked series of activities taken over time. This may mean tracking the progress of individual students, or of cohorts of students; it may mean collecting the same examples of student performance or using the same instrument semester after semester. The point is to monitor progress towards intended goals in a spirit of intended improvement. Along the way, the assessment process itself should be evaluated and refined in the light of emerging insights.

Assessing in groups is more visible, open and public compared to the more closed, sometimes secretive individual assessment. If undertaken online, it can be faster and more available to review and audit. There needs to be a degree of openness in the sharing of data, whether it is about written work or personal behaviour. Assessing in groups raises questions and open debate on what education is all about and more specifically about what the learning outcomes of a course are: how explicit they are; what encouragement and support the students get in attaining them; and how responsibility may be shared for their assessment.

Assessment in groups brings with it a fundamental question: who is qualified to make that assessment? The word 'qualified' here has two dimensions, one to do with being a valid observer and the other with being properly trained in the assessment role. When leading a discussion a tutor or e-moderator is in a position to make some evaluation of students' contributions, but what can he or she say about students involved in any of the structured activities or group projects discussed in Chapter 6 where they do not have access to the process of each group? Then there is the question of reliability. If a tutor is part of the group, is his or her judgement alone adequate? Does what the tutor observes tally with what is noticed by the rest of the group? A student who constantly confirms the tutor's stand or is always ready to give an academically sound response may restrict the contributions from the rest of the group. The argument for including the students in their own assessment is therefore a compelling one.

There are probably four major areas in which groups can be engaged in assessment: where they are used *for* assessment; for written or spoken presentations; for functions or behavioural skills that help group discussion; and for contributions to project teams.

Groups used for assessment

There are situations where groups may be formed purely for assessment needs, either on grounds of economy or student preference.

An example of this procedure is in Grant (1996) who describes a form of viva voce, or oral assessment for an in-service diploma course for teachers in which the group served as a context in which individual assessment took place. Students had already been given the option of being assessed by written examination or orally in a small group of four or five. The idea of using a group in this way was based on view that teaching is a cooperative activity.

Prior to the assessment, students were given planning sheets with the learning outcomes of each unit of the course and a set of questions to help them focus on the sort of questions they might be asked. The structure of the assessment process was made clear beforehand as a way of reducing anxiety, and every effort was made to create a physical environment which was as relaxing as possible. Before they started their assessment students were reminded of the ground rules: they had to speak from their own experience, making 'I' statements, as the assessors were mostly interested in what the students actually did in their own teaching. They were also encouraged to interact with each other in the group and add to each other's contributions: the event was intended to be a learning experience as well as an assessment. The two assessors made notes on the achievements of each student against the prepared criteria and whenever they were satisfied that these had been met for any one unit, they moved on to the next, the choice of this sometimes being given to the students. The students knew in advance the areas in which they would be assessed. Once the assessors felt they had enough evidence from any particular student on which to make their decision, the student was invited to give a brief oral self-assessment of their performance before being given feedback on how well they had performed. The assessors discussed their assessment openly in front of the other students.

The assessors asked challenging questions and had to exercise considerable group skills to ensure coverage of any learning outcome and to judge when to move on to another. A reasonable degree of objectivity was achieved by having one of the two assessors take notes which could be used as documentary evidence.

On some occasions the students were allowed to choose which colleagues they wanted be assessed with, but that was not always convenient and there was also a risk that a particular mix of group members might not be conducive to the task.

Groups can also be used to develop a deeper appreciation of criteria and standards in written work. Here is one example. Students are asked 'What are we looking for in a "good" essay/report/review' or other written work and, using a cumulative method like the snowball or pyramid, they then generate a set of criteria, one in turn from each of the final sub-groups. These can be compared with those of the tutor and moderated before the students go away to write their assignment. This work is brought to a subsequent group meeting and must have that is a self-assessment attached based on the criteria. The assignments are then handed to the group or sub-groups for circulation, each person giving the writer a grade and at least 50 words of feedback. The tutor then takes the assignments in and marks them with feedback not only to the writer but to the peer assessors. While this may seem to create a lot of extra work, it can pay enormous dividends in getting the students to internalise criteria and standards and thus relying less on retrospective feedback from the tutor. It can also serve to prepare the students for self- and peer-assessment of future written work.

The main principle in using groups for this kind of assessment is that, by comparing self with others and by identifying with peers in familiar and similar situations, students are opening themselves to a wider range of possible skills and behaviours. This is particularly so when seminar presentations are assessed. As we have already noted, seminar presentations are often poorly executed by anxious students to a group of peers who are likely to be equally anxious on their behalf. There are ways to reduce this anxiety, such as the role play described on page 267, but there is still the problem of how students can learn to present more effectively. Here again a 'front-end investment' of a brief training session can be of great benefit. The Back-to-Back exercise on page 311 in the Appendix, requiring only 30 minutes to run, will give students enjoyable practice and a set of criteria with which to prepare their presentations. A more specific tool such as the Seminar Peer Assessment Form (Figure 9.1) or the Seminar Presentation Mark and Feedback Sheet (Figure 9.2) may then be used for an assessment. Note that both of these include items concerned with skills in handling group discussion.

Patchwork texts

> The patchwork text deconstructs the essay's monolithic finalising unity into a series of fragments, with a possible overall pattern that is waiting to be synthesised by means of a personal journey of exploration. Thus, it embodies a model of learning as an act of imagination, i.e. as an essentially creative process of discovering links between matters that may seem initially to be separate.
>
> (Winter 2003)

The value of formative feedback is central to this innovatory form of assessment. Rather than writing a sizeable end-of-term assignment, students are required to build up their assignment through a series of varied writing tasks which are successively marked and finally incorporated into a composite whole – the patchwork. In most cases students working in groups share their work progressively and get peer feedback. They are thus able to reflect, refocus and develop their skills, style and argument with consequently less and anxiety; the tutors are able better to gauge the students' progress and encourage a clearly articulated development. And the tutor is able to feel a direct and contributory

STUDENT .... SEMINAR PRESENTER					
	Excellent	Good	Adequate	Poor	None
1 Quality of preparation Handouts, advanced reading, briefing, support and advice *Comment*	2	1½	1	½	0
2 Quality of explanation Clear grasp of topic clear answers to questions *Comment*	2	1½	1	½	0
3 Quality of sources Wide range of relevant sources. References provided for reading *Comment*	2	1½	1	½	0
4 Quality of presentation Good use of AV aids, handouts, pace, lively *Comment*	2	1½	1	½	0
5 Quality of discussion Interesting and effective group methods used, all took active part *Comment*	2	1½	1	½	0
Overall comment:	**Total** ☐ (Maximum 10 marks)				

Figure 9.1 Seminar peer assessment

part in that process. One who conducted a comparative study of 'intercultural' student groups doing patchwork assessments with those doing an essay assignment (Illes 2003) noted:

> I had the feeling that all the essays were rather similar in structure and style and had a sense of uniformity about them, whereas [with] the patchwork assignments . . . visual images of students started to appear in front of my eyes. Their work revealed many of their individual thoughts, their beliefs and values. Often it felt as though the student was guiding me through a personal journey through their culture.

She also noted that group norms influenced those who were not fully committed to the approach and that those more competent in English started to act as coaches with those less fluent in the language.

Criterion	Mark	Comments

Content:
  clarity of argument,
  understanding,
  overview, conclusion
	0% 1% 2% 3% 4% 5%	

Soruces:
  breadth and relevance
  acknowledgement
  references
	0% 1% 2% 3% 4% 5%	

Presentation:
  voice, use of AV aids,
  pace, variety, notes
	0% 1% 2% 3% 4% 5%	

Group skills:
  structuring, engaging
  questioning, answering
	0% 1% 2% 3% 4% 5%	

Total (maximum 20%		
Your best skills		
Your weakest skills		
How you might improve your performance		
Tutor .... Date		

Figure 9.2 Seminar presentation marks and feedback

The nature of the final 'patchwork' may vary – literary, visual , interactive, online – all are possibilities, sometimes determined by the nature of the student's work, sometimes prescribed.

The patchwork text has radical implications for:

- The presentation of learning in writing.
- The integration of group and developmental learning.
- Assessment of learning processes as well as the learning 'product'.
- Supporting a variety of learner styles.
- The integration of academic and creative writing development.
- Facilitating autonomous learning.

- Widening access and building on prior experiential learning.
- Academic literacy for academic and professional practices.

USING NEW TECHNOLOGIES IN ASSESSMENT

Learning technologies offer us new ways of thinking about assessment of individuals and group learning and achievement. Just like teaching and learning processes, assessment can take place entirely online or blended with more traditional approaches. Alignment can be achieved by using online assessment where all or part of the learning takes place virtually (Gibbs 2004).

Assessment consumes a large part of staff teaching time and rarely achieves economy of scale. However, just like teaching and learning online, simply 'applying' technology merely achieves worry and frustration – it cannot be a magic bullet (Davies and Graff 2005). A fair measure of rethinking the approach needs to lie alongside the practical process.

Some of the benefits of introducing e-assessment into group work are:

- Devising more efficient assessment programmes that balance summative assessments with formative assessments, through the virtual learning environment. Most of the more popular VLEs offer tools to assist with assessment.
- Developing students' self-assessment and peer-assessment skills systematically from their first year onwards and if possible, maintaining a record in an e-portfolio.
- Balancing e-assessment demands across the timeline of a course, by offering small but frequent online assessment tasks. Students work consistently and with purpose, in and out of class, and receive regular motivational feedback on their performance.
- Realigning how tutors deliver feedback by integrating feedback into teaching and learning processes. Online offers ways of providing quick and easy feedback which students enjoy and tutors find efficient to offer.
- Creating conditions in which feedback is attended to and acted upon by students – perhaps linking future group work to individual feedback.

TECHNOLOGIES TO SUPPORT E-ASSESSMENT

- *Classroom communication technologies*: technologies that facilitate interaction in large lecture classes. Tests are presented in class and student respond using electronic handsets. Electronic voting systems (EVS) are popular with staff and students. These technologies have great potential to provide immediate feedback and they support self- and peer-assessment and small group discussion in large classes.
- *E-portfolios*: electronic portfolios support personal development planning and self-regulated learning by students. Learners reflect on and select learning outputs to record and monitoring of work by staff.

▼

- *Online simulations and games*: provide intrinsic and dynamic feedback to students often embedded in real-life examples, e.g. problem-solving, and decision-making in business. Simulations help integrate knowledge from different disciplines and enhance motivation.
- *Online exemplars and models* of written work, such as essays and reports, with feedback. Groups can use these to help understand their task and what counts as 'good performance'. They might be asked to compare their work with exemplars to encourage self-assessment and self-correction.
- *Databases and lists of frequently asked questions (FAQs)*: a form of self-assessment with feedback. Students select questions that they wish answers to and receive feedback results.
- *Answer gardens*: a way of building up answers to questions previously asked by students and formulating these into online reusable resources. Typical questions and answers can be carried forward from year to year and module to module. It is important that they are grouped and classified and searchable.
- *Online questions posted by students*: if done before lectures or tutorials this form of feedback helps staff to tailor the teaching to students needs.
- *Online diagnostic tests*: short tests used to gauge classroom understanding at key points during the course.
- *Online tests*: provide immediate feedback, repetition and reinforcement. They are useful in skills learning where practice is essential such as problem solving and as a self-assessment task to help develop autonomy.
- *Databanks of feedback comments*: can be used by tutors to respond to students' written work more efficiently.
- *Peer marking and assignment distribution management software*: helps tutors manage peer-marking processes. It supports anonymous sharing of students' work amongst peers and the collation and distribution of peer feedback.
- *Plagiarism detection software*: can automate some of the work required by staff to ensure that assignments submitted by students are actually produced by them.

Many thanks to Dr Gillian Roberts from Caledonian Business School and her insights into the SHEFC E-learning Transformation Project: Re-engineering Assessment Practices in Scottish Higher Education.

ASSESSING GROUP SKILLS

The skills required for effective participation in groups are complex and inter-relating but as we have seen in Chapter 2 there are some very clear functions which can be identified and thus promoted. Much interest in the past ten years in the UK has centred on the development of transferable or key skills. Whether skills are in reality transferable or not is discussed thoroughly by Neath (1998), who concludes that they are transferable only in the sense that people who have well-developed problem-solving skills are able to interpret a new situation and find the necessary skills to match it.

The need for skills in group work to be embedded in the curriculum is portrayed in the TDMA model in Figure 9.3. If a skill is to be effectively developed the students must first receive some *training* in it – they cannot all be expected to possess it to the required degree – and it seems unfair to allow the experience of a group or project team to suffer as a result. If they are to apply what they have learned from the training the students will need to practise the skill, and in the competing priorities of student life there must therefore be a *demand* for its use and for appropriate learning time to be allocated to tasks in which the skills are employed. The acquisition of skills is, as we already know, an uncertain process in which other factors like anxiety and surprise can have a profound effect; and it does not take place as an immediate consequence of a training exercise. Skills continue to develop over a period of time until they become embedded in the subconscious, but that development needs *monitoring* through rehearsal, feedback and review. Self-assessment can, in the context of group feedback, be especially valuable here, and it is *assessment* that provides the final element in successful skill development, given that so much student learning is driven by assessment. The team-based learning model (page 213) embodies many of the principles of TDMA.

However, whether we describe items as skills, behaviours or functions, they cannot operate without a recognition of concomitant dispositions and values. Someone who is a brilliant initiator or clarifier in terms of the content may be so arrogant or unaware of colleagues' contributions that discussion is uneasy and tense.

At Alverno College, Milwaukee, a distinction is made between a task-oriented group model and an interpersonal problem-solving model, the primary goal in the former being the achievement of the task and in the latter, the relationship between group members, although each has the other as a

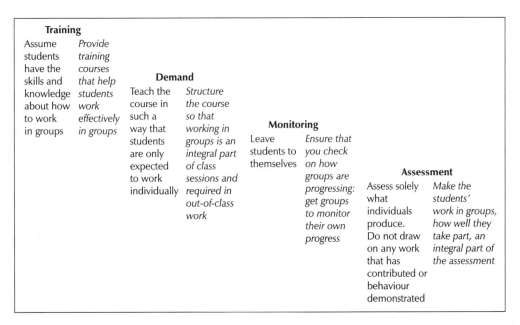

Figure 9.3 The TDMA model for developing skills (traditional practice in plain type; preferred practice in italics)

secondary goal. In task-oriented groups it is assumed that 'efficient and effective group process is possible when group members collaborate through a series of interdependent behaviours to accomplish the task in hand'. Students are assessed on their group skills, using a checklist which includes the following stages:

- *Orientation*: Leading (initiating), information/opinion seeking, information/opinion giving and reinforcing (encouraging others).
- *Examination*: advocating, challenging mediating and reinforcing (supporting the opinions of others).
- *Synthesis*: summarising, evaluating, leading (consensus and the consequences of decisions).
- *Termination*: closure, reinforcing (giving recognition to others).

In addition to these positive behaviours Alverno includes a set of blocking behaviours – attacking, dominating, interfering, withdrawing and being defensive – that undermine group effectiveness.

The assessment is done by self, peers and a member of the local community called the 'off-campus assessor'. All three parties are given training in assessment processes. The actual event, which Alverno has demonstrated at their summer workshop, has each group in turn seated at a round table with the task of reaching consensus on a given problem. External assessors for each students are also present. As soon as the task is completed or the allocated time is up, the external assessors leave the room while the self- and peer-assessment takes place. In another room the external assessors meanwhile come to a consensus about the students' effectiveness or less productive behaviours and agree on the main areas to discuss with each of the two students they have observed. Each assessor then provides feedback privately to one student. The succession of events was: discussion, self-assessment, peer-assessment and external assessment, each done independently and revealed in that order. The student's self-assessment of the group interaction and the external assessors' feedback are entered into the student's digital diagnostic portfolio. and as the student progresses through her programme of studies, she enters selected performances and her self-assessments of them. Faculty and external assessors also continue to enter selected feedback into the digital portfolio. The student can look at her self-assessments or feedback over many performances and see how she is developing, and so she can compare how she interacted in a group assessment in her first semester with an assessment in her third semester and so on.

The skills identified for the interpersonal problem-solving model at Alverno are:

- *Personal statements* (or 'I' Statements): reflect own thoughts, feelings, beliefs, ideas.
- *Expression of feelings*: identifies emotional responses to problems; expresses relevant feelings.
- *Perception checking*: reflects tentatively what other person expresses and confirms its accuracy.
- *Paraphrasing or active listening*: restates other's comments in own words.
- *Empathic statements*: give insight into other's concerns, gets 'into' other's perspective.

- *Open-ended questioning*: asks questions that allow other to explore viewpoints.
- *Behavioural descriptions*: describe observable actions of another without judgement or interpretation.
- *Appropriate nonverbal behaviour*: demonstrates congruence between oral and body language.
- *Physical attending*: leans towards, maintains eye contact with other; open, relaxed posture;
- *Listening*: pays careful attention to spoken and unspoken communication.
- *Avoiding giving advice*: elicits solutions from other, brainstorms alternatives.
- *Constructive confrontation*: tries to help others to examine consequences of their behaviour' requests change in specific behaviour.
- *Monitoring verbal and nonverbal congruence*: identifies discrepancies and points them out using behavioural descriptions and constructive confrontation.
- *Positive reinforcement*: uses verbal and non-verbal support; avoids making judgements of others.

In formal discussion groups where there may be more emphasis on academic discourse a slightly different set of criteria may be more relevant. The following list, a favourite of mine (for which credit to an anonymous author), describes 'the important things students do for which they should be given credit'.

General	Discussing this list with peers
	Attendance and attending
To do with the content	Preparing for the session by thinking and/or reading
	Asking questions
	– clear questions
	– open questions
	– creative questions
	Clear explanations, definitions of terms
	Making logical connections
	Keeping to the topic
	Condensation (being succinct)
To do with the process	Intellectual risk-taking
	Not dominating or oppressing by speaking too loud, too long or too oppressively in any way
	Expressing appropriate emotions
	Thoughtful, comfortable silence

	Altruism, sharing
	Bringing others in by verbal and non-verbal means
	Awareness of group dynamics for self and others
Personal matters	Willing to speak personally and bring personal experience as well as cognitive stuff into the discussion
	Acceptance of all group members
	Equal rights for self and others
	Finding and using own voice
Other comments	

Whatever the complications of organising the assessment with such a rich array of criteria, it is easy to see that what the students learn in discussing and agreeing them will make a substantial contribution to an effective learning process in the group. Such is the power of openness and the sharing responsibility.

A simpler and equally productive form of self (and possibly peer) assessment might be simply to raise both individual and group awareness of what skills and qualities are likely to help each member, and the group as a whole, to gain more from the group process in terms of both learning and teamwork. In this, the group is told that each member will be asked to self-assess using the checklist in Figure 9.4 at the start, the middle and the end of the term or semester with the added requirement of checking this with a different peer each time. Even if the assessment is solely for personal feedback, students will be thus encouraged give more attention to their own behaviour and that of others as the group progresses.

THE SKILLS OF ASSESSMENT

As we have already noted (Chapter 3) self- and peer-assessment are very influential in the promotion of metacognition. To assess oneself and a peer, and to draw comparisons between the two, causes a level of thinking in which one goes 'beyond' and 'without' the problem identified. In other words one is thinking at more than one level in both time and space. Students can perform a variety of assessment tasks in ways which both save the tutor's time and bring educational benefits. They need to develop their ability to make this kind of judgement and to give constructive feedback, and this takes time and practice. They need to be convinced of the value, and validity, of self-assessment. For this reason it is safer to start with self- and peer-assessment for the purpose of feedback rather than to get involved straight away with marking which counts towards a final qualification. It is important that students have a chance to test and refine their judgements and marks against those of the tutor before their own marks are taken into account. It also makes sense for tutors to provide their own criteria when trying out self-assessment for the first time before allowing students to use their own criteria.

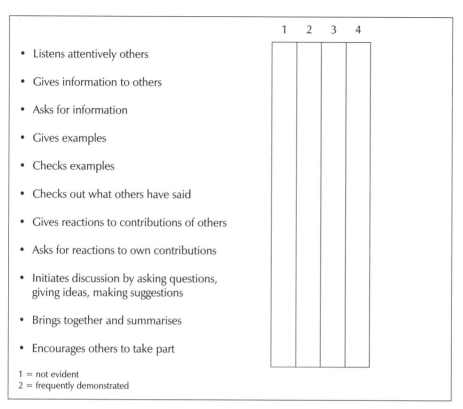

	1	2	3	4
• Listens attentively others				
• Gives information to others				
• Asks for information				
• Gives examples				
• Checks examples				
• Checks out what others have said				
• Gives reactions to contributions of others				
• Asks for reactions to own contributions				
• Initiates discussion by asking questions, giving ideas, making suggestions				
• Brings together and summarises				
• Encourages others to take part				

1 = not evident
2 = frequently demonstrated

Figure 9.4 Skills for student participation

There are many possible stages and choices in this self- and peer-assessment, each of which involves some form of delegation or relinquishing of control to the students; and they can be mutually exclusive. For example students can be offered a choice of assessment tasks or invited to set and conduct the assessment. They may be invited to discuss prepared assessment criteria or to set them. They can give feedback to themselves or their peers with or without giving marks. They can assign marks, suggest marks for the tutor to moderate or negotiate them with the tutor. Assessment by oneself, a peer and the tutor can be 'triangulated' between the three parties.

All of these practices can be part of a process for the students in which they learn more about group skills and about the task of giving a fair assessment based on them. Boud (1991) describes research which indicated that two of the most important skills for professional work (which are incidentally two of the most underemphasised in higher education) are teamwork and the ability to assess one's own and others' contribution to it.

The evident fact that to engage in self- and peer-assessment, to any of the degrees suggested above, can be very complex and time-consuming if done properly has to be seen in the light of the learning benefits that can nevertheless accrue. In their handbook 'Student Assessment as Learning' the Alverno College Faculty (undated) promote the view of assessment as a 'multidimensional process, integral to learning, that involves observing performances of an individual learner in action and judging them on the basics of public developmental criteria, with resulting feedback to that learner'. They ask fundamental questions like:

- How do we know a given performance is representative?
- Is the student having an unusually bad day?
- Can she exhibit the same abilities under different circumstances?
- How varied need the samples be to suggest the complexity of an ability?

and they pose the further questions:

- Are the abilities being assessed *integrated* (with values, attitudes, behaviours)?
- Are they *developmental* (can they be extended, inferences made)?
- Are they *transferable* (preparing students for new and different roles and settings)?

The Alverno assessment process is so central to the learning strategy of the college that all concerned are given rigorous training in the designing of learning outcomes, criteria, modes of assessment, assessment and feedback strategies.

Self- and peer-assessment can be used in at least two other ways that promote metacognitive learning: assessment of the written work of each of the other members of the group, and one group conducting the assessment of another – a 'fishbowl' assessment.

A full, fair and rigorous assessment is never a straightforward task; one reason for the continued existence of the traditional system of essays, reports and exams is that it has been thoroughly tried out and has stood the test of time, at least in the sense that all involved appear to be familiar with its processes and procedures. But another reason may be to do with the fear of losing control by using unfamiliar and more visible methods: to involve students intimately in the process is to lose some of that control and with it some of the arcane aspects of the relationship between tutor and student. That aside, it is apparent that participatory assessment can be a complex process and that the justification for it must be in the learning value of it and the greater sense of student commitment (Creme 1995), democracy and fairness that can or should accompany it. This is certainly true for the assessment of group projects which we shall look at now.

Assessing group projects

The kinds of behaviour valued in project work differ in many ways from those of discussion and therefore require somewhat different criteria. Projects are of necessity more task-oriented, using a wider range of skills such as problem-solving, organising, chairing and editing. They are not subject to a regular timetable, nor are they accessible to regular observation by the tutor. Their autonomous nature means not only that the groups themselves are often (but not always) the best judges of how effectively they have worked, but the tutor may have to rely principally on what the group reports rather than on live interactions.

Assessing the contribution of individuals within a group

Where group projects are undertaken the work is often assessed as the single product of the group and each individual within the group gets the group mark regardless of the value of their individual contribution. In terms of the values already expressed in this chapter an appropriate assessment would be one which would retain the value placed on group cooperation and the submission of a single group product for assessment but also add a dimension of individual assessment which:

- Provides a sense of fairness to individuals such that good students don't have to 'carry' or get dragged down by poor or lazy students.
- Takes into account the different levels and qualities of contribution which individuals can make to their group.
- Serves as guide to the students on the behaviour, skills, attitudes and work styles likely to lead to the successful completion of the project.

The methods described all assume that the group still submits a group project report of some kind. The group mark is then added to or modified by one or more of these methods: shared group grade, peer assessment of contribution to the group, peer feedback on contribution to the group, project exam and oral assessment.

Shared group grade

A major difficulty in assessing the contribution of individuals within a group is that the tutor may not have much idea about which individual students have done what. However, the students themselves are in a very good position to make such judgements. Although the tutor can only award a mark to the group, the members of that group can be left to distribute the mark between themselves in a way which they think reflects the relative contributions of individuals. For example if a group of five students were to be awarded 60 per cent for a group report, they would be given $5 \times 60 = 300$ marks to distribute amongst themselves.

There are three ways in which groups tend to react in this situation:

- Some groups will agree at the start of the project that all marks will be shared equally at the end, in order to avoid unpleasantness. Such groups must face the prospect of individual group members doing little work, safe in the knowledge that they will get the same mark as the rest of the group.
- Other groups will not discuss assessment at all until it comes to dividing up the marks. They then find that they disagree about the basis upon which the marks should be divided. Some will value creativity, some will value workload, some will value leadership, some will value the ability to communicate the project outcomes, and so on. Without prior agreement about criteria there are likely to be arguments about who should get what marks for which contributions.

- Some groups will sit down at the start and decide what criteria they will use in allocating marks, and will keep to these criteria. Everyone will be clear about what their contribution ought to be, and will be more likely to accept the final allocation of marks.

This third way of dealing with shared group grades is clearly the most satisfactory and the tutor can help students by organising discussion and negotiation of criteria at the start of the project. If time doesn't permit this, the tutor can impose her/his own criteria which the students then use to allocate the marks. It is crucial, however, that the criteria are made clear and accepted at the start of the project, and not pulled out of thin air at the end. There are two rather different ways in which criteria can be used:

- Students may naturally adopt different working roles within the group, or the project may even specify such roles. For example one student may become the chairperson, one the note-taker, one the data-analyser, one the report-writer, one the 'ideas person' and so on. In this case assessment criteria can focus on how well each student performed his or her different role.
- Every student may be expected to contribute equally to all aspects of the project (for example, each writing one section of a group report). In this case each criterion should be applied equally to each student.

Figures 9.5 and 9.6 are more explicit and perhaps more 'user-friendly' proformas for assessing individual contributions to the report which can, of course, be helpful indicators of desirable skills and attributes if shown and tested early in the project.

Project exam

One way to test an individual's knowledge when group work has been assessed is to set an exam. However, conventional exams, with their tendency to emphasise memorising and regurgitation of factual information, are quite unsuitable for a project-based course. They can completely distort the aims of the course by distracting students from their project work because they know that they are not going to be tested on it in the exam. However, there are forms of exam which avoid these problems by asking students questions directly related to their project work.

For example on an estate management course students undertook a substantial case study involving the simulated purchase of a building site and its subsequent commercial development. This they wrote up in a report consisting of a log of their calculations, decisions, problems, etc. The examination questions took the form:

Q. If there was a three month national building strike starting on week 3 of the simulation, how would this affect your handling of the case?

Q. If outline planning consent were granted for a competing major shopping precinct at the north end of the High Street on week 14 of the simulation (see details below), how would you advise your client?

ROBERT GORDON UNIVERSITY
School of Computer and Mathematical Sciences

CONFIDENTIAL
PEER GROUP ASSESSMENT FORM

Bsc in Mathematical Sciences with Computing – Mathematical Models and Methods

Please assess your colleague by giving a mark of 1–5 (by ticking the appropriate box) in each of the following 10 categories

NB This form will be treated in strict confidence

Name (of colleague being assessed):

	5	4	3	2	1	
Regularly makes a useful contribution in group discussion						Finds it difficult to be a contributing group member
Can be relied upon to carry out allocated duties accurately and without supervision						Needs more supervision than most in carrying out instructions assigned to him/her
Works amicably with others as a member of a team						Has difficulty in working with colleagues and is sometimes not accepted as a member of the team
Responds well to instructions/advice/criticism						Resents criticism and is reluctant to accept advice
Is consistently courteous and helpful to colleagues						Appears off-hand and casual in dealing with colleagues
Shows excellent ability to plan and complete own work						Has not yet learnt to organize own work effectively
Is outstanding in ability to organize and supervise work of others						Is not able to organize and supervise work of others
Grasps essentials very quickly						Has difficulty in recognizing essentials
Successfully anticipates the requirements of new situations and takes appropriate action						Has difficulty in recognizing implications of new situations
Is good at solving problems						Has difficulty in suggesting solutions to problems

Comments:

Your Name: **Date:**

Figure 9.5 Peer assessment of contribution to group

Bsc in Mathematical Sciences with Computing – Mathematical Models and Methods

Please assess your colleague by giving a mark of 1–5 (by ticking the appropriate box) in each of the following 10 categories

NB This form will be treated in strict confidence

Name (of colleague being assessed):

5 4 3 2 1

Demonstrates awareness of the structure and presentation requirements of report writing	Seems unaware of the structure and presentation requirements of report writing
Shows excellent ability to plan and complete own elements of written teamwork	Has not yet learnt to organize self as part of a writing team
Keeps colleagues informed about progress of the task	Appears casual in dealing with colleagues
Successfully anticipates requirements of a situation and takes appropriate action	Has difficulty recognizing implications of a situation
Is outstanding in ability to integrate and can amend and check written work	Is not able to integrate or amend and check written work

Comments:

Your Name: **Date:**

Figure 9.6 Peer assessment of group activity pro forma

Students had their log books and other case material to hand and were expected to use these in answering the questions. Such questions cannot be answered from memory, or even directly from this information, but only from students' experience and understanding of the case study.

In this first example, all students undertook the same project work individually. In the second example, below, students had been working in separate groups and individuals had been awarded a group grade. The exam in this case was designed to test individuals' understanding and to produce a mark for each individual student. The context was a catering management course in which groups of eight students tackled a simulated management problem. Within the groups students performed different roles (for example secretary, report-writer) and so they almost certainly learned different things. The course was designed to apply management principles to a specific and complex situation. An exam was used to test individuals' ability to apply these principles to the work of their own groups.

The exam question took the form:

Q. How can pricing and marketing policies influence other management decisions concerning catering outlets? Give specific examples from the simulation to illustrate your points.

The first part of this question is general, in that it is based on management principles learned at an earlier stage in the course. It is the second part which tests students' ability to apply these principles to their project work. This type of exam has the added advantage that if students know at the outset that they will be expected to answer questions of this form, they are more likely to be reflective about theory and general principles during the simulation than to get overwhelmed with practical details and forget the purpose of the exercise.

Oral assessment of projects

This serves the same function as a project exam: it allows individuals to be questioned about their understanding of the group's final report. This can be done quickly and flexibly in an interview. An interviewer can ask about:

- The content of the report.
- The group processes involved in creating it.
- Problems encountered and how these were overcome.
- The particular elements of the group's work for which the individual was responsible (and not responsible).

The interviewer would have the marked group report to hand in order to ask specific questions possibly using the same model as described on page 232. Marking could be undertaken in one of two ways:

- The group report is marked out of 80 and the project viva out of 20 (or some other balance such as 60/40). The individual student gets the group mark plus his or her project viva mark.

■ The group report is marked out of 100 and the individual mark is arrived at by modifying this up or down up to 10 per cent according to how well the student performs in the viva.

Assessment of group process

A major aim of some projects is to develop the students' cooperative groupwork skills and an accompanying awareness of how groups operate effectively. If students are going to take this aim seriously then the group process, rather than only the product of the group's work, needs to be assessed in some way. If process issues are to be assessed, then some mid-project feedback to groups is probably necessary to guide groups in the right direction.

Assessing process is often trickier than assessing an end product, partly because process is more transitory, partly because both lecturers and students lack experience in the assessment of process and partly because it is not so readily accessible to a second opinion . Whatever methods are tried are likely to suffer from unexpected problems to some extent. The choice and operation of assessment methods will need to be kept under review. The crucial measure of the success of the introduction of the assessment of process will be evidence of students' increased awareness of, and attention to, process issues in the ways they run their groups, and a corresponding improvement in group performance. Assessment methods need not be particularly reliable or valid to achieve this. The following options may be used for assessing group process.

Observation of process

The tutor sits in on each group once and assesses the way they conduct and plan their business. The group is not warned when this will be, but receive explicit criteria in advance. One of the checklists on group process in this chapter for example could be used, modified as below in order to grade the group on each rating scale. This would give a total score out of 35.

Assessment interview on process

Each group could be interviewed about how they had operated as a group and carried out the project. It should become clear whether a competent leader is 'faking good' to cover up the failings of weaker group members. Such an assessment interview could be undertaken by one of the other groups, given appropriate briefing.

Presentations on process

Groups could be asked to each give a 20-minute presentation about the way they operated, the problems they encountered working together, how they tackled these problems and what they have learnt. These presentations could be assessed by the tutors or peer-assessed by the other groups. Each group could discuss the presentation for five minutes and give a group grade. The group giving the presentation would get the total of these grades (4 and 2 are simply intermediate positions):

5 = group showed great awareness of group processes, tackled process problems with vigour, sensitivity, imagination and demonstrable success.

4 =

3 = group showed moderate awareness of group processes, tackled some problems with some signs of sensitivity, but with limited vigour and imagination and with limited proof of success.

2 =

1 = group showed little awareness of group processes, appeared not to tackle problems, or tackled them half-heartedly and/or insensitively and with no sign of success.

With five groups of eight, each group would be graded by four groups, giving a maximum score of 20.

This presentation and peer-assessment could be undertaken (without contributing to the final mark) mid-way through the year in order to tune the groups in to process issues and demonstrate effective and ineffective ways for groups to pay attention to process issues.

Process review

The groups could have a review of their group processes with a tutor prior to any of the other assessment processes (e.g. prior to *presentations on process*). This would not itself be assessed, but act as a tutorial for groups so that they can prepare themselves for the assessment of process more effectively.

Essay on process

Groups could be asked to submit an essay, at the end of the year, based on the diaries of individuals in the group, on the process issues which have arisen and been addressed by the group through the year. A brief essay or report could be written by each group and shared between groups half way through the year. This would not be for marking, but, again, in order to tune the groups in to process issues.

Final report: section on process

One section of the final group project report could be on process issues. The number of marks allocated to the discussion of process issues out of the total allocated to the report could be specified (e.g. 20 per cent).

Use of diaries or logs

The diaries themselves could be assessed in terms of the awareness and analysis of process issues of individuals as revealed by entries throughout the year. Some of the other assessment processes described here (e.g. interview on process) could contribute to diaries and the diaries could be assessed rather than the contributing events. There is a danger with assessing individuals' reports of group processes that they may invent, idealise and blame others in ways which a whole group would not.

Assessment criteria

Whatever assessment process is used (exam, essay, report, presentation) criteria should be specified explicitly and include those concerned with awareness and analysis of process issues. The criteria may be pre-determined, negotiated with all the groups or negotiated with each group while including a core of common criteria. The process of proposing and negotiating criteria can be of great help in the students' awareness and ownership of group process. Typical criteria for group assessment (Heathfield, in Brown and Glasner 1999) might be:

- Regular attendance at the group preparing material for the task.
- Contribution of ideas for the task.
- Researching, analysing and preparing material for the task.
- Contributing to the cooperative group process.
- Supporting and encouraging group members.
- Practical contribution to the end product.
- Competitive cooperation.

Figure 9.6, a proforma used in assessing group activity, illustrates both the factors that contribute to successful teamwork and a wider range of behaviours that can be used in peer assessment than can ever be observable by a tutor.

Profiles

A list of specified desired group behaviours could be drawn up and groups assessed by writing up a profile rather than by awarding a grade. This might involve one of the checklists on pages 232 to 234. A description of the strengths and weaknesses of the group as a working group may be more valuable to the group than a mark. Each student could also have a profile drawn up to compare with that of the group as a whole.

Conclusion

So the assessment of groups, far from being an optional extra, has an important and integral role to play in the all-round education of students. It raises the awareness in students of their own responsibility for making the process work and, if we include self and peer assessment and feedback, to learn about two salient professional skills – *teamwork* and the *ability to judge the work of self and others*. By focusing on collective outcomes, the students can achieve more in comparing and contrasting themselves than they would as individuals working alone. What is perhaps even more important is that they are likely to give any assessment of their group skills and their contribution to the work of the group much more notice, to the extent that they feel some ownership of the process and identification with each other in it. And we should not forget the benefits to the tutor too: it can (indeed should) lead to a raised sense of autonomy and improved quality of group work as students continue on the course; and the tutor will have less marking to do with a consequent reduction in the demand on resources.

EVALUATING GROUPS

Whenever two or more people interact they are in some sense evaluating one another. Tutors do it of students, students of teachers, each of their own colleagues. Although the tutor's job is to make judgements about students, we may not feel so happy about students openly reciprocating the process and judging something we feel responsible for. Something much more precious and sensitive seems to be at stake: our self-esteem. There are, too, understandable doubts among teachers about any evaluation which attempts to judge complex phenomena in simplistic terms. Teachers, as Miller (1975) remarks, are sceptical that the intricate network of their experience, which contributes to their concept of themselves as a teacher, can be encompassed in some kind of measurement which is either meaningful or helpful. Yet even if a suitable kind of measurement were available, the probability is that some teachers would find 20 good academic reasons why their self-image should not come under scrutiny.

The major part of this problem is possibly that a sense of being judged is likely to create a defensive reaction. In the view of Gibb (1961), a defensive climate results from the sort of communication which displays evaluation, control, strategy, neutrality, superiority or certainty. Supportive or coop-erative climates, on the other hand, have the following qualities: description, problem-orientation, spontaneity, empathy, equality and provisionalism. Each of these corresponds to its equivalent defensive quality taken in the same area. Thus it is more supportive to say, 'Just then, it seemed as if you were having difficulty with students who wanted to go their own way in the discussion' (provisionalism), rather than, 'You can't control discussions!' (certainty).

The way in which evaluation is handled is clearly of great importance if the results are to be accepted and acted on positively. A lot of the threat can be taken out of an evaluation if as much initiative and responsibility as possible rests with the person being evaluated, as may be seen in the approach for a tutor with a group in Figure 9.7. This process need not be just for the tutor. It could be used for any student or to the whole group.

The value of this approach is that, in first requiring a description of events, it is less threatening to the person being evaluated and should develop a greater awareness among all concerned of process as it occurs. Then, in commenting first, that person can anticipate the potentially hurtful things others might say or might feel inhibited about saying. Last, in having negative points converted into problems, a constructive future-orientated view is encouraged.

The timing of evaluation is important too. We do not like to hear something critical of ourselves, either when we feel vulnerable (e.g. when something has just gone wrong and there is an audience watching) or when it is too late to do much about it (e.g. at the end of a course). A 'formative' evaluation – that is, one done in order to achieve useful changes for those involved – is generally less threatening and of greater learning value than a 'summative' one, completed at the very end of a course.

Who initiates the evaluation? Who conducts it? Who processes the results and how? Where is it done? Who else is doing it in parallel? All these questions may also be of consequence in determining how efficiently an evaluation is carried out and, more importantly, how conscientiously its results are implemented. More significantly, where evaluation is seen as more of a regular process in which all group members view themselves as contributors and take responsibility for outcomes, there is more

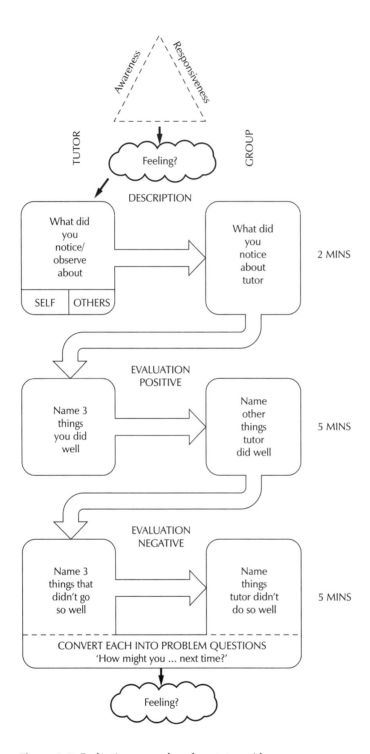

Figure 9.7 Evaluation procedure for a tutor with a group

chance of change through cooperation. Five minutes set aside at the end of each meeting to review how things went are therefore likely to be of greater benefit to all concerned than any formal, externally applied, procedure.

EVALUATION AS LEARNING

Johnson and Johnson (1987) observe that 'a productive group is one that realises that there will be process problems and is willing to evaluate its progress in managing these problems effectively'. Evaluation presents an opportunity not merely to gauge the quality of group work but to give individuals the chance to reflect on their own behaviour in groups, even, and especially, when there is no assessment of this. In this sense they comprise a creative source of learning, one that informs both individuals and the group as a whole about their part in its work and suggests ways in which they can contribute to the needs of the group.

Significant developments in the evaluation of teaching will not come from staff thinking about their own courses, nor from students as consumers expressing their judgements about the courses which are provided for them, but by an integration of evaluation into the learning process so that an important part of the students' learning is in fact coming to understand their own strengths, weaknesses, inhibitions and styles of thinking and working in relation to the varieties of constraints and opportunities presented by the course (Cox 1978).

Evaluation, whether it be of individual students, the group, the tutor or all of these, is likely to improve the prospects of training and improvement:

■ If it enhances the experience of teaching by creating a climate of openness and honesty where there might otherwise be a sense of secretiveness and mistrust.
■ If it is organised as a cooperative act in which both teacher and students articulate their experience and learn from it.
■ When there is no question of its being used for promotion or other public purposes, except where this has been clearly opted for.
■ Where it is organised at stages in the life of a group rather than at its conclusion, and all concerned can have the opportunity to develop and change for mutual benefit.

As Miles (1981) comments, group members feel better about evaluation when they see the specific methods as clear and sensible, and recognise that it is an integral part of training programme that feeds directly into improvements.

EVALUATION METHODS FOR GROUPS

The method or technique that one chooses to evaluate group work must, of course, be established and agreed within the context of the group and the overall climate of the learning situation. The consequences of unacceptable evaluation can be disastrous. Before evaluating, questions like 'Who is it for?', 'How is it to be used?' and 'How honest can we be?' have to be faced and answered.

Observation

Although the observations of an evaluator external to the group may to a certain extent be invalid and superficial, a collection of such views, provided they are to do with the group as a whole and do not refer to the behaviour of individuals, can form a useful basis for appraisal of the group's success. The fishbowl technique can therefore be a useful device for face-to-face groups. In this, one group arranges itself concentrically round the other and the outer group acts as observer, and evaluates. This relationship is reversed to allow the second group to be observed.

Diaries

Whenever the life of a group extends over a period of time, members can derive great benefit from keeping diaries in which they can record: what ideas, concepts, principles and information they learned; what they learned about their own ability to discuss, agree and express ideas, as well as their own contribution to the group process; how they saw the group as a whole. Rainer (1980) offers a host of ideas on diary writing. If these diary comments can be shared in the group even on a selective basis, many helpful insights can be gained by students and tutors alike. Blogs can be usefully used as online diaries.

Reporting back

At the beginning of each group meeting, 5 to 10 minutes may be allocated to one or two members who report back on what happened in, and what they gained from, the previous meeting. Staged reflections provide similar insights for online groups.

Paired appraisal

This process lies somewhere between assessment and evaluation in that its primary focus is on individual needs, though it can be expanded to include the whole group. For paired appraisal, students work with an appropriately chosen partner (perhaps the 'learning partner' described in Chapter 6). Each of them prepares a set of written answers to questions such as:

> How is the group working out for you?
> What about your own part in it?
> Is their anything about the way you are in the group that you'd like to change?
> What kind of things are you learning about groups?
> Is there anything about the group that you'd like to change? How might you do that?
> How effectively are you learning?
> What seems to be getting in the way and how could you deal with that?
> Putting all this together, what do you plan to do, by when, and how, if you want, can I be of help to you in this?

It is not the job of the appraiser to comment or advise. The process is then reciprocated. Each appraiser can report back on any generic issues that came up such that the group can become more aware of how it is seen by its members and what they want of it. Paired appraisal can take place at different times through a course.

Checklists

Any group is, of course, free to determine its own criteria and marking system for evaluation of its performance. On pages 249–51 are five schedules for use in groups and workshops. They are valuable as triggers for discussion as much as for a thorough evaluation. They may be used by the group itself or by another group in a 'fish bowl' arrangement.

'Do-it-yourself' checklist

Using the 'snowball' technique (pages 123–4), individuals are asked to write down a maximum of three statements worth making about the group/class/course, and these are successively pooled and refined in sharing them with a progressively larger number of colleagues. Finally the whole group is asked to draw up a list of statements (which must be shorter than the aggregate number produced if any real discussion is to occur). These are written on a board or newsprint on public view or electronically on a bulletin board. Each statement is then given a three- or five-point scale from 'strongly agree' to 'strongly disagree' and everyone marks their rating for each statement with a blob to make the weighting or preferences more visually apparent (Figure 9.8).

The great virtue of this technique is that everyone contributes and the results are immediately visible. The group can thus quickly discuss some of the salient features of the ratings, particularly those where close agreement is apparent and those where there appears to be a fairly equal balance between opposing views.

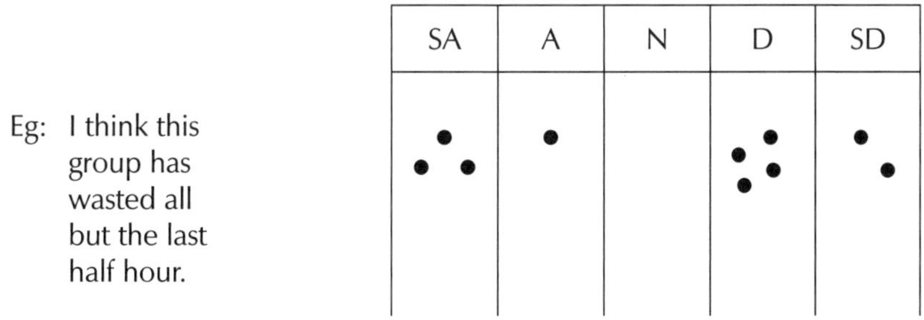

Figure 9.8 Statement ratings for group evaluation

Temperature reading

This comprises a set of special headings under which members may contribute:

- *Appreciations*: An expression of what each person has valued about the group and any of its members.
- *New information*: Anything anyone would like to share with others, any information they would like to have.
- *Puzzles*: Anything they still can't work out or would like to know before they leave.
- *Complaints with recommendations*: Expressions of what was not so valuable, enjoyable, helpful, BUT it must be accompanied by a recommendation. The ground rule is 'No complaint without a recommendation'.
- *Wishes, hopes, dreams*: Visions for the person contributing or for the group as a whole.

Temperature reading can occur as a group round for each category in turn or with all five categories for each person in turn.

Interviews

While one-to-one interviews for all students are hard to justify in terms of time and energy spent they can be of unpredictable benefit, both in what they can reveal of the less-than-conscious experience of students and tutors, and in the way they help students to integrate their learning; interviews require participants to reflect intensively and comprehensively. One-to-two interviews are more economical but not so confidential, while one-to-group interactions can reveal to the interviewer a lot about how effectively the group operates. Who conducts the interviews is of course a problem; given an open and trusting relationship between tutors, how-ever, there is no reason why one should not interview members of another's group. It is not our purpose here to learn interview techniques but it may be helpful to indicate to budding interviewers some of the sorts of questions which might stimulate revealing answers (though they may not all be suitable for every situation):

How did the group go for you?
What did you like best about it?
What did you like least about it?
What sort of things, apart from content, do you believe you learned from it?
How would you describe the climate of the group?
How would you describe this group, as distinct from any other you've experienced?
Any suggestions on how the tutor might improve the handling/the work of the group next time round?
Anything you would like to have said to the tutor at the time but preferred not to?
What else stood out for you?

Questions of this kind are usually sufficient to provoke a wealth of comment on group experience. With the additional use of 'eliciting' questions (see pages 19–20 and 188–9) there should be little problem in getting a comprehensive picture of what went on. Interviews work well by e-mail too.

Pass-round questionnaire

Each student is asked to divide a sheet of paper into three areas to cover:

> things you found most valuable, and why,
> things you found least valuable, and why,
> ideas for improvements,

and to write responses to each. Once completed, each sheet is passed round the group and read quietly in succession by the other students. When the sheets have circulated to the last person before returning to their author, students are invited to read out or recall any comments they agreed or disagreed with or which stood out in any other respect. Finally, the authors receive their sheets back and add any further comments to their sheet before it is collected for processing. You can undertake this process successful by e-mail or on a bulletin board.

Self-made evaluation

More sophisticated groups may be asked to split into two or more sub-groups, each of which has to devise a technique of evaluation which it will use on the other sub-group(s), and then to administer it. It could choose from one of the above techniques or create an original one. Whether the self-made evaluation is set up as a regular monitoring task throughout the life of the group or is organised only at the end is a matter of choice, but it does have the enormous virtue of being good fun and thus raising spirits at the end of a course when they are typically at a low ebb. Such processes can work well at the end of a successful online course. It's important not to let them just 'fizzle out'.

Video playback

Provided the group can be recorded in its natural setting, video recording and playback can serve to alert everyone in the group to behaviours and events which they may have failed to notice at the time they were recorded. A consultant from outside the group can be brought into start and stop the playback at the behest of the group and to ask facilitating questions about the interaction:

> What was going on there?
> What were you thinking/feeling at the time?
> What effect did that have?
> What did you fear might happen?

What was your strategy?

What do you think he expected of you?

and so on. Alternatively, the playback could be sprinkled with questions such as on the checklist on pages 251–2.

Online reflections

Post a question at regular intervals throughout the process: weekly if the course lasts more than three weeks. Ask for self and group evaluation against structured questions. If appropriate, feedback a summary and ask for comment.

If you have asked for individual or group objectives for the online course at the beginning, ask participants to revisit and comment on their achievement, or how they would change them.

Ask each participant to choose one e-tivity, or one from each week of the course, and comment on whether they feel they or the group achieved the stated purpose. Ask them to comment what they learnt from the 'spark' of information provided and what from the group discussion.

MANAGING THE EVALUATION

Evaluation works best if it is seen as a continuous process engaged in by all those who contribute to the setting up of and participation in the group rather than it being left to others to deliberate over or, where it is in a summative, end-of-course form, for a new group with less commitment to experience. It makes a lot of collaborative sense to conduct group evaluation in such a way that results can be fed back to all concerned in time for improvements to be put in place, experienced and reviewed. Such a procedure is known as formative evaluation.

'When the cook tastes the soup, it is formative evaluation; when the dinner guest tastes the soup, it is summative evaluation' (George and Cowan 1999). Formative evaluation is designed to pick up information and concerns which can be addressed and acted on as a course progresses.

Questions to consider:

What clues are you picking up from week to week in the group?

How appropriate are the demands implied by the aims and learning outcomes?

How do any assessments match the learning outcomes/aims?

How open is the group to consideration of its effectiveness and progress?

How 'constructively aligned' are the group methods and tasks to the learning outcomes?

How aligned is the group's work with the other learning activities in the course?

How effective are the tutors/moderators in supporting the students' achievement of learning outcomes?

How appropriate are the methods of feedback and evaluation?

What processes are there in place for action and development based on evaluative feedback?

It is easy for an evaluation of group work to resolve itself into a critique of the tutor rather than of the whole group. Certainly, the tutor will in most cases feel responsible if things go 'wrong' but, recognising the mutual nature of human interaction for being what it is, we must avoid the temptation of judging the success of a group in terms of the tutor's skills alone. This notion becomes more compelling when we understand the value of the students themselves learning about their own group skills through the process of evaluation.

Many of the evaluation methods or instruments included in this chapter can be used equally well for training purposes. The choice of which one to use may depend on the preferences of the group, the style of its operation or the kind of problem that seems to beset it. The group may choose to develop new instruments and methods more responsive to their immediate situation. Whichever approach we use, we must be aware of the sorts of bias to which evaluation may be subjected, particularly the wish to please (or displease). For this to be revealed for what it is, the 'results' of the evaluation must be processed through discussion in an open climate where a balance of support and challenge can create the possibility of change (see Smith 1980). The way in which results are presented is therefore of the utmost importance; this may be another matter to be determined by consensus in the group.

Checklists for evaluation

The following series of checklists for use in evaluating groups, based on the observation of the discussion. It would need appropriate modification for online groups.

Objectives

- What was the purpose of the discussion?
- Was it clear to the participants?
- Did they accept it?
- Is the teaching method appropriate for these objectives?

Setting

- The room itself – what associations does it have? Does it encourage intimacy and relaxation?
- Seating – are the chairs comfortable? All the same? Draw a plan of their arrangement. Note empty chairs, distances between participants, prominence of any one group member, including the tutor.
- Online, what features of the environment supported and enabled, and what got in the way?

Role of the tutor or e-moderator

- What role seemed most dominant – facilitator, chair, instructor, etc.? (See pages 173–4 on the role of the tutor.)
- Was the tutor's role clear, accepted, appropriate?

- What kind of questions were asked – open, factual, personal reactions, critical, appropriate to the level of the students, loaded . . .?
- For what proportion of the time did the tutor talk?
- What techniques were used to involve group members? What use was made of praise and encouragement?
- Were students discouraged from participating? How and why was this done?

Roles of individual students

- What interpretations (if any) can be made about individual students' characteristic behaviour?
- What observable effects do they have on relations within the group (including the tutor)?
- What role does each student have (e.g. leader, playboy, passive observer, clarifier, consensus-taker, reconciler, etc.)? Are these roles temporary, changing or permanent? Are they sought, accepted or thrust upon them?

Dynamics

- Length and frequency of each member's contributions.
- What status does each group member have? (n.b. – the tutor is a group member.)
- Is the group harmonious or competitive? How were conflicts dealt with? Were denial, avoidance, or repression made explicit and worked through?
- What emotions or motives are aroused? (e.g. Do questions produce fear, curiosity, laughter . . .?)
- What are the goals of group members? Do they coincide with the tutor's objectives? How much commitment?
- Did the group stay formally as one or did it split up for different phases? What effects were produced by the changes or lack of change?
- What rules appeared to prevail? What behaviour is appropriate in the group? (e.g. order of speaking, not disagreeing with tutor, avoiding specifics?)

Checklist for Group-based Learning

Does the tutor ...

Ensure the venue is suitable in
terms of seating, heating, lighting etc.?
Establish a congenial atmosphere in which
students' viewpoints are valued?

1. Venue and climate

Ensure that students understand
the aims of the session(s)? And how
these relate to other parts of their course?
And what they can expect to achieve
from the session(s)?

2. Aims and purposes

Make sure the students know what is
expected of them by way of preparation?
That they understand when it is appropriate
to contribute, to raise a question or to
challenge points made by others?

3. Ground rules

Select tasks appropriate to the aims
of the session? Do the tasks offer the
students a variety of learning experiences
(e.g. the chance to draw on their own
resources and experiences, but also share
with and learn from others)?

4. Planning tasks

Ensure tasks early in the session(s)
enable all to be involved? Make sure
the outcomes from one task lead to
another? Give clear and succinct
instructions? Set and keep to realistic
time allocations for tasks?

5. Structuring and sequencing tasks

Give positive attention to what
students say? Express readiness to
listen in verbal responses and in body
language?

6. Listening

Use a varity of questioning strategies
in a sensitive and flexible manner?

7. Questioning

Allow students space to attempt tasks
or think about questions before giving
own explanations? Build students' ideas
into own explanations?

8. Explaining and clarifying

Figure 9.9 *continued*

Encourage all students in the group
to contribute, to talk to each other (as
well as to the tutor)? Avoid dominating
the proceedings? Intervene appropriately
(e.g. to restrain the vociferous, to encourage
the silent, to defuse unhelpful conflict)?

9. Encouraging participation

Act sensitively towards students as individuals
(i.e. taking into account their backgrounds
and prior knowledge)?

10. Responding to students as individuals

Provide opportunities for the group
to take stock and to review its effectiveness
as a learning group?

11. Monitoring

Make provisions for summing up what has
been achieved? Establish what is necessary
to follow up the session and consolidate
what has been learned?

12. Closing

Figure 9.9 Checklist for group-based learning

DISCUSSION POINTS

- What are the principal risks in evaluation for (a) the person giving the evaluation and (b) the person(s) being evaluated? What happens to these risks when these two are the same person?
- Choose one or more of the evaluation measures to review the work of your group(s). What makes the one(s) you choose more useful or valid than any other? How might you administer it? How did it work out? In what ways could (or did) the evaluation serve to integrate learning in your group?
- How would you describe the principal differences in the group dynamics of discussion groups and project groups? How does that affect the way they are assessed and evaluated?
- What ways can you use the online environment to assess or evaluate the achievements of your groups?

CHAPTER TEN

CASE STUDIES OF GROUP TEACHING AND LEARNING

In this chapter we explore how different academic teachers incorporate principles of group learning into their courses. Many of the principles, concerning group dynamics, communication, learning and its assessment are exemplified in the context of both virtual and face-to-face environments.

TRANSFERABLE SKILLS

University College London initiated a programme intended to equip undergraduates with a range of personal transferable skills which could subsequently be useful to them both during their university studies and thereafter. The focus of the programme was on teamwork, leadership, communication and project management skills. The resulting personal development programme was designed:

- To be college-wide, and to work in collaboration with employers.
- To act as a 'seed' activity from which experience could be gained and cascaded down the departmental structure, in order, eventually.
- To embed these skills in the curriculum.

Group work skills were applied in a variety of situations designed to illuminate the dynamics of a group and the roles individuals take, including aspects such as problem-solving, planning, communication, the functions of leadership, and the organisation of information, material and people in order to achieve specific tasks.

The pilot course included:

- *Introduction to teamwork*: intended as an opportunity for participants to develop their understanding of group processes and the elements of leadership through a series of exercises and reviews.

- *Teamwork and leadership*: a challenging series of practical, team-based exercises offering leadership opportunities to all participants, including reviews, and reflection and action planning.
- *Communication skills*: video-recorded oral presentation skills training with group feedback and team-based role play in a variety of communication settings.
- *Project management*: to develop an understanding of the processes of managing a project: individual time management and project management, concluding with a complex competitive team exercise involving all the preceding skills.

Assessment was formative and conducted by facilitated peer review during group review sessions. At the end of the course the facilitators wrote open references for each of the participants. This served a dual purpose: it formed a basis for discussion in a final course interview in which performance was reviewed; and it was available to the student to use in support of subsequent applications for employment or further education.

Participants reported an increase in their self-confidence, particularly with regard to oral presentations and in negotiations of various kinds, and said that it helped them to make decisions that they might not otherwise have made (course changes, career decisions and so on).

Because the personal development programme was based on group work and extended right across University College London it proved it to be a vital mechanism in demonstrating the practical benefits of, and encouraging department interest in, group-based learning activities.

(Adapted from Guzkowska and Kent 1994.)

ASSESSMENT OF GROUP PROJECTS

The Diploma in Management Studies at the University of Teesside organised group projects using peer assessment, which they introduced because the previous system of personal interviews to establish individual contributions had come to be seen as ineffective. It involved group members in assessing the contribution of both themselves and each other on a variety of dimensions. There was no requirement for agreement on the final results: each person's assessment was made independently and in confidence. Peer assessment fed into the overall examination process, one of its main uses being as a mechanism to ensure equitable distribution of grades within a group.

The tool devised for this purpose examined the group processes under two headings: *task management* (behaviours that move the group towards the completion of its working goals) and *process management* (behaviours that determine the quality of the relationships between the group members). It also included consideration of *project output* (contribution to the task in terms of time and/or effort and/or quality) and an *overall evaluation* category.

Assessment of the group project fell into two main areas:

- The appraisal or a consultant-style report submitted on completion of the project, plus a video presentation of five to seven minutes' duration.
- Self- and peer assessment of learning from, and contribution to, the project activity.

Responsibility for final assessment rested with two members of staff, one the project tutor, who established the baseline of assessment and determined any variation in grade between individuals in the group. The latter relied on the tutor's knowledge of the individuals in the group, on factual evidence provided by the group or individual members, and on peer assessment. The peer and self-assessments both provided valuable input for the assessment process but were not the sole means of differentiation between individuals.

An analysis of the peer assessments provided some interesting revelations about student values.

- *Equality*. In some cases group members were so sure that they all contributed equally that they gave readings of 10 points for each and every area. It seemed that students were not willing to provide any information that might be detrimental to their fellows.
- *Normal distribution*. Group members in this case attributed a rating of between 5 and 15 on the dimensions. Although it seems unlikely that there was a genuine equality of input, group pressure and people's good will made this the most common alternative. It demonstrated a give-and-take within the group and a sensible distribution of workload and responsibility.
- *The reluctant finger*. Where there had been free-wheeling on the part of one member, the responses from other members showed a consistent level of under-contribution for that person and this might be mirrored by the individual's self-rating. It seemed that in most cases students would bend over backwards not to 'shop' their friends.
- *Stitch them up*. There was sometimes an apparent collusion between some of the group members giving a clear indication of poor performance on the part of one individual; this pattern was perhaps the most difficult to deal with as a tutor, and then the tutor might penalise the group as whole.
- *Out of kilter*. From time to time there were cases where the pattern of responses varied considerably within the group. The simplest case was where someone thought that they had done considerably more than anyone else. In this case the average of marks for reports of others gave a more consistent assessment.

The hardest decision to reach was to fail one individual and pass the rest of the group. The projects was, after all, a group project, and if individuals did not contribute to the group then this undermined the entire ethos of the strategy.

The project assessment focused on project output, task management and process management.

(Adapted from Mathews 1994.)

THE UPSHOT PROGRAMME

First-year business and accounting degree students at the University of Plymouth took part in an innovative business skills programme. It involved groups developing knowledge of the university campus and city. At an initial meeting in induction week students were asked to divide into groups of six and to choose a leader. Each group member was given different tasks and they were then asked to meet the following day when they would take part in a time-constrained group work exercise. The groups had to gather information and equipment from a variety of points in the university. They had to collect and solve cryptic clues; obtain and use maps of the campus and city; collect and follow instructions; take 10 photographs of the campus and/or city; and finally, select three of the 10 photographs to submit as the most effective and appropriate illustrations for insertion in the university prospectus.

Students were also expected to keep the team 'log' which was to include information such as the key decisions taken, and by whom, the problems encountered and interesting events. At the end of the exercise, students were required to complete individually a group behaviour questionnaire to help in analysing the effectiveness of individual and group performance. The students were also given reading material containing an overview of major theories relating to working in groups.

During the following three weeks, each group reconvened and planned a short video presentation summarising the exercise. They were also asked to use the team log, group behaviour questionnaires and further reading material to help them draw conclusions as to how effectively the group worked. Prizes were awarded to the winning groups and some of the photographs were used in the next university prospectus.

All students involved in the UPshot programme subsequently took the organisational behaviour module which builds on the group experience previously gained.

(Adapted from Guzkowska and Kent 1994.)

TEACHING CREATIVITY THROUGH GROUP WORK

At the Business School at De Montfort University in Leicester, UK, the recognition that qualities like creativity, intuition and originality are rarely developed through common pedagogical processes led to the design of a business game in which group work, decision-making and creativity were developed in a non-deterministic fashion. Each tutorial group had to demonstrate the application of basic marketing, personnel, managerial and accounting techniques to situations which developed as they introduced change into the company. Students were expected to work under sustained and increasing pressure of deadlines and organisational constraints. The accent was on the decision-making, forcing students to experience both the process of, and solutions to, the business problems.

Students began by organising themselves on company lines, electing their managing director and other senior staff from within their tutor group, with areas of responsibility given to individual managers and departments. Each group had responsibility for choosing the products and markets in which the firm operated, but the business had to be a manufacturing company and its span of operations broadly consistent with an inherited balance sheet. Successful groups selected, for example, paper cartons, industrial toasters and garden gnomes.

Information inputs of strategic marketing, finance and manufacturing were given through formal lectures and appropriate videos, and practice in skills development through workshop tutorials. Each group had access to a tutor acting as facilitator through 'open' tutorials. To give immediate relevance to the programme, each group visited a local manufacturing firm to get hands-on experience of production, engineering and capital investment, and their inherent advantages and problems.

Creativity, innovation and communication of mission and objectives were all heavily weighted in the assessment.

Students were expected to finalise their plans, and a series of meetings were videoed. In these meetings, a strategic decision at board level was transformed into operational plans at department level – including negotiation with the workforce in the production department. A final meeting was necessitated by an unexpected emergency which required immediate action.

The prime aim of the assessment was to focus the group's mind on the decision-making processes rather than on the plan itself.

(Adapted from McHardy and Henderson 1994.)

CREATIVE WAVES

In 2005, Rick Bennett of the University of New South Wales in Sydney offered one of the authors (Gilly) and her small team of online researchers access to his project, called 'Creative Waves'.

Creative Waves was the first in a series of free fully online projects for students located anywhere in the world, studying graphic design, photo-media and visual communication. Over a seven-week period in March and April 2005, Creative Waves formed the largest multi-cultural community of student designers ever to work together in a totally online context. Participants interacted in creative exchanges, responded to challenges by unfolding design briefs and engaged in dialogue, discussion and collaboration to produce visual outcomes.

Students represented education institutions from across six continents and worked together in small mixed teams. They were joined by special guests, professional designers, writers, theorists and teachers. The community consisted of 100 participants from 22 countries. Typically the students had grown up within the digital world and were used to surfing and working online – just the kind of people we call digital natives! However, most of the professionals and teachers who became involved found themselves heading rapidly for a new and somewhat unfamiliar beach – the digital immigrants!

The digital native's perspectives

Even the 'cool' digital natives who formed the student participants knew that the Creative Waves experience was something special. They said:

> It's like being in the Matrix. Totally plugged! We've got very encouraging mentors and coordinators and not to mention the brainstorming between us Alyans. Discussions on Branding! It's been really good learning experience and tons of knowledge. (Participant Team Alya)

> There were times that I was really excited about . . . being creative with people from around the globe, e.g. clicking our cameras at the same time all around the world. I mean how cool is that! I have never done anything like that before and that really pumped me up! (Participant Team Hyades)

The digital natives worked well together, in spite of the absence of any overt or planned team-building. All of the participants were very task-orientated, focused and self-sufficient, even without regular mentoring input. They got down to the task quickly and single-mindedly, without any preliminaries, by-passed small talk and the 'getting to know you' stages. They concentrated successfully on the immediate tasks to the exclusion of distractions. In effect, ice breaking was a by-product of their tasks. At some level this was admirable. At another we thought that a little more attempt to understand and appreciate each others' strengths and potential contributions from the start would have enhanced the collaborative outcomes.

The digital immigrants

The teacher-mentors were unsure about their role and less confident to just 'jump in' compared to the participants, although many were as excited by the potential of the project as their participants.

> I log onto Creative Waves at least once a day. This project is more complex and time consuming than I ever imagined, I'm still unclear of my role as mentor (maybe I missed that class!) and whether I should be doing any of the graphic work also, or trying to keep discussion alive, or be a sounding board for you guys, to critique work in progress or what. . . . (Mentor Team Alya)

We felt that there could be much greater coordination or division of labour between mentors. They needed briefing, effective online training before the participants arrive, and tips on effective time management and on a division of labour between them. They needed a facility in the software for feedback, summarising and archiving messages at the end of each week.

Polishing the surf boards

You might be interested in the researchers' recommendation to the e-learning design team. They felt that six weeks was about the right length of time, but that the time online could be better used with more structured planning, to provide fewer tasks, more simply presented, a better flow between the tasks and a simple model of the creative and collaborative process to follow e.g. divergence and convergence. There was no systematic tracking, monitoring, support and encouragement of lurkers, laggards and drop-outs. A more collaborative and supportive environment and a better, fairer, shared experience for all participants could have been created through such a system.

A final quote from a digital native:

> For me it's been a really positive experience. Everything has been really amazing and I feel really lucky to have all these resources at my fingertips, in the form of readings, lectures, galleries, chat sessions, feedback from coordinators and also other participants. The way it has all been brought together is just great, in fact I struggle to think of any negatives . . . probably the only one I can think of is that the chat is a bit unpredictable but that's only minor tech stuff. This site is totally addictive, I must admit I probably spend a bit too much

time in it, but I can't help myself, I have learnt so much and can't wait to find out what happens next! I will miss it when it's all over. . . . (Participant Alya)

Such enthusiasm was infectious and unmistakable! The researchers' view is that some small changes across a number of fronts, together with more explicit, clear supportive human intervention from trained mentors, could make a big difference if the Wave rides again.

The Omnium Project (Australia) hosted the Creative Waves project on behalf of the International Council of Graphic Design and their worldwide education network (IEN). The project can be found online at www.omnium.edu.au.

PROJECTS IN AEROSPACE DESIGN

As the culmination of three years of study towards the BEng in aerospace engineering students at the University of Hertfordshire undertook a group aircraft design study. During the project students found that the difficulty of problems of group dynamics rivalled that of the technical problems of aircraft design. The course aimed to simulate the situation which occurs in the industry during the early stages of a new aircraft design. At that time there are relatively few engineers involved but they will have a good deal of experience. Political and economic factors will invariably be present and will tend to produce obstacles only overcome by the most persistent design organisation.

The task specified for the project was topical in that it involved one of the most critical issues facing the aircraft industry at the time, namely the development of an aircraft for the regional airline. About a hundred students operated in groups of five or six, their work being largely self-directed, with staff acting in a consultative or advisory role. The project represented one module of student work.

The work requirement for each student designer was individually defined. Each student was expected to work as a collaborative partner within his or her team, to face the technical issues together, and to share the decision-taking. The student team leader, responsible for organisation and management, played a unique role in promoting the harmony of the team and had to be elected by the group with some care. The design groups were expected to imagine that they represented an international consortium of manufacturers, with the necessary financial capacity to launch a new aircraft.

A member of staff was attached to each project group, on a five-week rota. Within this regime it was possible that a group wanting to do aerodynamics work would have a supervisor who was an expert instructional design. It would then be important that the group made full use of the advice immediately available, while ensuring that some group members pursued aerodynamics by self-directed reading and research.

The project was timetabled to operate for three hours a week. The programme was divided into four phases of supervision, the last week of which was for staff/peer assessment of each student's effort. The course concluded with submission of portfolios of work and group presentations.

Assessment marks came up from four individual phase assessments of 12 per cent each, a group presentation representing 22 per cent and an individual portfolio of work which carried a 30 per cent of the box. The emphasis on team activity was thus reflected throughout the assessment.

(Adapted from Pressnell 1994.)

SETTING UP INDEPENDENT FIRST-YEAR SEMINARS IN ITALIAN

This case study involved the first year of an Italian course in which students had weekly seminars for the historical component. Throughout the year the students would take turns to give seminar presentations. In the past the seminars had gone very badly, with little interest or preparation from anyone other than the seminar presenter, poor-quality presentations and a very unproductive atmosphere in the groups.

Eight parallel independent seminar groups of eight were set up for a class of sixty-four students. A training day (page 261) was run during the students' induction week, to help the groups to form, discuss how they wanted to operate, and practise giving seminars. The programme for this day is reproduced below. Second- and third-year students were invited to share their experience of dreadful seminars in the negative brainstorm exercise.

In the practice seminars students chose their own topics (such as 'Rock bands in the 70s') and prepared overhead transparencies, flip-chart posters and handouts. They gave the seminars as pairs to reduce the stress involved and increase cooperation.

The handouts 'Improving Seminar Presentations' and 'Involving Students in Discussion' (in Gibbs 1995) were used in briefing students about how to run their seminars. The practice seminars all took place in one large room, and with no involvement whatsoever on the part of the tutor. The students' first experience of seminars in higher education was therefore of independent groups where the groups themselves had total responsibility for their own operation. The handout 'Seminar Presentation Feedback Form' was used by the groups to give feedback to the seminar presenters.

The day ended with each student making a statement about what they had learnt about seminars or about what they would do to make their seminar groups more pleasant and effective. Each seminar group formulated plans for monitoring their own performance as a group.

SEMINAR GROUP TRAINING SESSION

Aims

- To introduce students to each other.
- To establish effective seminar groups.

- To develop effective seminar group working practices.
- To develop seminar presentation skills.
- To establish a method for giving feedback to seminar presenters to improve their presentations.

Programme

10.00 Introduction

10.10 Team formation. Establishment of seminar groups of eight and a team-building exercise in which students had 30 minutes in which to turn themselves from an anonymous cluster into a functioning team.

10.40 Doing it wrong. A negative brainstorm and discussion of how to make tutorials dreadful, helped by second- and third-year students, followed by a display of posters.

11.00 Coffee

11.20 Doing it right . . . Ground rules. Groups discuss the opposite of how to make seminars dreadful in order to establish the ground rules they wish to work to. Each group displays and signs their own set of ground rules on a poster.

12.00 Effective presentations and discussions. A very brief presentation based on a handout.

12.20 Preparation for seminars in the afternoon. Each pair in the seminar groups of eight will have the chance to give a 20-minute seminar: ten minutes of presentation and ten minutes of discussion, followed by five minutes of feedback. The pairs have until 2.20 to prepare.

2.20 Practice seminars. Each seminar pair is given 25 minutes.

4.00 Tea.

4.20 Closing exercise. Each person in turn completes one of the following the sentences:
'Something I'm going to do to make my seminar group work well is . . .'
'How I feel about being in my seminar group is . . .'
'Something we have learnt as a group is . . .'

4.30 Close.

(Gibbs 1995)

VOYAGE OF DISCOVERY

In 2005, although other professions were experimenting with online working, learning and support, not much work had been done amongst the clergy, who have an increasingly demanding role in the society of the twenty-first century. Tom Leary, a Church of England minster of religion working in South London, who is also a psychotherapist and experienced group work facilitator, first trained as an e-moderator to prepare himself for developing online working in his context.

Tom wrote:

> It was apparent that there were new skills to learn. On the other hand there were skills which were familiar to me from counselling and psychotherapy training. The most important issue was to learn the difference between face-to-face learning and e-learning. There was also the necessary task of building up my confidence within the online environment.

Tom secured some funding to pilot an online process to provide a short support course for clergy. With the help of Gilly and David Shepherd from All things in Moderation Ltd (www.atimod.com), he designed a five-week, entirely online, process based on the five-stage model and the e-tivities framework which he called 'Beyond Pastoral'. We published the course on a VLE called Janison. He managed to recruit nine eligible participants and the course started in April 2005.

Here is what actually happened:

Week 1

At the end of the first week the participants had joined the forum and were getting familiar with the online environment. There were mostly individual responses with only a little interaction between the participants. It was clear then that by the beginning of the second week the behaviour of certain members of the forum was diverging from that of others. Some like A and I were offering some important thoughts and ideas, while others like D and J were more pragmatic.

Week 2

It was clear that the participants' behaviour was changing. There was more self-disclosure in a discussion about dreams. E-tivities and discussions around pastoral situations generated considerable interest, with participants contributing ideas and support to each other. They also offered practical technical suggestions. There was also more sharing of their individual hopes and fears. However, by this time some participants were finding it difficult to find the necessary time to log on regularly to take part and some longer gaps between log-ons emerged for four participants, and one withdrew at this point. One participant lost access because his computer was stolen. Tom, as e-moderator began, summarising many of the messages. They quickly learnt that more concise messages evoked better responses from others.

Week 3

During week 3 an extensive discussion ensued about the pros and cons of the online environment. There was a recognition that the online forum does have emotions, can be intimate, allows for freedom of expression and reflection. It is always available to all participants and it allows great flexibility, and all that has been written is available to everyone all the time. However, the number of people logging on at one point of week 3 was minimal and at another point the whole forum was in danger of faltering. Fortunately the e-moderator was able to entice them back and the discussions took off again, which included offering some visible pastoral support to each other and some deep insights into the nature of ministry. It was noticeable that certain sentences of brief comments sparked a large and sometimes deep and emotional response, but others were merely passed by. It became clear in some discussions that two more experienced clergy were assisting a less experienced colleague. It also demonstrated how support could be offered in ways in which the design had not contemplated.

Week 4

The e-tivities this week were a little more complex, with the use of quotes and metaphors. The metaphors enabled participants to take the discussions in a variety of ways they felt appropriate. They generated a wide range of interested, interesting and complex responses. There was evidence of participants auditing and reworking their own messages and the messages of others, acquiring and demonstrating the skills of summarising and weaving for themselves, and in particular looking for themes and commonalities to assist their understanding. During this week some very personal illustrations and examples emerged from the lives of the participants. There was depth and seriousness in many of their contributions. Critically, not only were the members of the Beyond Pastoral project able to share with each other, they could also empathise, show care for each other and even bring practical ideas and humour to the 'table'.

Tom noted at this stage that in therapy, or in a face-to-face group, unconscious phenomena from experience can be explored. It is noteworthy that these concepts can emerge, or be elicited from the online environment. He also says: 'The response to the "past and present" e-tivity illustrated that what has happened to us personally in the past affects us pastorally in the present. It would not have been possible, in my view, to have explored this so clearly in a face-to-face group.'

By this stage, the participants had developed into being able to share and support one another online. The freedom of the online discussion means that not everyone has to agree with one another and yet there is no difficulty in holding together whilst still expressing different experiences and insights. This is markedly different from a face-to-face group where feelings can often paralyse the group members and sometimes overwhelm them.

Week 5

During this week, as the project drew to its close, there was considerable challenge occurring amongst participants. The forum took on the role of mediating teaching and learning and imparting knowledge and insights, all of which was linked to personal self-disclosure. It is this combination of different facets that make it so interesting. The role of the e-moderator became less obvious: much less so than the role of a leader in a face-to-face group.

Participants were invited to look over the whole project. As a response they posted messages that showed how those who had put a lot into the forum were the same who got a lot out of it.

Here the participants speak for themselves:

> Since this has all been a voyage of discovery for me, technically and in some ways personally, I have enjoyed the fact that the pace of online working and progress is dictated by the structures.

I have been thinking about using the time online effectively, there have been times when a chat would have been good, but then it takes time and we need to be on line at the same time. I suspect that its very rare to be around at the same moment. Parish work varies so much from day to day!

This is a protected environment. I feel I have made cyber-friends, and it's been great. Thanks.

I agree with you very much about the 'no seeing' and judgement bit – it has felt like quite a pure reflective medium to me.

Like others I didn't start out with any particular expectations but it has been a fascinating journey. I've realised retrospectively that just posting a note about something that's happened was very cathartic. Whether or not anyone else directly responded didn't actually matter – it was just helpful to be able to share it – and know the sharing of it was safe. So often I hold on to things because there is nowhere safe or nobody to tell it to and having somewhere to put things down has been an unexpected outcome.

Many thanks to Rev. Tom Leary for permission to quote from the Beyond Pastoral Project

STUDENT FORUMS WITHOUT A TUTOR

Oxford Brookes University experimented with students running their own discussion sessions in English Studies as a supplement to the existing patterns of lecture, seminar and office hours. The experiment was marked by both glittering triumphs and 'howling disasters'. The basic pattern of teaching and learning we have adopted is in three parts as follows:

- A staff lecture introducing terms, techniques and theories relevant to a specific topic.
- A student forum (without tutor but with guidelines) which had the task of engaging in a preliminary discussion of this topic and framing a provisional critical agenda.
- A seminar (with tutor present) in which the preceding agenda was modified and put into practice, with the tutor supplying further guidance and information.

In practice, occasionally, this format worked wonderfully well. All three parts interlocked productively and the result was, in the words of the tutor 'a genuinely empowered student group and a really energised and purposeful final seminar'. More often, however, students seemed confused or uncertain about their roles and responsibilities in the student forum, and did not contribute fully – or simply failed to turn up.

All this prompted some changes in the second run-through. The guidelines on how the sessions were to be organised were firmed up, with clearer advice on appointment of chairperson and secretary and a stronger insistence on the responsibility to produce a properly framed and reasoned agenda. A subsequent redrafting of the guidelines took place, with a member of staff attending at least the first student forum to help get it going, and who might even drop in periodically later to help sort out continuing organisational problems. The tutor was against the idea of a register to enforce attendance. ('A session is either worth attending or it isn't.') He and his colleagues remained convinced that if 'student-centred' was to mean more than the usual 'blast of flatulent rhetoric', some such experiments in the transfer of responsibility and power were necessary.

(Contributed by Rob Pope, Oxford Brookes University 1994)

A BLEND OF SUCCESS

Tony Churchill of the University of Leicester's Staff Development Centre describes a blended campus and online process.

The Academic Practice award at Leicester University was created for people new to lecturing in Higher Education and attracts around 70 participants each year. It combines a virtual learning environment (VLE, using the Blackboard platform) with campus-based face-to-face groups. Since 2002 the blend of e-learning into this post-graduate course has become progressively richer – changing from a means of raising lecturers' awareness of online learning to becoming an integral part of the course process.

Initially, the virtual environment was used for distributing course information and to provide resources for participants to explore. Early uses of the online communications functions were primarily for awareness raising of the VLE's potential, but bulletin boards and e-mail have increasingly been used for communications and course support. Despite regular face-to-face meetings, the course team found that the VLE could be successfully deployed to provide an up-to-date e-mail list for all participants, a synchronous virtual classroom and an asynchronous discussion board. From the outset the 'Groups' function in the VLE helped with course administration – overcoming shortcomings of other systems for e-mailing the cohorts and then replacing e-mails with discussion boards as a source of advice on assignment completion. As the use of the online environment increased and the blend became richer, the VLE brought considerable added value to the course by promoting the reflective process and collaboration. A recurrent theme in courses such as this one is the need for individuals to develop a reflective approach to their teaching. Some participants find personal reflection challenging and welcome the opportunity to read the thoughts of others before sharing their own. The course discussion board provided an excellent forum for reflective interchange of that kind.

Perhaps the example that best illustrates the evolving course blend is the changing approach to 'handouts'. There were concerns among the course team about the limitations of the ubiquitous PowerPoint handouts. Concerns that needed to be addressed included poor accessibility and loss of meaning if print-outs of PowerPoint slides are offered without the context normally provided by the speaker. The team therefore produced word-processed alternatives including background information and more detailed explanations of content along with space for note-taking, exercises and screenshots of diagrams. The change not only drew on research into supporting on and offline learning but also on best practice in supporting students with accessibility issues e.g. adapting text or using screen-readers. The approach adopted provided for simple and quick conversion to standard presentations.

Another significant consideration was that the greater detail in such handouts provided the basis for the 'storyboards' needed to create online resources.

Whatever their mode of attendance and interaction with their peers, participants now benefit from a range of online support resources. These cover the full-spectrum of interactivity from static materials such as Blackboard Learning Units (consisting of sequentially presented materials) to multimedia presentations. Throughout, the resources are linked to structured discussion boards encouraging collaborative reflection on the content.

Early in the move towards blended learning, postings to discussion boards were limited to 'enthusiasts', with the majority either lurking or opting out. This was addressed by creating an online introduction for subsequent cohorts based on Salmon's networked learning model. Working in small groups, participants addressed tasks on e-learning and its use, posting their agreed collaborative 'e-reflections' for all participants to see. This overcame many of their concerns about working in groups in this online medium and led to significantly higher participation rates.

The success of such group work led us to more experimentation across the course including the approach to the course glossary. This was always intended to be far more than just a list of definitions. Tutors added references in both web and paper-based format but the demands of workload inhibited the glossary's development. It became more dynamic as the discussion boards became busier, with the glossary acting as a repository for the ideas and resources posted by participants. The latest change at the time of writing is that it has been converted to a wiki format enabling participants to directly amend the web pages. Groups of participants will research and update entries, incorporating evidence of their work in their individual e-portfolios.

The blended delivery now enables the course to meet the needs of wider audiences – including more experienced staff, the university's associates supporting distance learning courses and colleagues in other Higher Education institutions, in the UK and beyond. Online resources enable tutors to give the options for more experienced lecturers to be involved and monitor teaching developments without the requirement for them to attend all sessions. Hence, increasing numbers of experienced lecturers have used the course as a means of continuing personal development whilst gaining Higher Education Academy membership and a recognised qualification.

The extension of the programme to Diploma and Masters qualifications has also been heavily influenced by the blended delivery. The blended model adopted means that all key resources and interactions take place online but we still offer face-to-face sessions – especially in the early stages – as they further enrich the course blend. The face-to-face sessions are also publicised as 'stand-alone' staff development events for everyone in the university. This means that the online interactions play a crucial part in building the 'identity' of the course group. They also generate further resources for those participating solely through e-learning. A blend and reinforcement for all participants!

The blended approach has enabled wider and deeper participation through the creation of a strand that consists entirely of distance learning and through a greater emphasis on reflection and collaboration in groups. The impact of this richer blend has seen the Academic Practice award expand and diversify.

NO TASTE FOR ACCOUNTING?

Imagination and excitement are not normally terms associated with subjects like Accountancy and Financial Management. But at Oxford Brookes University in the School of Hotel and Catering Management the introduction of role play coupled with presentation helped to create seminars that stimulated enormous interest and controversy among the group. The combination of the two approaches kept the academic integrity of study and research while facilitating communication and interaction in a live scenario to the benefit of both presenters and peer group.

Students in a class of up to 24 were asked to research an agreed topic in teams of two or three, submit their findings to the tutor in the form of a seminar paper, together with a one-page executive summary containing the key issues. Each team was then required to present a role play to the group, comprising one or more aspects of their findings and using a scenario of their own choice. The role players were expected to involve their peer group by encouraging members to question, challenge and engage in a discussion of the topic. The seminar paper was graded by the tutor while the role play presentation was peer assessed against predetermined criteria. The assessment form is reproduced on page 268.

An example of a topic would be 'Is it possible to predict financial distress or failure of businesses in the hospitality industry?' One scenario selected for the concomitant role play comprised an examination of multi-variate models through a client meeting in the office of a firm of consultants. Two consultants were confronted by an angry restaurateur who had recently become insolvent, despite prior reassurances on the reliability of the prediction models. In another session on company mergers and takeovers, two students took their idea from the film *Romuald et Juliette* and posed (and dressed up, complete with mops and brushes) as two cleaners who had discovered, in clearing out office waste bins, some papers about a secret deal by a senior executive to leak information to a rival, predatory firm.

Even animals were not excluded from presentations: two pandas at a zoo arrived on one occasion to engage in an animated discussion on the problems of labour turnover at their zoo.

(Contributed by personal communication from Peter Harris, School of Business, Department of Hospitality, Leisure and Tourism Management, Oxford Brookes University.)

PASSPORTS FOR SEMINARS

Absenteeism and poor preparation by some members can demoralise a seminar group. This double problem was dealt with in an unusual and imaginative way by Paul Gaffney at the School of Business at Oxford Brookes University. Faced with 'increasingly-decreasing' numbers – a 60 per cent attendance apparently being connected with inadequate preparation, low energy and a poor quality of discussion on the part of some of them – the rest of the students started to 'vote with their feet'. When attendance dropped to 25 per cent and pleas had failed to make much difference, the tutor decided, paradoxically, to make it more difficult for students to attend rather than easier by introducing a 'passport system'. He notified students that in future no one would be allowed into the

Criteria:

Introduction
Setting the scene,
identifying the roles

Excellent   Poor

| 5 | 4 | 3 | 2 | 1 |

Comment:

Creativity
Innovative, imaginative,
surprising

| 5 | 4 | 3 | 2 | 1 |

Comment:

Convincing
Acting out the role,
maintaining the scenario

| 5 | 4 | 3 | 2 | 1 |

Comment:

Communication
Clear, well-presented

| 5 | 4 | 3 | 2 | 1 |

Comment:

Technical Content
Relevant to the topic,
use of theory

| 5 | 4 | 3 | 2 | 1 |

Comment:

Audience Management
Quality of discussion,
questions

Excellent   Poor

| 5 | 4 | 3 | 2 | 1 |

Comment:

Total score [ ] (Maximum 30 points)

Figure 10.1 Peer assessment for a role play seminar – 'No tase for accounting'

seminars unless they presented a 10 cm by 12.5 cm card with both sides filled with notes from their reading of the recommended texts. He promised them he would collect these, listed under each name, and return them to the students when they were seated in their end-of-term exam (there were no exam rules that banned the use of specified and scrutinised notes.) Proxy submission of the cards was not permitted.

Attendance shot up rapidly to 90–100 per cent, the discussion was energetic and well-informed and students evaluated the seminars positively and enthusiastically. Moreover students with high anxiety about exams claimed that they felt more relaxed and were therefore able to perform better.

The interesting feature of this strategy was that, far from changing the overall system, it used it to advantage and gave the students the sort of connectedness between their discussion and assessment that is not easy to achieve within an otherwise fairly traditional course.

ASSESSING POLITICS

In Politics seminars run by Helen Irving at the University of Technology, Sydney, several facilitator students (about 10 per cent) are responsible every week for preparing to lead the discussion; each then launches and facilitates discussion in small sub-groups. Helen designed the approach to avoid the tedium of awful seminar presentations by the presenter with the other students being unprepared, being passive or not turning up at all when it was not their turn to be the presenter.

Typically, as part of their preparation, the facilitator students write a seminar paper but they do not read it out to the group. After the discussions, these students finish writing up their seminar papers, and include their notes and critique of what's been discussed in their small groups and the larger group. Students hand in their papers and notes the day after the seminar – so they have 24 hours to tidy up their notes and do some integration into their paper, but are not expected to do huge amounts of further research. Helen's assessment criteria require that students include their discussion notes and show evidence of linking them into their papers. The following week a different group of students would be responsible for preparing.

During the first seminar of the semester, Helen leads a discussion about ways of facilitating the small group discussions. At the beginning of each new session she tends to give some very broad cues by saying something like 'Last week we talked about X, so as part of your discussion you might like to explore the question of. . . .' So if the student facilitator really hasn't thought of a starting question (and they're supposed to do this as part of their preparation) they could always start there, but it is more often a question which emerges in the middle of discussion. The students are not allowed to just read their paper – so that kind of anxiety and boredom is avoided. In fact, peer expectations encourage most of the non-facilitators to prepare – as each student has to take a turn at being the presenter, and as they have to incorporate other students' comments, they know that if they don't contribute then they can't expect their peers to contribute to discussion in the sessions they will facilitate.

Another version has the facilitator students working in a group to prepare and being able to give a five or ten minute overview (timed), but then having to lead discussion for the remaining time and incorporate the results of the discussion in their assessed work. This has a side benefit in that tutors have to learn about small group discussion facilitation approaches so that they can help their students to use them.

(Compiled from Video Case Studies: Teaching Matters, University of Technology, Sydney and personal communication with Helen Irving.)

GRADING CONTRIBUTIONS

Smith (1992) asked students who participate in groups to give a note of what they said or thought to the tutor at the end of the class. Then he graded the slips as soon as possible after a class, while the class content was still fresh in his mind. Grades were limited to three points per class session so as to discourage excessive participation. The slips were returned at the next class with feedback comments. Most slips contain valid material and thus received one credit per item.

A claimed benefit of this method is that the students tended to rethink and rewrite what they said and in so doing reinforced their learning. It was also very useful for shy or quieter students who were allowed to write down what they were thinking or would like to have asked, and thus did not need to feel so excluded. Moreover the tutor had the opportunity to include many of these ideas in the subsequent class so as to give more confidence to such students that their ideas were valued.

A NEW WAY WITH DEBATES

Students involved in an English degree at Anglia Polytechnic University on a 'Gender sexuality and writing' module found themselves in groups of 20–24 dealing with a large amount of poetry and some prose. They also had to cope with some rather 'turgid and lengthy' prose fiction often in a highly opinionated form, i.e. women's equality and 'the woman question' of the later nineteenth century. Initially the tutor feared that the students would not read the material – there were hundreds of pages of it – and would be unable to move away from mere opinion into using the material to really engage with arguments made at the time (rather than contemporary). The tutor could also envisage a class in which there was far more tutor talking than desired, which would give the tutor too much authoritative and authoritarian control of what went on.

So the tutor divided the group into four units: two groups for equality for women and two against. For an hour one week they worked together, minus the tutor, but with detailed instructions and the texts. Together they read through and processed the different prose essays for and against, and marshalled arguments, while at the same time taking note of any ideas that could be put up by the 'other side' and how to counter them. They were told they must use the texts in all their points, quoting and referring, in order that opinion did not take over from the use of argument and reference.

The following week started with 20 minutes devoted to putting the two sets of groups together, making one group for and one against. Students had to handle this pulling together of ideas and points together – this negotiation and explanation. They elected a speaker and seconder from each of the (now) two groups, and everyone else knew they must plan a question, with back-up evidence quoted and referenced, or plan a point to make, or one which could be made against a point raised by the other side. The rules were:

1   Roles and comments and positions are decided by teamwork.
2   The speaker and seconder must not dominate once the debate is underway.
3   Everyone must speak once the debate is underway and others must help to prompt and bring in their colleagues where appropriate.

4   The comments made, questions asked, etc. must always be backed up by textual references.
5   No mere opinion!

One person was elected as chair to help run it, and the tutor stayed on the sidelines.

One of the surprising results was that sometimes the group (largely female) 'won' the debate with a strong argument against women's equality, thus proving that they could argue even when they did not themselves believe in what they were arguing for (always an issue in debates). The dynamics and interaction was high, the use of text well handled, and everyone took part.

In the de-brief the group looked not only at the process and teamwork which led to it, but at the 'graduate skills' which they had demonstrated during the course of the debate and build up to it. These included:

■   Teamwork.
■   Communication and interaction.
■   Synthesis and engagement with knowledge and primary sources to develop their own learning and arguments.
■   Oral presentation skills.

One of the other achievements of this session was that the tutor as teacher remained on the sidelines and did not enforce her/his readings or authority – the students ran it themselves, and clearly learned how to handle evidence and referencing in argument, and the skills of sharing out work, roles and points between them.

HANDLING CHANGE

The foregoing case studies include a cross-section of several different but interrelated elements: subject area, activities, organisation, planning and evaluation – all within the context of various aims and purposes. There should be sufficient reference points for readers to recognise or identify with similar concerns in their own institution. The case studies are in the main not so much a description of problems but of their solutions. If any of them seem to fit your own concerns and inspire some sort of action, that is all to the good, but beware! Colleagues might not share your analysis of the problem any more than your proposed solution. Your understanding and handling of a wider group process may be well and truly tested in your attempts to introduce even small changes to the system. So the best way forward is likely to be:

■   Start where you can.
■   Start small and simple.
■   Find allies.
■   Start planning longer-term change.
■   Produce documentation.
■   Collect evaluation evidence.

If you experiment and it doesn't work out well, do not despair; it's part of the rich tapestry of teaching. The problem is that it is not a problem external to us: our own ego is on the line. But let me end, at the risk of mixing metaphors, with a quotation from Brookfield (1990) in which he describes teaching as the equivalent of white-water rafting:

> Periods of calm are interspersed with sudden frenetic turbulence. Boredom alternates with excitement, reflection with action. As we successfully negotiate rapids fraught with danger, we feel a sense of self-confident exhilaration. As we start downstream after capsizing, our self-confidence is shaken and we are awash with self-doubt. All teachers sooner or later capsize, and all teachers worth their salt regularly ask themselves whether they are doing the right thing. Experiencing regular episodes of hesitation, self-doubt and ego-deflation is quite normal. Indeed the awareness of painful dilemmas in our practice, and the readiness to admit that we are hurting from experiencing these is an important indicator that we are critically alert.

DISCUSSION POINTS

- What principles of learning in groups seem to be evident in the various case studies? Can you draw up a classification chart?
- How do these relate to the strategic issues in group leadership as described in Chapter 7?
- Which of the experiences do think you might find most easy/difficult in persuading another group of students to participate in?
- What forms of evaluation would you propose for (say three) different case studies that would be congruent with, and possibly add to, the learning processes?
- To what extent do you think the effectiveness of any of the methods used is dependent on a shared culture of innovation rather that just individual enterprise? Or would be if repeated elsewhere?

CHAPTER ELEVEN

DEVELOPING GROUP LEARNING

This chapter provides a collection of practical ideas for training others in group work and leadership and a range of opportunities for staff development with tutors and e-moderators.

How can we learn about groups and our own part in their process and achievement? This book has offered many ideas, practical and theoretical, to that end. However, no amount of reading is sufficient without reflection, monitoring and feedback on our own experiences and the creative exchange of ideas with colleagues.

Four possible areas of opportunity suggest themselves:

- The *learning group*: seminars, tutorials, etc. in which the focus for learning about group process (and its assessment) is the tutor/student group itself through reflection and a collaborative ethos.
- The *task group*: for example, a staff working party or conference planning team who may, apart from their primary task, wish to learn how to work more effectively as a team.
- The *training group*: in which a small number of people (tutors and possibly students) come together to study group process either in a workshop or a regular series of meetings within a risk-free environment whose boundaries are sacrosanct; and the *training activity*, usually in the form of workshop led by someone with a training role.
- The *learning community or teaching team*: which may have a shared project, a learning task, can work online and face-to-face and if it is to work effectively, needs a clear allocation of time and working space.

Each of these has its own special features; each could complement the others as part of an integrated programme; and starting with one may well lead to the development of others.

Our title 'Learning in Groups' applies as much to university teachers as to their students. Both can learn so much through an awareness of themselves, and the effects they have, whatever the focus and purpose of the group may be. The principles of practice for good teaching and learning, proposed by Prosser and Trigwell (1999), add a further dimension. University teachers, they say, must:

1   Become more aware of the way they conceive of learning and teaching within the subjects they are teaching.
2   Examine carefully the context in which they are teaching and become aware of how that context relates to or affects the way they teach.
3   Be more aware of and seek to understand the way their students perceive the teaching and learning situation.
4   Be continually revising, adjusting and developing their teaching in the light of this developing awareness.

RESOURCE 1: FACE-TO-FACE GROUPS FOR LEARNING

There are many opportunities for us to learn more about groups and our own part in them. Here are some possibilities, with suggestions on how to gain something from them while helping achieve whatever formal purpose they serve.

Learning groups

The opportunity for monitoring and risk-free experimentation can be created in a normal tutorial or seminar group. However, it is not easy to stand aside from the tutoring task and tutors may risk undermining their credibility if they were to expose their failings (and feelings) to general scrutiny. Nevertheless, if evaluation can be viewed as a learning rather than a judgemental procedure, then the possibilities are boundless. Any of the evaluation techniques described in the previous chapter could be employed, provided always that evaluation is used as a basis for developing more effective behaviours and processes in the group, and that it is conducted as a whole-group task rather than as one polarised between tutor and students.

Whether this work is done on a planned basis, or activated by critical incidents and crises as they arise, will depend on the kind of course being followed and the relationship between the tutor and the students. Action Learning Sets and even committees can provide sources of learning provided one can play the dual role of participant observer.

Task groups

Both tutors and students are frequently called upon to work on specific tasks with a view to developing some kind of end product. Staff working parties, course design teams and student project groups are examples of groups in action and they offer good opportunities to reflect on teamwork skills in working together, and to take some 'safe risks' in the improvement of skills as the work progresses. Cooperative behaviour may not always be easy to learn and practice in what is often a win-win climate.

Increasingly, however, the need for improvements in this basic management skill is being appreciated in solving problems in teamwork. Two successful approaches to learning teamwork studies 'in the saddle' are:

- Give team members a short induction in which they practise various training exercises (those on pages 283–303 for instance), in anticipation of problems to come. This could be followed by a shorter session in the middle of the project or task as a checking and topping-up exercise.
- Encourage the group to use simple evaluative measures, checklists, or diaries, and to meet at prescribed times to discuss teamwork problems and make explicit what they are learning from their handling of them.

Eitington (1996) suggests a range of ideas for the preparation and training of teams.

Training groups

You will by now be well aware that group processes embody a complex web of attitudes, under-standings and behaviours. Some of us learn to function effectively within this web quite early in life but for most of us, it appears there is a great deal of unlearning to do: shedding some of the expectations and stock responses we have developed over years of schooling, and acquiring new ways of listening, perceiving and acting in groups. Such changes involve considerable personal adjustment and many may argue that this is too much to expect of adults, especially those in a teaching role. Yet if the group itself is willing to act as a learning medium, more change is possible than many of us are inclined to think. The various exercises included in this chapter are all based on small group activity. They assume that the small cohesive group (five to seven) provides the most effective medium for personal understanding and growth in group skills, whether it results from a regular meeting of committed tutors, or as one of several sub-groups in a large-scale workshop.

The exercises are based on one further assumption: that participants are committed to improving learning in the groups of which they are part. This does not mean there is no value in one or two antipathetic members taking part. Far from it: one or two cynics may contribute hugely to the creation of a realistic group process provided they stay with the group and they may also induce their colleagues to take less for granted.

Whereas academic discussion in seminars often deals with content divorced in time and space from what is occurring within the group process, training groups have to focus much more on the 'here and now' experience of their members. Just as there is no way in which one can comprehend group dynamics without seeing it in action, so it is virtually impossible to become aware of one's own effect on a group, or to acquire new skills, without participating in the dynamics of a group committed to these tasks. In order to develop more effective group behaviours, the learner must have the chance to learn from doing, exploring, trying out and getting feedback on what he or she does. 'I want to try something different today and I'd be grateful for any feedback on it' is likely to produce more helpful responses that just sitting back and hoping people will notice.

But for this to happen, there has to be a climate with a degree of mutual trust and tolerance and where participants feel free to take risks in admitting failings and anxieties and in experimenting with newly learned behaviours. As feelings of safety and trust grow in a training group, it becomes increasingly possible for members to reveal their own observations about themselves and each other. Although this trust may grow quite naturally in a well-run group, there are helpful exercises in developing it, one of the most powerful of which is the Johari window (page 76). Nevertheless, an atmosphere of trust does not develop easily and it is often safer at first to employ distancing mechanisms (for instance video tape or role play), in which people can talk about their image or enactment. It is less threatening to learn about one's own group behaviour by watching and identifying with others in an enactment, whether those others are:

1   The group members themselves detached in time through the playback of interaction on video recorded shortly before; or
2   Involved in a role play or enactment in which members may (semi-legitimately) claim they were not being themselves.

Such activities, though always to be valued, become less and less necessary as the degree of trust develops, excepting always that a particular problem may generally or individually pose too great a threat for live confrontation, or that it is the only way of bringing an external scenario like a laboratory within the scope of the training group's immediate experience.

The central concern in training groups is to examine social rather than personal behaviour. The interpersonal has precedence over the intrapersonal (though the latter is of definite consequence). The training group is 'usually less concerned with the inner reasons for why someone does something and is more concerned with how they do it, what the impact is on others and how they can improve what they do to become more skilful' (Miles 1981). A person may, in the course of such a group, gain vivid insights into some inner problems, especially in the way they may hinder her or his effectiveness in relating to others, but this is incidental to the primary concern of the group.

The learning community

The potential for personal and professional development through a committed and active collaboration group of tutors focused on enhancing teaching and learning is enormous. A mix of seminars, online exchanges and activities that provide ideas and develop the scholarship of teaching and learning can reap great rewards for staff, students and the institution alike. Such communities are likely to be more productive if time-limited. A participant in a learning community may choose a course or project in which to experiment with innovations, and to assess the resulting student learning; alternatively the group may write and edit a booklet or manual of value to themselves and others; and all may agree to prepare a portfolio.

Some strategies for promoting teamwork across learning communities teaching teams suggested by Laufgraben and Tompkins (2004) include:

- Clear articulation of expectations for the teaching team.
- Recognising and rewarding planning efforts (planning lunches for teachers, stipends for summer planning time, professional development funds for travel to conferences).
- Providing examples of successful teamwork in learning communities.
- Avoiding (whenever possible) changes in teaching assignments once a team has formed and started its work.
- Having space where teaching teams can meet preferably away from individual offices or departments to allow for more focused, less interrupted team planning time.

RESOURCE 2: MOVING TO WORKING ONLINE

All educational institutions are facing acute demands for rapid upskilling and professional development of existing and new remote tutors to underpin and ensure the quality and success of their e-learning operations. We use the term 'e-moderator' to refer to the human intervention associated with designing for participation and intervening for learning in online groups. Currently, with a few exceptions, development of teachers, tutors, facilitators and trainers as e-moderators relies on training in the use of new technologies, typically virtual learning environments (VLEs) rather than new social, communication and pedagogical skills. However, all teachers and trainers in online or in blended situations need to understand that creating successful networking for learning is not merely about the choice of technology but also about critical human skills and understanding.

The more successful and scaled networked courses for teacher development use scaffolding (that is, intentional staged skill-building) approaches. Scaffolding is also a way of gradually moving from what we might call directed instruction to a constructivist approach, from short-term to longer-term needs and from immediate to more holistic learning. To engage the participants, there will be active but online involvement in negotiating meaning from the experience of working online in their context, interacting remotely with others, promotion of knowledge-sharing and support of the shared enterprise and purposefulness of the experience. They will learn about the use of computer networking *along with* learning about the topic and with and through other people. This approach will send a very strong and clear message to all participants about the capabilities of low cost networked technologies for learning.

The most important aspect of such online development is to promote skills and competencies that can be modelled and transferred from one learning technology to another (some of them not yet created), from one learning context to another, from formal to informal and vice versa and from one country or region to another. This can be done by offering key models and frameworks for human intervention presented through experience and enabling each individual teacher to create his or her understandings.

Professionals such as teachers, trainers, facilitators and academics need only a little specific knowledge about a new way of working, but then they must engage in dialogue to investigate its relevance and implications in their particular contexts. They must engage in actual practice but with the chance to reflect and collaborate. First, new skills must be acquired to enable them, both new and experienced and at all levels, to be able to create, manage and successfully promote participation in interactive conferencing online. Second, attention needs to be given to how they can maintain confidence and professionalism, and keep up to date. The mechanism for acquiring and continuing to develop should be through the medium itself and depend on the role of experienced facilitators and peers. Hence one of the authors (Gilly) has worked extensively to provide training and development online and in context, based on the five-stage model and e-tivities described in Chapter 2.

The most successful e-moderators have some particular skills: supporting learning in text-based communication, weaving, summarising and classifying participants' messages to promote knowledge-sharing and learning and motivating and developing learning groups without physical meetings. These skills and understandings can be best passed on in the online environment itself and from more experienced peers as the interaction develops.

One of the most successful ways of enabling the shift to online working is through a 'cascade' process. The intention can be to create a network of practitioners and advocates who are 'breakthrough thinkers' and have the ability to support and influence others. They will acquire not only the basic skills of designing for online networking participation and intervening for learning but also the capacity to recreate the experience for others within their span of influence, discipline, country or level of education. The key skills promoted should be simple and effective. They should include understanding of the sociological and psychological nature of the online environment and the special characteristics of handling time and group communication in asynchronous environments. They need to learn how to design in advance for participation and the success of groups and then intervene carefully and professionally during the course process. Of critical importance is their ability to weave messages together, give appropriate online feedback and summarise participants' messages.

EXAMPLE PLAN FOR A SHORT ONLINE E-MODERATORS' DEVELOPMENT COURSE

Overview

This course is aimed at online teachers and tutors with some experience as an online learner or teacher. It follows a three-week pattern of structured supported online work followed by a four-week personal development process and submission of portfolio. It is presented and run (e-moderated) by experienced peers who are provided with all the materials, e-tivities and resources in easily accessible format in the online environment. The course uses the five-stage model, e-tivities format and the latest version of the e-moderator competences table (Salmon 2002, 2004).

Objectives of the course

- Increasing recognition of the value of collaborative learning as the key e-learning paradigm in teaching and learning practices.

> Supporting development to enable participants to design for participation and e-moderate for learning in collaborative groups in online environments.

Organisation

0 Introduction: welcome.
1 Where are we and what do we need (days 1–5).
2 Designing for participation and understanding the online environment (days 5–10).
3 Managing group interactions (days 11–16).
4 Developing e-moderation skills (days 17–21).
5 Development focus: four-weeks 'window' when all resources remain available, community can continue interacting.

RESOURCE 3: PLANNING

Once a training group has been launched – or even before – someone will have the responsibility of preparing and planning, whether that person is a designated or a self-appointed leader. There are various concerns he or she will have to address, each of which may affect the quality of learning in the training group. Among these are:

- Assessing their own motives.
- Making judgements about the institutional context:
  - what attitudes and interests in group learning exist
  - what priority participants are likely to give it

- deciding:
  - who should plan
  - who should participate
  - timing and physical arrangements
  - roles of leader(s)
  - evaluation strategy

- Organising the content (a sequence based on psychological rather than logical criteria is usually more effective).
- Choosing ways of maintaining continuity between activities or separate meetings.

Above all, the programme for a training group should be amenable to change in response to members' developing needs and interests. Ideally, it should be planned and monitored by them in the way described as a 'peer learning community' (Heron 1999).

Facilitating

The role of facilitator in a training group (if of course it is relevant at all) need not be unlike that of the facilitator described in Chapter 7, but with a ready repertoire of techniques and skills to demonstrate in response to issues that arise in the group. As facilitators we must also be prepared to face considerably more challenge to our position than academic tutors, with their legitimated authority, might expect. We should not be put off our stroke by this, but rather see it as an opportunity for further 'here and now' discussion of the way a tutor might handle critical incidents.

For instance, if an incident arose in a training group the leader might ask 'How would you handle this if you were in my position?'

As training group leaders we may expect to be confronted with the following sorts of problems:

- Initial attack or challenge to our authority, or worse still, withdrawal.
- Being 'trapped' by anxiously dependent members: 'Tell us what the tricks of the trade are; how would you do it?'
- Conflict over expectations and aims, especially where there are involuntary members.
- Resistance to change: 'This is irrelevant, it doesn't apply to us', 'What's the theoretical justification of all this?' or long abstract discussions.
- Frustration: people feel they are not getting what they want from the group.
- Revolt, where a group wants to go its own separate way (fight).
- Cosiness: 'Aren't we a lovely group?' – which probably means that the conflict and pain necessary to learning and change are being avoided (flight).
- Low points, where spirits are flagging, can occur at any time but almost always do occur at the end when members are likely to be somewhat depressed that the life of the group is at an end, or merely that it's after lunch.

In tackling these problems the leader will have to draw on a range of skills, techniques and strategies, be alive to the need to maintain continuity and momentum, and be flexible in allowing reasonable changes of direction and alternative courses of action. Bramley (1979) gives several practical hints on handling these kind of problems, as does Tiberius (1999) in his trouble-shooting guide to leading small groups. But perhaps the simplest strategy is merely to offer a commentary on what is observable and leave the group to reflect on that. See also Resource 4 below.

Deciding on group sizes

You can usually choose the size of the group that you invite participants to work in. The choice will depend as much on the purpose of a particular exercise as on such principles as sequences in learning and variety of stimulus.

CHOOSING GROUP SIZES

Small groups (2–5) for:

- Intimacy and trust
- Warming up
  - feeling safe
  - taking risks
- Privacy in feedback
- Agreeing quickly
- Leaderless discussion
- Getting everyone involved
- Delegating facilitator 'control'
- Comparing details

Large groups (8–40) for:

- Variety of ideas
- Getting a wide perspective
- Keeping 'control'
- Making things public
- Processing what has happened
- Meeting, greeting and parting
- Experiencing a more complex dynamic
- Communicating with the whole membership

Inter-group processes for:

- Developing separate plans
- Producing a sense of competition
- Mixing cohesiveness with openness
- Building a sense of the whole group quickly

Examples of group structures

Small	Large	Inter-group
Pairs	Full circle	Fishbowl
Buzz group	Plenary	Pyramid
5-minutes each way	Line-up	Milling
Back-to-back	Brainstorm	Syndicates
Tutoring pairs	Circular questions	Crossovers

Changing group membership

It is sometimes beneficial to change the membership of small groups so as to:

- Discourage 'cosiness'
- Change visual and hence mental perspectives
- Energise people through physical movement
- Provide opportunities for people to meet new faces and ideas
- Break up dysfunctional groups

RESOURCE 4: HANDLING LARGER GROUPS

Large groups, as we have already indicated (on pages 11, 106 and 162), present their own special challenges, and it is how we deal with them that determines degrees of success. There are three main strategies for dealing with problems characteristic of large groups (Gibbs 1995).

1   *Don't start from here*. This refers to problems that occur because appropriate steps were not taken at an earlier stage. For example, the students may not have been introduced to each other, the purpose of the seminar may not have been made clear, the preparation that was required may have been unclear or impossible, or the ground rules of the session may not have been established appropriately. Until these are sorted out you may repeatedly find yourself trouble-shooting throughout the meeting and the incident will keep recurring.

2   *Use structures*. Unstructured large group discussions take a lot of skilful handling. As we have seen in Chapter 1, many incidents are an inevitable consequence of lack of structure. Both the process and the content need to be structured. Suggestions for structures can be found in Chapter 6.

3   *Make leadership interventions*. These are the really skilful things experienced tutors learn to say and do which subtly redirect groups, defuse situations, bring in quiet students and so on. In larger groups you may need to be less subtle and more emphatic in your interventions, and skills you have developed in small groups may not be as effective. You may need to be a great deal more explicit about what you are doing and what behaviour you are expecting, and you may need the cooperation of the group to tackle any problems.

1   *'Don't start from here'*

Consider all these before the group starts:

- Group composition
- Group size
- Room shape
- Furniture
- Preparation by you
- Preparation by students

- Learning tasks
- Expectations
- Check assumptions
- Draw up ground rules
- Agree contracts
- Use icebreaker/warm-up exercises

2   *'Use structures'*

- Buzz groups
- Pyramids
- Rounds
- Milling
- Circular questioning
- Fishbowl
- Games

- Line-ups
- Crossovers
- 5 minutes each way
- Role allocations (individuals or sub-groups taking different perspectives)
- Role plays (including 5-Minute Theatre)
- Brainstorming

- *Use exploratory questions* (for example, 'Does anyone have any experience of . . .?').
- *Look around the group* (to pick up signals and to avoid being visually locked in one-to-one exchanges).
- *Open questions to the whole group* (for example, 'What do the rest of you think about that?').
- *Bounce questions back* to the questioner (for example, 'Well, what do YOU think?').
- *Resist answering questions.*
- *Echo* (for example, 'Made no sense of the theory' (see pages 19–20 and 185).
- *Accept silence* (silently count to 10, 20 or even 30).
- *Bring in* (using hand gesture and, for example, 'What did you want to say Mo?').
- *Shut out* (using hand gesture and, for example, 'Hang on a minute Les, let's hear some other ideas first and we'll come back to you later').
- *Check for understanding* (for example, 'So what you are saying is . . .').
- *Describe individual behaviour* (for example, 'You nodded then, Chris').
- *Describe group process* (for example, 'I notice that a lot of people haven't spoken so far today').
- *Support, value, encourage* (for example, 'Thank you Jo, that's very helpful').
- *Self-disclose* (for example, 'I'm finding it difficult to hear everyone in this room today – are you finding it the same?').

RESOURCE 5: RUNNING TRAINING SESSIONS

The following examples of training activities are not in any sense a cookbook for improving group skills. Facilitators or tutors will need to adapt them to meet the immediate requirement in the light of their own abilities and the situation in hand. It would probably not be wise therefore to use the activities without reference to the rest of this book You will no doubt develop your own variations and create new exercises which make more sense in a particular setting.

The activities are designed for work with groups or sub-groups of no more than eight members, possibly in a workshop format. The aggregate number of sub-groups should not exceed four or five.

Starting

Paired introductions

Commonly in groups, individuals are invited to introduce themselves as a way of getting started. It is hoped thus that everyone will become more open and friendly towards each other and that defences will be somewhat lowered. Yet frequently people are either reluctant to say much about themselves or ramble on at an inconsiderate length about their own background and interests. Interpersonal boundaries often remain untouched. A procedure that appears to be much more successful in breaking the ice socially is as follows:

1   Ask everyone to look round and pick some one the don't know or would like to know better. In pairs A interviews B for two minutes about their background, interests and what they hope to get from the group or workshop, and something unusual about them. Suggest they do not write notes. B then interviews A. They will have one minute each to introduce their partner in such a way that the rest of the group can get to know them as a person. They are told that they will have one minute in which to introduce their partner to the group and that they must do so in such a way that the group will remember them (finding out something unusual is a useful device).

2   Each person then introduces their partner to the group (in no particular sequence) preferably 'as the spirit takes them'. A time limit of one minute is imposed on each contribution.

This complete procedure should be explained to everyone before they embark on it.

Walking interviews

With a larger group it is often desirable to encourage a level of mixing which seated positions do not allow. Walking interviews encourage people to mill and ask questions of each other that they might not otherwise consider. The procedure is:

0   Members are invited to write down one (or two) questions which they would like to ask every other member of the group.

1   They then mill around, locate a partner to put their question to and themselves answer questions from. (There is an explicit proviso that anyone may refuse to answer any particular question without any consequence.)

2   When a reasonable degree of mixing has been achieved, the group may be reassembled and asked:

   ■   Whether any general patterns of information emerged.
   ■   What specific items of interest people picked up.

You can find many other activities under 'Starting and Ending Groups' on the website.

Forming groups

When running a training event the problem of forming groups is one that has to be addressed. You can carefully designate group membership so as to break up cliques and ensure as heterogeneous a mix as possible by forming a line-up (pages 128–9) and asking them to number off from one end – 1,2,3,4; 1,2,3,4 etc. then getting all the 1s , all the 2s etc. into separate groups. Another method that combines randomness with purpose is:

1   Invite all participants to mill around the room briefly greeting non-verbally as many others as possible and to keep moving.

2   After two or three minutes, ask everyone to stop, to look around them and form clusters of whatever size you need for the event, again non-verbally.

3   Now in the groups, they may talk. Their task is: 'To become a group (or team) and to report after 30 minutes how they did this and how successful it was'.

4   The reporting takes place and can, of course, be part of the evidence of the success of the group.

If the groups seem to be having problems agreeing, you can give them a list of what to avoid, e.g.

- Theorising.
- Not listening to each other.
- Not trying to understand each other.
- Not taking risks.
- Chatting aimlessly.
- Avoiding the expression of feelings.
- Not finding out special things about each other.
- Keeping things to yourself.
- Withdrawing from participation.

and possibly, what to do:

- Finding out about each other.
- Doing something physical.
- Finding out how you came to choose each other.
- Taking some risks together.
- Changing places in the group.
- Trying something out.
- Identifying what skills each member has.
- Building something together.

RESOURCE 6: TABLE FOR COLLABORATING ONLINE

David Shepherd is an Associate Lecturer with the Open University Business School in London. He tutors in groups studying the university's Certificate in Management course. Study is undertaken through print, websites and tutorials are conducted through the online collaborative tool called FirstClass.

Here he describes his approach to encouraging groups, early in their development, to collaborate through the online environment. They work on comparing and contrasting application of key course ideas to their own work situations.

Members of my groups are already familiar with e-mail but few participants have experience in working in threaded online discussions. Following online introductions and an icebreaker, I set up a simple online collaboration exercise. Students know that they will need to collaborate for assessed assignments, so their motivation is high!

The task is to collaborate by exchanging information about their own organisations by applying two concepts or theories from their course books. They are then asked to establish one idea to improve identified problem areas or take advantage of an opportunity. Fellow students are asked to critique their proposals.

When I first attempted to enable students to work together this way in the online environment, I borrowed techniques that had worked well in face-to-face groups. I asked them to contribute in several stages:

My first attempt to achieve this level of interaction required several stages as follows:

1   Get together into small groups.
2   Share ideas about your organisations' missions.
3   Carry out a simple environmental scan using the commonly applied headings of Sociological, Technological, Economic and Political (STEP) factors.
4   Identify an idea for change or improvement.
5   Comment on two other students' proposals.

In practice, I underestimated the structure needed to carry out these tasks in the asynchronous online environment. I had made the assumption that, as the process worked well in a face-to-face situation, it would work online. Online all this was carried out in a single thread in the message board. Several activities take place in parallel. This caused some muddle. Although a few students worked through the process, most became confused. I found that the messages threads very quickly became confusing and too large. Messages appeared from participants questioning and clarifying entries in the tables but muddled in with apologies for not keeping up and promises to complete by the following day. The problem seems to be associated with time lags and the need for more precise instructions as well as offering a simple process on 'how' to share ideas, comment and present their contributions.

My next attempt at designing instructions that left no doubt produced instructions that were longer than the exercise itself and would have been daunting for a simple practice exercise. Structure seemed to be the key and eventually I decided to ask students to collectively build up a single table in a single thread.

Now I provide a table in Word with the stages (see below) in a single column and blank spaces for students to add their own information. Students then add their own information in a new column and post their updated table as an attachment. This process continues with each participant adding his or her own data in another column and then posting the further updated table. No timetable or sequence is suggested by me for individual completion, but the students pick up the idea quickly enough!

The table builds up over the week into a very rich matrix. Students question each other online via messages in the threads to gain clarification and to fill any gaps.

Information headings	Student A contribution (Write your name here)	Student B contribution
Say a little about what your organisation is about (e.g. mission)		
Scan the environment for factors that may be opportunities or threats under the headings below		
Sociological and cultural		
Technological		
Economic		
Political		
What is the most pressing factor that you could respond to?		
What action could be taken?		
Comment on other students' responses (only two)		

I find that, as a result of writing down their ideas in the table, they attempt a level of recorded detail that I have not seen in face-to-face groups working on similar topics, when, perhaps the pressure to take notes in real time and listen to discussions gets in the way of detail. Online all the information is there and in a form that is easy to cut and paste into their own assignments – with acknowledgement of course. Online each student can contribute and read several inputs in parallel at each online visit. In a face-to-face group, usually only one issue can be tackled at a time in a more linear fashion.

The tabular approach so works well that students transfer the process when faced with their next collaborative assignments on different topics. They collaborate using the online table method without any prompting. As a result they need much less input from me as the e-moderator and continue to produce a high level of accessible and shareable detailed information exchange.

RESOURCE 7: EXERCISES

Prepared DVD

The tape or films of an unfamiliar learning group is ideal for this activity. One procedure is to play it with yourself in control of the stop/start switch but ask anyone to signal when they notice anything and want it stopped. In the ensuing step-by-step discussion (see page 118) you can ask questions about the group on the screen on issues such as:

- Atmosphere.
- Expectations.
- Behaviour.
- Anticipated consequences.
- Alternative strategies.
- Physical layout.
- Relationships.
- Apparent statuses.
- How these affect interaction.

The most suitable points at which to ask these questions, and others which will certainly arise, will be evident in the screened action as it evolves. The timing is a matter of judgement, bearing in mind what is to come. Do therefore view the tape beforehand.

You could also set up a role play to explore alternative interactions.

Consultants and assessors game

We present this exercise both because of the variety of its applications but also as an example of a typical procedure for running and debriefing a game or simulation.

The class is split into two or three teams who take the role of consultants or experts working in parallel with one another with the task of providing a solution to a given problem. Their solution or proposal is presented to an assessors panel composed of one or two representatives who are themselves elected from each group; the assessors' job, in addition to making the final adjudication, is to set criteria for the acceptability of the proposals or solutions. The whole exercise should last one-and-a-half to two-and-a-half hours depending on the number of teams.

(Though no mention of competition or authority is made, a sense of intense rivalry between the teams and respect or resentment of the power of the assessors can develop. The format of the game, originally proposed as an exercise in intergroup relations by Kolb et al. (1984), provides a dynamic which can give poetic life to otherwise prosaic tasks. It may amuse you to speculate how many committee hours could have been saved over the years had their members, when confronted with a knotty problem, split into teams to work concurrently for an hour, rather than farming it out to a working party for two years – D.J.)

Here is the game in detail.

- *Aims*:
    - To experience working as a team on an agreed task within a limited time span.
    - To produce proposals or solutions on a given problem and to subject them to critical scrutiny.
    - To study some of the interpersonal behaviour and reactions arising from inter-group competition and perceptions.

- *Number of participants*: a minimum of 10 and a maximum of 25. All should have a reasonable level of experience in the field covered in the task (see organiser's instructions, paragraphs 2 and 3).
- *Time required*: a minimum of one hour, but preferably two-and-a-half hours (the smaller the total number participating, the less the amount of time needed).
- *Materials*: Whatever the teams require for the presentation of their proposals. Flipchart paper or OHP transparencies with pens will probably suffice.
- *Physical setting*: A room large enough to accommodate the teams and the assessors panel without undue mutual sound interference, otherwise separate rooms for each team; also a room (possibly one of the above) in which the formal presentations of the teams' proposals can be made.
- *What the tutor does*

(a) Explain the aims of the exercise and describe its structure by using the following diagram.
(b) Either announce a pre-selected problem or task to be worked on by the teams, or invite everyone present to suggest and agree one. The task should be one which the participants are competent to work on and which allows for a variety of solutions (for example, the design of a bridge or a study skills course, the formulation of a new law or a research submission). Agree with participants on sufficient background information to define the context of the problem. Remember that definition of too much detail: is time-consuming; can stifle a lot of creative thinking; can detract from the central task. For example, if the task is to design a study skills course the teams will

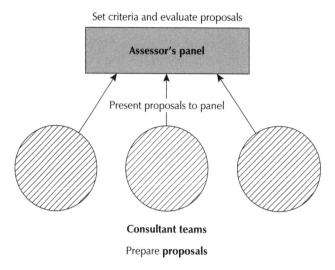

Set criteria and evaluate proposals

Assessor's panel

Present proposals to panel

Consultant teams

Prepare **proposals**

Figure 11.1 Consultants and assessors game

doubtless need to know how many students there are in the institution, what subject areas are studied and possibly how much money the team has; but other questions such as how long the course should be, how many tutors are available, whether any members of the team are to be the actual tutors, when the course should be held and so on may be left to the teams to decide within the ambit of their proposals. Having negotiated the task, form two or three teams (not more than eight in each) and set them up in separate working areas.

(c) Now distribute the consultants team instruction sheet.

(d) After about 20 minutes, remind each team to elect one or two members (depending on how many teams there are) who will jointly form the assessors panel. They will not represent the views of their original team so much as take them into account in determining criteria.

(e) Once the assessors panel is composed, find them a suitable place to meet. Give them the assessors panel instruction sheet.

(f) Announce a timetable and make it clear to all that it will be strictly adhered to. The timetable must allow at least 30 minutes total for the presentation and discussion of all the proposals. For example, if the overall length of the session is one-and-a-half hours, the following timetable might apply for three teams:

Introduction and negotiation	10 minutes
Teams work on proposals	45 minutes
Presentation and discussion	35 minutes

For certain problems a longer work time (and hence total time) may be needed if proposals of sufficient quality are to be achieved.

developing group learning

(g) Act as referee to ensure that the instructions are clear and being followed. You may need to make interpretations and variations from time to time. These should be within the context of the game and, unless there is good reason for not doing so, should be announced to all.

(h) You may also act as a neutral resource person in any way appropriate to the content of the exercise.

(i) The teams will invariably be oblivious to the passage of time. They will therefore need reminding of approaching deadlines and of any other responsibilities.

(j) Keep a check on any other decisions implied in the two instruction sheets.

(k) Debrief (at least 30 minutes). There are several ways in which the review session can be conducted. A lot will depend on whether the game was run primarily as an exercise in group and intergroup dynamics or as a way of producing a rich variety of ideas and plans on the problem under consideration; whether the emphasis was on process or product. The main thing is to give some recognition to things that will have gone on both within and between groups and the fact that the experience will have been both an intellectual and an emotional one for most participants.

Before embarking on any discussion of process or product you may find there are a few feelings floating around which may need to be defused. You might do well to ask 'How is everyone feeling – anyone want to get anything out of their system?' or something similar, but then, as soon as the immediate response to the question has taken place, quickly pass on to the process discussion.

After this you might adopt the following pattern:

■ Ask the teams separately to discuss and report back, in plenary, questions about: leadership and the distribution of tasks; how conflicts were resolved and decisions made; the effects of time pressure; the criteria by which Assessors were elected; how the Assessors felt during the presentation phase; how the Consultant Teams felt about the Assessors.

■ In plenary, draw out the answers to the above questions and try to build up a more generalised picture of the events in the game and then implications with questions about:

 – how easy participants would find it to join one of the other teams to implement the winning, or any other, proposal and what that implies;
 – what parallels there were with 'back-home' experiences, structures, relationships;
 – how they might use the format of the game in their own work;
 – what they learned from the game generally and about themselves;
 – what things they might wish to do or change as a result.

■ Then there are questions about the product:

 – what did they think of the quality of the proposals?
 – how did the proposals compare with equivalent ones 'back home'?
 – what improvements could they make to the proposals?
 – how might they use the ideas in their own work?

Of course the opportunity to ask questions at preordained times rarely arises. You will probably have to be fairly selective and pragmatic in the ordering of the above questions.

INSTRUCTION SHEET 1 – CONSULTANT TEAMS

Your main task is to prepare a proposal for solving the agreed problem and to present it to a panel of assessors at the appointed time.

After you have discussed the task for about 20 minutes you should elect two of your members to join others similarly elected on the Assessors Panel. You will have five minutes (ten if time allows – check with tutor) to present your proposals to the Assessors Panel who have the task of determining criteria for judging the merits of the proposals submitted. After your proposals have been heard there will be a question and answer session with the Assessors Panel, and they will then evaluate the separate proposals.

You should also decide how you are going to present your proposal, bearing in mind the strict time limit. The Assessors Panel has full responsibility for the conduct of the presentation session.

INSTRUCTION SHEET 2 – ASSESSORS PANEL

You are independent assessors and in no way represent the teams from which you were elected. Your task, while the teams are preparing their proposals, is to establish criteria for their evaluation. In addition you should agree a procedure for the adjudication.

Each of the teams will decide for themselves how they are going to present their proposal. They will each give a five-minute presentation followed by five minutes of questions and answers with you (times may be extended by the organiser). All the presentations should be completed before the question and answer session starts.

You should set up the room for the presentation roughly in the pattern shown by the organiser at the start and establish a reasonably formal atmosphere.

Once the presentations and questions are complete you will naturally wish to discuss your impressions and make the necessary decisions. This discussion should last no more than five minutes and should be conducted openly so that all the teams can hear.

The adjudication may take two forms. One is to announce one of the teams as the winner. The other is to discuss openly the relative merits of the proposals. In either case you should make public the reasons for your assessment and reveal the process of arriving at it.

You are responsible for the conduct of the presentation session.

Variations on Consultants and Assessors game

- *Increase competition*: Every participant puts a sum of money into a pool and the winning team picks up the total.
- *Adding simulation components*: Start the game with a comprehensive scenario and roles for the groups and/or separate players.

Focus on the various processes that form part of the game, such as planning, problem-solving, decision-making, teamwork, competition and the presentation of proposals.

Visual case studies

Aims:

- To provide a visual input to learning about groups.
- To study how someone else organises and handles groupwork with students.
- To compare and contrast different approaches to group discussion.

Materials: DVD or video case studies: 'Teaching Matters 2: Tutorials' and 'Teaching Matters 4: Assessment' with accompanying booklet obtainable from the Centre for Teaching and Learning, University of Technology, Sydney, Tennant, M., McKenzie, J., Moses, I. Scott, G. and Trigwell, K. (1993) and http://www.iml.uts.edu.au/learnteach/resources/tm/tmvideos.html.

Procedure: Choose one (or more) of the eight case studies and follow one or more of the following:

- Ask everyone to consider, as they view the case study, which of the strategies, methods, interventions and so on they think contributes to deeper learning approaches.
- Ask them which of the strategies, methods, interventions and so on they would feel confident in using, and which not.
- Give them the 'points to note' from the booklet and ask them to observe these in action.
- Ask them to note their own points and compare these with those from the booklet afterwards.
- Conduct a step-by-step discussion of the case study, stopping the tape whenever someone requests it.

Numbers game

A simple yet powerful game, this has numbers and algebraic symbols for the content.

Aims: To study the group process, and in particular the relation between individual and teamwork, when group members are faced with a simple yet ambiguous task.

Materials: A set of cards for each group – one for each member – on which is written one of a set of consistent simultaneous equations, for example:

$$A + B = 8$$
$$A + D + 2E = 11$$
$$A - E + B = 3$$
$$2C - A - D = 1$$
$$C - D + E = 10$$

Procedure:

(a) Teams of five are established.
(b) Each team is given, face down, their set of five cards.
(c) The teams are told 'You are to determine the value of the letter D, and you will be timed'. (The wording is quite important as we shall see).

The participants are puzzled. Do we cooperate in our team?' 'Have the other teams got the same equations?' 'Are we in competition with them?' 'What are we supposed to do?' The uncertainties are momentarily crippling. As organiser you can ignore these questions: the best you can do is to show no interest and look casually out the window, refusing to answer, while the teams learn to accept the ambiguity of the situation and get down to the task. When the first team shouts out the answer there is often agitation among the members of the other teams as they check their answers: they assume each team has been given the same set of equations.

Debriefing: Centres on how the players engaged in the task, what they thought the problem actually was, what assumptions they made about communication in and between groups, and how leadership, if any, was exercised.

Commentary: The Numbers Game is about the assumptions that people make in common social settings, particularly that in the educational classroom, e.g.:

- Competition is valued above cooperation.
- There is a single right answer to every question.
- Authority will always guide you if you are uncertain about where to go.

But it also exposes assumptions to do with teamwork and leadership:

- Each group has a leader.
- Teams function best when everyone is discussing the problem in hand.
- The set problem or task is the only one that needs to be solved.

If there is any discussion of the equations problem as such, it becomes quickly submerged in revelations about what went on in the teams. The content is so basic that participants soon come to realise that what happened was a result of their own interpretation and actions. They cannot blame the numbers for their own behaviour.

developing group learning

Do-it-yourself

An exercise in group teaching methods for tutorless groups

Aim: To introduce a wide range of group activities using some of the methods in Chapter 6 and to invite participants to make and critically discuss their choices

Materials: A copy of '53 Interesting Things to do in your Seminars and Tutorials' from Habeshaw, Habeshaw and Gibbs (1992) for each group

Handouts for participants as shown below (each handout on a separate sheet).

Time needed:

60 minutes for groups of six
90 minutes for groups of eight

Preparation:

For each participant make a copy of:

■ Handout for participants.
■ Contents page (from Habeshaw et al. 1992).

For each group one copy of:

■ Instruction for the announcer.
■ Instructions for the timekeeper.

Before the event:

■ Get a copy, or as many copies as you need to ensure that each group has a copy.
■ Physically pull the book(s) to pieces and lay out the 53 items on tables, or on the floor for each group.
■ On a side table lay out one copy of each of the Instructions for the Announcer and Instructions for the Timekeeper.

At the event:

■ Divide the participants into groups of six to eight.
■ Make sure that each participant has a copy of the Handout for Participants and the Contents Page.

HANDOUT FOR PARTICIPANTS

Glance quickly through these notes.

1 Please introduce yourself to the others or remind them of your name.
2 The person whose name comes *first* alphabetically should take the Instructions for the announcer.
3 The person whose name comes *last* alphabetically should take the Instructions for the timekeeper.
4 Everyone, including the announcer and the timekeeper, takes part in the exercise as an equal participant.
5 Enjoy yourself.

INSTRUCTIONS FOR THE ANNOUNCER

1 Glance quickly through these instructions.
2 When names have been exchanged get everyone's attention and read out the following message:

I am the announcer and I have to announce things to you. The authors of the book we will be using have sent this message to you:

'This session is about making seminars and tutorials go better. We believe that "experts" are not always useful during such discussions and we are confident that you can have a productive and enjoyable session by yourselves. If you have any queries about any of the ideas that arise, don't hesitate to contact one of us after the session!'

When the laughter and astonishment have died down read out the following statements:

There are no other instructions than these I am reading now. If you are confused, don't ask ME, use your common sense.

You have copies of the book *53 Interesting Things to do in your Seminars and Tutorials*. Your task is to select an idea you'd like to try out and to refresh your memory on it. The timekeeper will tell us when we've had 8 minutes, at which point we will come and sit in the circle of chairs. We are asked . . .

   to *explain* the item we've read;
   to *say what we like about it* in the light of our experience of seminars and tutorials;

- to *describe how we would use it and to open up the issues involved* with the others in the group, asking for their comments, and chairing any discussion which follows about the item.

OK. You have the list of contents – off we go.

REMEMBER TO PARTICIPATE YOURSELF.

3   After the timekeeper has announced 'You have had 8 minutes', please read the following:

I have an announcement. Just to remind you, when it's your turn, you should:

a   explain the item you've just read; then
b   comment on the item in the light of your experience of seminars and tutorials; then
c   ask 'Does anyone else use a method like this?' 'Could we use it more?', 'What problems can arise as a result of this method?' and 'What do others think?' Then chair the discussion which follows.

The timekeeper will keep track of each 5 minutes of time. We'll go round in a clockwise direction, starting with the person who is nearest the door.

4   When everyone who wants to has had their turn, read out:

I have an announcement. At this point we can either

a   select a second item from the book, read it, and have a second round of discussion,

or

b   move to the last stage of the session.

Which would you like to do?

Judge the feeling of the group. You already know how to handle a second round of discussion, simply by asking people to select another item and going back to 3.

For the last stage of the session, read out:

I have an announcement. To draw our personal conclusions from this session, the authors suggest that each of us in turn makes a personal statement starting with the phrase:

'One thing I intend to do in my seminars in future is . . .'

Please take 3 minutes to think about your personal statement.

After 3 minutes, say: 'That's time now. We'll go round anti-clockwise, starting with the tallest person here.'

At the end of the round of personal statements say: 'The authors would like to point out nine techniques, all detailed in the book, which were used in this session:

- 2 – *Learning names*: a very brief version to start off with.
- 30 – *Distributing group roles*: for the announcer and the timekeeper and the rotating chair for discussion.
- 35 – *No-teacher groups*.
- 31 – *Working alone*: to read items and prepare your presentation.
- 14 – *Breaking up the task*: dividing the material between all participants and dividing reporting into three stages.
- 22 – *Rounds*: to get everyone involved in the discussion, and in making personal statements at the end.
- 19 – *Furniture*: to create a set for display and a circle for discussion.
- 47 – *Open book tutorials*: since materials were available to everyone during the discussion.
- 51 – *Self disclosure*: in making the personal statements.

Thank you for participating. That is the end of the session.'

INSTRUCTIONS FOR THE TIMEKEEPER

Glance quickly through these instructions.

It is your job to inform others when the time allocated for a task has elapsed. Otherwise you should participate like everyone else.

STAGE 1

People have 8 minutes to read before coming back to discuss what they have read. Let them know when 8 minutes has elapsed by saying:

You have had your 8 minutes. Are you ready to start?

STAGE 2

When people are sitting down and taking turns to describe what they've read, let them know how much time they have had by saying:

'We have now spent more than 5 minutes on this item. Do you want to carry on with this discussion or move to the next item?'

Ask them again after another 5 minutes has been spent on the same item. Continue to do so until they decide to go on to another item or until the last 5 minutes of the session is reached.

STAGE 3

If the group decides to read a second item each, you will have to time them again for a further period of 8 minutes.

STAGE 4

Let the group know when there is only 5 minutes of the session left by saying:

'We have only 5 minutes left now.'

and then, when this time is up,

'That is the end of the session.'

Styles of teaching and learning

This exercise uses Gardner's Eight Intelligences.

Aim: To look at ways in which we approach a simple teaching task and the limits we set ourselves in defining the task of teaching and learning.

Materials: Ten index cards per group with one word on each (see below) or a set of ten random objects (some unusual). The Multiple Intelligences sheet. Observer's instructions.

Time required: One-and-a-half hours.

Class size: Any number.

Procedure:

1   Read the above aim and explain to participants that they will shortly be given a teaching task in which they can use some of the Multiple Intelligences activities as they choose. Invite two people to be teachers; three to six, students; the remainder to observe.

Hand the 'teachers' the cards or objects with the following verbal instruction: 'Your task is to teach these.' Give them cards or objects. 'You have 20 minutes to plan your teaching and 20 minutes to do it! The task is clearly stated and there should be no discussion about its interpretation.'

Hand the observers their checklist.

2   While the 'teachers' are planning their teaching, ask the 'students' to consider their thoughts and feelings about their impending class.

3   After 30 minutes precisely has elapsed call a halt to the teaching and ask the observers to use the questions on their checklist as a basis for discussion with the 'teachers' and 'students'. This should take another 20 minutes.

Possible words:

METAL   SUBCULTURE
GROUPS   MACHINE
FACULTY   MOLECULE
POETRY   RELATIONSHIP
EXPERIMENT   CAVITY
HEGEMONY

Possible objects: One of the best places to find objects is the office stationery cupboard.

Note: The teachers will want to ask questions such as can they have longer, what is expected of them, what can they use apart from the objects or words. Tell them the time is fixed but they have to decide on the other issues.

Debriefing

Ask the teachers:

1   What did you think the task was?
2   What teaching strategy did you use?
3   In what way did you involve the students?
4   What was your impression of the students?
5   How did your perception of the task and the students influence your behaviour?
6   What limits to the task did you assume and why?
7   How did you feel about the teaching?
8   How well did you operate as a team?
9   Which of the multiple intelligences did you find best matched the students' needs? Which did you find easiest and most difficult to use?

Ask the students:

1   What did you think or talk about in anticipation of the teaching session?
2   How was the learning task presented to you?
3   How did you perceive the task: meaningful, useless, how?
4   What was your impression of the 'teachers'?
5   How did your perception of the 'teacher' and the task influence your behaviour?
6   What limits did you assume in your learning and why?
7   How did you feel as learner?
8   Which of the approaches to learning did you find worked best for you?

Leadership exercise

The behaviours described on page 283 while simple in principle are not so easy to put into practice especially in a familiar and habitual context. They all require attention to the group process as well as the content and judgements as to their appropriateness may not at first be easy to make. This exercise is designed to help not only in practising the interventions but in deciding when and how to use them through feedback from observers and the group.

Aims: To give practical experience of group leadership interventions and feedback on how appropriate and well timed they are.

Materials: Chart set out overleaf.

Time required: One hour.

Task: One member of the group is invited to generate a participatory discussion involving the *whole* group and in so doing consciously practise some or all of the behaviours listed below. The topic should be either one that is topical for the group, or preferably one that is well known to the person leading the group but that the rest of the group may expected to be less familiar with.

The group members can be advised that the learning may be maximised if they can responsibly simulate some of the common characteristics of the kind of groups relevant to the leader and the context of the training.

Observers, who can be the participating members of the group if numbers require this, check with a tick in the relevant box each time a particular behaviour is demonstrated.

Debrief:

1   Invite the 'leader' to do a self-assessment referring to the checklist: 'What I think I did and how well it worked'; 'What I found difficult'; and 'Opportunities I missed and what I would like to do 'next time'.
2   Invite the observers' (if outside the group) comment on 'What the leader did effectively', followed by 'Opportunities he or she seemed to have missed'.
3   Repeat 2 with the group members and add 'And how it felt to me' to each of the above statements.

Behaviour	Comments
Uses exploratory questions	
Looks around group	
Opens questions to the whole group	
Bounces questions back to the questioner	
Resists answering questions	
Echoes	
Accepts silence	
Brings in	
Shuts out	
Checks for understanding	
Describes individual behaviour	
Describes group process	
Support, values, encourages	
Self-discloses	

Figure 11.2 Leadership exercise

Powerful ideas in teaching

How to get workshop people engaged in processing written text is always a bit of a challenge in training events, especially where they would rather do something more active than just read. This exercise (a kind of role play) is based on *11 Powerful Ideas from Preparing to Teach* (Gibbs et al. 1992).

Aims:

- To encourage deeper assimilation of a set of principles on teaching and learning.
- To demonstrate how reading can be integrated into a group activity.
- To illustrate the use of role differentiation and play in giving a sharper focus to learning.

Materials: Copies of the *11 Powerful Ideas*, edited as necessary and copied onto cards, enough for each person to have a copy of at least one of the 'Ideas'.

1   Each person picks up a card and reads their chosen copy in order to answer questions on it. If more than one person has the same 'Idea' they can discuss it with those holding the same card for 5 minutes.

2   The reading done, the first card holder volunteers to give the rest of the group a 30-second summary (not read) of their Idea.

3   The task of the rest of the group is to act as students who are potentially interested in the course but have suffered from the inadequacies that the Idea is designed to remedy.
    The exercise continues with the rest of the 'Ideas' taken in a random order.

4   On completion hold a discussion on which of the 'Ideas' the whole exercise exemplified and how, as a model it could be varied and improved.

Outline of workshop for group leaders/tutors

Leading group discussion

Programme

0930   Paired introductions and checking of assumptions.
1000   Aims and related tasks for groups: reading the chart from page 91, Chapter 5, and discussion in pairs.
1030   Problems with groups 1: the checklist (see page 302) is completed individually then compared in pairs.
1045   Coffee.
1100   Problems with groups 2: consultancy groups of 4/5 with self-assessment (Chapter 9, Exercise 2, pages 320–3).
1230   Trident: a three-pronged strategy: presentation of Handling Problems in Larger Groups (pages 282–3).
1300   Lunch.
1400   Structures for large groups: practice with Circular Questioning and Fishbowl methods (Chapter 6) using the topic chosen by the group led by the facilitator.
1445   Interventions with large groups: demonstration and practice using Leadership Exercise (page 282).
1530   Tea.
1545   Assessment with groups: (video/DVD of the case study from page 293) and sample checklists.
1615   Evaluating groupwork: two evaluation checklists from Chapter 9 used as in Chapter 9, Exercise 3 or in shorter form by doing only (a), (b) and (c) in the exercise.
1700   Action plans: 'What I intend to do as a result of this workshop, who can help me, what could get in the way, and what I might do about that.' Individuals complete and are checked and supportively challenged by a partner in pairs.
1730   Adjourn.

Learning outcomes

By the end of this workshop participants should:

■   Be more able and feel more confident in the use of a wider range of group techniques.

- Be more resourceful in finding suitable solutions to problems that may arise with larger groups.
- Have a wider repertoire of interactive skills.
- Have clearer plans for assessing and evaluating students in groups.

LEARNING THROUGH GROUPS

The activities described in this chapter represent only a sample of the many that are available to interested readers. Christopher and Smith (1991), Miles (1981), Eitington (1996), Napier and Gershenfeld (1999), Johnson and Johnson (1987 and 1990) and Thiagarajan (2003) all include further samples of well-tested training activities. Yet whatever games, exercises or methods we may use, there are certain assumptions and principles which perhaps need to be underlined.

1   The accent is on 'whole person' learning: learning that involves both thinking, feeling and behaviour.
2   There must be practice of behaviour and skills – practice that is informed by guided experience and constructive feedback (see page 77).
3   There should be a strong focus on the 'here and now'. The 'there and then' is great use with a video playback (Kagan 1982) but while it makes discussion of behaviour safer, it may also make it less immediate. The 'here and now' approach helps in the learning and monitoring of skills.
4   There should be general acceptance that everyone has unique styles of personal behaviour, different needs and their own way of seeing the world.
5   The emphasis should be on the 'social self' rather than on the 'inner world' of participants.
6   Personal change is best achieved where there is a judicious blend of support and challenge (Smith 1980).
7   The primary orientation should be towards the development of skills, but these should be seen within a wider framework of attitudes and values (Miles 1981).

DISCUSSION POINTS

- What principles of learning seem to be incorporated in the various activities included in this chapter?
- Draw up (and negotiate) a contract for the work of your group.
- You have been asked to design and run a one-day workshop on group teaching. What are you going to include? How will you sequence and thread together all the activities?

WORKING TOGETHER

We both know that there's a bit of irony about reading and writing about the concepts, principles and practice of learning and teaching in groups. It's something you need to live, reflect on, experience and explore. Done well, it's a life's work and a complete joy; done badly, see the rush back to screens and books rather than other people! We've tried to engage you in the potential and the pitfalls through sparks to light your group fires and offer you choices and options to make your own. You will see that we believe there is a myriad of possibilities, whether you're starting out on the learning in groups journey, or considering fresh pathways and need new vehicles. But now – just do it, please, and let us know how it goes.

You will have noticed that many of the principles, concepts and studies in this book have been around a while. Those that we have included are the ones we think are still valid, relevant and useful. Recently, research has been somewhat deflected by different agendas: e-learning for example. We expect that as you work with your own learning in groups you'll see gaps in our knowledge – why not consider trying to fill them and contribute to twenty-first-century understanding of learning together. It's a great moment in history for educators to explore new tools and techniques!

So here, at the end of the text, our job diminishes and yours begins. But there's a website: www.learningingroups.com. You can find us through there and we hope that you'll send us your experiences with the principles in the books, your applications and your cases studies. And of course your research ideas and findings.

EXERCISES

CHAPTER 1

1 Feedback on group behaviour

Figure 1.5 shows a chart of group behaviour.

Individuals in the group who perform these functions well

Task-based behaviour	Initiating	
	Giving and seeking information	
	Giving and seeking opinion	
	Clarifying	
	Building, integrating	
	Summing up	
	Consensus testing	
		Individuals in the group who perform these functions well
Maintenance-based behaviour	Encouraging, valuing	
	Mediating	
	Compromising	
	Releasing tension	
	Gatekeeping	

Figure 1.5 Feedback on group behaviour

1 Working individually, each member writes the names of group members on a copy of the chart who perform the particular functions well. They then mark, on another copy of the chart, how they see themselves in terms of each category.

2 When this is completed each member goes to a prepared flipchart and writes up the names in the appropriate boxes, indicating clearly the number of times that any name appears.

3 Each member in turn should then talk about how their self-assessment compared with the composite list and ask for any feedback that would help them understand any differences.

4 Finally the group can discuss what gaps there appear to be in the overall pattern and what might need to be done to remedy that.

2 Fishbowl

Ask the leader/tutor to leave the room for the first half of this discussion. The group divides to form a fishbowl (see page 124); in this the outer members act as silent observers while a discussion takes place in the inner one.

Conduct a discussion on authority/dependency and organisational structure or another psycho-dynamic concept in relation to the group you have been working in.

- How and when does the tutor exercise authority?
- What feelings does it engender?
- What do you learn for yourself from that?
- What would happen if the group as a whole had no tutor?

Meanwhile the outer group can be making notes on questions like:

- What *is* happening in the inner group without a tutor?
- How is authority assumed?
- Who takes initiatives?
- Is there any 'pecking order' in contributions?

When the tutor returns (after 30 minutes), the outer group explains to the tutor what they observed with the inner group remaining silent.

Finally the whole group re-assembles and the tutor joins in an open discussion based on the exercise.

CHAPTER 2

1 Places

- Ask group members to negotiate a change of place with somebody who is not sitting next to them and to describe the new experience to one of their new neighbours before speaking to the whole group about it.

- Ask each member to sit in a different place from their usual one as they arrive.
- Allocate places with numbered cards which members are presented with as they arrive.
- Re-arrange the furniture into an unfamiliar configuration.
- Explain the purpose and nature of the session and ask members to decide what arrangement of furniture would be most suitable.

2 Lines of communication

In a typical group, members are only half aware of how much they speak or to whom they direct most of their contributions; nor is the group as a whole usually aware what the pattern of communication is over time.

In this exercise two members of the group, or two outside observers, sit outside the group and on opposite sides, and draw a map of the group with everyone's names on it. Then over a period of time (say half an hour), as they observe the discussion, they draw lines with arrows to indicate, where possible, who has addressed or questioned whom and responded to whom. Against each person on the map they place a tick for every time they say something – so that when someone addresses the whole group the proportion of their contributions to individuals compared with the group should be visible on the map.

Once the observers have conferred, the group is shown the maps (preferably a copy for each member) and then invited to comment in turn on:

- the extent to which this tallied with their impression of themselves;
- what they learn from that.

A communication analysis such as this is easy online by virtue of the written record.

3 Secret leadership

Prepare as many folded slips of paper as there are members of the group and mark one of them with the letter 'L'. Tell the group that they are to take part in a discussion in which there will be a designated leader, whatever that may mean to them. Each of them is to be given a slip and whoever has one with an 'L' marked on it is to act as leader. Hand the slips out with the instruction that they must check their own slip privately and not reveal what is written on it to anyone. Online the instruction could be achieved by private e-mail (see the variations below).

After the allowed time, ask the group who they thought the designated leader was and for what reasons – what did they do, how did others relate to them that was different? Then ask the actual leader to reveal him or herself.

Discussion can then centre on how the leadership role was interpreted by the 'L' person, how comfortable they felt with it, and what others may have been doing in any form of competition for the leadership. Finally it may be useful to ask the group to generate freely a list of effective and ineffective leadership behaviours that they observed in the exercise, including any that were lacking.

Variations

- The task can be a practical or a decision-making one.
- You may choose who gets the 'L' in order to avoid any personal discomfort for any group member or for other reasons.
- Two slips could be marked with an 'L'.
- All the slips could be marked with an 'L'.

4 Norms exercise

Norms are mutual, unspoken expectations. They are mostly learned through what is *not* said or through non-verbal cues. They comprise the unstated do's and don't's of the group and may be held individually or by the group as a whole.

In groups of four, discuss:

(a) 'Norms in groups I belong to, lead, etc.' (10 mins)
(b) 'Norms in this group.' (10 mins)
(c) 'Norms I/we can change in our group and how.' (10 mins)

Draw up a personal list of norms for each of the three categories as you go along:

Norms in groups generally

. . . .
. . . .
. . . .
. . . .

Norms in this group

. . . .
. . . .
. . . .
. . . .

Norms to be broken, plus observations

. . . .
. . . .
. . . .
. . . .

Find a partner from one of the other groups

Share findings and discuss intentions for full group discussion which follows (10 mins)

Full group reconvenes

Open discussion (and observation of what happens in light of above insights) (20 mins)

CHAPTER 3

1 What makes learning effective?

Think back to an occasion in your life when you learned something really well, or which you remember vividly. It need not necessarily be when you were a student. Think of all the concomitants of the experience: what happened before and after, who was involved, the physical and social environment, your feelings, etc.

When you have done your reminiscing find a partner with whom to talk about it. Your partner will help you explore your recollection with questions about concomitants – the context, antecedents, consequences, significant people, etc.

Jot down any notes you may need to make as an aide memoire.

After 15 minutes join up with another pair and after describing your partner's experience, draw up a group list of completions to the sentence:

Learning is usually better when . . .

2 Surface and deep learning

Below you will see a list of factors that affect the quality of student learning. Indicate the degree to which each of them is characteristic of the modules/courses in your subject area/department, and then those on which you actually teach. 10 = high, 0 = non-existent.

Surface learning is likely to be encouraged by:	Dept	Your teaching
A heavy workload		
Relatively high class contact hours		
An excessive amount of course material		
A lack of opportunity to pursue subjects in depth		
A lack of choice over subjects and a lack of choice over the method of study		

Poor feedback on progress

Assessment methods that emphasise recall or the use
of simple, standard procedures

A threatening and anxiety-provoking assessment system

Deep learning approaches are likely to be encouraged by:	Dept	Your teaching
Clearly stated expectations and outcomes		
Teaching that focuses on student learning		
Opportunities to exercise choice in the content and methods of study		
Recognition and use of a range of learning modalities		
Encouragement of and demand for active learning		
Teaching and assessment methods that encourage active and lifelong engagement in the learning tasks		
Learning tasks that relate to the students' prior knowledge and future interests		
A tutor who shows enthusiasm and commitment		

CHAPTER 4

1 Back-to-back

An exercise in one-way communication

In this exercise a '*sender*' of information sits back-to-back with a '*receiver*' and has to communicate with the latter under a set of restrictive rules. (As with many such games it may be advisable with some students to give them a little orientation beforehand.) As an introduction to this game you could for example chat briefly about the reality of the communication process by suggesting that communication is a simple process of which we are all superb practitioners. Then give an example of exactly how simple it is with the situation in which the teacher says to a class: 'Does everyone understand?'

'What', you could ask students, 'do you think you would reply if you were the teacher? If you wanted to say "yes", would you? What would be the likely consequences of so doing? If you answered "no", what would be the implications of that? So what do you do? Look at the floor? Pretend you're reading your notes? So maybe the apparently simple question has another function'. And so on . . .

You might also ask them about the last time they were walking down the street and a car stopped to ask them the way. 'As you reached the stage of your communication where you said "and take the third exit from the roundabout, if you don't count the no entry sign" you can see the glazed expression coming over the driver's face as he or she reaches for the window winder. "Is that OK?" you ask. "Fine, thanks" the driver says and drives away. As you walk round the corner you see that the car has stopped again and another pedestrian is trying to help. So what goes wrong?'

So, on to the exercise. Person A, sitting back-to-back with person B, has to tell B how to draw an apparently simple figure, such as that shown in Figure 4.6, without any checking or communication back from B to A.

Subsequently the roles of A and B can be reversed using another figure (Figure 4.7). The simple rule of one-directional communication can be varied to include feedback, limited questions and so forth, but the basic exercise, though it may last no more than five minutes, almost invariably produces a plethora of ideas and insights on the problems of lecturing, phone conversations, or the giving of instructions. Having asked participants to draw up a list of guidelines to improve communication these can then be compared with a prepared list like the one that follows. It is also a useful way to demonstrate the experiential learning cycle.

To explain I instruct clearly you should:

- try to orient the other person to the task and to what is being communicated – have a clear picture of what you want the other person to understand;
- analyse your own feelings about the topic and the other person;
- assess your own and the other person's communication skills;
- try to identify yourself with the psychological state of the other person;
- make a realistic assessment of the degree of clarity obtainable in the given context: make the message relevant by using the other's language and terms – state ideas in the simplest possible terms;
- define before developing and explain before amplifying;
- make it clear when you are explaining as opposed to instructing;
- develop one idea at a time;
- take one step at a time;
- use appropriate repetition;
- review when relevant;
- compare and contrast ideas;
- use analogies;
- determine which ideas need special emphasis;
- use as many channels as necessary for clarity;
- pace according to the learning capacities of the other person;
- where any two-way communication is possible, watch for and encourage corrective feedback in as many channels as possible.

The dynamics of this game, though simple, are interesting in what they reveal about opportunity and risk in personal behaviour. During the exercise proper each pair is separate from the rest and has the reassurance of physical contact (their shoulders inevitably touch in the strain of trying to pick up words amid the background noise of all the other pairs) and the chance to avoid those embarrassing glances that go with failure and inadequacy when one is in eye-to-eye contact.

In the debriefing period the pairs themselves are asked to discuss problems privately before public discussion is invited. Anxieties and feelings can thus be shared in safety before being revealed, if so chosen, to the whole group. If anyone chooses not to, then they can silently draw comparisons between their privately shared thoughts and the public ones of others more bold or foolhardy than they.

Note: although this exercise may be difficult to operate online, the above list would be of relevance.

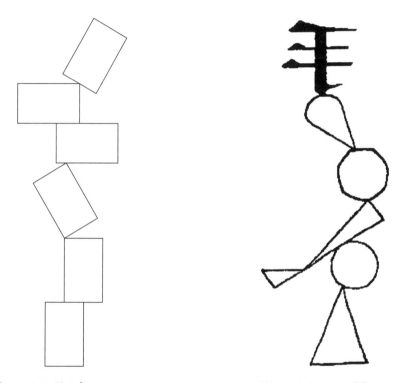

Figure 4.6 First figure   Figure 4.7 Second figure

2 Johari window

The Johari window, Figure 4.4, can be used to help group members develop insight into how their communication affects others in the group whether face-to-face or online.

1   Each person (the client), working alone, fills in quadrant 1 and as much of quadrant 3 as they are prepared to reveal.

2   Each client then chooses a partner and explains what they have written in quadrants 1 and 3 before inviting their partner to give them feedback for quadrant 2 for a period of 5 minutes (or longer if time is available). As the discussion takes place, the client may gain new insights in quadrant 4 and choose to make some notes to themselves.

3   The process is reversed with the other partner becoming the client for the same time period.

4   One of each pair moves clockwise round the group and for 5 minutes each way repeats the above process.

5   When members have finished receiving this feedback a group round takes place in which each member tells the group in one minute what they have learned, what they intend to do with that and what if anything they would like the group to do to help them in this.

3 Non-verbal communication

Organise the group into a fishbowl (see page 126), the outer group to observe the inner one. Give the inner one a suitable task, e.g. 'Discuss what you think this group is best suited for' or 'Agree an appropriate slogan for the group'. For a given time (e.g. 20 minutes) the outer group is asked to watch for and record non-verbal behaviour in:

- getting attention,
- expressing agreement,
- expressing disagreement,
- emphasising,
- showing puzzlement or confusion,
- stopping someone,
- cutting in,

and to look for any variations according to sex, order of speaking, position in group, etc.

The outer group, still in position, then feeds back what they observed, particularly picking out differences between members. They should be very conscious of the need for sensitivity in giving this feedback and of the principles described on page 77.

CHAPTER 6

1 Arranging the furniture

Figure 6.14 shows several possible arrangements of furniture in a classroom. Each chair with a 'T' in it represents a tutor.

Instructions

1   Working individually for 5 minutes, each person thinks about the configurations and asks themselves what kind of interaction these might promote.

- what task might you give the participants?
- how do you think they might respond?
- what improvements or alternatives can you suggest?

2   Now, groups of three, for 15 minutes, take each configuration in turn and discuss each person's ideas for it.

3   Now, groups devise one new configuration with a suggested task and each person draws a sketch of it, possibly on a flipchart.

4   Finally, either in a plenary forum with a flipchart or through crossover groups, each group's idea should be presented, with any provisos.

5   Finally each person completes the following sentences in a group round:

- ■   One arrangement I could use is . . .
- ■   I could do the following things with it . . .
- ■   I think the problems of using it might be . . .
- ■   I reckon I could overcome those by . . .

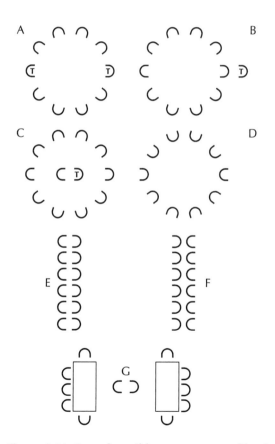

Figure 6.14   Several possible arrangements of furniture in a classroom

2 Group activities

Choose five of the group activities described in this chapter and list what problems these might address. Mark each 1, 2 or 3 according to how confident you feel in running it and add comments in relation to that.

3 Problems in groups

Problems in groups are notoriously difficult to pin down but if they are not dealt with speedily they may become part of a pattern of the group culture which then becomes hard to shift. What can you do to anticipate or tackle them as they arise? This exercise is designed to pick out some of the common problems and develop solutions from your own resources.

Task 1: Working by yourself, write down in the left-hand column as many problems or tricky situations that seem to occur in your groups. Do not at this stage fill in the right-hand column (3–5 mins).

Task 2: In groups, conduct a group 'round' to share what you have written down: one item per person in turn on a 'top-slicing' basis (each takes the top of the remaining items on the list each time round).

Task 3: Plenary session: each group in turn calls out a problem/incident to be listed on the board/screen (this can be omitted).

Task 4: In groups, each person chooses a particular problem/incident to address and has a 5-minute slot in which to solicit the help of the group in coming up with solutions. This requires one or two members of the group to act as 'consultant' to each 'client' in turn which will mean listening, clarifying and helping the client to come up with solutions of her/his own. Others may act as timekeeper and peer assessor. The facilitator may wish to model the consultant role, and also remind participants of Task 6.

Task 5: Plenary session: each group contributes, in turn, a chosen problem and the proposed solutions, a different group member contributing each time round. OR: Each group receives and reads the list of possible solutions and the facilitator checks out any unsolved problems.

Task 6: Group 'crossover', i.e. each group numbers its members and all the 1s, all the 2s, all the 3s etc. get together such that there are new groups with a mix of members from the previous groups. The task now is to conduct a self-assessment, completing the sentences: 'What I did well as a consultant . . .' and 'What I could improve on . . .' and then to compare this with the peer assessment.

Problem/incident	Possible solution/intervention

CHAPTER 7

1 Teaching small groups – checklist

Read the following. list of statements and tick the box which describes your own teaching best. Add four statements of your own.

1   I find it easy to learn students' names   ▪ ▪ ▪ ▪ ▪   I find it hard to learn students' names

2   My sessions start working slowly   ▪ ▪ ▪ ▪ ▪   My sessions start working quickly

3   I find it is easy to get students to contribute   ▪ ▪ ▪ ▪ ▪   I find it hard to get students to contribute

4   Most students prepare well   ▪ ▪ ▪ ▪ ▪   Most students prepare poorly

5   I find it easy to keep discussion to the point   ▪ ▪ ▪ ▪ ▪   I find it hard to keep discussion to the point

6   I find it easy to keep discussion going   ▪ ▪ ▪ ▪ ▪   I find it hard to keep discussion going

7   I speak more than I would like   ▪ ▪ ▪ ▪ ▪   I speak less than I would like

8   I find myself talking to one or two students   ▪ ▪ ▪ ▪ ▪   I find myself talking to the whole group

9   Sessions lack structure   ▪ ▪ ▪ ▪ ▪   Sessions are well structured

10   My students seldom express their own views   ▪ ▪ ▪ ▪ ▪   My students freely express their own views

11

12

Now write a statement of what you intend to do to deal with the problems implied by this checklist.

2 Group problems

Knowing what the problem is in a group does not necessarily mean that we have the resources to solve it. The incidents in the following list are typical of many student groups. What interventions might you use if you were the tutor in the situation? List as many possible ways as you can think of to deal with it. Add more incidents from your experience and describe how you have, or could have, handled them. When you have completed this, compare your ideas with those on page 319.

Incidents	Possible solutions
Group silent/unresponsive	
Individual(s) silent	
Students not listening to each other/not building/point scoring	
Sense of group secret/private joke/clique	
Sub-groups form/pair starts conversation	
One or two students dominate	
Students look for answers from tutor/too deferential	
Discussion too abstract	
Discussion goes off point/becomes irrelevant	
Attendance is poor	
Distraction occurs	
Preparation not done	
(Add more from your own experience.)	

Possible solutions to group problems above

Knowing what the problem is in a group does not necessarily mean that we have the resources to solve it. The following list of incidents and possible ways of handling them may give some clues.

1 *The whole group is silent and unresponsive*
   Use rounds, buzz groups or pyramids to get people talking and energised. Describe what you observe. Ask 'What is going on?' Ask fours to discuss what could be done to make the group more lively and involved and then pool the suggestions.

2 *Individuals are silent and unresponsive*
Use open, exploratory questions. Invite individuals in: 'I'd like to hear what Chris thinks about this.' Use buzz groups.

3 *Sub-groups start forming with private conversations*
Break them up into different sub-groupings with a task. Ask 'What is going on?' Self-disclosure. 'I find it hard to lead a group where . . .'

4 *The group becomes too deferential towards the tutor*
Stay silent. Throw questions back. Open questions to the whole group. Negotiate decisions about what to do instead of making decisions unilaterally thus having ownership.

5 *Discussion goes off the point and becomes irrelevant*
Set clear themes or an agenda. Keep a visual summary of the topics discussed for everyone to see. Say: 'I'm wondering how this relates to today's topic.' Seek agreement on what should and should not be discussed.

6 *A distraction occurs (such as two students arriving late)*
Establish group ground rules about behaviour such as late arrivals. Give attention to the distraction. Welcome late arrivals.

7 *Students have not done the preparation*
Clarify preparation requirements, making them realistic. Share what preparation has been undertaken at the start of each session. Consider a contract with them in which you run the seminar if they do the preparation, but not otherwise. Use 'passport' system (see page 267).

8 *Members do not listen to each other*
Point out what is happening. Establish ground rules about behaviour. Run a listening exercise.

9 *Students do not answer when you ask a question*
Use open, exploratory questions. Leave plenty of time. Use buzz groups.

10 *One or two students dominate*
Use hand signals, gestures and body language. Support and bring in others. Give the dominant students roles to keep them busy (such as note-taker). Use structures which take away their audience. Introduce ground rule or card system. See student(s) privately and ask to count up to 10 before speaking.

11 *Students complain about the seminar and the way you are handling it*
Ask for constructive suggestions. Ask students who are being negative to turn their comments into positive suggestions. Ask for written suggestions at the end of the session. Agree to meet a small group afterwards.

12 *Students reject the seminar discussion process and demand answers*
Explain the function of seminars. Explain the demands of the assessment system (if any!). Discuss their anxieties.

13 *The group picks on one student in an aggressive way*
Establish ground rules about respect. Ask 'What is going on?'. Break up the group using one or more structures from Chapter 6.

14 *Discussion focuses on one corner of the group and the rest opt out*
Use structures. Point out to the group what is happening. Check the layout of the room.

15 *You're running out of time*
Slow down!

A group-centred method for **Group Problems** is described below: section 2 'Dealing with difficult incidents in groups'.

CHAPTER 9

1 Principles of good practice for assessing student learning

Take each of the Principles of Good Practice for Assessing Student Learning on page 219 and write a brief account (20–30 words) on a single sheet of paper under each of the headings about how you would see this reflected in an assessment of group work, either in a discussion or a project format.

Pass the sheet round the group, inviting other members to write any comments before they pass it on. When, finally you receive your own sheet back, study it again before taking part in a group 'round' completing the sentence: 'What I've learned about assessment in groups is . . . and what I would like to see happen (or do) is . . .'.

2 Dealing with difficult incidents in groups

You can use the exercise on page 318 in a workshop format by organising groups of five to six and either giving them the list of problems (not the solutions!) or asking them to generate their own, allocating roles and taking them through the procedure.

1. Individually everyone marks up on the list the top three problems for them.

2. In each group members share their problems through a 'top-slicing' process – a group 'round' in which each person in turn describes what is successively the top item on their list – and the process is repeated around the group until all items are exhausted. They should not discuss the problems at this stage.

3. Each member then chooses one problem on which to focus, a different one for each person, which they would like to solve with the group's help.

4. Once the work 'GO' is given each person in their group will have 5 minutes (may be more if time permits) as a 'client' to briefly describe their chosen problem and enlist the help of another member (a 'consultant') in solving the problem. The person on the 'client's right should be the 'timekeeper', the person opposite, a 'consultant' with any remaining members acting as 'observers'.

> The task of the consultant is to help the client find their own solution to their problem. *They do this by exercising the skills of listening, exploratory questioning, clarifying, checking for understanding, giving full attention to the client and offering advice only at the end, having checked first that it is welcome.*
>
> The timekeeper must signal, preferably in a clear, non-verbal manner, 30 seconds before the allocated time is up as well as the completion.
>
> The task of the observers is to make an assessment of the consultant's effectiveness and skills using the assessment chart below, and to communicate this at the end of the 5 minutes. (This activity, that is 6 and 7 below, may be omitted if time is limited.)

5. The roles are agreed for the first of as many successive rounds as are necessary which will rotate round the group. The 5-minute consultancy now takes place.

6. Once the first consultancy is complete the consultant fills in her/his assessment sheet while the observer(s) show their peer assessment to the client and timekeeper for confirmation and addition (5 minutes maximum checked by the timekeeper).

7. When the consultant is ready the self and peer assessment sheets are exchanged and any problems of understanding clarified (5 minutes maximum checked by the timekeeper).

8. The exercise from 5 to 7 is repeated for each group member.

9. The 'Possible solutions to group problems' list on pages 319–20 is distributed for reading through followed by discussion.

10. An additional activity before the plenary if time permits is to use the 'crossover' method described in Chapter 6 such that new groups comprising one person from each original group is formed to share their received assessments and what they have learned from them.

Observer's sheet

Peer assessment of consultancy skills

Consultant's name ....

What the consultant did well

What the consultant could improve on

Any other feedback comments

Rating

Listening skills	1	2	3	4	5
Questioning skills	1	2	3	4	5
Overall as a consultant	1	2	3	4	5

Observer/Assessor's name ....

Consultant

Self-assessment

Please complete this as soon as possible after you have done your consultancy session.

What I think I did well

What I think I could improve on

Any other feedback comments

Rating

My listening skills	1	2	3	4	5
My questioning skills	1	2	3	4	5
Overall as a consultant	1	2	3	4	5

Comments

3 Deciding how to evaluate the group

Take two evaluation checklists (see also website to compare and contrast in the group).

(a) Each group member studies the two checklists with a view to their suitability for use in evaluating the way the group has worked.
(b) In a group 'round' each person briefly presents their view of the relative merits of the two checklists and how they might be used and processed in the group.
(c) The whole group then has to decide which checklist to use to evaluate the work of the group over the period of its existence and how it should be processed.
(d) The checklist is completed and processed in the group.
(e) If there is sufficient energy, the group may then use the other checklist to evaluate its work in (b) and possibly (c).

Finally, we thought it would be helpful to finish a book of similarities and differences with a summary of some of the relative merits of online and face-to-face group learning from David McConnell's *Implementing Computer-Supported Cooperative Learning*, reproduced by kind permission of the author.

FIVE-STAGE CHART FOR ONLINE GROUP DEVELOPMENT

Stage	Objective	Design	E-moderator Action	Typical problems	Solutions
1	Access to the system for all participants within a short period of time	Simple log on Clear intuitive navigation Clear instructions for help in case of difficulty	Welcome, Congratulate, Encourage, Reassure, Direct to online or telephone help	Participants' inability to diagnose source of access problems Emotional responses to IT failures	Provide human support Acknowledge feelings Provide really good joining instructions System thoroughly checked and independently tested before going live – 'right first time!'
	Motivate each participant to contribute (post a message rather than just read)	Provide an easy e-tivity to ensure an early posting Avoid requesting lots of personal information and photos	Acknowledge all successes Encourage participants to respond to each other	Worries about security, Reluctance to contribute to strangers	Reassure Scaffold all contributions so trust builds gradually and effectively
	Motivate to visit and contribute frequently	Make benefits of each task 100% clear Keep tasks simple and achievable at one log in Keep to only 2 or 3 tasks	Ensure all participants have posted in first few days and each has had responses to their contributions Follow up 'no shows'	Participants believe taking part is too time consuming	Avoid lots of reading in first couple of weeks Insert tips on how to manage time and use the software effectively Chase non-contributors through email or telephone
2	Build effective groups	Set up e-tivities that demonstrate the value of working together	Weave, Summarise, Feedback, Admire . . . but not too often Avoid overwhelming by constant interventions	Domination of the conference by one or two individuals	Encourage all participants to post *and* respond to others
	Set the stage for the learning	Ensure each e-tivity has a clear purpose and one straightforward task	Model supportive group processes	Lurking due to feelings of having less to contribute than others	Encourage each person to write from his or her own experience

Stage	Objective	Design	E-moderator Action	Typical problems	Solutions
3	Set up practice in online co-operation	Provide e-tivities that need small groups of around 6 persons to complete	Encourage participants to do their own weaving and summarizing but be alert and willing to 'teach' and comment where appropriate. Monitor group activity	Difficulties in organizing teams and working together such as unequal group size or late starts	Provide models of structured ways of working together. Pay attention to the group formation stage. Allow plenty of time but provide deadlines for paced completion of activities
	Set up use of information for learning	Use small 'sparks' of interesting content that promote dialogue between the group	Provide direction through the material if asked but avoid constant interventions	Participants become overwhelmed by the delivery of 'content' and/or constant e-moderator interventions and requests	Design each e-tivity so it uses content but leads to exploration of the topic
4	Enable collaborative working	Provide structure with flexibility. Encourage groups to work to realistic deadlines and paced outcomes	Provide information and support where and when necessary	Intermittent log ons. Some groups falter	Encourage the group to self manage, by provide pacing and deadlines. Use tracking in the software to see who is logging on when
	Enable knowledge construction	Use more demanding e-tivities that encourage creative, practical and critical thinking	Hand over weaving and summarizing process but also provide timely feedback on outcomes	Passivity or lurking	Encourage participants to become 'authors' and contributors rather than receivers of information and encourage questioning by all participants
	Enable groups to work more independently	Provide very good sparks. Ask for collaborative outcomes	Show that e-moderator is available to support and help and visits often but avoid the temptation to intervene	Time management. Uneven contributions from individuals	Provide practice earlier in process to build confidence and remote team working and models of exchanging information

5	Promote self and group reflection	Set up e-tivities that invite reflection on whole process Encourage individuals to consider personal development	Offer personal feedback if requested and appropriate	Ensuring a suitable ending	Provide clear e-tivities that indicate the ending of the group with an opportunity to 'sign-off' and say goodbye
	Promote critical thinking	Provide e-tivities that give structure to review process and outcomes	Be willing to comment/ offer constructive criticism	'Surface' (as opposed to deep) responses	Encourage all participants to post their intentions for actions with commitments to action plans to apply the learning and to engage in further collaboration with other participants, where appropriate
	Enable application of learning	Provide e-tivities that offer opportunities for indication of application, use and development of learning	Provide feedback	Usual feelings of 'missing the group'	Encourage to apply individual learning and each participant to post what s/he will do next

REFERENCES

Abercrombie, M. L. J. (1969) *The Anatomy of Judgement*, London: Free Association Books.

Abercrombie, M. L. J. (1979) *Aims and Techniques of Group Teaching*, 4th edn, Guildford, Surrey: Society for Research into Higher Education.

Allan, J. (1994) *Record of Achievement Project*, Wolverhampton: University of Wolverhampton.

Allen, K. (2005) Online learning: Constructivism and conversation as an approach to learning, *Innovations in Education and Teaching International* 42(3): 247–56.

Alpay, E. (2005) Group dynamics processes in e-mail groups, *Active Learning in Higher Education* 6(1): 7–16.

Alverno College Faculty (undated) *Student Assessment-as-Learning at Alverno College*, Milwaukee, WI: Alverno Productions.

Amaria P., Biran, L. and Leith, G. (1969) Individual versus cooperative learning 1: Influence of intelligence and sex, *Education Research* 11(2): 95–103.

American Society for Engineering Education (ASEE) (1976) *Experiential Learning in Engineering Education*, Washington, DC: ASEE.

Bales, R. (1970) *Personality and Interpersonal Behaviour*, New York: Holt, Rinehart and Winston.

Banet, A. G. Jnr and Hayden, C. (1977) A Tavistock primer, in *Annual Handbook for Group Facilitators,* eds W. Pfeiffer and J. Jones, San Diego, CA: University Associates Inc.

Barrows, H. and Tamblyn, R. (1980) *Problem-based Learning: An approach to medical education*, New York: Springer.

Beaty, L. and McGill, I. (1992) *Action Learning: A practitioner's guide*, London: Kogan Page.

Becher, T. (1989) *Academic Tribes and Territories: Intellectual inquiry and the cultures of disciplines*, Buckingham: Open University Press.

Belbin, R. (1981) *Management Teams*, Oxford: Butterworth-Heinemann.

Bennis, W., Benne, K. and Chin, R. (1985) *The Planning of Change*, New York: Holt, Rinehart and Winston.

Berne, E. (1968) *Games People Play: The psychology of human relationships*, Harmondsworth: Penguin.

Biggs, J. (2003) *Teaching for Quality Learning in Higher Education*, 2nd edn, Buckingham: Society for Research into Higher Education and Open University Press.

Bion, W. (1961) *Experience in Groups*, London: Tavistock Publications.

Bligh, D. (1986) *Teach Thinking by Discussion*, Society for Research into Higher Education, London: NFER Nelson.

Bligh, D. (1998) *What's the Use of Lectures?*, Exeter: Intellect Books.

Bligh, D. (2000) *What's the Point of Discussion?*, Exeter: Intellect Books.

Bligh, D. et al. (1981) *Teaching Students*, Exeter: Exeter University Teaching Services.

Bligh, D., Jaques, D. and Piper, D. W. (1981) *Seven Decisions When Teaching Students,* Exeter: Exeter University Teaching Services.

Bloom, B. S. et al. (1956) *Taxonomy of Educational Objectives* Vol. 1, London: Longman.

Bloom, B. S. et al. (1964) *Taxonomy of Educational Objectives* Vol. 2, London: Longman.

de Board, R. (1978) *The Psychoanalysis of Organisations: A psychoanalytic approach to behaviour in groups and organisations*, London: Tavistock Publications.

Bonwell, C. and Eison, J. (1991) *Active Learning: Creating excitement in the classroom,* ASHE/ERIC Higher Education Report No.1, Washington, DC.

Boud, D. (1981) *Developing Student Autonomy in Learning*, London: Kogan Page.

Boud, D. (1991) *Implementing Student Self Assessment*, HERDSA Green Guide, 2nd edn, Birmingham: Staff and Educational Development Association.

Boud, D. (1995) *Enhancing Learning Through Self-assessment*, London: Kogan Page.

Bramley, W. (1979) *Group Tutoring*, London: Kogan Page.

Brookfield, S. (1990) *The Skillful Teacher*, San Francisco, CA: Jossey-Bass.

Brookfield, S. and Preskill, S. (1999/2005) *Discussion as a Way of Teaching: Tools and techniques for democratic classrooms,* Society for Research into Higher Education, Buckingham: Open University Press; 2nd edn, San Francisco, CA: Jossey-Bass.

Brown, G. (2004) *How Students Learn,* http://www.routledgefalmer.com/series/KGETHE/resource.pdf.

Brown, G. and Atkins, M. (1999) *Effective Teaching in Higher Education*, London: Routledge.

Brown, S., Armstrong, S. and Thompson, G. (1998) *Motivating Students*, London: Kogan Page.

Bruner, J. (1977) *The Process of Education*, Cambridge, MA: Harvard University Press.

Candy, P. C. (1991) *Self-direction for Lifelong Learning*, Higher and Adult Education Series, San Francisco, CA: Jossey-Bass.

Chickering, A. and Gamson, Z. (1989) *7 Principles for Good Practice in Undergraduate Education* Racine, WI: Johnson Foundation.

Christopher, L. and Smith, L. (1991) *Negotiation Training Through Gaming*, London: Kogan Page.

Collier, K. G. (1983) *The Management of Peer Group Learning: Syndicate methods in higher education*, Guildford, Surrey: Society for Research into Higher Education.

Cooner, T. S. (2005) Dialectical constructivism: Reflections on creating a web-mediated enquiry-based learning environment, *Social Work Education* 24(4) June: 375–90.

Cornwall, M. C. (1979) *Students as Teachers: Peer teaching in higher education*, COWO, Amsterdam: University of Amsterdam.

Cox, R. (1978) The evaluation of teaching, in *Improving Teaching in Higher Education*, eds D. Jackson and D. Jaques, London: University Teaching Methods Unit.

Creme, P. (1995) Assessing 'seminar' work, in *Assessment for Learning in Higher Education*, ed. P. Knight, London: SEDA/Kogan Page.

Crystal, D. (2001) *Language and the Internet*, Cambridge: Cambridge University Press.

Davey, A. G. (1969) Leadership in relation to group achievement, *Educational Research* 11(3).

Davies, J. and Graff, M. (2005) Performance in e-learning: Online participation and student grades, *British Journal of Educational Technology* 36(4) July: 657–71.

Day, K., Grant, R. and Hounsell, D. (1998) *Reviewing your Teaching*, Edinburgh and Sheffield: University of Edinburgh, TLA Centre/CVCP UCoSDA, p. 25, www.tla.ed.ac.uk/resources/ryt.

Dence, R., Cann, A. and Mobbs, R. (2006) Piloting innovative uses of informal repositories in campus-based student assessment and associate tutor communities of practice, Proceedings of ALT-C, Edinburgh, September.

Denzin, W. (1969) Symbolic interaction and ethnomethodology: Proposed synthesis, *American Sociological Review*, 34 December: 922–34.

Deutsch, M. (1949) Experimental study of effects of cooperation and competition on group process, *Human Relations* 2(3): 199–231, also in *Group Dynamics: Research and Theory*, eds D. Cartwright and A. Zander (1968), New York: Harper and Row.

Dewey, J. (1916 and 1944) *Democracy and Education*, New York: Free Press.

Dewulf, S. and Baillie, C. (1999) *CASE: Creativity in Art, Science and Engineering*, Department for Education and Skills, UK.

Dolmans, H., Snellen-Balendong, Wolfhagen and Van Der Vleuten (1997) Seven principles of effective case design for a problem-based curriculum, *Medical Teacher* 19(3): 185–9.

Donaldson, A. and Topping, K. (1996) *Promoting Peer-assisted Learning amongst Students in Higher and Further Education*, Birmingham: Staff and Educational Development Association.

Downing, K. and Chim, T. (2004) Reflectors as online extraverts?, *Educational Studies* 30(3): 265–76.

Edirisingha, P., Fothergill, J., Salmon, G. and Traxler, J. (2006) IMPALA: informal podcasting and learning adaption, Proceedings of ALT-C, Edinburgh, September.

Edwards, J. (1980) The Engineering Syndicate Study, *Proceedings of the Institution of Electrical Engineers* 8, November.

Eitington, J. (1996) *The Winning Trainer*, 3rd edn, Houston, TX: Gulf.

Entwistle, N. (1981) *Styles of Teaching and Learning*, London: John Wiley.

Entwistle, N. (1998) Motivation and approaches to learning: Motivation and concepts of teaching, in *Motivating Students*, eds G. Thompson, S. Armstrong and S. Brown, pp. 15–24, London: Kogan Page.

Errington, E. (2005) *Creating Learning Scenarios: A planning guide for adult educators*, New Zealand: CoolBooks.

Exley, K. and Dennick, R. (2004) *Small Group Teaching*, London: RoutledgeFalmer.

Exley, K. and Moore, I. (eds) (1993) *Innovations in Science Teaching*, Standing Conference on Educational Development (SEDA).

Fazey, J. and Marton, F. (2002) Understanding the space of experiential variation, *Active Learning in Higher Education* 3(3): 234–50.

Felder, R. and Brent, R. (2003) Learning by doing, *Chemical Engineering Education* 37(4): 282–3.

Fink, L. (2003) *Creating Significant Learning Experiences: An integrated approach to designing college courses*, San Francisco, CA: Jossey-Bass.

Fink, L. (2004) Beyond small groups: Harnessing the extraordinary power of learning teams, in L. Michaelsen, A. Knight and L. Fink (eds) *Team-based learning: A transformative use of small groups in college teaching,* Sterling, VA: Stylus.

Forster, F., (1995) 'Tutoring in Arts and Social Sciences', in *Tutoring and Demonstrating: A handbook,* eds F. Forster, D. Hounsell and S. Thompson, Edinburgh and Sheffield: University of Edinburgh, TLA Centre/CVCP UCoSDA, pp. 11–24, www.tla.ed.ac.uk/services/tutdems/handbook.htm.

Freud, S. (1921) *Group Psychology and the Analysis of the Ego*, edited and translated by Strachey, (1975), New York: Norton.

Galanes, G. (2003) In their own words: An exploratory study of bona fide group leaders, *Small Group Research* 43(6): 741–70.

Gardner, H. (1993) *Frames of Mind,* London: Fontana Press.

George, J. and Cowan, J. (1999) *A Handbook of Techniques for Formative Evaluation: Mapping the student's learning experience*, London: RoutledgeFalmer.

Gibbs, G. (1981) *Teaching Students to Learn*, Buckingham: Open University Press.

Gibbs, G. (1984) Using role play in interpersonal skills training: A peer learning approach, in *Learning for the Future,* eds D. Jaques and E. Tipper, SAGSET, Loughborough: University of Loughborough.

Gibbs, G. (1990) *Improving Student Learning Project: Briefing Paper*, Oxford: CNAA / Oxford Centre for Staff Development.

Gibbs, G. (1992) *Improving the Quality of Student Learning,* www.53books.co.uk.

Gibbs, G. (1994) *Learning in Teams (Tutor Guide, Student Guide and Student Manual)*, Oxford Centre for Staff and Learning Development, Oxford: Oxford Brookes University.

Gibbs, G. (1995) *Discussion with More Students*, Oxford Centre for Staff and Learning Development, Oxford: Oxford Brookes University.

Gibbs, G., Habeshaw, S. and Habeshaw, T. (1989b) *53 Interesting Ways to Appraise Your Teaching,* Bristol: TES Publications.

Gibbs, G., Habeshaw, S. and Habeshaw, T. (1992) *Preparing to Teach,* www.53books.co.uk.

Gibbs, G., Habeshaw, S. and Habeshaw, T. (1994) *53 Interesting Ways to Teach: 12 do-it-yourself staff development exercises*, Bristol: TES Publications.

Goldschmid, B. and Goldschmid, M. (1976) Peer teaching in higher education: A review, *Higher Education* 5: 9–23.

Goleman, D. (1995) *Emotional Intelligence*, London: Bloomsbury.

Goodlad, S. (1978) Projects, in *Improving Teaching in Higher Education*, London: Centre for Higher Education Studies.

Gordon, W. (1961) *Synectics*, New York: Harper and Row.

Gordon, W. (1981) *The Basic Course in Synectics*, New York: HarperCollins.

Gordon, W. and Poze, A. (1981) *The New Art of the Possible: The basic course in synectics*, Cambridge, MA: Porpoise Books.

Grant, P. (1996) Oral assessment in groups, *The New Academic* 5(2).

Guirdham, M. (1990) *Interpersonal Skills at Work*, Englewood Cliffs, NJ: Prentice Hall.

Guzkowska, M. and Kent, I. (1994) Facilitating teamwork in the curriculum, in *Using Group-based Learning in Higher Education*, eds R. Thorley and L. Gregory, London: Kogan Page.

Habeshaw, S., Gibbs, G. and Habeshaw, T. (1992) 53 *Problems with Large Classes: Making the best of a bad job*, www.53books.co.uk

Hanlon, T. and Thomas, C. (2002) *Integrating Environmental Science and Humanities through Team Teaching*, www.ferrum.edu/thanlon/ecology/teamteach.htm.

Harris, T. A. (1973*) I'm OK – You're OK*, London: Pan Books.

Heathfield, M. (1999) Group-based assessment: An evaluation of the use of assessed tasks as a method of fostering higher-quality learning, in *Assessment Matters in Higher Education Choosing and using diverse approaches*, eds S. Brown and A. Glasner, Buckingham: Society for Research into Higher Education and Open University Press.

Hedley, R. and Wood, C. (1978) *Group Discussion for Seminar Leaders*, Mimeograph, University of Manitoba.

Heron, J. (1976 and 1989) *Six-Category Intervention Analysis*, Human Potential Research Project, Roehampton: University of Surrey.

Heron, J. (1981) Assessment revisited, in *Developing Student Autonomy in Learning*, ed. D. Boud, London: Kogan Page.

Heron, J. (1999) *The Facilitator's Handbook*, London: Kogan Page.

Hill, W. F. (1977) *Learning Thru Discussion*, London: Sage.

Honey, P. and Mumford, A. (2005) *The Learning Styles Questionnaire,* www.peterhoney.com.

Hussey, T. and Smith, P. (2002) The trouble with learning outcomes, *Active Learning in Higher Education* 3(2) November: 220–33.

Huston J. D. (1995) Managing large classes, in *Inspiring Teaching*, ed. J. Roth, Bolton, MA: Anker Publishing.

Illes, K. (2003) Reflection and cooperative cultures, in The patchwork text: a radical re-assessment of coursework assignments, eds R. Winter, J. Parker and P. Ovens, *Innovations in Education and Teaching International* 40(2).

Jackson, N. (2004) Developing the concept of metalearning, *Innovations in Education and Teaching, International* 41(4): 391–403.

Jaques, D. (1980) Students' and tutors' experience of project work, in *Higher Education at the Crossroads*, ed. R. Oxtoby, Guildford, Surrey: Society for Research into Higher Education.

Jaques, D. (1981) Behind the Scenes*, Report to the Nuffield Foundation*.

Jaques, D. (1988) *Supervising Projects*, Oxford Centre for Staff and Learning Development, Oxford: Oxford Brookes University.

Jaques, D. (1989) *Independent Learning and Project Work*, Oxford Centre for Staff Development, Oxford: Oxford Brookes University.

Jaques, D. (2005) Facilitating games and simulations, *Training Journal* 19, Ely: Fenman.

Johnson, D. W. and Johnson, F. P. (1987) *Joining Together: Group theory and group skills,* Englewood Cliffs, NJ: Prentice Hall.

Jones, K. (1988) *Interactive Learning,* London: Kogan Page.

Kagan, N. (1982) *Interpersonal Process Recall: Basic methods and recent research*, Mimeograph, University of Michigan.

Kimball, L. (2001) *Boundaryless Facilitation: Leveraging the strengths of face-to-face and groupware tools to maximize group process*, www.catalystonline.com/about_us/pdfs/cct_maximizing_team_learning.pdf.

Kindley, R. W. (2002) Scenario-based E-learning: A step beyond traditional E-learning, *ASDT online magazine – Learning Circuits*, 3(5), May.

Knight, A. B. (2004) Team-based learning: A strategy for transforming the quality of teaching and learning, in *Team-based Learning: A transformative use of small groups in college teaching,* eds L. Michaelson, A. Knight and L. Fink, Sterling, VA: Stylus.

Knowles, H. C. and Knowles, M. (1972) *Introduction to Group Dynamics,* Chicago, IL: Association Press/Folletts.

Kolb, D., Rubin, I. and McIntyre, J. (1984) *Organizational Psychology: An experiential approach,* 4th edn, Englewood Cliffs, NJ: Prentice Hall.

Kuhn, T. (1973) *The Structure of Scientific Revolutions,* Chicago, IL: University of Chicago Press.

Laufgraben, J. and Tompkins, D. (2004) Pedagogy that builds community, in *Sustaining and Improving Learning Communities,* J. Laufgraben, N. Shapiro and Associates, San Francisco, CA: Jossey-Bass.

Lewis, V. and Habeshaw, S. (1995) *53 Interesting Ways to Promote Equal Opportunities in the Curriculum,* www.53books.co.uk.

Luft, J. (1970) *Group Processes: An introduction to group dynamics,* Palo Alto, CA: Mayfield.

Luker, P. (1987) Some cases of small group teaching, unpublished thesis, University of Nottingham.

MacGregor, J. (2000) *Teaching Communities within Learning Communities,* http://learning commons.evergreen.edu/pdf/springb.pdf.

McConnell, D. (2001) *Implementing Computer-Supported Co-operative Learning,* London: RoutledgeFalmer.

McGill, I. and Beaty, L. (2001) *Action Learning: A guide for professional, managerial and educational development,* London: Kogan Page.

McHardy, P. and Henderson, S. (1994) Management indecision: Using group-work in teaching creativity, in *Using Group-based Learning in Higher Education,* eds R. Thorley and L. Gregory, London: Kogan Page.

McLeish, J., Matheson, W. and Park, J. (1973) *The Psychology of the Learning Group,* London: Hutchinson.

McLuckie, J. and Topping, K. (2004) Transferable skills for online peer learning, *Assessment and Evaluation in Higher Education* 29(5) October: 563–84.

Mager, R. (1961) *Preparing Instructional Objectives,* Pal. Alto, CA: Fearon Pubs.

Mama, R. (2001) Preparing social work students to work in culturally diverse settings, *Social Work Education* 20(3): 373–82.

McNiff, J., Lomax, P. and Whitehead, J. (1996) *You and Your Action Research Project,* London: Routledge.

Marris, P. (1965) *The Experience of Higher Education,* London: Routledge and Kegan Paul.

Marton, F. and Säljö, R. (1976) On qualitative differences in learning I and II, *British Journal of Educational Psychology* 46(1): 4–11 and (2): 115–27.

Marton, F., Hounsell, D. and Enwistle, N. (eds) (1984) *The Experience of Learning: Implications for teaching and studying in higher education,* Edinburgh: Scottish Academic Press. Revised and expanded 1997 edition on free download from http://www.tla.ed.ac.uk/resources/EoL.html.

Massy, W., Wilger, A. and Colbeck, C. (1994) Overcoming 'hollowed' collegiality, *Change* 26: 11–21, American Association for Higher Education, July/August.

Mathews, B. (1994) Peer evaluation in practice: Experience from a major group project, in *Using Group-based Learning in Higher Education*, eds R. Thorley and L. Gregory, London: Kogan Page.

Michaelson, L. Knight, A. and Fink, L. (eds) (2004) *Team-based Learning: A transformative use of small groups in college teaching*, Sterling, VA: Stylus.

Miles, M. (1981) *Learning to Work in Groups: A program guide for educational leaders*, 2nd edn, Columbia, New York: Teachers College Press.

Miller, C. (1975) Evaluation of teaching and the institutional context, in *Evaluating Teaching in Higher Education*, ed R. Cox, London: Centre for Higher Education Studies.

Miller, C. and Parlett, M. (1974) *Up to the Mark: A study of the examination game*, Guildford, Surrey: Society for Research into Higher Education.

Miller, N. (1993) Perspectives on experiential group work, in *Using Experience for Learning*, eds D. Bond, R. Cohen and D. Walker, Oxford: SRHE and Oxford University Press.

Napier, R. W. and Gershenfeld, M. K. (1999) *Groups: Theory and experience*, 6th edn, Boston, MA: Houghton Mifflin.

Neath, M. (1998) The development and transfer of undergraduate group work skills, unpublished thesis, Sheffield Hallam University.

Nicol, D. (1997) Research on Learning and Higher Education Teaching, *UCoSDA Briefing Paper 45*, Sheffield: Universities and Colleges Staff Development Agency.

Nuhfer, E. (1995) *A Handbook for Student Management Teams*, Office of Teaching Effectiveness, University of Colorado.

Olivera, F. and Straus, S. (2004) Group-to-individual transfer of learning: Cognitive and social factors, *Small Group Research* 35(4): 440–65.

Osborn, A. (1963) *Applied Imagination: Principles and procedures of creative problem solving*, New York: Scribners.

Palmer, P. (1998) *The Courage to Teach*, San Francisco, CA: Jossey Bass.

Parker, J. C. and Rubin, L. J. (1966) *Process as Content: Curriculum design and the application of knowledge*, Chicago, IL: Rand McNally.

Parlett, M. (1977) The department as a learning milieu, *Studies in Higher Education* 2(2): 173–81.

Parlett, M. and King, R. (1971) *Concentrated Study: A pedagogic innovation observed*, Guildford, Surrey: Society for Research into Higher Education.

Parlett, M., Simons, H., Simmonds, R. and Hewton, E. (1988) *Learning from Learners: A study of the student's experience of academic life*, London: Nuffield Foundation.

Perry, W. (1970) *Forms of Intellectual and Ethical Development in the College Years*, New York: Holt Reinhart.

Pfeiffer, W. and Jones, J. (1974) *Annual Handbook for Group Facilitators*, San Diego, CA and Mansfield, UK: University Associates Inc.

Pressnell, M. (1994) A case study of a group project in aerospace design engineering, in *Using Group-based Learning in Higher Education*, eds R. Thorley and L. Gregory, London: Kogan Page.

Prince, G. M. (1972) *The Practice of Creativity*, New York: Harper and Row.

Pring, R. (1973) Objectives and innovation: The irrelevance of theory, *London Educational Review* 3: 46–54.

Pring, R. (1978) Teacher as a researcher, in *Theory and Practice of the Curriculum*, ed. D. Lawton, London: Routledge and Kegan Paul.

Priola, V., Smith, J. and Armstrong, S. J. (2004) Group work and cognitive style: A discursive investigation, *Small Group Research* 35(5): 565–95.

Prosser, M. and Trigwell, K. (1999) *Understanding Learning and Teaching: The experience of higher education,* Buckingham: Society for Research into Higher Education and Open University Press.

Rainer, T. (1980) *The New Diary: How to use a journal,* London: Angus and Robertson.

Rainsbury, E. and Malcolm, P. (2003) Extending the classroom boundaries: An evaluation of an asynchronous discussion board, *Accounting Education* 12(1): 49–61.

Ramsden, P. (1984) The context of learning, in *The Experience of Learning*, eds F. Marton, D. J. Hounsell and N. J. Entwistle, Edinburgh: Scottish Academic Press.

Ramsden, P. (1993/2003) *Learning to Teach in Higher Education*, London: Routledge, 2nd edn, Buckingham: Open University Press.

Richardson, E. (1967) *Group Study for Teachers*, London: Routledge.

Richardson, J. (1994) Cultural specificity in approaches to studying in higher education: A literature survey, *Higher Education* 27(4): 417–32.

Rogers, C. (1983) *Freedom to Learn in the 1980s*, Columbus, OH: Merrill.

Rossen, E. (2001) Trust in virtual teams, in *Proceedings of World Multi-conference on Systemics, Cybernetics and Informatics*, Orlando, Fl.

Rowan, J. and Reason, P. (1981) *Human Inquiry: A sourcebook of new paradigm research,* London: JohnWiley.

Rowntree, D. (1981) *Developing Courses for Students*, London: McGraw-Hill.

Säljö, R. and Marton, F. (2005) Approaches to learning, in *The Experience of Learning*, eds F. Marton and R. Säljö, Edinburgh: Scottish Academic Press.

Salmon, G. (2002a) Mirror, mirror on my screen exploring online reflections, *British Journal of Educational Technology* 33(4): 383–96.

Salmon, G. (2002b) *E-Tivities: the Key to active online learning,* London: RoutledgeFalmer.

Salmon, G. (2004*) E-moderating: The key to teaching and learning online*, 2nd edn, London: Routledge Falmer.

Salmon, G. (2005) Reclaiming the territory, *Journal of e-Learning and Knowledge Society, The Italian e-Learning Association Journal* 2, September: 219–22.

Salmon, G. and Lawless, N. (2005) Management Education for the 21st Century, in *Handbook of Blended Learning: Global Perspectives, Local Design*, eds Bonk and Graham, San Francisco, CA: Pfeiffer Publishing.

Savin-Baden, M. (2000) *Problem-based Learning in Higher Education*, The Society for Research into Higher Education, Buckingham: Open University Press.

Savin-Baden, M. and Major, C. M. (2004) *Foundation of Problem-based Learning*, The Society for Research into Higher Education, New York: Open University Press and McGraw Hill Education Press.

Savin-Baden, M. and Wilkie, K. (2006) *Problem-based Learning Online*, Milton Keynes: Open University Press.

Schellens, T. and Valcke, M. (2004) Fostering knowledge construction in university students through asynchronous discussion groups, *Computers and Education* 46, November: 349–70.

Schroder, H. and Harvey, O. (1963) Conceptual organisation and group structure, in *Motivation and Social Interaction*, ed O. Harvey, New York: Ronald Press.

Shaffer, J. and Galinsky, M. (1974) *Models of Group Therapy and Activity Training*, Harlow: Prentice Hall.

Shepherd, D. (2004) The challenge of moving collaboration into the online environment, *Proceedings of Online Education*, Berlin, December.

Shuell, T. (1986) Cognitive conceptions of learning, *Review of Educational Research* 56: 411–36.

Slavin, R. (1990) *Cooperative Learning: Theory, research and practice*, Englewood Cliffs, NJ: Prentice Hall.

Smith, D. (1992) Encouraging Students' Participation in Large Classes: A Modest Proposal, *Teaching Sociology* 20(4) October: 337–9.

Smith M. (1994) *Local Education: Community, conversation, praxis*, Buckingham: Open University Press.

Smith, P. (1980) *Small Groups and Personal Change*, London: Methuen.

Stahl, G. (2005) Group cognition in computer-assisted collaborative learning, Journal of *Computer Assisted Learning* 21(2): 79–91.

Stanford, C. and Roark, A. (1974) *Human Interaction in Education*, Boston, MA: Allyn and Bacon.

Stenhouse, L. (1972) Teaching through small group discussion: Formality, rules and authority, *Cambridge Journal of Education* 2: 18–24.

Stenhouse, L. (1975) *Introduction to Curriculum Development*, London: Heinemann.

Stewart, I. and Joines, V. (1987) *TA Today: A new introduction to transactional analysis*, Nottingham: Lifespace Publishing.

Tannen, D. (1990) *You Just Don't Understand; Women and men in conversation*, New York: Morrow.

Tennant, M., McKenzie, J., Moses, I., Scott, G. and Trigwell, K. (1993) *Tutorials: Teaching matters, videos and booklets*, Sydney: University of Technology.

Thiagarajan, S. (2003) *Design Your Own Games and Activities: Thiagi's Templates for Performance Improvement*, San Francisco, CA: Jossey-Bass.

Thomas, L. (2002) Student retention in higher education: The role of institutional habitus, *Journal of Education Policy* 17(4): 423–42.

Thomas, L., Cooper, M. and Quinn, J. (eds) (2003) *Collaboration to Widen Participation in Higher Education*, Stoke-on-Trent: Trentham Books.

Thorley, L. and Gregory, R. (1995) *Using Group-based Learning in Higher Education*, London: Kogan Page.

Tiberius, R. (1999) *Small Group Teaching: A trouble-shooting guide*, London: Kogan Page.

Toohey, S. (1999) *Designing Courses for Higher Education*, Buckingham: Society for Research into Higher Education and Open University Press.

Treadaway, J. (1975) Do Seminars Work? *Institute of Education Reporter*, University of London.

Trelfa J. and Feaviour K. (2002) Lecture notes as part of *Interpersonal Communication and Group Work*, Personal communication.

Wellington, P. (1998) Multidisciplinary student teams motivated by industrial experience, in *Motivating Students*, eds S. Brown, S. Armstrong and G. Thompson, London: Kogan Page.

Wenger, E. (2005) Seminar at the UK Open University, 5 October.

Wilson, A. (1980) Structuring seminars: A technique to allow students to participate in structuring of small group discussion, *Studies in Higher Education* 5(1), March.

Winter, R. (2003) Contextualising the patchwork text: Addressing problems of coursework assessment in higher education, *Innovations in Learning and Teaching International*, Routledge/SEDA.

Yamane, D. (1997) Group projects: Problems and possible solutions, *Teaching Professor*, Madison, WI: Magna Pubs.

Yazici, H. J. (2004) Student perceptions of collaborative learning in operations management classes, *Journal of Education for Business*, November/December 80(2): 110–18.

Zinkin, L. (1994) Exchange as a therapeutic factor in group analysis, in *The Psyche and the Social World: Developments in group analysis theory*, eds D. Brown and L. Zinkin, R. London: Routledge.

FURTHER READING

Angelo, T. and Cross, P. (1993) *Classroom Assessment Techniques*, San Francisco, CA: Jossey-Bass.

Barr, R. and Tagg, J. (1995) From teaching to learning: A new paradigm for undergraduate education, *Change*, November/December.

Baume, D. and Baume, C. (1996) *Running Tutorials and Seminars*, Oxford Centre for Staff and Leaming Development, Oxford: Oxford Brookes University.

Beard, R. and Hartley, J. (1989) *Teaching and Learning in Higher Education*, London: Harper and Row.

Biggs, J. (1982) *Evaluating the Quality of Student Learning: The SOLO taxonomy*, London: Academic Press.

Boud, D. (ed.) (1985) *Problem-Based Learning in Education for the Professions*, Higher Education Society for Research and Development of Australasia.

Boud, D. and Feletti, G. (eds) (1991) *The Challenge of Problem-based Learning,* London: Kogan Page.

Brookfield, S. (1997) *Developing Critical Thinkers,* Buckingham: Open University Press.

Brown, G., Bull, J. and Pendlebury, M. (1997) *Assessing Student Learning in Higher Education*, London: Routledge.

Brown, S. and Glasner, A. (1999) *Assessment Matters in Higher Education: Choosing and using diverse approaches,* Buckingham: Society for Research into Higher Education and Open University Press.

Bryan, C. (2004) *Assessing Group Practice*, SEDA Paper 117, London: Staff and Educational Development Association.

Cameron, B. (1999) *Active Learning*, STLHE Green Guide No. 2, Halifax, Canada: Society for Teaching and Learning in Higher Education.

Cannon, R. and Newble, D. (2000) *A Handbook for Teachers in Universities and Colleges*, London: Kogan Page.

Cross, K. P. and Steadman, M. Harris (1996) *Classroom Research: Implementing the scholarship of teaching.* San Francisco, CA: Jossey-Bass, also in *Accounting Education News*, Spring 1998.

Davison, A. and Gordon, P. (1978) *Games and Simulations in Action*, London: Woburn Books.

Easton, G. (1982) *Learning from Case Studies*, New York: Prentice Hall.

Erikson, E. (1971) *Identity: Youth and Crisis*, London: Faber and Faber.

Fink, L. (2002) *Significant Learning*, http://www.ou.edu/idp/tips/design.htm

Fleming, H. (2004) *Peer Assisted learning*, http://www.peerlearning.ac.uk/

Fry, H., Ketteridge, S. and Marshall, S. (2000) *A Handbook of Teaching and Learning in Higher Education: Enhancing academic practice*, London: Kogan Page.

Gibbs, G., Habeshaw, S. and Habeshaw, T. (1995a) *53 Interesting Ways to Assess your Students*, www.53books.co.uk.

Gibbs, G., Habeshaw, S. and Habeshaw, T. (1995b) *53 Interesting Ways of Helping your Students to Study*, www.53books.co.uk.

Hartley, P. (1997) *Group Communication*, London: Routledge.

Hinett, K. and Thomas, J. (eds) (1999) *Staff Guide to Self and Peer Assessment*, Oxford Centre for Staff and Learning Development, Oxford: Oxford Brookes University.

Hounsell, D., McCulloch, M. and Scott, M. (1996) *The ASSHE Inventory: Changing Assessment Practices in Scottish Higher Education*, Edinburgh and Sheffield: University of Edinburgh, TLA Centre/CVCP UCoSDA, pp. 51, 53 and 149, republished electronically in 2002 by the Learning and Teaching Support Network, and subsequently by the Higher Education Academy, www.heacademy.ac.uk/asshe/.

Hounsell, D. and Entwistle, N. (2005) *Enhancing Teaching-Learning Environments in Undergraduate Courses* (ETL Project Final report), http://www.ed.ac.uk/etl/publications.html #occasionalpapers

Jaques, D. (2003) Learning in groups: ABC of learning and teaching in medicine, *British Medical Journal* 326: 492–4.

Jenkins, A. M. (1992) Encouraging active learning in structured lectures, in *Improving the Quality of Student Learning*, ed. G Gibbs, Bristol: Technical and Education Services.

Johnson, D. and Johnson, F. (1990) *Learning Together and Alone: Cooperation, competition and individualisation*, Englewood Cliffs, NJ: Prentice Hall.

Johnson, D. W., Johnson, R. T., and Smith, K. A. (1998) *Active Learning: Cooperation in the college classroom*, 2nd edn, Edina, MN: Interaction Book Co.

Jones, K. (1991) *Icebreakers*, London: Kogan Page.

Jones, K. (1995) *Simulations: A handbook for teachers and trainers*, 3rd edn, London: Kogan Page.

Juwah, C., Macfarlane-Dick, D., Matthew, B., Nicol, D., Ross, D. and Smith, B. (2004) *Enhancing Student Learning Through Effective Formative Feedback*, York: Higher Education Academy.

Kennedy, G. E and Cutts, Q. I (2005) The association between students' use of an electronic voting system and their learning outcomes, *Journal of Computer Assisted Learning* 21(4): 260–71.

Knight, P. (ed.) (1995) *Assessment for Learning in Higher Education*, London: SEDA/Kogan Page.

Knowles, M. (1975) *Self-Directed Learning: A guide for learners and teachers*, Association Press/Chicago, IL: Folletts.

Knowles, M. (1979) *The Adult Learner: A neglected species?* Houston, TX: Gulf.

Knowles, M. (1986) *Using Learning Contracts*, San Francisco, CA: Jossey-Bass.

Kolb, D. (1984) *Experiential Learning*, Harlow: Prentice Hall.

Kukulska-Hulme, A. and Traxler, J. (2005) *Mobile Learning: A handbook for educators and trainers*, London: RoutledgeFalmer.

Lago, C. and Shipton, G. (1995) *Personal Tutoring in Action*, Sheffield: University of Sheffield Counselling Service.

Lewis, R. and Mee, J. (1981) *Using Role Play: An introductory guide*, Cambridge: National Extension College.

Light, G. and Cox, R. (2001) *Learning and Teaching in Higher Education: The reflective professional,* London: Paul Chapman.

Lin, S. S. J., Liu, E. Z. F and Yuan, S. M. (2001) Web-based peer assessment: Feedback for students with various thinking-styles, *Journal of Computer Assisted Learning* 17(4): 420–40.

McNamara, D. and Harris, R. (eds) (1997) *Overseas Students in Higher Education*, London: RoutledgeFalmer.

Matthews, R. (1996) Collaborative learning: Creating knowledge with students, in *Teaching on Solid Ground: Using scholarship to improve practice*, eds R. Menges and M. Weimer, San Francisco, CA: Jossey-Bass.

McKeachie, W. and Svinicki, M. (2005) Teaching Tips: Strategies, Research and Theory for College and University Teachers, Boston, MA: Houghton Mifflin.

Menges, R. and Weimer, M. (1996) *Teaching on Solid Ground: Using scholarship to improve practice,* San Francisco, CA: Jossey-Bass.

Millis, B. (1994) Formats for group work, *The Teaching Professor*, May.

Nias, J. (1993) *The Human Nature of Learning – Selections from the work of M. L. J. Abercrombie,* Buckingham: Society for Research into Higher Education and Open University Press.

Nicol, D. and Macfarlane-Dick, (2004) Rethinking formative assessment in HE: A theoretical model and seven principles of good feedback practice in *Enhancing Student Learning Though Effective Formative Feedback*, eds C. Juwah, D. Macfarlane-Dick, B. Matthew, D. Nicol, D. and B. Smith, York: The Higher Education Academy.

O'Rourke, K. (2003) *Learning Based on the Process of Enquiry*, http://www.intranet.man.ac.uk/rsd/ci/ebl/examples.htm.

Piccinin, S. (2003) *Feedback: Key to learning*, STLHE Green Guide No. 4, Halifax, Canada: Society for Teaching and Learning in Higher Education.

Pretty, J., Guijt, I., Thompson, J. and Scoones, I. (1995) *Participatory Learning and Action: A trainer's guide*, London: International Institute for Environment and Development.

Prince, S. and Dunne, E. (1998) Group development: The integration of skills into law, *The Law Teacher* 32 (1): 64–78.

Race, P. (2000) *500 Tips on Group Learning,* London: Kogan Page.

Race, P. and Brown, S. (2004) *500 Tips for Tutors*, 2nd edn, London: Kogan Page.

Rudduck, J. (1978) *Learning Through Small Group Discussion*, Guildford, Surrey: Society for Research into Higher Education.

Ryan J. (2000) *A Guide to Teaching International Students*, Oxford Centre for Staff and Learning Development, Oxford: Oxford Brookes University.

Shaw, M. E. (1977) *Group Dynamics: The psychology of small group behaviour*, New Delhi: Tata-McGraw-Hill.

Sherpa, C. (2000) *Assessing Group Work*, http://learn.lincoln.ac.nz/tls/groupwork/assessment/assessment.htm.

Smith, P. (1973*) Groups within Organisations*, London: Harper and Row.

Squires, G. (2003) *Trouble-shooting Your Teaching,* London: Kogan Page. [Also available in ringbinder format to allow photocopying for teaching purposes.]

Stefani, L. and Nicol, D. (1997) From teacher to facilitator of collaborative enquiry, in *Facing up to Radical Changes in Universities and Colleges,* eds S. Armstrong, G. Thompson and S. Brown, London: Kogan Page.

Stein, M. (1975) *Stimulating Creativity, Vol 2: Group procedures*, New York: Academic Press.

Talbot, M. (1994) Learning journals for evaluation of group-based learning, in *Using Group-based Learning in Higher Education*, eds R. Thorley and L. Gregory, London: Kogan Page.

Van Ments, M. (1983*) Effective Use of Role Play*, London: Kogan Page.

Watzlawick, P., Bavelas, J. and Jackson, D. (1962) *Pragmatics of Human Communication*, New York: W. W. Norton.

Zuber-Skerritt, A. (1992) *Action Research in Higher Education: Examples and reflections,* London: Kogan Page.

INDEX

346